168 SONGS
OF HATRED AND FAILURE

168 SONGS
OF HATRED AND FAILURE

A HISTORY OF
MANIC STREET PREACHERS
KEITH CAMERON

**WHITE
RABBIT**

First published in Great Britain in 2025 by White Rabbit,
an imprint of The Orion Publishing Group Ltd
Carmelite House, 50 Victoria Embankment
London EC4Y 0DZ

An Hachette UK Company

The authorised representative in the EEA is Hachette Ireland,
8 Castlecourt Centre, Dublin 15, D15 XTP3,
Ireland (email: info@hbgi.ie)

1 3 5 7 9 10 8 6 4 2

A CIP catalogue record for this book is
available from the British Library.

ISBN (Hardback) 978 1 3996 0740 7
ISBN (Export Trade Paperback) 978 1 3996 0741 4
ISBN (Ebook) 978 1 3996 0743 8
ISBN (Audio) 978 1 3996 0744 5

Typeset by Input Data Services Ltd, Bridgwater, Somerset

Printed and bound in Great Britain by Clays, Ltd, Elcograf, S.p.A

www.whiterabbitbooks.co.uk
www.orionbooks.co.uk

'For us, music and words came first, and everything else was secondary.'

– Richey Edwards, 1993

Introduction

'Hatred and failure go perfectly together
Like the quick and the sand, beautiful and damned.'
  – Manic Street Preachers, 'Between The Clock And The Bed'

The straightforward explanation for this book's title is it was too good to go to waste. In 2011, Manic Street Preachers toyed with making an album called '70 Songs Of Hatred And Failure'. Sadly, common sense prevailed and the idea mutated into the more feasible concept of the separate but concurrently made *Rewind The Film* and *Futurology*. Two great albums, one great lost album title.

But why 168 songs? Because in Manic folklore, the number 168 has special significance. According to 'Motown Junk', the band's third single and their first song to impact beyond the margins, '168 seconds' is the length of time a love song 'stops your heart beating . . . [and] your brain thinking'. In 'Motown Junk's synthesis of iconoclastic punk rock throttle and Marxist theory, where 'songs of love echo underclass betrayal', a single of 2 minutes 48 seconds' duration is the perfect pop form. So although at the time of writing there have been 319 officially released Manic Street Preachers songs, only through a selection of 168 can we find the essence of this remarkable group.

And why hatred? Because hating and being hated have always been integral to the band's ethos. Manic Street Preachers were born out of working-class rage and a defiant self-sufficiency. The first song they wrote was called 'Aftermath', a lament for their home town of Blackwood, gravely wounded like many others across the South Wales Valleys by the brutal 1984–5 miners' strike – the closest Britain had come to civil war in 400 years. All aged between fifteen and sixteen at the time, all intimately connected to a community whose entire existence was predicated

1

on digging coal out of the earth in order to make a living, each member of the band was profoundly hurt by the strike, be it the daily drama of its conduct or the agony of its outcome. 'Being part of that living newsreel will be with us for ever,' says James Dean Bradfield. 'It made you feel like you were the vanquished.'

Thus began the failure, a condition that, for all the band's subsequent victories – the multiple awards, headlining every major UK music festival, an ongoing string of hit records – remains a constant worm in the Manic Street Preachers' gut. As Sean Moore once observed, 'We're an experiment gone wrong.'[1]

Four kids from an obscure locale, drunk on the residue of punk's idealist/nihilist elixir and bonded by ties of blood and friendship into a tight unit, each with strictly demarcated roles: cousins Bradfield and Moore would be the musical engine, while Richey Edwards and Nicky Wire supplied the intellectual fuel, weaving dense political and philosophical theories into slogans-cum-lyrics, while constantly feeding the media an inflammable mix of conviction and provocation. The Manics pledged to release just one multi-million-selling double album then split up, having obviated any need to make another, leaving behind an indelible cultural legend. They signed a record deal with Sony, titled their definitive opus *Generation Terrorists*, and affirmed the purity of their kamikaze mission when Richey Edwards cut '4 Real' into his arm with a razor blade while chatting to *NME* journalist Steve Lamacq.

But reality bit hard. The apocalyptic spectacle gave way to the attritional grind of the rock 'n' roll trenches, dragging a patchy second album to mid-sized venues with chart numbers rattling around the lower end of respectable, playing the game to diminishing returns. Something had to give. And despite the initial burst of Situationist rhetoric, it would be their Valleys hinterland's traditional moral code and ingrained work ethic that saw them through: the Manics kept digging, and eventually found their true voice.

'I think if you can come back from failure, as a human being or as a band, or both in my case, then it just makes your life richer,' says Nicky Wire. 'When bands are on a linear line of perfection and success, it's not that interesting. [The Clash's] *Sandinista* always came across as a disaster when you read about it: lost money, no hits, didn't sell. But through time it became really influential. We always knew that there was going to be a lot of fucked-up failure in the band and massive highs and lows were going to be in our DNA.'

I first met a Manic Street Preacher in early February 1994, at the newly rebranded *NME* 'Brat' Awards ceremony in London. The event coincided with the first flush of Britpop: Suede, Elastica and Radiohead were among the winners, while members of Blur sauntered about the place, drinking in the buzz around the imminent release of their new album *Parklife* and confident that this time next year it would all be about them. There were no awards for Manic Street Preachers, however, who attended the evening purely to honour the memory of their manager Philip Hall, who had died two months earlier and in whose name a special 'Best New Act' category had been created. Wandering the edges of the post-show party, I bumped into a colleague searching for a quiet corner to do an interview with his companion, who was unmistakeable in spite of his wearing what looked like a vintage police jacket.

'It's very nice to meet you,' said Richey Edwards. I began to apologise for the crass and ill-considered review of *Gold Against The Soul* I'd written the previous year, but seeing Richey's gaze drift down to the floor, I instead offered my condolences about Philip and we went our respective ways. Within two weeks, Richey and his bandmates took up residence in a cheap studio on one of Cardiff's meaner streets and began recording *The Holy Bible* – the album that would turn me from a Manics sceptic into a believer.

Three years earlier, wowed by 'Motown Junk', my view of the

band had been somewhere in between. The UK music weekly *Sounds* gave the Manics their first magazine front cover in late January 1991. As *Sounds'* Reviews Editor, I was subsequently invited onto the BBC daytime television chat show *Kilroy* to debate the role of politics in pop music, alongside card-carrying Tory prog-rock god Rick Wakeman, socialist comedian Mark Steel, a member of Liverpool band The Real People, and what seemed like a sizeable delegation of Jehovah's Witnesses. Asked to justify championing a group which sang 'Repeat after me, fuck Queen and country', I replied that the Manics were intelligent young men simply doing their job and that we needed 'more of this sort of thing', much to Rick Wakeman's evident distaste.

By the time of *Gold Against The Soul*, however, the struggle to marry the conceptual rhetoric with an expedient musical vehicle had led the Manics to an impasse. *The Holy Bible* would resolve that: for all its jagged edges and inner torments, this was the sound of a band truly at ease with itself. 'The lesson was that we were a rock 'n' roll band – we weren't an art installation,' James Dean Bradfield later reflected. '*The Holy Bible* might be deeply skewed and twisted but it's still a rock 'n' roll record. And Richey was really on-message with never censoring himself. It was a good, healthy environment.'

Soon enough, Richey Edwards's health became the dominant narrative around Manic Street Preachers. Six months after the encounter at the *NME* Awards, I interviewed James and Nicky for the first time, shortly before the release of *The Holy Bible*. Richey was absent, having been admitted to The Priory, a private psychiatric facility in south-west London that specialises in treating addictions and eating disorders. The band played four festivals as a trio in order to pay for his care. With Edwards restored to the line-up, the Manics then undertook three months of touring, finishing with a residency at the London Astoria, smashing all their equipment at the end of the third night, 21 December 1994 – Richey's final public act as a Manic Street Preacher.

The disappearance of Richey Edwards continues to be the casual observer's main reference point for the band. Add this to the bittersweet miracle of the remaining trio not only surviving but prospering – in less than five years they had two million-selling albums and sold out Cardiff's Millennium Stadium – and it's easy to mistake their ongoing presence as an inevitability. There's a sense that the Manics' musical achievements are taken for granted, a byproduct of the fact they never broke up, even at the moment when their situation appeared utterly broken. Also, because their individual components are so idiosyncratic, the Manics have had a surprisingly limited musical influence. Apple Music's 'Inspired By Manic Street Preachers' playlist is thinly spread over fifteen tracks of mostly generic nineties alt-rock, and even features one solo track each by James Dean Bradfield and Nicky Wire to bulk up the numbers.

On the other hand, a search for 'Manic Street Preachers' on the academic digital library JSTOR brings 858 results. More scholarly papers have been written about the Manics than bands formed in emulation. This partly explains why other groups of their generation are playing stadiums on the nostalgia circuit, yet the Manics have always dealt in a different currency. Anyone seeking to fathom today's contemporary landscape of tech-dysfunction and resurgent fascist demagogues could do worse than sift these 168 songs for clues from history. Educators as well as entertainers, there's something glorious about their desire to continue the dialogue. As Sean Moore says, 'To achieve the perfect song – that's the only thing that keeps us going.'

Songs made the Manics, offered them a means to escape, to transcend and to celebrate themselves, and songs saved them and sustain them still. The moment they finished making their fifteenth album, 2025's *Critical Thinking*, thoughts turned to what lies ahead. James tells a great anecdote about his teenage self writing a fan letter to Mike Scott, after an all-night session listening to The Waterboys, even burning the edges of the paper to make it look ancient. Many years later, he found himself on the same plane as Scott, and after some agonised deliberation went over to introduce himself. Scott looked up and said, 'I got your letter.' More recently, asked to describe how The Waterboys' 1984 album *A Pagan Place* had affected him, Bradfield replied, 'Mike Scott's not trying to romanticise reality, *it's how he sees the world.*'[2]

James might as well have been talking about his own band. Manic Street Preachers built their own reality, then rebuilt it multiple times. Hopefully this book will explain how and why.

1.

Suicide Alley

Recorded: Sound Bank Studios, Blackwood
Producers: Glenn Powell and Tony Wilson
Released: Autumn 1988 (single, SBS Records)

'Hell, I tried – didn't I?'
> – R.P. McMurphy in *One Flew Over the Cuckoo's Nest*

For a little group of glam-punks being chased by the local toughs, 'Suicide Alley' was both a state of mind – 'where I can be what I want to be' – and an actual physical space: an escape route off Blackwood's main drag, just up from the Pizza House (where, as James Dean Bradfield recalls approvingly, 'the cheese wasn't Mozzarella, it was cheddar').

The debut Manic Street Preachers single gave this place a soundtrack. Its vision of rackety poundshop punk rock was written by James Dean Bradfield in his parents' front room at 20 Sir Ivor's Road, Pontllanfraith, one of the satellite communities clustered around Blackwood. The first version of 'Suicide Alley' came together on a farm in Mynyddislwyn – 'Islwyn Mountain' – where recording engineer Glenn Powell and his friend Tony Wilson had a studio, Sound Bank, a five-minute drive up twisty, ever-narrowing roads from Pontllanfraith. Although a rush-job, the recording still got the Manic Street Preachers their first play on BBC Radio Wales, which on Saturday mornings aired demos from new bands. 'That was "Suicide Alley" by a band from Blackwood up in the Valleys,' the DJ announced, 'called the Man Who Eats Peaches.' Bradfield flinched. Still, he thought, it had sounded amazing.

By June 1988, Sound Bank had moved two miles down the

Sirhowy Valley, to the basement of Cwmfelinfach Workingmen's Institute. Powell suggested that the Manics re-record 'Suicide Alley' 'properly' – 'as in, "that was the demo, but this is your breakthrough song",' says Bradfield. The process took two days, the first of which was wasted in a wholly counter-intuitive attempt to record each instrument in isolation, starting with the individual components of Sean Moore's drum kit. This might have been how Mutt Lange worked with Def Leppard, but the method was incompatible with the song's frantic energy and the band's rudimentary abilities. Taking a simpler approach on day two brought results. 'The moment we started playing "Suicide Alley" on the second day of that session, I felt we were going somewhere straight away,' says Bradfield. 'I actually felt really comfortable in the band, like we were meant to be here. I felt like we all understood each other – which is fifty per cent of whether a band's going to work or not.'

The mutual understanding extended to the fact that Nicky Wire isn't on the final recording – with the clock running down, Bradfield did as Steve Jones had done in the Sex Pistols and quickly added bass, thereby establishing a precedent for the Manics whereby the individual's role was subservient to the collective. Likewise, the division of labour, with Bradfield singing Wire's internal monologue, proclaiming this vision of 'a Scorsese-esque journey through a one-horse town', as Wire now puts it, revelling in the danger of daring to stand out from the herd, the tension of walking down Blackwood High Street on a Friday night and being asked why he was wearing a blouse. 'It was a celebration of "othering",' says Wire. 'Which seemed really prevalent when we were growing up. You didn't want inclusivity, you wanted exclusivity – "I don't want to be part of this shit."'

The song is elevated beyond high-velocity routine by a key-shift in its final third, suggested by Moore, accompanying Bradfield in the front room at 20 St Ivor's Road on a Casio keyboard. 'Sean said, "You haven't used this lyric: 'You can't eat away at my mind with your ideas of decency.'" I said, "Yeah, I couldn't fit those in." He said, "What about this?!" He went from the E major to the G sharp. So Sean wrote the outro. We just sat there, about six o'clock on a summer evening, and I thought, "Wow – that's how collaboration works."'

The idea of adding a guitar solo to counterpoint the outro's vocal – a conscious mirroring of the duel between Mick Jones and Joe Strummer at the end of The Clash's 'Complete Control' – came from Richey Edwards. Still yet to join the band, Edwards's input and presence were already key to its aesthetic direction. Older than the others by six months (Moore) to over a year (Bradfield and Wire), he provided a confident, calm presence in the studio. He also took the photograph of Bradfield, Moore and Wire standing in 'Suicide Alley' that would appear on the record's sleeve, echoing the image of Jones, Simonon and Strummer on The Clash's debut album: a temporary trio awaiting its essential fourth component. 'We looked ready,' says Bradfield. 'Ready to go into action.'

2.

Tennessee (I Get Low)

Recorded: Sound Bank Studios, Blackwood
Producers: Glenn Powell and Tony Wilson
Released: Autumn 1988 ('Suicide Alley' B-side,
    SBS Records)

'There ain't nothin' more powerful than the odour of
mendacity . . . It smells like death.'
                            – Tennessee Williams, *Cat On A Hot Tin Roof*

Although in its quaint way a perfect initial declaration of self, 'Suicide Alley' was a musical dead-end. Its B-side, on the other hand, had ambitions wider than mere utilitarian Clash homage: the hanging power chords and shrill distorted guitars suggestive of The Jesus and Mary Chain covering The Who, while Moore broke out of his punk regimentation with flailing drum rolls, driving a narrative of escape and fearlessness.

Philosophically too, the song reached beyond Blackwood and its enclave mentality, taking inspiration from a trip to the US undertaken by Wire's brother Patrick Jones in 1987 as part of his American Studies degree. Patrick returned with his head full of romantic adventure (he'd secretly got married), bags of Beat Generation literature, and a cassette of *Warehouse: Songs And Stories*, the valedictory double album by Minneapolis trio Hüsker Dü. Wire soaked it up into a love lyric that coupled the road's simmering promise of eternal redemption with intimations of drug tragedy: 'Take those pills and now she'll dream on/Tennessee's eyes orange once blue'. The overdose and the reprised verse's declaration 'I'll never forget you' echoed two songs, 'Pink Turns To Blue' and 'I'll Never Forget You', from *Zen Arcade*, an earlier

Hüsker Dü double set that reframed The Who's existentialist saga *Quadrophenia* for the post-punk era. 'The Who were a huge influence, much bigger than we admitted,' says Wire. 'Brutal yet so artistic.' Bradfield's reading of the lyric – 'a long-time longing, emotional pathfinding, trying the key that blocks the secret of everything' – prompted his suitably heroic chord shape: 'I put a G against a floating suspended A, and I'm thinking that's kind of "I Can See For Miles", sounds amazing. Nick says, "Oh, that's 'Just Like Paradise' by David Lee Roth . . ." You wanker!'

Although a favourite amid the band's shows during 1989–90, little of 'Tennessee (I Get Low)'s transcendent yearning spirit survived its subsequent makeover, as simply 'Tennessee', on *Generation Terrorists*. In Richey Edwards's rewrite, corrupted innocence became 'ultimate nihilistic love', with side helpings of American race-hate ('The white man is disease'), and all dynamic nuance vacuumed away amid producer Steve Brown's preferred template of turbo-rock gloss and programmed drums – much to Bradfield's subsequent dismay. 'There are only a few moments in our career where I can actually remember *not* being into it. And that's definitely one of those. The original "Tennessee" felt like a new way of expressing ourselves and we had to chase it. I don't think the rewrite does it any favours.'

3.
New Art Riot

Recorded: Workshop Studios, Redditch
Producer: Mark Tempest
Released: 25 June 1990 (*New Art Riot E.P.*, Damaged
    Goods)

'I don't want charity, just half a chance.'
                              – The Mighty Wah!, 'Come Back'

Manic Street Preachers were blessed and cursed from the very start. Cursed to come of age in South Wales just as the region's descent into the post-industrial economic darklands was hastened by the outcome of the 1984–85 miners' strike. And blessed by the binding ties of family and collective purpose that tradition-ally define working-class communities, for better and worse, in good times and bad. Together, these forces instilled a blinkered sense of defiance and esprit de corps that would sustain the band throughout its existence. It was blazingly evident even amid the scrawny routines of their early records, beginning with 'New Art Riot'.

Among the first three lyrics co-written by Richey Edwards and Nicky Wire, 'New Art Riot' was the most striking, and the first truly emblematic example of what soon became a Manic hallmark: a metrically convoluted jostle of philosophical and political placards, given plausibility by the music's heroic uplift. When Bradfield read the lyric sheet, one line in particular leapt out: 'Hospital closures kill more than car bombs ever will'. He recognised at that moment that his band were at complete vari-ance with the entirety of the UK's musical landscape, in particular the druggy hedonism of acid house and Madchester. 'It was the first song that felt like a manifesto,' he says. 'It's a misconception to think that statement was there to shock. It's just saying, "This is the people we are, this is where we come from and this is our intent." It put across how brutal Thatcher's government had been to us, literally coming into our town and going, "Fuck you, you're useless."'

With Moore now 'more in girlfriend territory than me', Bradfield wrote the music alone in his bedroom at Sir Ivor's Road, during early 1989. 'I had my little tape recorder, my goldfish – well, Sean's goldfish which he made me look after – and words from Nick and Richey. I had a ball for about a month.'

Seeking 'an emotional motivation' worthy of the verses' Year Zero indictments and exhortations ('Revolution soon dies, sold out for a pay rise'; 'Wipe out aristocracy now/Kill kill kill-kill-kill!'), he prefaced a gyroscopic chord sequence with a brace of staccato stabs, a structure considerably indebted to My Bloody Valentine's 1986 EP track 'Lovelee Sweet Darlene'. The more oblique chorus ('Museums are dead, take a new art stance/ Paint mass suicide on the aspiration diktat') was shored up by a series of choppy downstrokes, while a bridge section overlaid the verse with a brief solo guitar flare-out. 'The music had to be "bam-bam-bam", but I didn't want to just chug like Sham 69,' he says. 'I loved the way "(I'm) Stranded" by The Saints had such freedom to it. I thought "New Art Riot" was on the way to showing how the art and the politics are going to bleed into each other.'

Although the recording still erred on the side of homespun, 'New Art Riot' represented a considerable upgrade from its predecessor, with Bradfield in particular benefiting from Blackwood musician Reno Lusardi lending him an early sixties gold top Gibson Les Paul. Lusardi ran the Dorothy café on Blackwood High Street, where the fledgling band would meet to scheme up their next move, and he also sold copies of 'Suicide Alley' from behind the counter. Grateful as they were to such staunch local champions, the Manics were determined that their second release would be with a bona fide record label.

Ian Ballard had seen the Manics' first London gig, 22 September 1989 at the Horse and Groom pub on Great Portland Street – the set opened with 'New Art Riot', which was also one of the slogans spray-painted on the band's shirts and guitars – and subsequently offered to release a single on his east London-based retro-punk imprint Damaged Goods. Despite sending copies of 'Suicide Alley' to every major record label in London, no other offers were on the table, so in spring 1990 the band found themselves in a studio in the West Midlands town of Redditch that Damaged Goods had used previously. 'We slept in a school gymnasium,' says Wire. 'The owner of the studio had the keys. He said, "I'll put you up in here, on the floor." I think we had sleeping bags. I remember thinking, "How are we going to get out if there's a fire? What are we actually doing here?!" It was odd. Nice guys. But the sound was just so *indie*. There's no frisson in any of the recordings at all.'

'New Art Riot' was too awkward to qualify as regulation ruminant agitpunk, nor did it fit with anything else in 1990's Summer of Love Redux. Which was exactly how the Manics felt too. 'We knew it was gonna be hard to pull this off when we were completely on our own,' says Wire. 'It wasn't like there wasn't anything happening in Britain at that point, it was actually really exciting. But we thought a title like that had to be worth it. "New Art Riot" is probably the first great lyric we wrote.'

Having quickly fallen out of setlists by the end of 1990, 'New Art Riot' was rarely played live thereafter, barring a brief return in 1994 and a solitary reprise in Tokyo on 18 May 2012. In the era of Brexit, however, the song was revealed to be surprisingly prescient. In 1990, twelve gold stars on a blue field was not a common cultural signifier, and with little obvious indication that it would become so. The 'New Art Riot' sleeve featured 'Collapsed European Stars', a representation of the Flag of Europe. In conjunction with the back cover's statement that 'Nationalism Is An Invented Product', the song's opening lyric – 'Vintage aromas and vintage ideals/Old men greying to a dying country's needs' – suggests that whatever an 'aspiration diktat' might be, its repercussions continue to be felt well into the twenty-first century.

4.

Strip It Down

Recorded: Workshop Studios, Redditch
Producer: Mark Tempest
Released: 25 June 1990 (*New Art Riot E.P.*, Damaged
    Goods); Live version: 7 May 1991 ('You Love Us'
    B-side, Heavenly); 14 July 2003 (*Lipstick Traces*, Epic)

'But still, we must forsake all to win.'
    – Dexys Midnight Runners, 'Let's Make This Precious'

As with 'New Art Riot', the finished recording of its more tightly structured EP companion left the Manics feeling dissatisfied. 'Strip It Down' was an important song, one in which they felt emotionally invested: an exercise in deriving strength from the despair of their mid-eighties environment. 'We'd seen defeat in front of our eyes,' says Bradfield. 'It was a bitter irony – to feel as if we were a backwater, never mentioned in films or music or literature, and then we're on TV. Why is that? Because of the miners' strike. We're watching our own defeat, on TV and in real life. So we were trying to carve out something new for ourselves from the ruins around us: bad fashion, bad music and bad political decisions.'

The creative fuel for the Manics' latest counterblast was, once again, The Clash – but 'Strip It Down' was a long way from 'Suicide Alley', much as 'White Riot's spindly rush had muscled up into the siren power of 'Complete Control', The Clash's first recording with drummer Topper Headon and the point at which they were revealed as a multi-faceted rock band, instead of 'mere' punks. 'Sean had a real Topper groove on "Strip It Down",' says Wire. 'The amount of Sex Pistols and Clash we were listening to then, and absolutely loving, it had such a subconscious stain on our musicality and our lyrics. We weren't purposely trying to rip stuff off, it was just really deep in our veins.' The Pistols' nihilistic yang to The Clash's yin was evident in the Edwards/Wire lyric, broadly a critique of consumerism's dehumanising subtext: in particular, 'Hate is art and we steal cars/Decaying flowers in the playground of the rich', recalled 'God Save The Queen's 'flowers in the dustbin', while the phrase 'cheap appeal' echoed another Pistols song, 'EMI' (indeed, *Never Mind The Bollocks*' closing track would find its way into another key early Manics song soon enough; see 'You Love Us', page 37).

By fusing the two bands' distinct ethics, Manic Street Preachers synthesised their own: 'Denialism', which according to Bradfield, meant abjuring 'happiness' and other typical teenage distractions. 'We wanted to try and get rid of all decadence, in our souls, to have a sense of purpose.' In the case of 'Strip It Down', denialism extended to the absence of a chorus. Its four verses, with their clipped, military bearing, said all that was required.

'Strip It Down' stuck around in live setlists until the end of 1992, far longer than many of its contemporaries. The band's frustration at its recording was evident when a live version from Bath Moles Club on the Motown Junk tour was released as a B-side in 1991 (and later included on the *Lipstick Traces* compilation). Although lacking the original's exultant group shout of 'strip it down', it's otherwise the closest to a definitive version that exists – a steaming blast of the pure stuff. 'I wish it had been on the first album,' says Bradfield. 'It was one of our great live songs.'

5.

Motown Junk

Recorded: Power Plant Studios, London
Producer: Robin Evans
Released: 21 January 1991 (single, Heavenly)

> 'Let that shit die
> And find out the new goal.'
> — Sonic Youth, 'Kill Yr Idols'

By the summer of 1990, the Manics' resourceful self-promotion had begun to open doors out of Blackwood and into the UK music business. Published in August 1989, *NME*'s Single of the Week review of 'Suicide Alley' opened with writer Steven Wells citing an accompanying letter sent to him by James Dean Bradfield ('We are the suicide of the Non-Generation . . .')[1] before he eventually considered the merits of the music itself ('Retrogressive, exciting and inspired. You'll probably hate it').[2] A month later, on 22 September, Manic Street Preachers played their debut London gig, thanks to fanzine editor Kevin Pearce, a regular recipient of impassioned missives from Richey Edwards, inviting them to open for his band The Claim in the upstairs room at the Horse and Groom.

One of the few witnesses that night was journalist Bob Stanley, whose subsequent gig review in *Melody Maker* instigated a regular correspondence between himself and Richey, eventually resulting in the Manics' first national press interview, published in April 1990 under the headline 'Manic Street Preachers – The Ugly Face of the New Art Riot'. Now officially a band member, Edwards was the only Manic quoted in Stanley's short feature article, dispensing Marxist critique of the burgeoning Madchester scene – 'Everyone likes Happy Mondays 'cos when the working class dance nothing changes except prole fashion'[3] – and a geopolitical assessment of the band's home town: '[Blackwood is] a soul-destroying place, we'd rather say we're from Europe.'[4]

Edwards's first letter to Bob Stanley had been a brief, simple challenge: 'Dear Bob, inspire me, Richey.'[5] Stanley was so inspired by Edwards that he formed the band Saint Etienne, 'despite not being able to play an instrument'.[6] Another journalist in the band's sights was Steve Lamacq. *NME*'s news editor had already been sent a copy of 'Suicide Alley', with an accompanying letter that featured a photograph of himself cut out of the paper's singles reviews page and inscribed 'Cheekbone Charisma', and in due course received a cassette of demos, including 'New Art Riot', which his friend Ian Ballard would soon release as a single. Lamacq also commissioned the *NME* 'On' section, devoted to discovering the week's most exciting new acts, where Bradfield had read about a certain 'Philip Hall' representing a band named Loves Young Nightmare. Noting that *NME*'s masthead printed staff members' direct phone numbers, Bradfield decided to give Lamacq a call. By the end of their conversation, he had secured the address of Hall's PR company, Hall Or Nothing.

A former publicist at Stiff Records, Philip Hall's artist roster included The Pogues and The Stone Roses, and he was now also seeking a band to manage in partnership with his brother Martin. Whereupon a foaming communiqué arrived in Hall Or Nothing's Fulham Broadway office with a South Wales postmark – the Richey Edwards letter that would change the lives of all concerned.

'It basically said, "We are your future,"' Martin Hall recalled. 'A load of mad stuff, like "thin-skinned exhaustion", and there was a photograph of all of them wearing leather jackets, standing against a wall and smoking. Which was ironic, because none of them actually did smoke. Looking hard. The music was OK, but Philip was intrigued by the letter and he said, "Why don't you follow it up with a phone call?"'

It was Edwards's mother who answered. *'"Richard! Phone for yooou!"* He was über-polite,' Hall said. 'We arranged to see them rehearsing in Newbridge, at a little primary school in the Valleys.'

The initial meeting with the Halls was tinged with farce. Nervous, the band rehearsed beforehand, during which Wire cut his head open on a tuning key while practising his Paul Simonon bass moves. 'So they walk in and Nick is streaming blood,' Bradfield recalled. 'Richey was completely open and started spouting an essay in their faces. Sean didn't speak to them, and I walked past them because I was incredibly shy, but they just thought I was being aggressive.' Martin Hall was aghast. 'Five minutes,' he muttered to his brother, 'then we're back in the car.'

But Philip Hall got it, smiling as the band tore through a brief set – 'New Art Riot', 'Repeat' (with its refrain 'Repeat after me, fuck queen and country'), 'Faceless Sense Of Void' (which later became 'Love's Sweet Exile'), and 'Motown Junk'. He was still smiling during a lunch of chicken curry and chips in the nearby Plas Hotel in Blackwood, where Edwards and Wire went into manifesto overdrive. 'Philip didn't seem intimidated by any of it,' Bradfield said. 'I remember Martin saying, "There's only one song in there, 'Motown Junk', I think you need to write more songs." And I could tell Philip didn't care, he thought the songs would come. He thought they're just such a mad bunch of unfashionable Welsh dickheads that something good's gonna come of this. Good stuff happens when it seems improbable.'

On 30 August 1990, Manic Street Preachers had mid-billing at the Rock Garden, a cattle-market-level music industry haunt on London's Covent Garden Piazza, where bands typically paid to play. Among the handful of people watching were Bob Stanley, the Hall brothers, and Jeff Barrett and Martin Kelly, whose new record label Heavenly had recently released the first Saint Etienne single.

'We'd heard noises about the Manics from Kevin Pearce,' Kelly recalled. 'I saw a couple of these impassioned letters they'd written to him. We knew Philip, and he asked us to go down and see them at the Rock Garden. I reckon there were literally eight people in there. Maybe ten. Just me and Jeff and a few tourists who happened to be in Covent Garden at the time. And out came the Manics, who blazed like they were playing a stadium. Pulling shapes, jumping around . . . Jeff and I were pissing ourselves laughing. Not because they were shit – we thought they were brilliant, but it just seemed so mental, this band burning with so much conviction in front of an audience of none.'

An amiably intense advocate for rock 'n' roll righteousness, at twenty-eight Barrett had already self-taught himself across various roles in the record industry's service sector: retail buyer, gig pro-moter, and latterly publicist – his Capersville agency represented Primal Scream, The KLF, Happy Mondays and New Order. With hedonistic appetites to match those of his illustrious clients, and an enthusiastic convert to the ecstatic communion of rave culture and acid house, Barrett's label didn't seem the natural home for a group of punk rock denialists. Approaching the Manics at the Rock Garden, he and Kelly were initially scorned, until the word 'Heavenly' was mentioned.

'They became instantly friendly,' Kelly says, 'because they really liked Saint Etienne. We did a deal very quickly with Philip, for two singles. They were always very straight with us, told us they wanted to be on a major label, they didn't want to be an indie band – they wanted to be huge. It was a really weird band for anyone to sign at that time, me and Jeff got ridiculed by lots of people. Acid house was prevailing, the Mondays and the Roses had broken through, it seemed so out of step that four kids from Wales should be doing this. They were completely out of step with everything. And that was what Jeff and I loved.'

In Heavenly, the Manics were aligning with another outsider clique influenced by punk and its mischievous deployment of gesture politics. There was also a pragmatic consideration: they didn't have any other offers. Applying a publicist's instincts to his first foray into management, Philip Hall regarded the band's incongruity with Heavenly's other acts – the twenty-four-hour party animal house of Flowered Up, Kelly's Byrdsian janglers East Village, and Saint Etienne's elegiac synth-pop – as a talking-point, and therefore an asset.

'As soon as we were on Heavenly, people thought, "Perhaps there's something else to this band rather than just being derivative Welsh punks,"' Bradfield says. 'Heavenly helped overcome people's perception of us. Which was part of Philip's reasoning. There was something quite maverick about them. Plus, Philip loved Jeff and Martin, especially Jeff. He only liked characters. At this point Jeff had long Robert Plant hair – that was shocking! Philip was a quintessential inscrutable Englishman but with a lot of charm – on paper they would have been a mismatch, but they really got on. Having started out at Stiff, Philip's raison d'être for being in the record industry was to hang out with functioning nutters.'

Hall felt confident that the band's musical capabilities would soon match their brains and ambition. Until then, and indeed to accelerate the process, those latter qualities were to be unleashed into the public arena, be it on stage or in the press. One month before the Rock Garden meeting with Heavenly, Hall had flexed the credit that came with representing The Stone Roses – the UK's hottest band, at that moment enjoying a Top 5 hit single and having just played to 25,000 at Spike Island, the Madchester generation's Woodstock equivalent – and secured the Manics interviews in the main three weekly music papers. 'At our second ever meeting with Philip, he told us his plan,' Bradfield remembered. 'He said, "You've got to play lots of gigs, and journalists have got to meet Nick and Richey. Talk to them like you talk to me." That's what I liked about him – he understood. The band I was living in had these two mad intellectuals with Tourette's syndrome, and Philip got that.'

Confronted with Steven Wells, *NME*'s gonzoid amalgam of

Lester Bangs and Leon Trotsky, an erstwhile ranting poet and member of the Socialist Workers Party who valued a rock band's revolutionary potential far more than specific musical attributes, Edwards and Wire funnelled years of wishful schemes into pithy self-mythology. 'We wanna be the biggest rock 'n' roll nightmare ever and we wanna take the monarchy and the House of Lords with us . . . We've spray-painted our school shirts to wipe out the brainwash and the boredom . . . When we jump onstage it is not rock 'n' roll cliché but the geometry of contempt.'[7] Wells was bedazzled. 'They have more energy and anger and intelligence than any other band I have ever interviewed,' he declared.

Melody Maker's Bob Stanley was treated to similar hot metal gold: 'We want to set fire to ourselves on *Top of the Pops*!'[8] Meanwhile, Andy Peart of *Sounds* asked where the Manic Street Preachers might be in twenty years' time. 'In the grave,' Wire declared, with Richey adding: 'Hopefully.'[9]

Bradfield and Moore were content to sit quietly and watch the blitzkrieg unfold, productively channelling any qualms that the bad's next record might struggle to match such rhetoric. In the end, 'Motown Junk' proved good enough. 'It was down to us being ready,' Bradfield said. 'We'd rehearsed a lot. We made sure that we were prepared, because we were nervous. We knew that Philip, Martin and Terri were pulling us favours and that we were going to a proper studio.'

Thanks to Philip Hall's wife, Terri, whose company This Much Talent managed the in-house producers at Power Plant on Willesden High Road, north-west London, Manic Street Preachers recorded their third single in the same room where Rod Stewart made 'Maggie May', on a Harrison console described as 'full of beefy goodness' by the Power Plant owner Robin Millar, whose own production credits included Sade's *Diamond Life*.[10] Bradfield played a vintage Gibson Les Paul Standard owned by musician Pete Brown, whose sister, the renowned singer Sam Brown, was married to the session's producer Robin Evans. 'As soon as I picked it up it sang to me,' says James. 'I'd never played a guitar that good before.'

Aware that this was, in every sense, a long way from the Workshop in Redditch, let alone Cwmfelinfach Workingmen's Institute, for the duration of the session the band slept in their van, parked in the street outside the studio, despite the fact that Bradfield had a bad cold. 'It was freezing,' he said. 'And a bit hairy round there. We were valley boys, slightly fish out of water. But we walked in and there's a big twirly staircase that went up to our studio. It was like *Stardust* or *Rock Follies*, everything I thought a studio should be.'

The 'one song' Martin Hall rated at Newbridge School, 'Motown Junk' had evolved considerably by the time it got to the Power Plant. An initial draft lyric dated from the same period as 'Tennessee (I Get Low)' (see page 10), and was likewise a Nicky Wire solo effort, with strong hits of doomed Beat romance. The lyric printed in the twentieth-anniversary edition of *Generation Terrorists* opens: 'I only ever wanted to be with you/Last words of your life spoken in blue'. As with the original 'Tennessee', this version can be read as a cautionary drug lament, with 'Motown junk' literally heroin from 'Motortown' (that is, Detroit), and the lines 'Motown junk it gets so vicious/Stops your heart beating for 68 seconds' suggesting an accidental overdose.

'At the time, my lyrics were much more influenced by American literature, because my brother had brought all this stuff back in particular,' says Wire. 'I came up with the title "Motown Junk". And Richey moulded it into a much cleverer lyric than it was.'

Even in the familiar Edwards/Wire version, 'Motown Junk's opening lyric – 'Never ever wanted to be with you' – reads like a declaration of thwarted love. (Wire: 'It might not even have been *that* deep.') Thereafter, however, it throttles swiftly into the accusatory rebellious jukeboxing that was already the band's hallmark, albeit now with heightened impact. Wire's revised 'Stops your heart beating for 168 seconds/Stops your brain thinking for

168 seconds' couplet referred to 'some spurious theory in the *NME* where that was the perfect length for a pop single', a pop single quite possibly released on Motown. Therefore, at 2 minutes 48 seconds' duration, both Smokey Robinson & The Miracles' 'I Second That Emotion' and 'You're All I Need To Get By' by Marvin Gaye & Tammi Terrell would fit the bill perfectly. The Temptations' 'My Girl' and The Four Tops' 'I Can't Help Myself (Sugar Pie Honey Bunch)' came agonisingly close at 2:45, with The Supremes' 'Stop! In The Name Of Love' a mere four seconds too long. All these and a great many more were grist to the song's hard-but-fair Marxist takedown: 'Love songs echo underclass betrayal.'

When he was handed the finished lyric, Bradfield's first thought was: '"Great title, but . . . I *love* Motown." Then I read the lyric, and of course I got it straight away. It was the right song, a very concise message, with some great lines. "All your slut heroes offer is a fear of the future" – it's such a lovely, beautifully scanned line. Nick and Richey are just bouncing off each other in a beautiful way.'

'Motown Junk' features hardly any of the awkward metre that Bradfield and Moore would often be tasked with turning into songs. In terms of awkwardness, however, one Richey Edwards line would duly earn lasting notoriety: 'I laughed when Lennon got shot'. 'The mad thing is, I don't even think we had a second thought about it at the time,' Wire says. 'There was never any discussion. Certainly no regret, not until much later on.'

Bradfield began self-censoring the lyric in live performance by the mid-nineties, roughly the point when The Beatles had become decisively re-canonised by contemporary enthusiasts from Oasis downwards. 'The line does cause harm,' he says. 'And we do regret it. "I laughed when Lennon got shot" – it's awful. We came out trying to prove too many things to too many people too quickly. I don't even like thinking about that line.'

Jeff Barrett and Martin Kelly appreciated the logic behind the band's reflexive assaults on rock's high temple. As James recalled: 'Richey would say things like, "We fucking despise Bob Dylan" to cause a reaction. I remember Jeff saying, "We know why you're saying that and we're going to let you get away with it."' The proposed sleeve art for 'Motown Junk', however, went too far – and in this instance the transgressors weren't the band. A collage by Heavenly associate Paul Cannell, the central image was a photograph of John Lennon and Yoko Ono, with a gun pointing at Lennon's head. The artwork's other main detail accrued eerie prescience following the 9/11 attack on New York: an airliner flying towards one of the World Trade Center's Twin Towers.

'It was presented to us and we were like, "Well, it looks good, but we can't use it,"' says James. Instead, the band collaborated with Simon Ryan on an alternative design featuring a watch found amid the ruins of Hiroshima, its hands burnt to a stop at 8:15, the time when the atomic bomb was dropped on 6 August 1945. Although the Cannell design literally referenced the song, the released artwork delivered a more nuanced jolt to an acquiescent pop culture, while also invoking themes that would recur in the band's work.

However offensive to some, claiming to have laughed at the murder of John Lennon seems a straightforwardly blunt, if extreme, example of the heresy that was the lingua franca of the Manics' punk forebears – The Clash's song '1977' declared 'No Elvis, Beatles or Rolling Stones', despite the band's fond appreciation of at least two of the three. Nicky Wire recalls Edwards describing 'I laughed when Lennon got shot' as the Manics' 'Pol Pot moment': an act of generation terror, negating the old order in the style of Johnny Rotten singing 'I am an antichrist' or wearing his 'I hate Pink Floyd' T-shirt. Three months after the single's release, the Manics opened their debut New York gig with Nicky declaring, 'The best thing that New York ever did was kill John Lennon', to audible gasps from the sparsely attended Limelight club. Yet given its subsequent notoriety, it's interesting to note how little media comment the lyric provoked at the time of 'Motown Junk's release, when interviewers seemed more preoccupied with the feasibility of the band's self-proclaimed kamikaze mission: 'The most important thing we can do is get massive and throw it all away . . . One double album that goes to Number 1 worldwide. Then we split. If it doesn't work, we split anyway. Either way, after one album, we're finished.'[11]

Manic Street Preachers placed a premium value on fuelling the music press sausage grinder. Each week had the potential to create new stars from well-turned hyperbole and a half-decent single. So perhaps the most shocking aspect of 'Motown Junk' was just how good a record it was. Post-Newbridge School, a demo version had been recorded in south-east London. Although in Bradfield's estimation 'a bit slow and ponderous', the Hall brothers remained convinced the song was fit for purpose – effectively the band's second debut single. And at Power Plant, Robin Evans's balance of technique and art contrasted with the more rigid sensibilities of their previous engineers. 'He was amazing, instinctive and skilled,' Bradfield says. 'And he believed in us straight away. Robin could hear the chemistry between us. He said, "I love the songs, you're not writing like anybody else at the moment, this is going to be amazing. Please, just trust me."'

Bradfield wanted to embellish the brief guitar solo following the first chorus, but Evans demurred. 'He said, "No, that's a really natural, off-the-cuff solo, like somebody's confident they've got something else in their locker – it's perfect as it is."' Amid the discordant bridge after the second verse and chorus, Bradfield flipped his pickup selector, Pete Townshend-style, then asked to re-record it. 'Robin went, "No, it drags your ear to it, you're thinking something's gone wrong – there's chaos, it's good." He was confident in everything we did.'

'Motown Junk's recording fed off the ghosts in the room – before 'Maggie May', the former Morgan Studio 1 had played host to Free's 'All Right Now' and The Who's 'Pinball Wizard' – as well as the Manics' own slut heroes. Bradfield's cold slightly deepened his normal vocal register, lending 'a little bit of Joe Strummer hoarseness'. The decision to add a layer of Hammond organ, played by the studio's rookie tape operator Dave Eringa, was taken only after debating whether, in Bradfield's words, 'it might be going outside the bounds of what The Clash would do at that point in their careers'. Even Eringa's presence as assistant engineer at the session came framed by The Clash: 'Terri Hall asked me did I want to make tea for the new Clash, and I thought, "That'll be good."'[12]

Although their public statements soon began to repudiate The Clash – in favour of Guns N' Roses and Public Enemy – 'Motown Junk's key sonic influence was clear enough. After running his guitar parts through one of the studio's old Marshall amps, James asked Robin Evans: 'Have you got something with a bit more gain to it, a bit more . . . *fizz*?' By way of reference, he then dug out a cassette and played the producer The Clash's 'Complete Control' and 'Tommy Gun'. The collective space inhabited by those two contains 'Motown Junk's brawny, fissile guitar tones – now played through the studio's Burman amp – as powered by Sean Moore's martial drumming and pliant, textural bass that belied the notion of Nicky Wire as little more than a rudimentary player. The band's first quantum leap forward, 'Motown Junk' distilled a fresh vocabulary for rock from a young lifetime's worth of accumulated emotion, its kinetic surges and melodic élan ultimately transporting the likes of 'Twenty-one years of living and nothing means anything to me' beyond utopian rhetoric and into the realm of the possible . . . if only for 238 seconds.

Bradfield: 'Everything lined up. You won't hear me say it much, but "Motown Junk" is perfection.'

It wouldn't resolve the debate over the perfect pop single's optimum duration, but 'Motown Junk' did provide its creators with a daunting new benchmark. Had they never made another record, here was a definitive declaration of self, even down to the fine details of the two samples which open and close the song: a looped shout of 'revolution!' from Public Enemy's 'Countdown To Armageddon' counterpointed by the mechanised guitar clang of Skids' 'Charles', a song about a factory worker turned into a robot, which slows down into obsolescence after Bradfield's valedictory chant: 'We live in urban hell, we destroy rock and roll'. Revolution come and gone in just under four minutes – a very Manics metaphor for the human condition.

'I don't think we ever sounded like that again,' Wire says. 'Nothing's ever been as good as that was . . . that moment.'

6.
Sorrow 16

Recorded: Power Plant Studios, London
Producer: Robin Evans
Released: 21 January 1991 ('Motown Junk' B-side,
    Heavenly); 14 July 2003 (*Lipstick Traces*, Epic)

'There was nowhere to go but everywhere,
so just keep on rolling under the stars.'
                                    – Jack Kerouac, *On The Road*

On the day of 'Motown Junk's release, the Manics were given a two-minute segment of BBC's *Snub TV*, featuring live footage from a spectacularly chaotic London gig six weeks earlier, and a group interview-cum-monologue. Among the many verbal hostages to fortune was Nicky Wire's 'We will never write a love song, ever. Full stop.' He'd already said as much on 'Sorrow 16': making his first Manics vocal interjection, Wire appended the refrain 'I feel like falling, feel like falling' with a gleeful 'in HATE!'

The recording provided an early textbook example of how fruitfully the band's intense creative chemistry could translate to a studio. After the final take of 'Motown Junk', everyone looked to the control room gallery, expecting Robin Evans to beckon them up for a listen. Instead, the producer insisted: 'Stay in the groove and do "Sorrow 16".' Evans was keen to slipstream the session's first-day momentum and sprinkle some 'Motown Junk' gold dust on an older song – about which Bradfield, at least, felt ambivalent.

'For me, "good" punk was a kind of classic rock 'n' roll,' he says. 'Like the Pistols, The Clash, Buzzcocks, The Saints. I didn't like things that were *too* punk, whether it be Abrasive Wheels,

Slaughter & The Dogs, Sham 69 . . . So I had a bee in my bonnet about "Sorrow 16" being too suburban-band-in-blues-club punk, just chugging all the way through. I wasn't happy about recording it, and I let Nick and Sean take control.'

On a bootleg recording of the 22 September 1989 Horse and Groom gig, there's certainly not much to differentiate the song from hi-velocity scrappers like Anti-Love and Destroy The Dancefloor. But the Power Plant version, where Sean Moore instils focus with half-time beat, shows why 'Sorrow 16' was still being played live regularly into 1993 while its lumpen bedfellows never made it beyond the toilet circuit. Amid the lyric's mostly routine Beatnik-into-Mod nihilism – 'Cut your hair in front of businessmen', suggests disillusioned Jimmy, the hero of The Who's *Quadrophenia*, singing 'Cut My Hair' – and residual echoes of The Jam ('too many numbers'), a string of unexpected musical flourishes elevate 'Sorrow 16' to its place of modest transcendence, notably the Kerouacian regret of 'Oh the road is beautiful' crowned by Bradfield's spelling out the word 'B-E-A-U-T-I-F-U-L', marking the first instance of a recurring Manic trope. Even the singer came round in the end and stretched his creative loins, enthusiastically playing slide guitar and becoming his own mini-choir for the 'I feel like falling' section.

'Robin Evans suggested that,' Bradfield says. 'I had a background in choir, so I knew how to harmonise. By the end of that second day we'd put a lot of overdubs on "Sorrow 16", and there's been a bit of serendipity at play. I didn't like what Nick and Sean had done with the half-time and the chugging, but I could see it had started to work. I realised that's what band dynamic is: you do what other people want sometimes and you fit around them, and then they bring something out of you. That's what it's all about.'

The title, incidentally, isn't mentioned anywhere in the lyric. 'It was originally inspired by The Pretty Things' *S.F. Sorrow*, says Wire. 'I'd always wanted to get "Sorow" in, because it's one of my favourite words. And "16" is the age – 16 being peak. "The wall is a reason to believe" – that was Richey's line. It's a youth song. Some great in-the-pocket guitar solos on this as well.' He laughs. 'Before James got too fast!'

Even more incidentally: The Pretty Things' 1968 psychedelic rock opera *S.F. Sorrow* initially went unreleased in the US. It eventually appeared in mid-1969 on Rare Earth – the newly launched and ultimately ill-fated rock imprint of the Motown Recording Corporation.

7.

We Her Majesty's Prisoners

Recorded: Power Plant Studios, London
Producer: Robin Evans
Released: 21 January 1991 ('Motown Junk' B-side,
  Heavenly); 14 July 2003 (*Lipstick Traces*, Epic)

'She looked young: for a moment she had turned back
from a figurehead into the young woman she was, before
monarchy froze her and made her a thing, a thing which
only had meaning when it was exposed, a thing that
existed only to be looked at.'

– Hilary Mantel, 'Royal Bodies'

In some respects, 'We Her Majesty's Prisoners' perfectly fits the
profile of an anti-royal family song by the young Manic Street
Preachers. If 'Motown Junk' was their best possible tribute to
The Clash, then its B-side invoked the Sex Pistols, specifically
'God Save The Queen'. No mere 'fascist regime', however, here
Elizabeth II is equated to an actual Nazi concentration camp ('So
celebrate Buchenwald as her majesty's heir'), bolstering a shock
quotient that was already rising nicely thanks to the chorus
refrain 'ceremonial rape machine' – originally the song's title
until Heavenly gently suggested considering an alternative. The
monarch is repeatedly indicted for being an all-pervasive agent
of colonial oppression ('England's glory lives on in worldwide
genocide'), inequality ('Underneath silk riches 66 million giving
slaves') and mass delusion ('Faces pressed at gates of anniversary
torture'). For good measure, the charge sheet adds the monarch's
role of *fidei defensor* ('This needle of religion's gonna rust in my
skin'); antipathy towards religion, state-sponsored or otherwise,

would become a familiar Richey Edwards preoccupation.

For all its intemperance, however, the lyric is structurally disciplined: three compact four-line verses, a four-line bridge and four iterations of a repeated two-line chorus. Its only rogue element comes just before the first refrain when Nicky Wire steals forward gleefully to command, 'Bow down!', like an overexcited theatre prompt.

'It's definitely a 75–80 per cent Richey lyric,' says Wire. 'Fair play to him – it's brilliant. I'm not sure how James wrote it, because the lines are quite hard to sing. I don't think we ever played this together until we recorded it.'

Bradfield was immediately enthused upon receiving the lyric. The Manics already had an anti-royal song in their live set, the route-one rabble-rouser 'Repeat' ('Fuck queen and country!'), and he was keen to try a different approach. 'Already the response to "Repeat" was, "Oh, they're just doing that do get a reaction . . ." No, we actually felt like that. I've truly got great distaste for anything that mob, those German cattle rustlers, are connected to. So I thought this lyric wasn't as obvious, but still as deeply felt.' Bradfield was particularly struck by the line 'Leaving us like butterflies trapped in the frost', the first instance of a recurring Manic trope: animals pitifully depicted as an analogue for human pain. 'It was something a bit more abstract,' Bradfield says. 'This song wasn't so linked into a punk methodology.'

In both the languidly menacing opening riff and the chorus's tingling piano underlay, the obvious musical reference is The Rolling Stones in all their late-sixties satanic majesty – although Edwards teased Bradfield that the riff more closely resembled 'Rock And A Hard Place' from 1990's *Steel Wheels*. 'Richey said, "You've not just copied the Stones, you've copied the shit modern Stones!" Stuff goes in by osmosis, obviously,' James says, 'but I would never have done that.' The piano, recurrently giving voice to a character never actually seen, was inspired by Nicky Hopkins in the outro of 'Street Fighting Man'. 'We recorded this song because we didn't have any others ready,' Bradfield admits, 'but it was exciting not knowing what it was going to be. Nobody's locked in with each other, everybody's floating in their own space.'

That space, rushing over and beneath the song's taut-yet-loose groove, possibly owed something to Bradfield's shifts behind the bar at Newbridge Memo Hall, a bikers' haunt where resident DJ Disco Dick would plays lots of Hawkwind. There's even a touch of the Charlie Watts drag to Sean Moore's drumming. 'Sean's not really accenting the vocals like he would have something else,' Bradfield considers. 'He's not locked in with Nick, everyone's quite free. Robin Evans jumped straight on that, he went for a very minimalist approach, a very pure sound on the rhythm section.'

Evans ('kind of an old hippy who knew punk,' says Wire) also felt the whiff of Hawkwind, and encouraged the psychedelic noise section which comprises the atypically long song's final third, wrapping Bradfield's guitar solo in echoey doom courtesy of an AMS digital delay unit. Amid the tumult, gleeful MC Wire pops up once again, cooing, 'Hello future, you're my lover'. Despite Richey's protestations that 'we don't do trip-outs' (as denounced in the band's *Snub TV* manifesto along with love songs and ballads), it was the perfect finale, contravening the band's own self-declared Magna Carta even as the ink dried on the parchment.

In asserting the right to break their own rules, 'We Her Majesty's Prisoners' is the last critical element in the Manics' first essential artefact. Untypical of the group's material at this stage, its proximity to 'Motown Junk's clarion conviction saw it overlooked and rarely ever performed live. Yet it was a key signifier that there was more going on here than first appeared, perhaps more than even the Manics themselves were ready to admit or embrace: the music's elegiac qualities counterpointed the harsh words, evincing ambiguous feelings, even sympathy, for the devil.

So yeah, fuck queen and country, but . . . Accompanied by that eerie piano – played by Dave Eringa – and Bradfield's wounded supplicant howl, 'Ceremonial rape machine/Love won't corrode you', could read as a feminist critique of monarchy, pitying the royal women valued only for their bodies' reproductive function, lamenting the lead-lined cruelty of an institution that owes its longevity to 'fake images'.

'It's the eternal jubilee,' says Wire. '"Repeat"'s obviously much more direct, but there was more existential threat to "We Her Majesty's Prisoners", it says something more about hierarchical society. Whenever I listen to it now, I'm quite startled at the classicism of it, and the playing. I didn't feel like we were capable of that.'

8.
You Love Us

Recorded: Power Plant Studios, London
Producer: Robin Evans
Released: 7 May 1991 (single, Heavenly)
Second version recorded: Black Barn, Surrey, August–
    December 1991. Producer: Steve Brown. Released:
    20 January 1992 (single, Columbia); 10 February 1992
    (*Generation Terrorists*, Columbia)

'What is this shit?'
> – Greil Marcus, review in *Rolling Stone*
> of Bob Dylan, *Self Portait*

After 'Motown Junk's sleeve evocation of nuclear Armageddon, the next Manic Street Preachers single went straight back to hell. 'You Love Us' opens with a sample of *Threnody To The Victims Of Hiroshima*, Krzysztof Penderecki's 1960 composition for fifty-two string instruments, famed for its extreme dissonance. The fifteen-year-old James Dean Bradfield came home from school one day to find Sean Moore listening to the piece as part of his A-level music studies at Crosskeys College. 'It was exactly at the point where the strings are being plucked and they're supposed to be like flesh dripping, which is obviously horrific. It had a massive effect on me – like, this is what people can do with music.'

An attempt at emulating with acoustic instruments the electronic sounds Penderecki discovered while studying at Warsaw's Polish Radio Experimental Studio in the late fifties, *Threnody* was a radical piece of music. Penderecki had a traditional conservatory education, but after hearing Karlheinz Stockhausen and *musique concrète* he sought to create a new, freer form of classical music, focused on texture and rejecting traditional notation. Originally titled *8'37"* – in reference to John Cage's *4'33"* – the composer dedicated *Threnody* to Hiroshima's victims after he witnessed the raw, disturbing emotional power of the performed piece. Some orchestras refused to perform it, with one Italian radio ensemble claiming the unorthodox percussive techniques would destroy their instruments. Which was exactly the kind of vehement reaction the Manics hoped to provoke with 'You Love Us'.

If 'Motown Junk' was the breach in the wall, then its follow-up had to be the vanguard of full-on cultural revolution. Or at the very least, a Top 40 hit. 'This is a song that was self-anointed as our big single, as soon as Nick and Richey wrote the lyrics, without us even writing any music,' Bradfield says. 'Which shows the way we thought – especially the way Nick and Richey thought.'

Bradfield and Moore knew the stakes were high when they saw the title, an inversion of 'We Love You', The Rolling Stones' somewhat half-baked attempt to join 1967's Summer of Love carnival. A quarter of a century on, the Manics wanted to invoke a Summer of Hate, to shock the post-acid house indie generation out of its loved-up loose-fit complacency. 'Nowadays it's all about the audience,' Wire says. 'You know, "The audience is amazing, they make the gig." We were the exact opposite of that. We were searching for the ultimate nihilistic statement, and we couldn't get it. When Richey came up with "you love us", that was a real light-bulb moment, and there was a fair bit of lyric rewriting at that point.'

Faced by hostility from live audiences and scepticism from music journalists, the Manics now reflected back the adversarial energy, a textbook punk move derived from Sex Pistols manager Malcolm McLaren's fascination with obscure sixties, European intellectual provocateurs the Situationists. In 'You Love Us', acid was no longer the euphoric 'Aciiieeed' but a weapon 'thrown into your face'. The Manics would 'pollute' the pilled-up drones' 'mineral water with a strychnine taste'. A classic yin/yang Edwards/

Wire collaboration, with a generous pinch of Public Enemy's '911 Is A Joke' in the couplet 'Parliament's a fake life saver/You better wake up and smell the real flavour', for the most part, however, it's the most utilitarian Manic Street Preachers lyric of the period, built around relentless repetition of a chorus – which itself was simply a repetition of the title. 'Richey was trying to get some extra words in,' says Wire, 'but we wanted a Pistols-esque yob rock thing.'

Bradfield and Moore delivered that much at least from their regular writing lair in the kitchen at 20 Sir Ivor's Road, Pont-llanfraith. 'Sean wrote the verse – F-C-G – and then we both stumbled upon the bridge, D to B to C,' James recalls. 'I already had the chorus, a Pistols sliding-into-the-main chord thing. We were dead happy with ourselves – the whole riposte to the Stones' "We Love You", refracting that working-class arrogance through our young crazy narcissism. I remember practising it in my living room with the boys, thinking, "Yeah! This is as good as anything the Pistols ever did!" before going downstairs and cooking the fish finger sandwiches. And then we went back to the Power Plant.'

Returning to north-west London, to the scene of 'Motown Junk', with the same producer and engineer, all made perfect sense. Even the freezing cold weather did its bit to replicate the circumstances of that previous session. This time, however, the Manics were in the Power Plant's second studio, known as the Jade Room, as opposed to Studio 1, the 'Maggie May' room. 'Everybody said it was the better room, the desk was better, it had flying faders, all that,' says Bradfield. 'But as soon as we starting recording "You Love Us", I knew it wasn't as good, the drum sound wasn't as good, it was a bit more processed. All the way through the session, I was thinking "I wish we were in the big gallery room." So I was worried.'

Misgivings led to overcompensation. Bradfield did some guitar harmonics through the chorus – Wire: 'I liked it, but it wasn't very Pistolsy' – which Robin Evans said sounded '"a bit like Eddie

Van Halen".' Adding 'ooh-ooh-oohs' to the verse didn't exactly boost the *Bollocks* quotient. Even the Penderecki sample, albeit a startling gesture, felt like putting vinaigrette on a bag of chips. That the song had already become a live favourite, the setlist opener on the January/February Motown Junk tour, only heightened frustration in the studio. An outro section was cooked up, wherein James spiels nihilistic insurrectionary jivetalk ('Fall out scream, death melody'; 'Hey passive electorate, die die die!') over a sample of Iggy Pop's 'Lust For Life'. 'I thought it was a bit too cheeky,' says James, 'I was like, "I'm not sure about this, boys." But Nick and Richey were saying, "Ah, fuck it."' Ironically, the outro had the crunch the rest of the recording lacked. For a final coup de théâtre, the cheapest guitar the band owned, a blue Aria pro, was smashed and its dying groans added onto the end. The Manics were, as Bradfield acknowledges in baseball parlance, 'swinging for the fence' – and it would not be the last time.

The Heavenly version of 'You Love Us' inadvertently confirmed 'Motown Junk' had been a case of supernatural alchemy. That Pistols-esque yob-rock vision turned into something closer to the camped-up glammery of Malcolm McLaren's original Situationist pop project, the New York Dolls: an overthought, undercooked indie record that can't quite realise its grand vision. 'I don't know what happened,' Wire says. 'Everything sounds like it's recorded with a tea towel over it.' On 15 May, one week after releasing an interesting indie artefact rather than the soundtrack for cultural erasure, overcompensation took a disturbing turn when Richey warmed down from an interview with *NME* journalist Steve Lamacq by razoring a chunk of 'You Love Us' ('Our voices are for real') into his left forearm. Days later, however, he was all smiles as the band signed a six-figure deal with Columbia, the world's oldest and most prestigious record company. After posing for photographs in the label's London boardroom, the band played a gig at the Marquee club. 'You Love Us' both opened and closed the set. The following week, the single entered the UK chart at number 62. Nicky Wire felt 'disappointed'.

As 1991 progressed, the band struggled to reconcile the recorded incarnation of 'You Love Us' with the song's central role in their self-mythology. During the Power Plant session, Robin Millar had been passing the Jade Room and listened for a moment or two. 'That song's a hit,' he confided to Dave Eringa. 'Not yet, but it will be.'

Inevitably, they took another swing at it during the *Generation Terrorists* album sessions. At Black Barn Studios in Surrey, under the sharp-eyed auspices of producer Steve Brown – maker of hits for Boomtown Rats, The Cult and Wham! – 'You Love Us' was transformed from gauchely artful glam-pop into tungsten-veined testostorock. There was no room for subtlety, no guitar harmonics or ooh-oohs. Out went Penderecki, in came the annihilatory pounding of programmed drums and multiple guitar parts so glossy they stung. The new coda saw Iggy replaced by Slash, as Bradfield effectively rewrote the ending to 'Paradise City', Guns N' Roses by now firmly installed as the Manics' new last gang in town. Even James himself wondered if this final piece of rock 'n' roll onanism was too much.

'I remember thinking, "I'm surrounded by nutters." I came in from one of those solo takes and Steve Brown was going, "Nicky, I've worked with Lemmy, I've worked with Elton John, I've worked with George Michael. I've met a lot of leopards in my life – and you, my friend, are a rock 'n' roll leopard!" Nick and Richey were egging me on, Sean was a bit circumspect, but Steve was just blazing. I love playing guitar, it was just that end section I wasn't sure about. But Steve did a good job – he did what the record company wanted him do.'

On 1 February 1992, Robin Millar's prediction came to pass: 'You Love Us' entered the Top 30 and Manic Street Preachers duly made their debut appearance on *Top of the Pops*, the BBC-approved portal to the Great British Living Room. Nicky went down on James's guitar à la Bowie/Ronson, Richey threw immaculate shapes, James changed 'mineral water' to 'marijuana', and from his giant riser Sean had the best view of the pyrotechnics. Mission accomplished.

Ultimately, neither version of 'You Love Us' adequately conveys just why it's been performed more than any other Manic Street Preachers song, featuring in almost every setlist since January 1991. Which may explain its durability: it continues to make demands on both the performer and the audience. The band can't fake it, because there is no definitive 'it' to fake – it's got to be *for real* every time. The fans, meanwhile, never tire of living up to the core provocation – can they prove they're really worthy of this? 'Every line is a killer,' says Wire. 'To this day it makes me wince, which is a good sign. You're playing a song that you're expecting a lot of your audience to accept.'

9.
Spectators Of Suicide

Recorded: Power Plant Studios, London
Producer: Robin Evans
Released: 7 May 1991 ('You Love Us' B-side, Heavenly);
     14 July 2003 (*Lipstick Traces*, Epic)
Second version recorded: Black Barn, Surrey, August–
     December 1991. Producer: Steve Brown. Released:
     10 February 1992 (*Generation Terrorists*, Columbia)
Third version recorded: Door To The River Studios,
     Newport, 2020. Producer: Loz Williams. Released:
     17 December 2020 (download, Heavenly)

> 'All that was once directly lived has become
> mere representation.'
>
>   – Guy Debord, *The Society of The Spectacle*

On 28 September 1990, Nicky Wire received a book that changed
his life. 'To Nick love Richey, James and Sean', read the inscription
on the inside cover. Published in July 1989, *Lipstick Traces* was the
latest volume of cultural archaeology by American music journalist
Greil Marcus, an epic trek across the twentieth century discovering connections between politics, art, philosophy and music: in
particular the Dadaist avant-garde, the utopian Marxist ideas of a
tiny intellectual sect called the Situationist International, and the
Sex Pistols, the band that Marcus contended had stripped rock 'n'
roll 'down to essentials of speed, noise, fury and manic glee'[1] and
whose first record, 'Anarchy In The UK', 'launched a transform-
ation of pop music all over the world'.[2]

Along the way, he pointed out that the 'Holidays In The Sun'
lyric 'A cheap holiday in other people's misery' was adapted from

a Situationist slogan written in graffiti during the May 1968 Paris uprising, the event that catalysed a generation of malcontents, notably frustrated Croydon School of Art student Malcolm McLaren.

Marcus's levitational text fizzed through the Manics' collective brain until it blew open. 'It persuaded us that we could attempt to create art that just might deeply resonate with people in the way that the book had resonated with us,' Wire wrote in a foreword for the twentieth-anniversary edition of *Lipstick Traces*, where he acknowledged the traces left by the book throughout his band's work, particularly in this foundational period – beginning with 'Spectators Of Suicide'.[3]

The song's title derived from *The Society of The Spectacle*, the 1967 text by Situationist International founder Guy Debord, which critiqued advanced-stage capitalism's alienating impulses in a numbered series of 'Theses', aphorisms and slogans. Chapter I ('The Culmination of Separation'), Thesis 34 states: 'The spectacle is capital accumulated to the point where it becomes images'.[4] Debord was essentially updating Marx for the age of mass media and its visual fusillade of advertisements, inducements, nudges. 'The domination of the economy' had progressively degraded life from 'being into having'[5]; technology was now evolving the misery of item commodification on to the passive consumption of images, ideas, culture. The Situationists' response to the spectacle was typically esoteric: they urged its negation, via the *détournement*, or diversion, of events or language – as per 'Cheap holiday in other people's misery', which hijacked the sales pitch for Club Med, the French tourist company owned by banker Edmond de Rothschild.

In contrast to their interviews' gung-ho rhetoric, 'Spectators Of Suicide' suggested the Manics felt the condition diagnosed by Debord overwhelmed any feasible solutions. Beyond Moore's opening rolls over a sample of Black Panther Bobby Seale in exhortatory mode ('We're going to walk on this racist power structure and say to the whole damn government, "stick 'em up motherfucker"'), this was an elegy for the vanquished, all hope crushed by the sheer weight of circumstance. With a requiem for a chorus – 'Spectators of suicide/Exploding in society's eye/ Spitting glass from our mouths/Dying like yesterday' – here was a first flowering of the luxuriant grace, both lyrical and musical, that would become a defining characteristic. Indeed, 'Spectators Of Suicide' was itself an example of *détournement*: a lyric directly inspired by an invocation of punk's disruptive energy set to music that didn't sound punk at all.

'When I started reading the lyric, obviously I recognised the Guy Debord stuff, the society as spectacle,' says Bradfield. 'It was wantonly placing "us" – the few people we knew that we thought were like-minded, and *us* in particular – as the resistance in the supposed wasteland that we were living in at the time. But musically I was looking for something that had a bit more air and space in it, a dreamlike quality. I had this fear that we were just going to be called a punk band as soon as we left the gates, which proved to be true. Because I had massive ambitions for us being lots of things. We all did. So I was always trying to write something that would redefine, so people would think they could expect more from us.'

The basic riff repurposed the older Colt 45 Rusty James – inspired by Francis Ford Coppola's film adaptation of S.E. Hinton's novel *Rumble Fish*, 'a vignette, rather than a proper song', according to Bradfield, which never made it past the demo stage – but as 'Spectators Of Suicide', retitled by Edwards and with a lyric substantially rewritten under the aegis of Greil Marcus, the song had real presence. The naive Who shadings of 'Tennessee' now had sharper definition, and Moore's drums locked in tightly as Bradfield tracked acoustic and electric guitars playing the same part for the first time. 'I remember thinking, "Oh, that's what Johnny Marr does" – that was a lightbulb moment for somebody as inexperienced as me.' The mood spoke to producer

Robin Evans's 'hippy instinct', as Wire puts it. 'James's guitar work is really beautiful, it doesn't sound like he has up to that point. In some ways it was a false dawn, because it's not like we kicked on with that at all. It's quite Pink Floyd – actually, very Dave Gilmour. James would hate me for saying that . . .'

On the contrary, Pink Floyd was exactly the template for the spectral quality Bradfield was after, albeit covertly, lest he breach the 'no trip-out' party line. 'Robin Evans said he had an effect that would make me sound like David Gilmour. I was like, "Shut the fuck up, Robin, if you say that any louder you'll get us in trouble." Bear in mind, I hadn't played with any pedals at all except for distortion at that point. But he pulled the effect up and I just flipped out, absolutely loving it. I remember thinking Heavenly might really like this one. So "Spectators", [laughs] despite the lyric, gave me quite a lot of hope.'

Jeff Barrett and Martin Kelly's reaction to the finished recording was one of awe tinged with regret. 'Spectators Of Suicide' signified a band with a far richer musical aesthetic than their records or pronouncements up to that point had suggested, yet Heavenly were well aware that with the fulfilment of their two-single deal the Manics' next record would be with a major label. 'When we heard "Spectators Of Suicide", that was a big moment,' Kelly says. 'I remember James saying, "Ah, that's easy shit, that is." Little did they know they would make their trademark with that sound, it's almost like a blueprint for *Everything Must Go*. They weren't afraid to do a song like that, they definitely had ambition. I would have loved to have had that first album on Heavenly. I think it would have been quite a different record.'

Given how intrinsic the song was to their collective ethos, it makes sense that the band would re-record 'Spectators Of Suicide' for their self-decreed one-shot-to-the-moon debut album. The original could certainly have benefited from Bradfield's verse vocals being more prominent. It made no sense, however, for the song to be rearranged into a vaguely funky ballad worthy of a cruise liner Guns N 'Roses tribute act. Gone was the Heavenly version's psychedelic rush, replaced by synthetic bongos and claves, and blues-wailing 'vibes' from the hack rock school of songwriter-producer Desmond Child. Although artistically contentious, most of Steve Brown's production implants to the core Manics sound could at least be justified on commercial grounds, if not always complete efficacy. This, however, was simply bizarre. 'It's an abomination,' says Bradfield. 'An absolute crime on every level.'

Compounding the affront to the original, Edwards rewrote some of the lyrics, generally erring on blunt spectacle over poetry. 'Spitting glass from our mouths/Dying like yesterday' became 'Democracy is an empty lie/Dead like our yesterdays tonight.'

'I don't know what we were doing,' Wire says. 'Trying to pad the album out, plus Brownie was keen to get some words that also fitted better – he was trying to smooth out a lot of rough edges, let's face it. Richey was always willing to rewrite stuff, and he was probably just bored. There's no redeeming features to it.'

Sullied in the minds of all concerned, the song would not be played live until 2008, when the Manics appeared as part of Forever Heavenly, a celebration of their former record label's twentieth anniversary at London's Royal Festival Hall. The six-song set comprised the entirety of their Heavenly catalogue, beginning with 'Motown Junk', ending with 'You Love Us', and the penultimate 'Spectators Of Suicide' now revealed as a cosmically charged electric folk anthem worthy of Sonic Youth. Four years later, the Heavenly version's inclusion on a *Generation Terrorists* box set reinforced the original's virtues in unforgiving proximity to the re-recording's clave calamity.

At last, in December 2020, almost thirty years after it was written, the song came home. To honour the publication of a Heavenly book written by long-time consigliere Robin Turner, the Manics recorded a third 'Spectators Of Suicide' in just two live takes at their own Door To The River studio near Newport.

The original's brittle grace was now powered by the weight of three decades' worth of life experience, embellished by hammered dulcimer, and transported to the upper echelons of the band's finest work with a guest vocal by Gwenno, a twenty-first-century Heavenly star (Wire: 'I'd say Gwen's version has reclaimed it'). She even sang a version in Welsh. The spectacle finally found its definitive voice.

'We thought Gwenno could sing this song perfectly, and she did,' Bradfield says. 'It just shows that song is in our bones. It's always had an ease to it. On the wrong day, I could have written something very much more *Holy Bible*-esque to that lyric. But it caught me on a good day! I think we did a good job.'

10.
Stay Beautiful

Recorded: The Manor, Oxfordshire
Producer: Steve Brown
Released: 29 July 1991 (single, Columbia); 10 February
    1992 (*Generation Terrorists*, Columbia)

'Better a spectacular failure than a benign success.'
                                        – Malcolm McLaren

During spring 1991, on the assumption that their next single
would be with a major label – and so, effectively, their third
debut – the Manics tasked themselves with writing an impactful
mission statement that would play well on radio to an audience
potentially hearing the band for the first time. They earmarked
'Generation Terrorists', a chunky slab of Sex Pistols-lite which
had been debuted live in January and subsequently demoed at
Marcus Studios in Fulham. It was this demo that Steve Brown
heard when he first met the band with a view to producing a
single and thence, providing all went well, the debut album.

'As soon as he walked in the room, I thought, "He's cool!"'
Bradfield says. 'Because he seemed a bit left over from the
eighties, still had long hair. He looked us right in the eyes and
answered every question we asked. He said, "Well, as long as
the song you play me doesn't say 'Fuck off' . . ." Then we pick
"Generation Terrorists", and there's "Why don't you just fuck
off" in the middle of the chorus.'

Under Brown's tutelage, working sixteen-hour days amid
The Manor's quintessential seventies record-industry-comfort,
the serviceable but textbook Situationist-glam-punk of 'Generation Terrorists' was reshaped into the elegant 'Stay Beautiful'.

Ironically, without the original's sneery patina and profane chorus, the song became more fit for its subversive 'culture of destruction' purpose. The shift was crystallised in changing the coda's chant from 'Destroy all bands, baby' to 'Destroyed by madness', a nod to Allen Ginsberg's 'I've seen the best minds of my generation destroyed.'

Edwards and Wire reworked some other lyrics: 'Find your faith in cocaine/The only god I need is a brain' got cut; the 'everlasting kiss' quote from Bruce Springsteen's 'Born To Run' stayed. Nicky's 'All we love is lonely records' made way for Richey's arguably less poetic 'All we love is lonely wreckage' (Bradfield sometimes reverted to the earlier line when playing the song live). Moore's playing got so tight he was soon accompanying his own programmed drum parts. Wire's bass hit the root notes with jaunty precision, as per Brown's guide reference of AC/DC. For Bradfield, the producer utilised the best aspects of old-school ways, as much psychologist as technician. He hired a vintage Gibson Flying V and told James: 'You're going to be playing the solo on this – but only if it's a good solo.' Bradfield appreciated the slightly cornball sentiment and duly spent half a day constructing a brand-new part which in the finished recording occupied no more than fifteen seconds – albeit fifteen irrefutable seconds.

'He was all about the fun, *and* the fucking work,' Bradfield says. 'It always felt like he was teaching me but not preaching to me. He said if you like Slash don't just [play] blues scales, pick out notes from the edge of the pentatonic scale and bend them – make it feel a bit awkward but beautiful. "Awkward but beautiful" was a nice phrase. He had a really good way of speaking to you like that. Never condescending. He wanted me to play a bit more like Starship in the bridges, because I wanted them to be a bit more pensive, before the "fuck off" which is not going to be a "fuck off". I said I wasn't sure about the Starship reference. And he went, "What about the little bits of guitar at the start of [Don

Henley's] 'Boys Of Summer'?" "OK, I like that song." Just good prepping. We were a good match.'

'Stay Beautiful' entered the UK singles chart at Number 44, then rose four places the following week – the Manics were now officially a Top 40 band. 'It felt like a massive breakthrough,' Wire says. 'We'd had a lovely recording session, just a bit of bliss, thinking something good is going to happen. And it was a brilliant radio record: driving, not threatening. That was the point. It didn't need to be deep or weighty, it just needed to work.'

The song's last line, 'Anxiety is freedom', was adapted from Søren Kierkegaard's maxim 'Anxiety is the dizziness of freedom'; the Danish philosopher's definition of absolute liberation was the feeling of being stood on the edge of a cliff. A successful synthesis of art and expediency, 'Stay Beautiful' landed Manic Street Preachers on the edge of something. To find out exactly what that was, however, would require them to jump.

11.
Repeat

Recorded: Black Barn, Surrey
Producer: Steve Brown
Released: 28 October 1991 (single, Columbia);
    10 February 1992 (*Generation Terrorists*, Columbia)

'Here the rabble comes, the kind you hoped were dead
They've come to chop, to chop off your head.'
                        – McCarthy, 'Charles Windsor'

Possibly the fact that 'We Her Majesty's Prisoners' had already been released meant the Manics overthought the recording of this older, more brutish anti-monarchy philippic. 'There was an idea that we had to add something, to try and make ourselves excited,' Nicky says. 'Which is a shame, because the original demo was amazing.'

The concept for the song was a haiku. 'Either Nick or Richey said that,' Bradfield remembers, 'then the other added "like a *war* haiku". That is, very short and succinct. So we did a demo up in Mynyddislwyn at SBS where we did 'Suicide Alley', and it really was brilliant. Not too much structure, just repeating, repeating, repeating. Like an army battalion – going forward, going forward.' Recorded in late 1989, the demo version of the song then known as 'Repeat After Me' has a feral energy completely absent from its later iteration, and not just because Steve Brown's production aesthetic inevitably favoured order over chaos. 'Repeat After Me' had a structural masterstroke, in holding back the song's vanguard lyric – 'Fuck queen and country' – until the initial stop-start call and response had been subsumed by the raw, broiling forward momentum. Brown's approach made sense in the broader context of the album, but fell short when confronted by a relatively primitive composition. 'We said this song's important, it needs to be on the album,' Bradfield says. 'And he was like, "But it needs to be more formed. 'War haiku'? What's that? Fuck that!" So he wanted to make it a bit more AC/DC! He said, "They have these rudimentary chords but the singer, whether Bon or Brian, has a way of giving it musical life, and you've got to do that." I'm like, how? The words are what they are. When it came to the "Useless generations, dumb flag scum" sections I had to express it a bit more. So it's a bit of a fail. We should have stuck with war haiku.'

By parachuting 'fuck queen and country' into the top of the song and actually increasing its repetition in the name of a conventional structure, not to mention the cheesy samples of rioting and gunfire, the remodelled 'Repeat' actually lacked the subtlety of the raw and raging 'Repeat After Me'. Quite a feat.

'It's a shame we couldn't coalesce Brownie's version with the magic of the original,' says Wire. 'When me and Richey wrote the words together at Swansea Uni, it really felt like we were writing our "God Save The Queen" or "Anarchy [In The UK]". It feels surprising talking about punk like that, because the artistry of it has almost been forgotten. The Pistols had an innate swagger which we barely even touched, though we tried really hard, and we probably had a chance with "Repeat". It's a missed opportunity.'

12.

Democracy Coma

Recorded: Black Barn, Surrey
Producer: Matt Ollivier
Released: 28 October 1991 ('Repeat' B-side, Columbia);
    14 July 2003 (*Lipstick Traces*, Epic)

'Inglan is a bitch
Is whey wi a goh dhu 'bout it?'
           – Linton Kwesi Johnson, 'Inglan Is A Bitch'

As the *Generation Terrorists* recording sessions stretched towards the end of their second month, Steve Brown took a weekend off and went home to London. Faced with nothing to do except 'beat Richey at Sega Spider-Man', and aware that a B-side would be required for the next single, James Dean Bradfield elected instead to work up a song that had been 'hanging around', with Black Barn's staff engineer Matt Ollivier sitting in for the producer. Its genesis may have been low-key, but 'Democracy Coma' vindicated taking an alternative approach. Instead of following Brown's policy of painstaking sonic separation built around entirely programmed drums, Ollivier recorded the band playing live.

'It actually turned out really well,' Wire says. 'Brownie was pretty intractable in terms of the way he worked, and "Democracy Coma" was really organic but classy as well. People forget how good we were live at this point, we all knew what we were doing, even Richey. Dare I say it, like a really good punk band.'

Sean Moore clearly relished the opportunity to hit real drums as opposed to push buttons on the Alesis SR-16, which may have been state-of-the-art technology but still sounded inescapably like a drum machine. His half-time groove was cut from the classic Topper Headon mode, instilling 'Democracy Coma' with a carefree energy that withstood the layers of slabwork stacked on top. Wire's bass was also released from the album's freeze-dried aesthetic and carried the melody line in the verses before ceding to Bradfield's power chordage in the chorus. James, meanwhile, added declamatory piano in the middle-eight, then a guitar solo that was doubly effective for being atypically modest. It was all oddly suggestive of a marriage between *Reckoning*-era R.E.M. and Guns N' Roses.

Even the lyric, superficially another regicidal broadside ('Sovereign fingers scrape our lives until we are bought'), benefited from a less neurotic focus on the set texts. 'To me the coronation's another auto-da-fé' went beyond the Debord crib-sheet into the realm of surreal theatre; 'In Walkman sounds hear Sony control' wryly critiqued both the infotainment culture and the Manics' place within it, signed as they were to a record label owned by the Japanese corporation. 'I don't see happy homes but the Belfast wall', meanwhile, referenced the band's visit to Northern Ireland earlier that year.

Ending on a sample of Allen Ginsberg reading from *Howl*, 'Democracy Coma' both acquiesced to and subverted the *Generation Terrorists* era's party line – a tantalising vision of an alternative path never taken. 'Matt Ollivier did a great job,' Bradfield says. 'If that weekend Steve had taken off had come a month earlier perhaps one or two more of the songs on the album would be a bit freer. I love that song. I remember saying to Richey, "Oh, auto-da-fé, that's a Tennessee Williams play" – because I was doing drama at O-level. And he was like, "Yeah, I like that play" – hell, I've got nothing on this guy – ". . . but that's not in the song because of Tennessee Williams." O-*kay*!'

13.

Slash 'N' Burn

Recorded: Black Barn, Surrey

Producer: Steve Brown

Released: 10 February 1992 (*Generation Terrorists*,
    Columbia); 16 March 1992 (single, Columbia)

'Corporations have neither bodies to be punished, nor
souls to be condemned, they therefore do as they like.'

– Lord Thurlow

A year or so before the Manics began recording their debut album,
a battle took place for the soul of the band. On one side, James
Dean Bradfield and his chosen weapon, *Appetite For Destruction* by
Guns N' Roses. On the other side, Sean Moore, with his copy of
I Am A Wallet, the debut album by McCarthy. Both records had
been released in 1987, but occupied different galaxies: GN'R's
strutting LA amalgam of seventies Rolling Stones riffology and
rock 'n' roll carnality versus an east London indie band's spiralling
guitar chimes and dense Marxist lyrics chastely sung by a man
called Malcolm Eden.

McCarthy had been a foundational Manics influence in 1986,
alongside the likes of Jasmine Minks, Big Flame, The June Brides,
The Loft, Tallulah Gosh: bands whose brittle, self-produced, often
self-released 7-inch singles James and Nicky would buy with the
proceeds from their Saturday busking sessions outside Spillers
Records in Cardiff. During the summer of 1988, however, the
foundations began to shift. With Nicky and Richey at university,
James busied himself by upping his guitar proficiency. When the
pair returned from Swansea for the holidays they found that
Bradfield had taught himself to play *Appetite For Destruction* in its

entirety, a record they too had been absorbing in their student digs. James recalls Richey coming back 'transformed, more glam. Without us actually talking about it, it was almost as if the Guns N' Roses aspect had infused us while they were at university and I was at home.'

Subsequently, as the band's '68-in-'88' rebel stance coalesced, their naive musical roots were deemed insufficient. Although some demo recordings from the period still carried traces, the official group discourse and sonic template now emphasised punk, hip-hop and, increasingly, red-blooded hard rock. 'One of Nick's favourite phrases throughout the band's history has just been the "fantasy" of something,' says Bradfield. 'There's an amazing fantasy to *Appetite*: there's glamour, and aggression. As soon as you heard the album you knew there was a big dose of punk in there. The lyrics were amazing. "Welcome To The Jungle" is a classic small kid arriving in a big city alienation song. "Paradise City" is somebody stamping their mark on the world. "It's So Easy" – the lyrics are questionable, to a certain degree, but as nihilistic as anything NWA were writing. My argument was we've gotta actually feel as if we're ready to go into war. And the simplest way of doing that is to rock – I felt the power and the glory of it, I was completely wrapped up in it.'

James still enjoyed listening to The June Brides and Big Flame and My Bloody Valentine, but was able to censor his own tastes so barely any of that was discernible in the music he was writing, encouraged by Nicky's own metal predilections – an inheritance from elder brother Patrick's teenage record collection – and Richey's propagandist eye for the spectacle. Sean Moore, however, hated Guns N' Roses. Outvoted and frustrated, he actually smashed his cousin's copy of *Appetite For Destruction*. 'I said it's just cock rock shite and I don't want to have anything to do with it. Which is a bit petulant, but you are when you're in your late teens. Even to this day, I don't listen to those records through choice.'

In this context, Moore's contributions to *Generation Terrorists* were all the more remarkable. Faced with Steve Brown's insistence on using drum machines, he determined not to rely on a programmer and within a matter of days had trained himself to the requisite professional standard. 'I would go in late evening, work through the night and have something for James to work on when he woke up in the morning. That was pretty much it for the whole album. It's got its sticky moments, it's naive, big on ambition, could have been mixed a lot better – but that's the price you pay with debut albums.'

GT opened with its fantasy rock apotheosis: a composite of Warholian pop product placement ('Madonna drinks Coke and so you can too') and eco-political polemic ('Drain your blood and let the Exxon spill in') wrapped in a riff fit for eternal repeat play by a Duracell bunny transmogrification of Keith Richards. With cowbell. 'Slash 'N' Burn' was born in the Bradfield family kitchen at Sir Ivor's Road, then enhanced under's Brown's amiably Stakhanovite work ethic at a pre-production demo session in The House In The Woods, a studio in the Surrey village of Bletchingley, where the song's critical element emerged. 'We had the verse and we had the chorus, but I didn't have a riff,' Bradfield says. 'So Steve said, "I'm gonna go away. I'll be sat in the kitchen, drinking pots of tea. And when I hear you do a riff that goes over the top of this, I'll come barging through the door."' One hour of playing his guitar later, Bradfield, by now capable of drilling along note perfect to GN'R and the entirety of *Exile On Main St.*, landed upon a quicksilver ascending/descending pattern in the classic Rolling Stones style. Steve Brown put down his tea mug and yelled: 'Hey!'

'A nice way of working,' says James. 'So I felt like king of the world – and then he's like, "Now you've gotta write a middle section." *Fuck's sake!*' Bradfield duly built a reverberant pizzicato'd mezzanine space for the 'Madonna drinks Coke' verse – an extra lyric Brown had demanded from Wire and Edwards – whereupon he was next tasked with delivering yet another part, to plot an exit destination from the middle section's orgasmic Robert Plant wails. 'Which is where,' Bradfield notes, 'it all goes a bit Michael Schenker Group. Sean put an extra beat in halfway through the bar, so it sped up and made it better.' Wire actually thought the subsequent proto-heavy metal drilling unnecessary, yet couldn't deny the preposterous logic of the finished recording. His methods may have been contentious, but Brown's vision for ushering Manic Street Preachers' dream album into reality was vindicated by this song alone.

'I love "Slash 'N' Burn",' Wire says. 'It probably goes too far, but what a riff. The dexterity! I remember being quite amazed when he played it. Although obviously Guns N' Roses were a big influence for us at the time, this song's got a lot of Stones in it. A lot of James's riffs are more roll than rock, plus I loved all the little extra bits he does that most guitarists wouldn't do, all the little trails. Only John Squire [then with The Stone Roses] was doing that at this point. There were no guitar heroes left, it was all gone.'

The deployment of the main riff bears closer examination, for it was highly strategic. The song opens with Bradfield's un-accompanied electric guitar figure repeated once: eight bars of 4/4 time. The next eight bars are a repeat of the first eight, but now accompanied by the other instruments' aerobic throb. Regulation stuff in the rock idiom: 'Paranoid' by Black Sabbath does it; so too 'Pretty Vacant' by the Sex Pistols, or 'What Difference Does It Make?' by The Smiths. Next, we have the first verse of the lyric, without the riff, building to the chorus and the climactic first appearance of the song title, where we might expect the riff to reappear – after all, that's what happens in 'Sweet Child O' Mine' by Guns N' Roses. If it's good enough for Slash . . .

But no – the riff comes back *after* the chorus, for an eight-bar reiteration of its earlier accompanied appearance, before exiting for another eight bars of verse/chorus. This sparing use of such a potent weapon is beginning to feel perverse, but wait: after the second chorus, instead of detouring into a traditional middle-eight section, the riff returns for another eight bars – unaccompanied, save for a cowbell clanging out the beat like 'Honky Tonk Women' at last orders. And then, a masterstroke: the ensemble crashes back in, still with the riff, but this time Bradfield is singing, at the top of his register, 'That's all you need!' So the song effectively now has two choruses, and this new one is a hymn to its raison d'être. Thence we progress through the none-more-metal middle-eight, back into the first chorus, and end with one final blast of the second.

'All down to proper pre-production with a great producer,' says Bradfield. 'Doing demos with him, then taking all the fruits of that to the recording and doing it easily.'

The title was obviously a pun coupling of the song's subject matter with Bradfield's guitar hero du jour. One other Guns N' Roses reference was more inadvertent: Bradfield tuned down his guitars a tone so that he could sing the chorus, which otherwise would have been pitched exceptionally high. 'Every song on *Appetite For Destruction* is tuned down one,' he says. 'When Slash is playing an E it's actually an E flat. The way Axl wrote his vocals they go to such a high margin that just taking one note away from that scale helps. "Slash 'N' Burn" is the same.'

The lyric's original inspiration came when Nicky heard a radio documentary about *Silent Spring*, the landmark 1962 book by Rachel Carson which exposed the environmental impact of pesticides such as DDT and the co-dependent relationship between the scientific and military industries. (In 2016, David Attenborough cited *Silent Spring* as the book that changed the world most after Darwin's *On the Origin of Species*.) Beyond the specific reference to 'Exxon', which had topicality due to ongoing repercussions from the 1989 *Exxon Valdez* oil spill in Alaska, Wire and Edwards applied a broad-brush treatment, positing humanity's eco-selfishness as a metaphor for capitalism's imperialist exploitation of developing economies ('Third world to the first'), whereby the poor pay for the greed of the rich. Amid some ear-catching singalong lines – 'Worms in the garden more real than a McDonald's' – its overall message gets a little lost in the all-pervasive hysteria. Ultimately, 'Slash 'N' Burn' was all about the inescapable logic of that four-bar motif, preferably with added cowbell.

'I was extremely excited by everything about "Slash 'N' Burn" once we were done,' Wire says. 'Obviously it's the naivety, the youth and the glory – the vainglory – but it still lifts me when I hear it. Because it's so overreaching. A band trying so hard to be something that they actually can't be, that they're never going to get to, even now.'

Notoriously, it was one of the four *Generation Terrorists* tracks that were remixed for the album's abridged US edition and with live drums added by ace session player Zack Alford. Ironically for a song that anticipates today's world asphyxiating amid its 'gorgeous poverty of created needs', the organic treatment lacked the heart and soul of the original. 'Slash 'N' Burn's brilliance lay within its immaculate interface of the fake and the real: it was machine-tooled but human-driven. Tasked with opening the debut album that could conceivably also be their last, this wry critique of over-indulgence proved the Manics' perfect hybrid vehicle.

14.

Nat West-Barclays-Midlands-Lloyds

Recorded: Black Barn, Surrey
Producer: Steve Brown
Released: 10 February 1992 (*Generation Terrorists*, Columbia)

> 'Banking establishments are more dangerous
> than standing armies.'
>
> – Thomas Jefferson

In 1999, *The Observer* published an article about the extent of Barclays Bank's collaboration with the Nazis in occupied France during the Second World War.[1] Revelations included the manager of Barclays' Paris branch 'volunteering' information to the German Bank Comptroller about Jewish employees, and the same branch accepting a deposit of 290,000 francs in July 1944 from the cashier at Drancy transit camp – the money had been seized from French Jews interned there before deportation by train to Auschwitz. It was also discovered that the branch manager, Marcel Cheradame, who was retained by Barclays until his retirement in the 1960s, helped finance increased quarrying of French lime for use by the German steel conglomerate Reichswerke Hermann Göring.

Coincidentally – or not – one month after *The Observer*'s article, Barclays announced a redesign of its spread-eagle logo, which although pre-dating the Third Reich by over 200 years bore more than a passing resemblance to the German coat of arms that the Nazis augmented with a swastika in 1935. Barclays' new logo removed the heraldic bird's talons, and smoothed off its sharp-edged beak and wings. 'We need to refresh the corporate approach and to some degree the old identity has been struggling to keep pace with the 20th century,' project manager Kate Thomas said.[2]

By 2012, the year of Barclays' implication in the Libor derivatives scandal and amid the ongoing global recession caused by 2008's financial crash, skewering banks' amoral practices had become common cultural currency. Twenty years earlier, however, the Manic Street Preachers were ahead of the game. 'Nat West-Barclays-Midlands-Lloyds' was first played live in April 1991 and although an audience favourite for its singalong qualities, its representation on *Generation Terrorists* soon came to exemplify the album's perceived design flaws, as well as highlighting ideological inconsistencies. *Rolling Stone*'s David Fricke was not alone in wondering: 'Are the Manics the only ones who don't see the irony of railing against the economic fascism of Nat West, Barclays and Lloyds while enjoying the generous bankrolling of Sony?'

From a Situationist perspective, the song succeeded precisely because its baleful depiction of capitalist abundance was released by one of the world's largest corporations. Yet 'Nat West-Barclays' was effective on more relatable criteria too. Its lyric – 90 per cent written by Richey Edwards, according to Nicky Wire – was a succession of blunt indictments, some poetic, some arcane, some satirical. 'Barclays iron eagle, '33 injection' juxtaposed the bank with the year Hitler became German Chancellor. 'Black horse apocalypse/Death sanitised through credit' evoked the famous emblem of Lloyds Bank as an equine harbinger of doom, dispensing cheap mortgages and manipulating interest rates (Wire: 'Surely that must have made people who thought we were po-faced smile?'). Nicky estimates he contributed just two lines, but like Edwards, his phraseology was frugal and efficient: 'They give and take away, repossess and crucify/The more you own the more you are, lonelier with cheap desire'.

Musically, a rolling thunder of elegiac arpeggios cut through the piston-pumped production, particularly in the middle section breakdown, where Bradfield's mournful upper register lends real pathos to the potentially hazardous lyric: 'Prosperity, Mein Kampf for beginners'. A solo piano outro, meanwhile, was played by Dave Eringa, 'an *homage* to "Epic" by Faith No More,' says Bradfield. 'It was a freer song originally, and then came Brownie's straight hard edges. But I used to love playing it live.'

'It resonates to this day,' says Wire. 'I remember Richey giving the lyric to me, more than half-written, with the title, and it made me smile. It's such an amazing idea. One of those songs that we were kind of derided for at the time, but it had a very long tail. The only thing that's been nationalised in the last fifty years is the banks – the irony of it. There's still a black horse apocalypse! Resilient fuckers.'

15.
Born To End

Recorded: Black Barn, Surrey
Producer: Steve Brown
Released: 10 February 1992 (*Generation Terrorists*, Columbia)

> 'The kids of the Coca-Cola nation are too
> doped up to realise.'
> — Southern Death Cult, 'Moya'

Having twice already evoked the USA's bombing of Hiroshima –
with 'Motown Junk's sleeve and the Penderecki sample in 'You
Love Us' – there was a macabre inevitability to 'Born To End's
referencing the subsequent destruction of Nagasaki on 9 August
1945. This time, however, the nuclear horror was prominently
invoked in the song's chorus lyric and imbued with a queasy
poeticism: 'H-bomb the only thing that will bring a freedom to
life/Underneath the blue skies, beautiful, empty, dying/Nagasaki
dolls are burning.'

Yet 'Born To End' went beyond mere Armageddon porn. The
title was a negationist twist on 'Born To Lose', Johnny Thunders' archetypal expression of nihilism, while the lyric illustrated
Richey Edwards's propensity to conflate his personal traumas and
self-harm with humanity's capability to harm itself: 'Get some
pain and I feel alive/Close my eyes overdose on hell.' With a
second verse lamenting 'free' post-Cold War Europe's subjugation
by consumerist fake desire – 'Images linger like repression' – this
was the power of negative thinking projected on a mass scale.

'At this point we were all pretty . . . I wouldn't say "happy"
is the word,' says Wire, 'but we're in a studio making an album,
backed by a massive company, telling everyone we're going to

conquer the world. I'd never be as big-headed to say I knew exactly what was going on in Richey's [mind], whether there was ever a part of him that was pushing it for its own sake, or that he was genuinely always feeling this bleak about things.'

The song certainly didn't sound bleak. Even in a demo recorded at the pre-album Marcus Studios session, it had a melody-soaked, tautly ragged internal combustion suggestive of Johnny Thunders' 'You Can't Put Your Arms Around A Memory', the original version of which featured The Only Ones' Peter Perrett, whose power-pop Stones aesthetic bled through into the *Generation Terrorists* version. Under Steve Brown's direction, an already strong song took on extra dimensions: a superior arrangement promoted the 'H-bomb' section from bridge to chorus, significantly added lyrics (hello 'Nagasaki dolls') and rewrote others ('Get some pain and I feel alive' superseded 'Cannot get no girl to look at me', revealing the lyric was originally rather more traditional in its preoccupations), enhanced the guitar solos, and unusually for the Manics, stacked backing vocal harmonies, all to heighten the sense of dark-side euphoria.

'Steve said, "The vocal and the riff have got to dance around with each other, gotta be like a tango, they can never hold hands",' Bradfield says. 'I had the motif, and he said, "OK to have a motif but you gotta put little Roman candles on it and shoot stuff off." Pictograms – I liked that. I think he recognised what kind of brain mine was: not exceptionally smart. He made me explode the solo a tiny bit, so it wasn't like a Mod solo. He did not like Mod – "It's not rock 'n' roll, James." He also had Sean do some more programmed toms, which made it more tribal. I wondered if that was from him listening to The Cult's *Dreamtime* before he worked with them on *Love*. I was always asking him about The Cult and he would give me examples of what Billy Duffy played. So maybe this was the stuff he tried to get The Cult *not* to do, now putting it back in with us. I always loved this song.'

Anomalous compared to its airless generic rock siblings yet still swallowed up by the album's monumental edifice, 'Born To End' bore another noteworthy trace of The Cult: the 1982 debut single by pre-Billy Duffy precursors Southern Death Cult was titled 'Fatman',[1] which happened to be the code name for the US bomb dropped on Nagasaki; the single's double A-side, 'Moya', featured the lyric 'Nagasaki's crying out'. It might seem surprising that 'Born To End' was particularly popular with audiences in Japan, or indeed that the band would even consider playing it at all. 'We did wonder,' says James. 'You know the intention of the song is appropriate, but is the situation appropriate? And then I saw the whole crowd singing "*Na-ga-sa-ki* dolls are burning" at us. They're enunciating the punctuation with their hands in the air. It was really strange.'

Perhaps the reaction was indicative of Japanese attitudes to death and spirituality, or simply down to the Manics' remarkable popularity there: *Generation Terrorists* attained gold status in Japan even before the band arrived for their first tour in 1992.

'[It was] one of those things you couldn't imagine happening, and then it did,' says Wire. 'That first tour to Japan was one of the greatest times ever to be in a band, because we'd mainlined into an aesthetic that was so appreciated, much more than any other country in the world. You do wonder why. Richey was really influenced by Mishima and a lot of Japanese literature, James was as well. And that idea of suicide in the Japanese culture actually being something to be admired. It sounds really harsh and cold, in terms of what played out. But we were all guilty of being attracted to it.'

16.
Motorcycle Emptiness

Recorded: Black Barn, Surrey
Producer: Steve Brown
Released: 10 February 1992 (*Generation Terrorists*,
    Columbia); 1 June 1992 (single, Columbia)

'Your mother is not crazy. And neither, contrary to
popular belief is your brother crazy. He's merely miscast
in a play. He was born in the wrong era, on the wrong
side of the river, with the ability to do anything that he
wants to do and finding nothing that he wants to do.'
                   – Father to Rusty James, *Rumble Fish* screenplay
                        by S.E. Hinton and Francis Ford Coppola

On 24 November 1991, Nirvana's 'Smells Like Teen Spirit' entered
the UK singles chart at Number 9. Four days later, the band's
appearance on *Top of the Pops* simultaneously mocked the show's
stilted format – Kurt Cobain singing his band's own version of
generation terrorism in a preposterously low register while his
colleagues hurled their instruments in the air, making no pretence at miming to the backing track – and heralded a musical
regime change. Into their fourth month of recording at Black
Barn, the Manics watched with a mixture of admiration and
disquiet.

'I'd been lost in making the record, so the first time I heard
"Smells Like Teen Spirit" was in the studio, when MTV played
the video,' James Dean Bradfield recalled. 'Richey came over and
said, "Look at this." I didn't admit it at the time, but it scared the
life out of me. We thought we were charging over the hill and
somebody's already at the top of it. I remember Steve Brown

looking over my shoulder and going, "Yep, that's really good, that." Terrifying.'

In July 1993, less than two years after 'Smells Like Teen Spirit', and its parent album *Nevermind*, had transformed the fabric of mainstream rock music, Kurt Cobain was repudiating his own act of cultural rupture. Pained by the fame he'd wished for but never expected to receive, he dismissed *Nevermind* as 'too slick', claiming, 'I don't listen to records like that at home.'[1]

A commercially expedient polishing of Nirvana's basic sound, *Nevermind*'s slickness was only relative. For instance, next to the contemporaneous *Use Your Illusion*, Guns N' Roses' twin-volume follow-up to *Appetite For Destruction*, the second Nirvana album felt raw and visceral. Either way, its act of singular genius was coating punk rock negaholia and alienation in a bubblegum wrapper, the product of its creators according equal merit to The Stooges and Abba. Here was rock's present and future, rather than a relic of its past.

Although it would displace Michael Jackson's *Dangerous* as US Number 1 in January 1992, and eventually sold over 30 million copies, at first *Nevermind* made only a modest commercial impact. It entered the UK album chart at Number 36, then dropped ten or more places for the next three weeks. One reason it didn't initially chart higher was the decision by Nirvana's label Geffen and its UK parent company MCA to concentrate their promotional and distribution resources on Guns N' Roses. To ramp up anticipation of *Use Your Illusion* finally emerging into the world after an agonised eighteen-month recording process, the albums went on sale at midnight on release day at major cities around the globe. Waiting in the queue outside Tower Records in Piccadilly Circus were James Dean Bradfield and Richey Edwards, having prevailed upon Black Barn engineer Matt Ollivier to drive them in his Mini to central London.

'It was a Sunday night and there was a tank going round with a topless woman on it,' James says. 'I remember Richey going,

"I hope *one* person recognises us in this queue." Then, lo and behold, a really vodka-sodden Hanoi Rocks fan went, "Hey dude! Man! You fuckin' rawk!" He was obviously from England . . . And I mutter to Richey, "OK, we've just been recognised – you happy now?"'

With *Use Your Illusion I & II* successfully bought, along with a CD for Ollivier to thank him for the lift (he chose Metallica's 'Black Album'), they drove back to Surrey and an expectant Nicky Wire for the two-and-a-half-hour listening session. 'We stayed up all night playing those albums,' Wire later recalled. 'It was really bad, because the first side of *Use Your Illusion I* is terrible, and we were like, "Fucking hell, what's gone wrong?"'

The malevolent energy of *Appetite For Destruction* was now barely visible beneath multiple layers of hack rock cliché and filigreed turgidity like 'November Rain'. 'Terrible' or not, however, the first week numbers for *Use Your Illusion I & II* were consistent with Guns N' Roses' status as the world's most commercially potent rock band, with sales of 685,000 and 770,000 respectively. The quality of the music was secondary to the fact of its actual existence: recording and mixing sessions overran so much that the Use Your Illusion tour began three months before the albums it was supposed to promote were even finished. But as time would prove, size matters only up to a point. When Nirvana arrived at MCA's London office in early November for a day of interviews before the European leg of the Nevermind tour, they were confronted with a wall-sized poster honouring GN'R's 31 August gig at Wembley: 'Guns N' Fuckin' Roses! Wembley Fuckin' Stadium! Sold Fuckin' out!' Invited to comment on his labelmates' achievement, Kurt Cobain took a pen and added to the poster: 'Big Fuckin' Deal!'

So when the Manic Street Preachers watched Nirvana's *Top of the Pops* performance of 'Smells Like Teen Spirit', the disappointment of *Use Your Illusion* still ringing in their ears, they feared their high-gloss vehicle for rock revolution had already been overtaken by events. The *Generation Terrorists* blueprint adhered to the traditional dream and lie of rock 'n' roll; now Nirvana had blown it apart with a mere shrug. *Oh well, whatever.* Shaken though they were, however, the Manics kept the faith – not least because they had a song, one that Steve Brown felt convinced was 'pure greatness'.

'Seeing Nirvana knocked the confidence a bit,' Wire says, 'because you knew something seismic had happened. But just as we loved Happy Mondays and The Stone Roses, it was pointless us trying to be them, so we had to diametrically oppose everything else. I still believed. I genuinely thought "Motorcycle Emptiness" could take over the world.'

'Motorcycle Emptiness' wasn't played live until four months after its release on *Generation Terrorists*, a period during which the Manics toured the UK, Europe, Japan and the US. Asked about the song's absence by *NME*'s Stuart Bailie when he interviewed the band in Los Angeles, Nicky Wire explained: '"Motorcycle Emptiness" is one of the best records of the year, more than anyone ever expected from us, and that song is four years old. We never played it early on; when you're jumping up and down at the Rock Garden you're not gonna do something like that. We don't want to do it live until we can do it perfectly.'[2]

Although certainly untypical of the band's repertoire at the time, it wasn't quite true to say 'Motorcycle Emptiness' was four years old. Two of its constituent parts did, however, originate in the band's prehistory – ironically for a song considered an evolutionary leap forward. 'Go Buzz Baby Go' was demoed in the basement of Cwmfelinfach Workingmen's Institute, Sound Bank Studios' second location, in late 1988 or early '89. Worked out by James and Sean in the Bradfield family kitchen to one of the first lyrics Edwards and Wire wrote together in their student hall of residence in Swansea, the chord sequence is recognisably similar to that of the song it became – as well as faintly resembling a maudlin 1985 June Brides song called 'Josef's Gone' – minus the main guitar riff and the chorus. 'Behave Yourself Baby', meanwhile, is an incongruous piece of barbershop skiffle suggesting The June Brides' jauntier aspect, with a trumpet solo from Sean. The song didn't survive past the home demo stage, but its bridge melody and lyric – 'All I want from you is the skin you live within' – would both be repurposed.

Of these two prototypes, 'Go Buzz Baby Go' was the more evolved, and traces of its lyric would also resurface, notably the pre-chorus lyric 'Forever/Ever/Ever' – which at its last iteration changes to 'Motorcycle emptiness/Motorcycle emptiness/Emptiness' – and the opening line. It might seem a stretch going from 'Tumbling down your spine/Down through the cracks of your broken smile', to 'Culture sucks down words/Itemise loathing and feed yourself smiles', but great art requires graft as much as magic.

'You could tell there was something there,' Bradfield says. 'We just didn't know what it was yet. Nick was a really good magpie – me and Sean would come up with stuff and I'd say, "It's shit", but Nick would say, "No, let's keep it, we'll be able to use stuff from that." And of course, in the end it paid dividends.'

'Go Buzz Baby Go' was a legacy of the band's fealty to eighties indie's pure pop aesthetic, where the rebel/romantic archetypes of previous generations were rewound through a post-punk filter, first by the likes of Echo & The Bunnymen, Orange Juice, The Smiths and The Jesus And Mary Chain, all bands who conceived music as a grand vehicle to transcend their prosaic environments, and then their subsequent legions of imitators who traded with lesser degrees of purpose and commercial success.

'We were obsessed with having a motorcycle song, like The Jesus And Mary Chain,' Wire says. 'And there's one brilliant line – "Lacklustre nights bring hurricane days/Is this your way of saying this is the end" – that was really Ian McCulloch. I loved bits of "Go Buzz Baby Go", and I loved bits of "Behave Yourself Baby", which I think was me writing about a girl. Obviously,

Richey flipped it into something much better. But "Motorcycle Emptiness" is living proof that not all songs are a natural moment. The lyrics were rewritten three times, the song probably took two years, maybe three years to actually morph into something so pristine and beautiful and glacial.'

Superficially, 'Motorcycle Emptiness' doesn't deviate drastically from the *Generation Terrorists*-era core textbook. It's a Marxist critique of capitalist alienation and the anomie of the spectacle ('Culture sucks down words/Itemise loathing and feed yourself smiles'), a history of the working class ('From feudal serf to spender/This wonderful world of purchase power') soundtracked by heroic guitars. It's also a reprise of 'You Love Us' in issuing a provocation to both critics and fans ('All we want from you are the kicks you've given us'). Yet its predominant mood is downcast and resigned: those 'kicks' have already been received and worn like a badge; that cyclical riff embodies the lyric's lament for 'each day living out a lie'. As Wire notes, the rhythm guitar beneath Bradfield's tearful long-tail leads 'is probably one of the most "indie" things James has ever played, so beautifully tasteful – it *is* like The June Brides. It's less powerful than Orange Juice!'

Perhaps 'Motorcycle Emptiness' became the first Manics song to resonate beyond their hinterland audience precisely because its prelapsarian roots were deep enough to survive the evolution from soppy *C86* homage to *Generation Terrorists* manifesto. Or maybe the multiple edits and revisions undertaken by Wire and Edwards together at a table on one of their purest collaborative lyrics simply pared down its didactic edges into something approaching poetry. Indeed, 'Under neon loneliness/Everlasting nothingness' was lifted from an actual poem: 'Neon Loneliness', written by Nicky's brother Patrick Jones in 1989 during his Jack Kerouac adventure living in Chicago.

'At that point everyone would claim our lyrics were just slogans gathered together,' Wire says. 'Whereas there's less specificity to this song than a malaise, the idea of images passing, recurring. Everything is filtered through a cinematic haze.'

The song's touchstone influence was indeed a film: *Rumble Fish*, director Francis Ford Coppola's 1983 adaptation of S.E. Hinton's young adult novel about a fractured fraternal bond amid the stylised urban wastelands of Tulsa, Oklahoma. Beautiful and doomed, the Motorcycle Boy is a 21-year-old former gang leader, portrayed by Mickey Rourke in a conscious evocation of Marlon Brando-as-Albert Camus. Having escaped the dead-end streets to California – where he met his estranged mother but never got to the ocean – he stuns his former acolytes by returning to be a spirit guide to his naive younger brother Rusty James (Matt Dillon), only to die in the cause of existential freedom.

Coppola's self-proclaimed 'art film for young people' was shot *à la* German Expressionism and the French New Wave in steaming black and white, featured an avant-punk-jazz soundtrack by Stewart Copeland, co-starred Dennis Hopper and Tom Waits, and blew the proto-Manic Street Preachers' teenage minds. Over time, they evoked themselves into its monochrome world until myth and reality became blurred. An early version of 'Spectators Of Suicide' was titled 'Colt 45 Rusty James'. Amid their mid-eighties Blackwood pop-art-poetry posse the 'Blue Generation', Patrick Jones's nom de plume was 'Rusty Blueheart'. On record sleeves from *Generation Terrorists* onwards, Richey Edwards would style himself 'Richey James'.

'We were all obsessed with *Rumble Fish*,' says Bradfield. 'We loved the idea of the Beat Generation madness of Motorcycle Boy and the innocent purity of Rusty James – they're brothers but they can't find anything that fits. We're all kinda disparate in the band, but we're brothers, yet we couldn't find [a] generation that fitted us, because we thought everybody was utterly wasted in an age of decadence and ignorance. That's what "Motorcycle Emptiness" was for me. As soon as I saw the new lyric and the title, I thought, "We're into something different now." It felt like an amazing song.'

Without Steve Brown, however, 'Motorcycle Emptiness' would quite likely never have existed beyond a feeling. At the pre-album session in The House In The Woods, the producer asked to listen to all the band's demos. 'He said, "There's lots of good stuff going on here, it's just going to go to waste if you don't use it,"' Bradfield says. 'He became quite frantic about it.'

In Brown's subsequent recollection, the band were at first reluctant to work on 'Motorcycle Emptiness' at all. 'The initial comment was, "Look, Steve, we don't really want to do this." It was the runt of the litter, because when I asked them why, I think it was mainly Nicky who was saying that some of the subject matter . . . he wasn't particularly inspired by it. I wanted to give it a shot.'[3]

Brown stayed up one night with Moore working on ideas for song structure and built a rhythm track (Bradfield: 'They agreed that, for want of a better word, it had to be slightly "baggy"'). They were still at it the next morning when Bradfield walked in and said he'd been dreaming about a guitar riff – at which point Brown deployed the same motivational technique which had already yielded 'Slash 'N' Burn'. 'Steve locked me in the studio control room and had me playing on repeat to that figure, the descending E going down to an A. "Keep going until there's a riff and then I'll come in." Took me about twenty minutes. He said, "That's exactly what we need!"'

Bradfield's dream riff fulfils the essence of the Nirvana = Stooges × Abba equation – indeed, there's even a hint of the unfurling string ascent into the chorus of 'Dancing Queen'. But it still wasn't enough for Steve Brown, who next tasked Bradfield to come up with a guitar solo, and then a middle section. James initially cried foul, but soon acquiesced to the producer's work ethic, delivering a bluesy solo ('rudimentary, E major going into G into A – not great, but it breaks the song up'), then taking the bridge from 'Behave Yourself Baby' and putting it in a different key. Finally, Brown was satisfied, though even at the mixing stage he found space to add strings and had session pianist Richard Cottle play 'a Jacques Brel-type affair' in the 'All we want from you' section.[4] The final version stretched beyond six minutes. 'He was relentless,' says Bradfield. 'And I knew he was right. That ethos of going into the studio, locking the door, playing to a loop and not coming out until something is finished, not to sleep on stuff, to chase something down – it really stuck with me. "Motorcycle Emptiness" became something that Steve Brown thought it could become. It kinda saved our skins.'

The dreamscape qualities that made 'Motorcycle Emptiness' almost uniquely anomalous on the album would also template an as yet unwritten future. Its reflective tone offered the Manics an alternative to being consumed by their own ideological inferno – 'survival's natural as sorrow' being a design for life by another name. The song's primary cultural source, meanwhile, was so resonant it could be inferred rather than broadcast: 'Drive away and it's the same' resembled one of the Motorcycle Boy's dime store aphorisms offered up for Rusty James, to be filed alongside the likes of 'If you're going to lead people, you have to have somewhere to go.'[5]

It's highly unusual for a sixth track culled from an album to shift so radically the critical consensus around a band, but that's what 'Motorcycle Emptiness' did when released as a single in June 1992. The song belied the then commonly held view of the Manic Street Preachers as a frivolous proposition. The promotional video had a suitably sorrowful elegance: directed by Martin Hall during their first Japanese tour, the band were filmed on the streets of Tokyo and in hotel rooms, aliens together amid a megacity, disconnected from the teeming life and sensation that surrounded them. Ten years later, the Academy Award-winning film *Lost In Translation* deployed strikingly similar moods, with one scene in particular uncannily echoing the 'Motorcycle Emptiness' video. One of the two principal characters, Charlotte, portrayed by Scarlett Johansson, sits on her hotel room windowsill, hugging her legs and gazing at the city, framed exactly like Richey Edwards in his neon loneliness. Perhaps the similarity wasn't so uncanny: *Lost In Translation* was written and directed by Sofia Coppola, whose father Francis Ford Coppola directed *Rumble Fish* and cast his then eleven-year-old daughter as the sister of Rusty James's girlfriend.

Rumble Fish ends with the Motorcycle Boy being killed after breaking into a pet shop and stealing the Siamese fighting fish, whose aggressive behaviour he suspects is a function of their environment: 'I don't think that they would fight if they were in the river . . . if they had the room to live.'⁶ Before he can complete his freedom mission, he's shot dead by his erstwhile police nemesis, Officer Patterson. Whereupon Rusty James scoops up the rumble fish and releases them into the river, then takes his brother's bike and rides out of town, past the graffiti 'The Motorcycle Boy Reigns', all the way out to the ocean. His cleansing odyssey feels reminiscent of the denouement to Bruce Springsteen's 'Racing In The Street', an anthem for doomed youth comparable in emotional scope to the Manics' epic. So vividly does 'Motorcycle Emptiness' conjure a state of mind, it might as well be an actual place, complete with map reference, microclimate, even its own smell – a unique kind of teen spirit.

'Everything was a build-up to this,' says Nicky Wire. 'It's probably the four of us at our peaks, four people coming together to create that landscape of existential despair, then Steve Brown transformed it into something spectacular and otherworldly – and timeless. There's something pretty special about it.'

17.

Little Baby Nothing

Recorded: Black Barn, Surrey
Producer: Steve Brown
Released: 10 February 1992 (*Generation Terrorists*,
    Columbia); 16 November 1992 (single, Columbia)

'People like you abused her and forced her to change.'
    – Stella Kowalski in *A Streetcar Named Desire*,
    Tennessee Williams

While 'Motorcycle Emptiness' evinced spiritual kinship to three mythic American totems – bikes, Beats and The Boss – the next *Generation Terrorists* track released as a single was explicitly indebted to the latter of the three. Bruce Springsteen had already received a Manics hat-tip in the lyric of 'Stay Beautiful', but that felt more like a cheeky aside, a knowing wink to the wise. 'Little Baby Nothing', however, had a Springsteen hallmark baked into its musical skin: guitars occupied a largely subordinate harmonic role while the melodic leads were taken by the piano, in the style of E Street Band keyboardist Roy Bittan on the likes of 'Thunder Road' and 'Jungleland'.

After 'Born To Run' had propelled Springsteen into the mainstream, its piano-prominent homage to Phil Spector's Wall of Sound became a familiar trope for artists seeking heightened theatricality. David Bowie's 'Station To Station' and Meat Loaf's 'Bat Out Of Hell' not only aped the style but got Bittan himself to play the part. Meat Loaf writer and producer Jim Steinman turned to Bittan again for Bonnie Tyler's 'Total Eclipse Of The Heart', a new benchmark for pop melodrama. For 'Little Baby Nothing', the Manics hired the services of a pianist au fait with the map co-ordinates for grandiosity: Spike Edney, an auxiliary live member of Queen since 1984. 'He knew how to drink wine and play piano at the same time,' James says. 'That's how the old school do it – they drink two bottles of wine and get better as they play.'

With introductory guitar chords hinting at Boston's 'More Than A Feeling' and the man who tinkled Queen's ivories at Live Aid on the ol' joanna, 'Little Baby Nothing' represented the Manics' peak episode of classic rock entryism thus far. The song's lyric was an indictment of misogyny and sexual exploitation, inspired by *SCUM Manifesto*, the 1967 polemic by feminist provocateur Valerie Solanas and her Society for Cutting Up Men which urged 'civic-minded, responsible, thrill-seeking females to overthrow the government, eliminate the money system . . . and destroy the male sex'.[1] What better vehicle for undermining patriarchal control than a grandiloquently produced slab of epic power balladry with the refrain 'Used, used, used by men'?

'Me and Richey had been reading a lot of Valerie Solanas,' says Wire, 'and James had been determined to write a Springsteen song – which, the more you listen to it, the more it is. He was obviously listening to "Born To Run", and put a lot into it, because all the segments fit really well together. The lyric was a proper collaboration – my title, the outro was me, whereas the body of the lyric is more Richey's. Some saw it as almost patronising in tone, white men talking about women, that sort of thing – but I think it was much more a self-condemnation of male power. You can't get much more explicit than the outro: "You are pure you are snow, we are the useless sluts . . ."'

Valerie Solanas attained notoriety with her 1968 assassination attempt on Andy Warhol, and although briefly a cause célèbre amid radical feminist circles, her subsequent life was a grim carousel of institutional abuse, and her 1988 death in a San Francisco budget hotel went largely unreported. Her reaction to 'Little Baby Nothing' can only be surmised, but she might have appreciated that its motivation was more sympathetic than Lou Reed and John Cale's subsequent vilification on their 1989 Warhol elegy 'Songs For Drella', or the 1996 Mary Harron film *I Shot Andy Warhol*. Indicative of the Manics' broad cultural hinterland, the lyric's other key influence was Tennessee Williams: 'Assassinated beauty/Moths broken up, quenched at last' paid homage to his poem 'Lament for the Moths', a hymn to the delicate creatures of the world and clearly one with which the Manics identified. The song was originally prefaced with a sample from the 1951 film version of *A Streetcar Named Desire*, where Kim Hunter as Stella Kowalski berates her brutish husband Stanley, played by Marlon Brando, for being an exemplar of male cruelty. Copyright issues meant the clip was omitted from subsequent pressings of the album, but the clip nonetheless demonstrated the daunting standards to which they willingly held their work.

Referencing the Society for Cutting Up Men and Tennessee Williams conclusively differentiated the Manics from the early nineties rock milieu, where male toxicity was barely acknowledged, far less confronted. Less certain, however, was the efficacy of the song on its own terms. Just as 'Motorcycle Emptiness's arrangement made narrative sense of a loosely related string of impressionistic images, here Bradfield's melodic instincts dignified a lyric that might charitably be termed 'well intentioned'. In their self-reproach at the male gaze and veneration of the divine feminine, such lines as 'Your pretty face offends/Because it's something real that I can't touch' veered towards the same objectifying perspectives. The saving grace was having a female voice responding to, and ultimately uniting with, Bradfield's: specifically a woman who could attest to the subject matter of commodification. The band originally envisioned Kylie Minogue, at that point still a prized asset for the PWL prefab pop stable, for whom she was currently making what turned out to be one last album. Head of A&R at Sony UK, Rob Stringer's enquiry never made it as far as Minogue herself. 'The song was pretty much written for Kylie,' Stringer recalled, 'but Stock Aitken Waterman were like: "We're not gonna do that – she's a huge pop star and this lot are a bunch of scumbags."'

Martin Hall and Sony US A&R Benjie Gordon liaised to present James with a less obvious, but even more appropriate duet partner: Traci Lords, the former underage porn star-turned-mainstream actress now attempting a career in music. 'We had no idea who she was – porn was not our world,' says Wire. 'But then it was explained to me and I thought it was a good idea. She was really nice – she flew to London and came to see our Christmas fan club gig, she had a leopardskin coat on like me and Richey. I can picture it now, everyone shuffling into place for a photo, and it did flash though my mind: this is slightly weird.'

'Little Baby Nothing' was initially put together by Bradfield and Edwards at Philip and Terri Hall's house on Askew Road in west London. Left to their own devices one evening while their manager and Wire attended a Heavenly record label event, James recalls they 'watched a bit of *Emmerdale*, made some food, then watched some of Phil's old Faces videos. And then about ten o'clock, Richey goes, "I've got this lyric . . ." It came really quickly.' Bradfield enjoyed singing differently for the female voice, and permitted himself some self-plagiarism by lifting the melody from 'Suicide Alley' for those verses. Wire returned, slightly tipsy, to find his bandmates with a completed new song. 'He went to bed,' says Bradfield. 'The only time in Manic Street Preachers history when Nick went out and got a bit drunk, and we stayed in and did some homework. Me and Richey thought it was brilliant, that we'd hit on something big time.'

Steve Brown felt similarly excited when presented with a demo of the song at Black Barn. Now deep into the second eight-week recording session, the sonic template for *Generation Terrorists* was by this point seamlessly embedded, with Sean Moore's programming so adept that even the delicate drum trills at the close of 'Little Baby Nothing' were executed with perfect verisimilitude.

'Steve thought getting Traci Lords to sing "Little Baby Nothing" was genius,' says Bradfield. 'There's production stuff on the album which is distinctly awful, and some stuff that considering what Steve was working with – us and our mismatched ambitions – where he did a brilliant job. And "Little Baby Nothing" is brilliant. Traci loved the song. She did talk about how she was sad – somebody had said to her what her gravestone would say, and that haunted her. She was definitely reflecting on everything. But she was really cool, her and Richey especially got along.'

In his desire to drape every corner of the song with heightened flourish, however, Brown did make what Bradfield considers the producer's one error on the entire album: having a professional singer 'ghost' some of Lords' vocals. 'Traci had a really good, almost female Joey Ramone vibe to her voice. And Steve had somebody sing along at points, and sometimes add a bit of vibrato, to make it a bit 'singerly'. So in the verses you are hearing one hundred per cent Traci, but when it goes "ooooh", that's a professional singing along. Which I thought was a mistake, because Traci had a great voice. I'm not sure if the song has weathered particularly well in the modern-day arena. But it was exciting doing it.'

Whatever Bradfield's reservations, 'Little Baby Nothing' was and remains a fount of Manic Street Preachers iconography, and has rarely left setlists for too long. The song's original concept was eventually fulfilled in December 1996 when Kylie Minogue, now freed from SAW's contractual restraints, joined the band onstage at London's Shepherd's Bush Empire; the following year she co-wrote two tracks with this 'bunch of scumbags' for her album *Impossible Princess*. The song's most recent female voice belongs to The Anchoress, who made her 'Little Baby Nothing' live debut in 2016 and has performed it with imperious grace regularly thereafter, living the dream of every Manics fan by declaiming its final couplet 'Rock 'n' roll is our epiphany/Culture, alienation, boredom and despair' like a philosophical roll call, the MSP equivalent of the Labour Party's Clause 4.

'The Anchoress really is the only person who's ever held the song as well as Traci Lords,' says Nicky. 'It's a regret that we've never done it live with her.' The regret appears to be mutual. On 16 November 2021, the twenty-ninth anniversary of 'Little Baby Nothing's release as a single, Traci Lords posted on Twitter: 'Beautiful haunting song. I loved singing on this track and I love you all. Happy Anniversary Manics', adding: 'I've been asked [to sing it live] in the past but had a schedule conflict. I hope this happens in the future.'

18.

Methadone Pretty

Recorded: Black Barn, Surrey
Producer: Steve Brown
Released: 10 February 1992 (*Generation Terrorists*,
   Columbia)

> 'When we were young, we had no history
> So nothing to lose.'
>
> — Swans, 'God Damn The Sun'

Boldly opening with a lyric co-opted from Karl Marx's *Critique of Hegel's Philosophy of Right* via Greil Marcus's *Lipstick Traces* – 'I am nothing and should be everything' – 'Methadone Pretty' was a fundamental 'Motown Junk'-era MSP song that didn't survive being machine-tooled into the skin of *Generation Terrorists*. 'When we used to play it live,' says Bradfield, 'if things were going well the crowd would just go mental even if they'd never heard it before. Which is exciting when you're young, it means you've got something. But it got straightened out on record, it lost something. I think we all knew it at the time too.'

On a good night, in its pre-recorded state 'Methadone Pretty' presented the Manics exactly as their idealised self-image: a hungry hellspawn of early Sex Pistols and peak Kit Lambert-vintage Who, its amphetamined co-option of 'I Can See For Miles' power surges aptly driving the lyric's equation of capitalism with opiate addiction ('Passive consumers with patrolled desires'). None of this jagged ebb and flow survived a routine swatting with the Steve Brown chamois, emerging as blanched as the song's victims, its serpentine riff forgotten about until too late, some superior T-shirt slogans trampled in the digital fog ('I accuse history'; 'Terminal young thing'; 'Mindless countdown to retirement'). Tellingly sequenced towards the end of the double-LP *GT*'s second disc, 'Methadone Pretty' wound up sadly fulfilling its own first line, an admission of defeat before the race was even run. 'We just lost faith in it,' Wire says. 'And I don't know why, because live it was probably our best song.'

19.

So Dead

Recorded: Black Barn, Surrey
Producer: Steve Brown
Released: 10 February 1992 (*Generation Terrorists*, Columbia)

'I am not stupid and I refuse to pretend to be.'

– Howard Devoto

One of the last songs recorded for *Generation Terrorists* – and one of only two never played live – 'So Dead' exemplifies the album's misalignment of ideas, vision and energy: an outburst of great individual components searching in vain for the appropriate vehicle to drive. Musically, its detente between the formative Manics' indie/metal culture clash suggested an alternative vision of The Cult, had Ian Astbury chosen Johnny Marr as his guitar player instead of Marr's longtime friend (and erstwhile Morrissey bandmate) Billy Duffy.

'Steve Brown went a bit Mutt Lange on me,' says Bradfield. 'He made me track an acoustic and an electric perfectly – every note of the arpeggios in the verses, he made me play the same thing every time. It'd be easy now, but at that age I was having to concentrate. He believed in sense memory – building stuff up and just knowing when things are right and dragging it out of yourself. I liked the verses, and this is the only lyric where Marilyn Monroe, such an important totemic character in our history, makes an appearance.'

Bradfield's open-G tuning effervescence suited a majority Nicky Wire lyric's clipped AABB rhyming scheme, lending a breezy subversion to such couplets as, 'No one fucks as good as Marilyn/ Plastic surgery sure cures your sins'. The narrative perspective switches from a consumerist demon sowing seeds of corruption ('You need a fix, I'm your prostitute/Repression says depravity's cute') to our jaded supplicant, numb at the altar of capitalism ('Eyes close down, I don't wanna see/Broken communion of the twentieth century'). The chorus reiterates the moral price of economic transaction ('Pay for it!') adding a defiant aside: 'You're gonna pay for my intelligence'. Most striking of all, however, was the admission, 'It's not that I can't find worth in anything/ It's just that I can't find worth in enough' – an early glimpse of a consumptively bleak existential purview.

'This was definitely more my lyric that Richey added to,' says Wire. 'It's not a benchmark song or anything, but it's definitely underexposed. Incongruous in terms of the album, because the jangly guitars aren't overpowering, James really just springs along, and I love the way he sings on this. He came up with the tune in Shepherds Bush – he was on a really hot streak in Askew Road. I still listen to this often, and I never stop thinking: why did we put that bit on the end?'

What would have been a perfectly impactful two-verse, two-chorus, 150-second palate cleanser at *GT*'s halfway stage was padded out with a holding-pattern guitar solo, and then overextended beyond all reason by a 45-second coda of generic Skid Row churn, with the repeated phrase 'You're so dead', apparently flown in from somewhere else entirely. In fact, the explanation is even more bizarre. The song was originally titled 'Pay For It', and had no coda until the September 1991 release of Lloyd Cole's second solo album *Don't Get Weird On Me Babe*, on which there was also a song called 'Pay For It'. Hunkered down in Black Barn, Wire and Edwards 'had one of our traumatic moments', and decided to change 'Pay For It' to 'So Dead', thereby requiring an additional part be written that contained the new title. 'The ending is shit,' says Wire. 'It just didn't need it. And it was definitely because of the title, we wouldn't have changed it otherwise. But there you go.'

20.

Condemned To Rock 'n' Roll

Recorded: Black Barn, Surrey
Producer: Steve Brown
Released: 10 February 1992 (*Generation Terrorists*, Columbia)

'Kill not the Moth nor Butterfly
For the Last Judgement draweth nigh.'
                        – William Blake, 'Auguries of Innocence'

By the time its last track was recorded, the Manics already sensed that *Generation Terrorists* was destined not to impact on the seismic scale they had promised. Two advance singles had failed to make the Top 20 – three, strictly speaking, as 'Repeat' came double A-sided with 'Love's Sweet Exile' – and upcoming tour schedules did not as yet include Wembley. Yet amid the confines of the church, they retained enough faith to see the mission through to a fitting close. 'Nick and Richey really wanted an opus,' says Bradfield, 'something overarching in its ambition. Something to frame our journey, which was supposed to end with this album. And if it's going to end with this album, it's gotta finish with a song that's some kind of doom-laden full stop, a heroic defeat.'

'Condemned To Rock 'n' Roll' was written at Black Barn from the ground up – no demos, no live prototypes – and yet it's perhaps the album's most directly emotive piece. The title came from Edwards, its lyrical biting point Nik Cohn's 1967 novel *I Am Still the Greatest Says Johnny Angelo*, whose title character, one of the inspirations for David Bowie's *Ziggy Stardust*, was a nihilistic pop idol who walks into his own violent death aged twenty-seven, having written his own epitaph: 'To all who pass that they may see – rock and roll was a part of me'. Edwards chose this as the song's sleeve quote. 'I actually don't like it,' says Wire, 'but that was a bit of a spark for Richey.'

Bradfield summoned a riff of Stygian gloom to suit a majority Edwards lyric that offers some striking depictions of existential misery ('The past is so beautiful/The future like a corpse in snow . . . It's a life sentence babe') and dissolution ('A line of vodka tears inside'), before collapsing into rather mundane relationship woe ('Masochistic love going nowhere'). 'It's the only time I find Richey's lyrics hard to deal with, because half the time he's just making shit up,' says Wire. 'He certainly didn't know how to behave with women.'

'Condemned To Rock 'n' Roll' reaches for transcendence one minute ('Oblivion's all we know') and moans about bad press the next ('Review with avant-garde lips, you're just a motherfucker'). If the kiss-off, 'There's nowhere I wanna see/There's nowhere I wanna go', was archetypal Wire curmudgeonry – 'Nothing much has changed!' he laughs – the song's opening line, 'Always feeling torn and slow', signposted Edwards retreating to the dark side; his default terminus soon enough. 'Condemned' shows he had plenty more where that came from, lamenting 'This fragile prison of sanity', an image with hints of Bowie's 'All The Madmen' and its assertion that mental asylum inhabitants were actually an insane society's greatest minds.

'I didn't like that line at all,' says Wire. '"Prisons" and "minds" never got on well with me. But that opener – written when he was twenty-two! In your prime! Richey's desperation . . . you know, I think I found it much easier because I was happy to be misunderstood, but he would talk so much about trying to explain everything. Obviously, you see that in the Steve Lamacq thing. I realised early on you just can't convince some people, but he couldn't let it lie. He just didn't seem able to let go. No matter how much you think you know someone, you just don't know how deep it runs. But there's a real sense of fun to the music of "Condemned To Rock 'n' Roll", however serious the words. You can't help but have a little smile to yourself at the never-ending guitar solo – why do one when you can do four?! James just went off. Like Jimmy Page and Slash combined. Rob Stringer didn't get it at all, that level of rock. Quite rightly, because it is . . . preposterous.'

After putting together parts for a verse, bridge and chorus, James Dean Bradfield knew by now what Steve Brown would say, so he duly delivered another section, built around a narrow-eyed approximation of the riff from Guns N' Roses' 'Rocket Queen' – which itself owed much to the high-velocity testostero-funk stylee Red Hot Chili Peppers – being fed into a woodchipper. Whereupon Brown asked for a further two parts, explaining that he'd heard an amazing track by LA punk-metallers Suicidal Tendencies and the Manics had to communicate with the West Coast skate kids. 'I said, "Are you fucking crazy?"' Bradfield remembers. '"There's not one skate kid in America that's ever gonna fucking know we ever existed!" And he's like: "Just for me?" So I did. And I'm glad I did, because it's kind of cool.'

Abetted by yet another Herculean feat of drum programming by Sean Moore, at the five-minute mark 'Condemned To Rock 'n' Roll' breaks through its heavy drapes and into a space that although not exactly sky blue still offers a glimpse of nirvana, crowned by Bradfield's jubilant declaration, 'Sterile like a line of piss, motherfucker!' It then descends via heroic Whovian yaggerdang – repurposing the chords to 'Behave Yourself Baby', bizarrely – to its end point.

'Condemned To Rock 'n' Roll' represented both destination nowhere and a foretaste of the band's as yet uncertain future: the phrasing of the title during the chorus would be echoed in 'From Despair To Where'. The song wasn't performed live in its entirety[1] until 6 November 2012, when Bradfield acquiesced to requests at a solo acoustic set promoting the twentieth anniversary edition of *Generation Terrorists*, and even then only on the proviso that the audience at London's Rough Trade East sing the words. It finally made its full band debut on 30 May 2015 in Edinburgh. Throughout the precision instrumental drive, Nicky Wire couldn't stop grinning; here, made flesh at last, was his sixteen-year-old self's dream of playing in a composite of Rush and The Smiths. 'We enjoyed it,' says Bradfield. 'A strange kind of release.'

21.

From Despair To Where

Recorded: Outside Studios, Hook End Manor, Oxfordshire
Producer: Dave Eringa
Released: 7 June 1993 (single, Columbia); 21 June 1993
  (*Gold Against The Soul*, Columbia)

'I cannot help it that my pictures do not sell.
Nevertheless, the time will come when people will see
that they are worth more than the price of the paint.'

– Vincent Van Gogh

During the summer of 1992, as they continued along the *Generation Terrorists* promotional treadmill, the Manics began building a future that would sustain them beyond the heroic rock 'n' roll moonshot exit that was now evidently never going to happen. Work began on 21 June in Soundspace, a small, modest studio in Cardiff's down-at-heel docklands, recording a version of 'Suicide Is Painless', the theme song from Robert Altman's 1970 film *M*A*S*H* – with lyrics written by the director's fourteen-year-old son Mike, who earned more from the song than his father did making the film – for a compilation to mark *NME*'s fortieth anniversary.

Although Steve Brown subsequently mixed the track, its creation was otherwise very different to the album: the band played together in a room, until they nailed it. Job done in a day at a cost of £80. So it was no small irony that when released as a single in September, the song went straight into the Top 10, thereby delivering what four months and £250,000 in rural Surrey had failed to do. Seeking to consolidate on this unexpected commercial breakthrough, Columbia chose 'Little Baby

Nothing' to be the seventh *Generation Terrorists* track as a single, so the band returned to Soundspace and the studio's engineer Alex Silva to record some B-sides, seeking the organic crunch that had characterised the previous session and somewhat restored the band's battered confidence.

'It wasn't just *Generation Terrorists*,' says Wire, 'but with the Heavenly "You Love Us" as well, we did start to think, "Was 'Motown Junk' just a fluke of recording?" Which it probably was in some ways. But all these little things: "Can we get the snare to cut through? Can we sound like a rhythm section?" Soundspace was tiny, but it had such a lovely drum sound, as soon as you went in it was life-affirming. A lot of the things we'd heard in our heads we thought we could now be capable of again.'

One of the two songs recorded with Silva was 'Dead Yankee Drawl', a muscly we're-so-bored-with-the-USA relic from 1989 setlists. More intriguingly, 'Never Want Again' suggested those evenings spent watching Philip Hall's Faces videos had not been wasted. This easy-paced rocker was of a different temperament to anything the band had recorded thus far, like an acoustic Stone Roses with fire in their torn-up hearts, a guitar solo that hit harder for being understated, and a Nicky Wire lyric replete with visions of sickness and malaise, or worse ('I smell death all around our name'). It also featured a slight return for the yearning vocal descent previously heard in the chorus of 'Condemned To Rock 'n' Roll' – a melodic orphan yet to find its forever home.

'This was start of the Wire misery lyric,' Nicky says, 'of feeling cursed, feeling ill all the time, we'd done a couple of tours where Richey was drinking catatonically, comatosely, just way too much. Plus I'm starting to miss home. I'd got engaged to Rachel, who I'd gone out with for a year when I was doing A-levels, and we got back together and I just wanted to be at home all the time. But "Never Want Again" was a nice little spot. It's breezy, very natural – a band actually sounding capable of doing something they'd sort of denied themselves.'

*

There wasn't much denial in evidence when Manic Street Preachers began recording their second album on 25 January 1993. For all that they loved the results they got at low-budget Soundspace in Cardiff's mean streets, their work and living place for the next ten weeks would be Hook End Manor in the south Oxfordshire countryside, equidistant from Goring and Henley-on-Thames. A sixteenth-century Elizabethan mansion, in the late eighties Hook End was sold by Pink Floyd's David Gilmour to record producers Clive Langer and Alan Winstanley, who ran it as Outside, a residential adjunct to their London-based Westside facility. According to Langer, 'Morrissey was the only person who could really afford it.'[1] The Manics were paying £1,500 a day, very much the going rate for a state-of-the-art studio housed in a Tudor pile offering clients four-poster beds, a gym, swimming pool, billiard room and, as experienced by Bradfield, the chance to meet a ghost. 'I didn't really believe in such things until it happened to me,' he says.

A haunted, uneasy mood would pervade proceedings generally. *Generation Terrorists* was made by a band driven to honour a utopian mission, fuelled by the momentum of two stellar indie singles and mountains of hysterical press clippings, and with a young lifetime's worth of points to prove. *Gold Against The Soul*, however, saw the Manics contemplating subsistence as a moderately successful career rock band, having thrown all their revolutionary fervour and songwriting fuel into its predecessor. The tanks were empty, the collective resolve battered, the esprit de corps fraying. *Generation Terrorists* was 'us against the world' – *Gold Against The Soul* was the world biting back. If, as per the Faust legend, every soul has its price, how prepared were the Manics to sell theirs?

'There was no coherent direction on *Gold Against The Soul*,' says Wire. 'Richey and I did a lot of the lyrics separately. The classic second album cliché – just scraping around. And we spent ten weeks in Hook End Manor, ridiculously, with Dave Eringa producing – and he'd never produced a record before.'

The choice of 21-year-old Eringa, supplier of tea, enthusiasm and Hammond organ during the 'Motown Junk' session, was certainly a risk. But as far as the band were concerned, this was a fellow true believer, whose attitude more than compensated for his inexperience. Eringa's epiphany came on a plane to Florida for a family holiday, where this twelve-year-old heavy-metal kid found himself sat next to 'a guy from America with really long hair who looked just like Sammy Hagar'.[2] In fact, Jeff Glixman was a rock producer whose credits included Georgia Satellites, Magnum, four albums by Kansas, Paul Stanley from Kiss's 1978 solo album and two Black Sabbath albums from the period where Tony Iommi was the only original member. By the end of the flight, having wrung out Glixman for war stories, Dave knew where his future lay. At eighteen he declined a place at university and set out to find work in a recording studio, landing a job as tape operator at Willesden's Power Plant, where in October 1990 he met the Manics, themselves only a couple of years older and barely more experienced.

'First time I saw him he had hair like Sebastian Bach from Skid Row, a Guns N' Roses T-shirt, Kiss buckle belt and cowboy boots – living the dream!' says Bradfield. 'A hopelessly optimistic Essex metal fan trapped in a Labrador puppy's body. He could have gone to Oxford or Cambridge but he gave it all up for rock 'n' roll. I loved that.'

For Sony to accept a relative novice producing conceivably the make-or-break record for a band that had already made one very expensive, only moderately successful album was testimony to the faith the record company had in the Manics – or perhaps more likely in Rob Stringer, who remained upbeat about his protégés' instinct and abilities, assuring the bosses that everything was going to plan.

Yet the plan was sketchy at best. The band arrived at Hook End Manor with demos of nine songs from three sessions spread over sixteen days in December 1992 and January 1993, with Eringa effectively auditioning to make the album. The second two sessions were at House In The Woods; the first, meanwhile, at Impact Studios near Margate in Kent, was primarily devoted to the song 'Patrick Bateman', a 6'34" evocation of author Bret Easton Ellis's eponymous *American Psycho*, with a couple of demos recorded as an aside. In the midst of these studio dates came the dire news that Philip Hall had been diagnosed with cancer. 'Never Want Again's spooked lyric now began to feel horribly prescient.

That 'Patrick Bateman's gratuitously profane ('I fucked God up the ass'), pitilessly rendered generic metal trudge was originally mooted as the Manics' next single indicates the mood of beleaguered fatalism within the group. It might as well have had 'career suicide' stamped into the 7-inch vinyl run-out groove. The song that eventually did announce the band's return was a far more adroit piece of work. 'From Despair To Where' successfully addressed both sides of the album title's art/commerce equation, where the music's woozy euphoria elevated a lyric of profound existential sorrow. Its opening lines established Richey Edwards's chastened mood – 'I write this alone in my bed/I've poisoned every room in the house' – then the second verse laid bare the sense of disillusioned innocence: 'There's nothing nice in my head/The adult world took it all away'. Meanwhile, the lyric's depictions of personal malaise and a life walking 'pale corridors of routine' echoed the title's specific reference to a band whose work defined the post-punk era more than any other: Joy Division. In just a few typewriter keystrokes, the epicentre of Manic Street Preachers' psychic landscape decisively shifted, as Edwards's preoccupations turned unflinchingly inwards.

'Richey was obsessed with the Joy Division song "From Safety To Where",' says Wire. 'But we understood pretty quickly that you can't try and sound like that band, they're so authentically true and original. So we took something from Joy Division and made it sound like the Faces.'

The Manics had become particularly drawn to 'True Blue', opener on 1972's *Never A Dull Moment* – notionally a Rod Stewart solo recording but in every unbuttoned swaggering detail a classic Faces song and performance. Sounding old before its time, 'True Blue' typifies the Faces' amiable earthy power: as Ian McLagan's electric piano tickles the itchy-toed Ronnie Wood groove in a rueful exchange with Ronnie Lane's freewheeling bass, Stewart a little improbably ponders the lot of a struggling vagabond minstrel ('Never gonna own a race-horse/Or a fastback mid-engine Porsche'), and tries to decide whether he should 'get myself back home'. On hearing the House In The Woods demo of 'From Despair To Where', Philip Hall was surprised but pleased.

'I remember him saying, "It's gonna be our transatlantic Number 1, like 'Maggie May'",' says Bradfield. 'I was like, "It's not . . .!" That was one of the first ones we did in Hook End Manor and the recording was amazing. Sean and Nick were so tight on that song, we'd done the demo, rehearsed lots, they were ready. There's a Mitch Ikeda photograph of Sean behind his drum kit at Hook End Manor, and it looks like a presidential press conference, he's surrounded by twenty-five microphones. Even Dave Eringa looks at that now and goes, "Fucking hell, what was anybody doing putting me in charge?" So that's my memory of recording "From Despair To Where" – even I knew there was a lot of microphones on the drum kit. But it sounded great, Dave made the right decisions.'

Eringa also contributed Hammond organ, amplifying the song's early-seventies-vintage British rock air. This, plus the string arrangement by the Royal Academy of Music's Nick Ingman, distinguished the song in the context of previous work – a useful quality for a comeback single tasked with heralding a new album and reasserting the band's ongoing vitality, especially a single with the word 'despair' in the title and depicting the diminished state of its majority writer.

'I'd say that Richey wrote this lyric thinking it would be for a single,' says Wire. '"I write this alone in my bed" is a really romantic first line, I could hear it on the radio straight away. The "cheap tarnished glitter" line was mine, but otherwise it was definitely Richey's lyric. "I try and walk in a straight line/An imitation of dignity" is great – the whole thing is quite concise for him. As with Kurt Cobain, there's a myth that Richey didn't want success, even though he was struggling at this point. He was drinking pretty heavily during the recording. If you see the interviews at that point, I don't think we were hugely confident with the record.'

One hopeful portent emerged while Dave Eringa was mixing the song at Olympic Studios in Barnes, south-west London, a studio forever associated with the legendary bands forged in the sixties British blues boom who went on to define rock for the ages: The Rolling Stones, Led Zeppelin, The Who (and indeed, the Faces). While Dave Eringa worked, out of the corner of his eye James Dean Bradfield noticed a man come into the room, who after listening for a minute or so had a brief word with Eringa, then left. Bradfield realised it had been Charlie Watts.

'I said, "What the fuck did he say, Dave?" Dave said, "He went – 'Fucking good'." I was like, "The mix good or the song good?!" "I dunno – mix and song good!" So we felt really happy at that point because Charlie Watts had come in. He had a lovely suit on . . . You know, we all could have done a better job. I thought I was singing brilliantly, but shortly after, I realised I'd gone over the top. My mum was really into music, and she said: "You're screaming it too much, what are you trying to prove?" "Oh, I don't know . . . everything?"'

With so much emotional and commercial investment in one song, 'From Despair To Where's chart performance dented spirits even further. Entering at Number 28, it crept up to 25, only to fall to 38 in the week *Gold Against The Soul* was released, and thence out of the Top 40, never to return.

'We knew then this is gonna be a bit tough,' says Nicky. 'I remember talking to Rob Stringer about it, and he's like: "We just gotta fucking crack on and dig in, Wire!" That was enough for me, to know that's what we had to do. You knew early doors you were in the trenches. With press, with tickets sales . . . A lot of bands would have just buckled at that point. But we kept digging! We dug so far we reached hell.'

22.

Sleepflower

Recorded: Outside Studios, Hook End Manor, Oxfordshire
Producer: Dave Eringa
Released: 21 June 1993 (*Gold Against The Soul*, Columbia)

> 'There is no such uncertainty as a sure thing.'
> – Robert Burns

Perhaps the second Manics album might be more favourably regarded if 'From Despair To Where' had been its opening track, as indeed it was on one provisional running order. Although more representative of *Gold Against The Soul*'s overall character, the song which eventually did take pole position highlighted some of the record's less coherent aspects and the band's conflicted impulses as they plotted a new route through a now radically altered musical landscape – one where mainstream rock strove to assimilate the version of raw authenticity proffered so successfully by Nirvana, Pearl Jam, Soundgarden et al.

Thus, 'Sleepflower' lives for and by its riff, a muscular serpentine phenomenon that as well as starting and finishing the song also runs throughout the verses, and recurs twice during an extended instrumental breakdown, instilling momentum and purpose. That one melodic device was tasked with so much – and succeeded so well – but left other components exposed. Most notably that breakdown section, which in its first half threw percussive clanks and what sounded like door chimes against acoustic guitar and plaintive wordless choral vocals. 'I wanted something a bit ethereal after all the macho bluster,' says Bradfield. The chimes came from a set of rusty tubular bells at House In The Woods, where a fully formed demo was recorded, while the section's second half offered syncopated drumming à la Stewart Copeland and notably well-articulated bass playing from Wire. It all evidenced a clear step forward from *Generation Terrorists'* synthetic patina to something more recognisably of the now; the efficacy of said progression, however, was debatable.

'I wanted that middle section to be more like Ruts DC's "West One (Shine On Me)", actually,' says James. 'But we were quite naturally hard rock at this point. Tight as fuck, snub-nosed, hard players. Pretty unsubtle, to be honest. When we remastered the album in 2020 my ears were in shreds. I called Nick up and said, "I can't listen to one of my own guitar solos any more."'

'Sleepflower's credentials as an album-herald were possibly overstated by Wire's habit of screaming 'Thunderstruck!' at the fingerpicked intro's resemblance to AC/DC's 1990 hit. The chorus had authentic rock mettle too, however unlikely the inspiration: a debate between Wire and Edwards over the merits of Def Leppard's most recent, ultra-lightweight material, which Wire contended made the erstwhile New Wave of British Heavy Metal flag-wavers' 1983 breakthrough hit 'Photograph' seem tough by comparison. 'Nick was saying to Richey, "You don't know much about Def Leppard . . ."' recalls Bradfield. 'And as the verse in "Sleepflower" was based on a riff and quite bluesy, I wanted the chorus to be anthemic. So because sometimes I just go the way of stuff we've been talking about, and they'd been having an argument about Def Leppard, I tried to write a chorus like Def Leppard.'

The Ruts, Stewart Copeland, Def Leppard . . . no wonder 'Sleepflower' doesn't quite add up. The lyric also spoke of a confused mindset: 'I feel like I'm missing pieces of sleep' was Edwards lamenting his mental turmoil caused by insomnia – 'a blind illness of my anxiety', symptomatic of adulthood's corrupted state. 'From Despair To Where's 'pale corridors of routine' now echoed to memory fading 'to a pale landscape'. Thus, 'Sleepflower' amplified the album's principal theme: loss of innocence. Edwards explained in a July 1993 interview: 'As a child you put your head on the pillow and fall asleep with no worries. From being a teenager onwards, it's pretty rare that you don't end up staying awake half the night thinking about bullshit.'[1]

A set-opener for most of 1993's live shows, 'Sleepflower' vanished from setlists in 1994 and wasn't performed again for thirteen years – much to the vocal displeasure of some. The band remain bemused by its hallowed status among the hardcore faithful. 'I don't think it's one of Richey's greatest lyrical achievements,' says Wire, 'but we can't deny it's a fan favourite. Bizarrely, it was released as a single in America, and at that time everything was based on how many "adds" you got on radio.' He laughs. '"Sleepflower" didn't get a single add to any radio station.'

23.
La Tristesse Durera (Scream To A Sigh)

Recorded: Outside Studios, Hook End Manor, Oxfordshire
Producer: Dave Eringa
Released: 21 June 1993 (*Gold Against The Soul*, Columbia);
26 July 1993 (single, Columbia)

'History is a combination of reality and lies.'
– Jean Cocteau, 'Journal d'un unconnu'

The sleeve of *Generation Terrorists* featured a quotation specific to each song, presenting the album as the musical sum of its literary and philosophical inputs. In contrast, *Gold Against The Soul* had just one: Auschwitz survivor Primo Levi's poem 'Song of Those Who Died in Vain', an indictment of war's political architects that gave voice to 'the innocents slaughtered . . . the conquered. . . [the] already dead', ending with the promise, 'If the havoc and the shame continue/We'll drown you in our putrefaction.'

Printed in full – clearance for which delayed the album's release by several weeks – Levi's poem wasn't linked to any one particular song, but seemed most apposite in relation to 'La Tristesse Durera (Scream To A Sigh)'. The song's title came from Vincent Van Gogh's final words (*'la tristesse durera toujours'*/'the sadness will last for ever'), albeit chosen by Nicky Wire for their poetic resonance rather than any desire to create a song about a suicidally depressed artist. 'I remember scrambling around, thinking I actually need to write a lyric about a subject, rather than just "culture, alienation, boredom and despair". Because there was still this idea that we were po-faced Marxists or something. And you know, the myth of war heroism and the way we treat old people is very much A Subject. So I wrote loads of the words and then Richey's definitely come in and added some.'

The fathers of both Wire and Edwards served in the army, and the lyric analysed the exploitation of military veterans ('I am a relic/I am just a petrified cry'), suggesting they were as much victims of war as the dead. The same political system that had previously scoured working-class communities for cannon fodder now had the survivors 'wheeled out once a year, a cenotaph souvenir', used as human shields by politicians who – as imputed by the song in juxtaposition with Primo Levi – were no less guilty of war crimes than the actual perpetrators. 'I think that line "I see liberals, I am just a fashion accessory" was quite daring,' says Wire. 'The way people were parading history without actually digging into the deeper meaning, or applying victimhood to someone rather than getting to the source.' Amid the litany of sparse, clipped verse, the toughest lines saw the old solider sell his medal: 'It paid a bill/It sells at market stalls/Parades Milan catwalks'. On an album where many lyrics were written separately, this was Wire and Edwards collaborating in the room together and reaping the creative benefits.

'I remember sitting down with Richey, finishing the words for this at a desk, in House In The Woods, in a bedroom. He just gave me a sheet and said, "I think this goes here, this goes there . . .". Richey wrote, "where they patronise my misery" and "parades Milan catwalks", which are great. The way Richey frames things adds a humanity to it. At times he was much more humane than me – the man who wrote "Archives Of Pain"! But we turned a corner with this song.'

Musically, 'La Tristesse Durera' was born in Wales, then began to take on recognisable shape at the Blooms Hotel in Dublin, where James Bradfield was holidaying with his girlfriend. He'd already received Nicky's initial lyric draft and had begun singing a verse in his head over the percussive instrumental 'Eve Of

Reality' from Arrested Development's album *3 Years, 5 Months And 2 Days In The Life Of . . .* Wherever this was leading to, he felt it was auspicious, and so made sure to pack his guitar. 'You just know when something's going to be really good,' he says. 'And it's good when it doesn't escape you. Sometimes it does.'

Upon release, more than one critic suggested the song was a belated 'baggy' anthem, which says much for the suggestive proximity of the Madchester era, and possibly the MSP–Heavenly connection too. In fact, Bradfield's vision was much closer to the band's foundational core, as the Arrested Development rhythm in his mind sped up and morphed into 'Car Jamming' by The Clash, a steamy beat gumbo which became the template for a Sean Moore full-kit showcase.

'We'd got a really good demo at House In The Woods, where I'd been singing the solo in my head. And then we get to Hook End Manor, where I've got a picture of Dave Eringa with a speaker out in the courtyard, to expand on the already big drum sound. I put a tiny bit of wah on it, just to get grooving a tiny bit more with Sean, who was playing a snare drum with the snare off, as a percussive thing, like Larry Mullen would do in some early U2 stuff. I was bouncing off the walls when Sean was playing – it was just brilliant.'

Adding to the percussive shakedown was Andrew Lovell, AKA Shovell from M People, who also played on 'From Despair To Where' and several other album tracks. No less unlikely a contributor than one of the UK acid house scene's latest crossover stars, however, was Richey Edwards himself. 'La Tristesse Durera' features the only instance of Richey playing guitar on a Manic Street Preachers recording: a single sustained barre chord, after the first chorus, heralding the wider arrangement of verse two. As Dave Eringa recalled, 'We cleared everyone out, and it was just me and Richey and he did pretty well. He was nervous – "Oh, we're going to be here all night, Dave" – but he just played it. No one laughed at him at all. Except Richey himself, of course.'[1]

'Richey had a good night doing that,' says James. 'I went in two hours later and he's like, "I'm still searching for the perfect chord . . ." He had a sense of humour about it. He never pushed to do anything else either, never said, "Can I play more guitar?" That was never an issue.'

In Richey's one-chord wonder and beyond, 'La Tristesse' proved the value of restraint – a quality conspicuous by its relative absence elsewhere on the record. While most songs betrayed the collective loss of nerve by layering on guitars, here there was a hole in the middle occupied only by a suspended flickering synth tone. 'It goes all through the song,' says James, 'almost like an accordion or a slowed-down version of [Tears For Fears'] "Everybody Wants To Rule The World". As soon as I played rhythm it just filled it up too much, so I needed something else and this little synth thing fixed it – it made everything come alive.'

The song's lone guitar solo is beyond question one of Bradfield's greatest. Yet even this, for all its heroic oscillatory spectacle, was a paradigm of less-is-more, despite James still heeding the advice of Steve Brown, not always a moderating influence. 'He said to me, "Not too many blue notes. If I want to hear shit blues guitarists I'll go to any fucking ents bar in Britain and listen to some student. Try and make your solo so you can sing it." So I started singing solos in my head and then translated to playing them. It's good advice.'

'La Tristesse Durera' does indeed endure: rarely dropped from setlists, it's reliably in or around the band's ten most played songs, latterly often as part of Bradfield's acoustic segment, a treatment that amplifies its empathetic qualities – particularly with the band's audience ageing with them in real time. Rock music intrinsically drinks from the well of youth, so it was indicative of the group's idiosyncratic vision that one of the Manics' key songs addressed the melancholia of growing old. As Edwards explained before the album's release: 'La Tristesse' is about 'the way life doesn't get any better as you get older. It's always a beautiful image every year when the war veterans turn out at the Cenotaph, and everyone pretends to care about them – but then they're shuffled off again and forgotten. I'm much more sympathetic towards older people than towards my generation – I think they have a lot more dignity.'[2]

Reproach at their own 'useless generation', with its apathy and solipsism, contrasting with respect for their parents' selfless embodiment of working-class rigour and decency would be a constant throughout the Manics' career. Likewise, 'La Tristesse Durera's parenthetical subtitle (Scream To A Sigh) made explicit an inner conversation – whether to rage against the dying of the light with a scream, or accept it with a sigh – that would subsequently inspire some of their greatest work, and still informs the band today.

24.

Roses In The Hospital

Recorded: Outside Studios, Hook End Manor, Oxfordshire
Producer: Dave Eringa
Released: 21 June 1993 (*Gold Against The Soul*, Columbia);
20 September 1993 (single, Columbia)

> 'Success makes life easier.
> It doesn't make living easier.'
>
> – Bruce Springsteen

No song on *Gold Against The Soul* better exemplifies the Manics' muddled impulses as they searched for a purposeful new direction. Titled from a line of dialogue in 1980 teen pulp film *Times Square* – its new wave soundtrack had already been pillaged for *Generation Terrorists'* throwaway 'Damn Dog' – 'Roses In The Hospital' was a refinement of the *Lipstick Traces*-inspired alienation technique, conflating personal and political malaise, to which the call-and-response lyric posited self-harming as a valid response ('Try to pull my fingernails out'; 'Stub cigarettes out on my arm'; 'The West scratches onto my skin'). There was even an insinuated critique of the 1980 Housing Act, the Thatcher government's contentious 'right to buy' legislation which incentivised council tenants to buy the houses they lived in, and became a cornerstone of Conservative hegemony ('All we wanted was a home/Now we are so strung out we wanna own').

Yet at the time, such subversive content went almost completely unnoticed, thanks to a curious shuffle-funk arrangement and its distracting resemblance to David Bowie's 'Sound And Vision'. 'It was obvious there was an echo straight away, there was no getting around it,' says Bradfield. 'It wasn't modelled on "Sound

And Vision", but it just happened. We did a demo at Impact in Kent, and it was awful. Really fucking bad. All neat and tidy, and *so* trying to be funky, but *so* shit and *so* white.'

Recorded during the 'Patrick Bateman' session, there are Ikea flat-pack shelves funkier than the first 'Roses In The Hospital' demo. Bradfield remembers Wire unfavourably comparing one section of sixteenth-note guitar buttquake to Nuno Bettencourt of Boston hard rock showboaters Extreme. 'Which was obviously a bit of osmosis – Richey at this point is playing Extreme around the place. So I thought, "That's got to go." We slowed it down, gave it a steadier undercarriage. If it was going to be funky, better to have that boom and bust "Sound And Vision" thing rather than too much slamming. Just go for the obvious influence. Everyone kept mentioning it, so OK, I'll stop denying it.'

Bizarre though it seems three decades later to have been embarrassed by the association, in 1993 David Bowie's cultural stock had yet to recover from the artistic nadir of *Never Let Me Down* and his abortive reboot as AN Other member of Tin Machine. Perhaps the Manics felt a certain beleaguered kinship: in the song's final version, the demo's iteration of the title as the last line of the chorus was replaced by 'We don't want your fucking love'. The shutters were coming down.

'Roses In The Hospital' sidesteps comparisons to anything else in the Manic songbook, the sound of a band lost in the fog and enjoying the jeopardy. To heighten the percussive clatter (M People's Shovell is prominent from the outset), Eringa fed Sean Moore's drums through a Leslie speaker and into the courtyard, albeit with the unforeseen drawback that the heavily compressed ambient microphones picked up the sound of Hook End Manor's ducks quacking, much to the drummer's irritation. However incongruous its party-hearty atmos, the clap-along dropout gave due prominence to a key couplet – 'This century achieved so much . . . To make a voice no voice at all' – and set up an extended valedictory lap of (dis)honour, built around the repetition of a resonant phrase that would subsequently reappear as both a song and album title: 'Forever delayed.' The closing flurry of ad libs, meanwhile, saw Edwards and Wire having fun with some of their pet hates ('Credibility? I'm yawning!'; 'Contagious, like a suntan!') and slyly flipping The Clash's 'Rudie Can't Fail' ('Rudie Rudie Rudie gonna fail!'), to which Martin Hall quipped: 'You know what they say, there's a time and a place for spontaneity.'

'Me and Richey worked hard together on this one,' says Wire. 'I think "Roses" stands up – it's ambiguous enough to be not too in your face. And I love "Credibility? I'm yawning!". We were pre-empting what was to come.'

In keeping with its black sheep profile, when released as the third single from a patchy album 'Roses In The Hospital' inevitably confounded expectations by entering the chart at Number 15. The highest placing for a Manics original single thus far, it would not be bettered until 'A Design For Life'. The band's performance on *Top of the Pops* featured another anomaly: the just-married Wire was absent, his place taken by the band's tour manager Rory Lyons wearing a Mickey Mouse mask. 'I was on honeymoon,' Wire says. 'In Swansea. For three days. Then we went on tour in Japan.'

25.

Gold Against The Soul

Recorded: Outside Studios, Hook End Manor, Oxfordshire
Producer: Dave Eringa
Released: 21 June 1993 (*Gold Against The Soul*, Columbia)

'This is a public service announcement – with guitars.'
    – The Clash, 'Know Your Rights'

The title track of *Gold Against The Soul* is the answer to an all-too rarely asked pop quiz question: what connects Madonna, Simple Minds and Union of Democratic Mineworkers leader Roy Lynk?

Created in mid-1985 at the end of the year-long miners' strike, the UDM was a breakaway from the National Union of Mineworkers and predominantly comprised miners from the Nottinghamshire area who had continued working throughout the strike, in contrast to miners in neighbouring South Yorkshire and the Manics' hinterland of South Wales, where support for the strike was as near-unanimous as the contempt for those erstwhile comrades who chose to break it. Roy Lynk was awarded the Order of the British Empire in 1990 in acknowledgement of his 'services to trade unionism': no less than he deserved for enabling the Conservative government under Prime Minister Margaret Thatcher to divide the miners, defeat the NUM, and implement its programme of colliery closures. Hence his citation in 'Gold Against The Soul's second verse: 'Close the pits/Sanctify Roy Lynk/An OBE'.

Although the events of 1984–5 and their repercussions had been sublimated in previous work – indeed, before the band's formation, Nicky Wire's first poem/lyric dated from this period and was titled 'Aftermath' – this was the strike's first specific appearance in a Manics lyric, one written predominantly by Wire with additions from Edwards, who described the song as 'an apocalyptic vision of Britain from the Thatcher years to the "caring '90s"'.[1] The words were arranged in dead-eyed dissociative epigrams, suggesting a news bulletin read by The Fall's Mark E. Smith ('Somebody told me to vote Conservative'; 'Fossilise, make Yorkshire into a tourist resort'). The lyric's purview cumulatively widened, encompassing different aspects of obeisance to free-market capitalism, like social prejudice ('Working-class clichés start here/Either cloth caps or smack victims'), or the hypocrisy of the white liberal who 'Hates slavery [but] needs Thai labour to clean his home'.

Musically, Bradfield's initial concept was no less arcane. At House In The Woods, he built a demo on samples of 'League Of Nations', from Simple Minds' art-rock apex *Sons And Fascination/Sister Feelings Call*, and Madonna's creepily lascivious proto-trip-hop single 'Justify My Love'. The demo has a feline menace, with grinding bass and sampled Solina synth draping the desiccated funk guitar and muted snare drum in Cold War intrigue. Sadly, the process of upgrading the song at Hook End Manor saw its more abstract qualities subsumed into the album's default hard rock veneer.

'I was trying to draw together stuff that shouldn't quite be with each other,' says Bradfield. 'And I do think the demo has a nice bit of old-school Simple Minds to it. But by the time we got to do it in the studio it just went wrong. For all Dave [Eringa]'s brilliant points, I don't think he was schooled enough in that kind of direction to know where we were trying to get at. Usually the title track of an album has got to be a triumph of some sort – something that could be a single. And that doesn't get close. So it's a fail. But an interesting fail. It was the last song we recorded, and there was definitely a sense of "that's as good as that one's going to be".'

'It's a strange way to end the album,' Wire considers. 'You can hear the Madonna sample . . . simulated sex doesn't really marry with Roy Lynk being a scab. People always say this song's "clunky". Well, when you're writing about "the now", it tends to be a bit clunky. It's like journalism. There's a reportage to our lyrics at times.'

Post-Madchester, mid-grunge, pre-Britpop, the rock 'n' roll landscape of early 1993 was a mostly politics-free zone. Even Billy Bragg had tired of picket line protest: his most recent album dwelt on domestic matters and featured a co-write with Johnny Marr called Sexuality. Only the Manic Street Preachers would consider a song inspired by a relatively obscure figure from an almost decade-old industrial dispute to be of 'the now'. Such was the profound, lingering impact of the miners' strike on the group's psyche. Or perhaps the Manics were just paying closer attention to the news than most. In October 1992, three months before 'Gold Against The Soul' was written, the soon-to-be-ex-leader of the Union of Democratic Mineworkers handed back his OBE, in protest at the Conservative government's announcement that seven out of the remaining twelve collieries in his Notting-hamshire backyard were to be closed amid a new programme of national cuts that would reduce British Coal's workforce by more than 50 per cent. The betrayer had himself been betrayed. But at least Roy Lynk now knew how much gold his soul was worth.

26.
Donkeys

Recorded: Soundspace Studios, Cardiff
Producer: Manic Street Preachers/Engineer: Alex Silva
Released: 20 September 1993 ('Roses In The Hospital'
   B-side, Columbia); 14 July 2003 (*Lipstick Traces*, Epic)

'I don't like people who have never fallen or stumbled.'
                           – Boris Pasternak, 'Doctor Zhivago'

Nicky Wire's 2004 description of Hook End Manor as 'a hollow arena to make arena rock' is a common hindsight view of *Gold Against The Soul*. But even in the immediate aftermath of its release, the Manics felt dissatisfied with the album and the compromises – artistic and commercial – it had entailed. Amid a tour schedule spanning four long months there were even a couple of bona fide arena rock gigs to play as the mid-afternoon opening act for Bon Jovi at the vast expanses of Milton Keynes Bowl, a confusing experience for all concerned. Jon Bon Jovi later thanked 'The Maniacs' for supporting, while James Dean Bradfield spoke for many when he said, 'It was obvious as soon as I walked onstage that I shouldn't be doing it.'[1]

The first tangible evidence of a desire to move the band's sound to a different place emerged from Soundspace, the scummy Cardiff antidote to Hook End's Home Counties opulence, where the band rehearsed and recorded several songs with Alex Silva during a few days' gap in the roadbook. 'Donkeys' paired an entirely Edwards-written lyric with a loping melody to anthropomorphise the band's current status as one of stoic acquiescence to the daily grind: 'Us donkeys wake up weary . . . Sweetness bent double, whole days making polite.' Such was the reality of 'digging in' and working their workmanlike rock album. Indeed, surveying the mountain of press coverage during this period, it's striking how collegiate the band suddenly appear, Edwards in particular. One month Richey was on the cover of *NME* to promote the Manics' UK tour alongside members of support bands Credit To The Nation and Blaggers ITA, while the next saw him in *Metal Hammer* magazine riffing with Wolfsbane's Blaze Bayley, Ginger Wildheart, Andy Cairns of Therapy? and Tony Wright from Terrorvision on the hot topic of the moment, 'Is Metal Alive & Well In The '90s?'. (Asked whether *Metal Hammer* should cover 'indie' bands like the Manics, Blaze laughed: 'Why not? They've got two guitars!').[2]

How fitting, then, that 'Donkeys' should articulate emotional shutdown with such affecting candour, its regretful aura minted from the very beginning by Bradfield's chord progression, ushering in an opening couplet ('Put some lipstick on/At least your lies will be pretty') worthy of its evoking the chorus of Bruce Springsteen's 'Atlantic City' (Bradfield: 'Richey was big on *Nebraska* by that point'). Intriguingly, all the song's ear-catching references were sourced from various different American heartlands. The hint of melancholy in the top line was a clear Pearl Jam evocation, with Moore's understated empathetic drums in comradely lockstep with some beautifully articulated Wire bass, which Bradfield particularly admired for its 'its lovely Duff McKagan clunk'. The guitar solo, one of Bradfield's very best, mapping the utopian arc of dreams always destined to fall short, owed its precision clarity to knowledge of how John Frusciante played his. 'It was the first time I'd used a Marshall shredder pedal on a dry channel – and I was playing a Strat for some reason. It was my whole Frusciante thing. I heard he had one dry channel on his guitar and then would just step on a gain pedal. Gives it more "headroom", as guitarists say.' The coda's impressionistic shimmers, meanwhile, had an Arcadian aura in which engineer Silva sensed Stevie Wonder's *Innervisions*, albeit not the hothouse funk of 'Higher

Ground' – the song that gave Red Hot Chili Peppers their first UK chart entry – but the pensive 'Visions', coalescing around the quietly devastating final lyric: 'Donkeys are only left with lies'.

'We all loved "Donkeys",' says Bradfield, 'we were just so absolutely together. It was a good run-up to us realising we could do another record with Alex Silva, a Cardiff boy with the right sensibilities. It fed into something.'

Three years later, it was the austere fortitude of 'Donkeys' that bequeathed what became the band's best-selling hit. 'The first two chords,' Bradfield affirms, 'nearly going into the third chord, are the same progression, with a different key and different overtones, as "A Design For Life". It would not have been born, musically, without "Donkeys".'

27.
Life Becoming A Landslide

Recorded: Soundspace Studios, Cardiff
Producer: Manic Street Preachers/Engineer: Alex Silva
Released: 7 February 1994 (single, Columbia); 21 June
    1993 (original version, *Gold Against The Soul*)

> 'Being another character is more interesting
> than being yourself.'
>
>   – John Gielgud

The *Gold Against The Soul* song that most bluntly expressed Richey Edwards's despondent worldview was released as the fourth and final single off the album a whole year after it was recorded, and exactly two months after the death from cancer of Philip Hall, the Manics' manager, mentor and friend. Nothing about the intervening twelve months had dissuaded Edwards from the diagnosis offered by 'Life Becoming A Landslide': a child enters the world crying and things only get worse from there. Assessing the band's future direction in a *Melody Maker* interview just before the single's release, Edwards paraphrased Henry Miller: '"At the edge of eternity is torture, in our mind's never-ending ambition to damage itself." That's what we would like to write about.'[1]

'Landslide' suggests they already knew the way to that grim locale but were still struggling to build an appropriate vehicle to take them. Bradfield's response to seeing the opening lines – 'Childbirth tears upon her muscle/Very first second a screaming icon' – was to reach for that renowned guide to sensitivity, Red Hot Chili Peppers' Rick Rubin-produced throb marathon *Blood Sugar Sex Magik*. 'Richey was obsessed with that album,' says Wire. 'And James was going through his massive John Frusciante

117

phase. We had dumped all our British influences at this point. It was Alice In Chains, Chili Peppers, Richey was listening to so much Skid Row . . . We cringe about *Gold Against The Soul*, but I think this song actually stands up.'

The specific mood template for 'Life Becoming A Landslide' was 'I Could Have Lied', one of the acoustic-based detours from *Blood Sugar Sex Magik*'s more typical phallocentric funk-offs like 'Suck My Kiss' and 'Sir Psycho Sexy'. For the plaintive opening Bradfield used a Lakewood acoustic guitar that Steve Brown insisted he buy after deeming the others substandard – 'He drove me to Anderson's in Guildford in his Range Rover, like a real producer would!' James recalls – then shifted through successively heavier tones for the subsequent verses. Bizarrely, the other main musical inspiration was The Clash's version of Willie Williams's Studio One reggae hit 'Armagideon Time'. 'I wanted the guitar and the bass to feel coagulated together, where you can't tell which is doing what,' says Bradfield. '"Armagideon Time" has that, even though it's a different pace. So that and "I Could Have Lied" were the two reference points. Which just doesn't make any sense when you say it out loud . . .'

That the Manics could bend such incongruous sources into a finished construct that resembled no one else speaks volumes for the robustness of the band's core aesthetic, as well as the quality of their wingmen. Nick Ingman's woody string arrangement rescued the chorus from the depths of extreme unction, while this song's surrogate Ian McLagan was Ian Kewley, a high-calibre Hammond session player and Paul Young's musical director. Yet for all the classy detail, 'Life Becoming A Landslide' ('I don't wanna be a man') never quite transcends the adolescent tendencies that its lyric – almost all Edwards's work – idealises. Although the House In The Woods demo's equivalence of 'Babies in line' with 'cattle in abattoir' didn't make the final cut, the song's keystone couplet is the equally jarring 'My idea of love comes from/A childhood glimpse of pornography'.

'We equated that line with how your sensibilities get so muddled by small corruptions of the way you should think when you're young,' Bradfield says. 'It's not something I really connected with. But I enjoyed playing this song – it felt like it turns around the sense of feeling there's no worth in anything.'

On 12 February 1994, 'Life Becoming A Landslide' entered the UK Singles Chart at Number 36, then swiftly dropped out. No invitation came to perform it on *Top of the Pops*. Two days later, the Manics began work on their next album, a record predicated on the belief that nothing could be gained from sweetening life's bitter pills.

28.
Comfort Comes

Recorded: Soundspace Studios, Cardiff
Producer: Manic Street Preachers/Engineer: Alex Silva
Released: 7 February 1994 ('Life Becoming A Landslide'
    B-side, Columbia); 14 July 2003 (*Lipstick Traces*, Epic)

'Displaying an interest in forward propulsion.'
                                    – Wire, 'Our Swimmer'

If nothing else, *Gold Against The Soul* successfully proved that Manic Street Preachers were the sum of their own contradictions – cognitive dissonance as rock 'n' roll. The album set gloomily sensitive lyrics of personal despair to blaring hard rock anthems. Its beautifully stylised front cover image was inspired by *Barakei* ('Killed By Roses'), a 1962 collaborative art book by Japanese author Yukio Mishima and photographer Eikoh Hosoe, while the music within referenced Red Hot Chili Peppers. Primo Levi? Meet Skid Row.

Yet the ongoing 'denialist' strategy of musical entryism wasn't really working, either in commercial or aesthetic terms. In this context, then, the B-side to the fourth single from a patchy year-old album heralded a significant tactical change. In one sense, 'Comfort Comes' was a throwback, its terse rhythmic guitar chops evoking Big Flame, the Manchester *C86*-era trio who ranked alongside The June Brides and McCarthy in the pre-denialism Manics' hall of fame. That version of the band, however, was lost to pre-history – and this song, recorded at the same Soundspace session as 'Donkeys', became a blueprint for the immediate future. Next to 'Life Becoming A Landslide', it might as well have been made by a completely different group.

'I remember Nick and Sean really rebelling against the rockiness of *Gold Against The Soul*,' says Bradfield. 'And not so much me and Richey. I'd started living back at my mum and dad's house, listening to my old records in my bedroom, playing Magazine and Wire, stuff like that. So the song started off as a post-punk exercise. Alex Silva was recording it, and he really liked it. Then *all* of us really got excited. It was nice to know we still had it in us.'

As part of this 'exercise', James had Nicky play a Rickenbacker – 'because it's plunkier' – while Sean pared down his kit to best assimilate a rudimentary post-punk sound. À la Wire drummer Robert Gotobed, cymbals were verboten. While mixing the track at Swanyard in London, Bradfield and Moore obsessively asked Silva to make the drums sound smaller and smaller. 'I wanted them so new wave that they disappeared into the oblique,' says James. 'Then I let rip with the guitar solo, which fucks up the post-punk exercise. But it's still a bit more framed, more McGeoch, more atonal. And we'd never really sounded like that. There's not much rock, it's smaller, more direct. It intends something different.'

Just how different is thrillingly demonstrated at the start of the final chorus, where Bradfield's solo crashes over and delays the re-entry of the vocal, a happy accident that the Manics in spiffy *GATS* mode would likely have gone back over and corrected. Silva, by contrast, simply smiled and cut the vocal.

'With *Gold Against The Soul*,' says Wire, 'the vocals were getting too over the top. Whereas I liked the tone of the voice here – much more claustrophobic. Also in that last chorus, I suspend the bass note and it really builds into a crescendo – a frenzy, but controlled, very small. It's a tense note.'

The tension mirrored the lyric, which was wholly Edwards's work, cutting to the core of his emotional black hole: 'I wish that someone would hold me/Wrap their arms around a shrinking somebody'.

'"Comfort Comes" is so minimal and miserable,' says Wire. 'It haunts me, it's so bare and raw. And honest. I always assumed it was his battle with alcoholism hovering over this. Although "reach out for the first person I see" – he never did that. He's not a "reach out" person. But that line about comfort, "Brutal and mocking but always there/A crutch for enmity's saddest glare" – brilliant. I don't know if there was a collective thought that this was the start of *The Holy Bible* when James wrote it. But when Sean and James mixed it in London and brought it back, it sounded like a template. It was exciting – we all listened together and thought: "This is the way to go."'

29.
Faster

Recorded: Soundspace Studios, Cardiff
Engineer: Alex Silva
Released: 6 June 1994 (single, Epic); 30 August 1994
   (*The Holy Bible*, Epic)

'Revolution starts at home,
preferably in the bathroom mirror.'
   – Hüsker Dü, sleevenote to *Warehouse: Songs And Stories*

Nicky Wire awoke on 12 May 1994 to the news that John Smith, leader of the Labour Party, had died of a heart attack, aged fifty-five.

Wire hadn't necessarily been John Smith's biggest champion. Since taking over from Neil Kinnock in 1992, the leader of the opposition's modest public profile and risk-averse strategy had thus far succeeded only in frustrating both the left and right wings of his party. Early into recording *The Holy Bible*, Nicky had been midway through a gesticulatory rant about how Labour would never win an election with Smith at the helm when he accidentally knocked over James Dean Bradfield's beloved white Gibson Les Paul. Both watched in horror as the guitar's neck snapped. But nearly three months on, Smith's sudden, wholly unexpected death struck Wire as symptomatic of a grievous prevailing mood. 'I didn't feel at all well around this time,' he says. 'For the rest of the year I thought *I* was going to have a heart attack.'

Smith's death occurred the morning after Manic Street Preachers returned from Braga in Portugal, where they had played their first show since Bangkok the previous month – a trip overshadowed by Richey Edwards slashing his chest in the Thai capital's MBK Hall dressing room with a set of ceremonial knives gifted to him by a young fan. Not for the first time, Edwards's act of self-harm had been witnessed by an *NME* journalist and photographer, thereby feeding the ongoing mythology of rock 'n' roll doom that seemed to swirl around the band. Portugal too had been traumatic, with Edwards's behaviour indicating Thailand fitted an ongoing pattern. 'Things were going awry,' Wire told *NME*'s Stuart Bailie. 'We had to put him to bed one night . . . he just burst out crying in the car.' James Dean Bradfield added: 'It was horrible. Richey was crying uncontrollably all the time.' The band members began to feel that Portugal was becoming their 'bogey country': during their previous visit, on 7 December 1993, they heard the news that their manager Philip Hall had died.

Shortly after the band returned from Thailand, one of Edwards's best friends from university killed himself. A couple of weeks earlier, as work on *The Holy Bible* neared completion, Kurt Cobain was found dead at his home in Seattle, aged twenty-seven. 'The zeitgeist of this year in general is fucking death and destruction,' said Wire. Bradfield phoned Edwards to tell him the news about Cobain. 'I can't pretend I remember what he said,' Bradfield later recalled. 'Not "good on him", nothing so easy to digest as that, but it was something which expressed admiration. [I remember] thinking: "Please just react in a human way rather than on an intellectual level. Just leave it as it is – if something is happening and it's bad, just leave it there."'

'Faster' was first played in public on 28 May, a week before its release as a single and a foretaste of *The Holy Bible*, when the Manics appeared at an Anti-Nazi League Carnival in Brockwell Park, south London. Richey's setlist was written on a sheet of headed notepaper from Forest Mere, a luxury health spa near the Hampshire village of Liphook which Edwards had first attended a year earlier upon completion of recording *Gold Against The Soul*, in an attempt to curb his drinking. Now, following the incidents in Thailand and Portugal, the band dispatched him there again, amid the sense that his various conditions – alcoholism, anorexia, self-harming – were degenerating out of control . . . and at dangerous speed.

As if to rebut this developing narrative, 'Faster' was a power-grab; its opening lyric, 'I am an architect/They call me a butcher', a counter-intuitive riposte to the assumption that Edwards was diminished by his inner torments and body issues. The subsequent lines – 'I am a pioneer/They call me primitive' and 'I am purity/They call me perverted' – reflected the certitude of the addict's perspective, however delusional, that what ostensibly diminishes them in the eyes of everyone else is actually a show of strength, an assertion of control that elevates the practitioner beyond the mundane. 'They' saw only the act of butchery, and its bloody aftermath, not the strength that 'I' summoned to commit it. Here was justification for Richey's '4Real' carve-up in self-aggrandising terms worthy of a Roman emperor.

Even though the lyric has its narrator acknowledging his benighted aspect ('I am idiot drug hive, the virgin, the tattered and the torn'), he remains unrepentant ('I do as I please'), culminating in the chorus's startling assertion of intellectual power: 'I am stronger than Mensa, Miller and Mailer/I spat out Plath and Pinter'.

'Faster's moral authority derived from its sense of beleaguered defiance, an exhilarating, faintly hysterical evocation of Freud's *Über-Ich* run amok in a library. Such agitated, confrontational posturing contrasted with the preceding Manics single, 'Life Becoming A Landslide', a poetically woebegone exemplar of the *Gold Against The Soul* era's disillusionment as the band felt their early dreams of effecting some glorious self-destructive art spectacle sucked lifeless by the deadening routines of a middling rock band career. Unlike many other songs on *The Holy Bible*, which were (or would become) inextricable from Edwards's physical and psychological state, 'Faster's lyric transcended the specific circumstances of its principal author. 'I know I believe in nothing but it is my nothing' was an affirmatory declaration of nihilism, an us-against-them exhortation, a song for the groundlings, the underdogs, the Davids against the Goliaths. 'I am all the things that you regret' had echoes of 'We're the flowers in the dustbin/ We're the poison in the human machine' from the Sex Pistols' 'God Save The Queen' – the definitive negationist redemption song – while the ensuing 'a truth that washes, that learnt how to spell' inculcated a broader societal subtext: the assertive voice of working-class intelligence. Indeed, 'Faster's radical credentials had already been established with the opening sample of John Hurt as Winston Smith addressing Suzanna Hamilton's Julia in the Michael Radford film adaptation of George Orwell's *1984*: 'I hate purity, I hate goodness! I don't want virtue to exist anywhere. I want everyone corrupt.'

Whereas the majority of *The Holy Bible*'s lyrics were written solely by Richey Edwards, 'Faster' was a collaborative effort – it would be the last song where he and Nicky Wire sat together and wrote in what had become their mutually supportive, ego-less fashion, exchanging material to advance or complete a train of thought. Wire had one fragment stuck in his head: 'So damn easy to cave in/Man kills everything'. He also had two aphorisms about conformity: 'If you stand up like a nail then you will be knocked down' – adapted from a Japanese proverb – and 'I've been too honest with myself, I should have lied like everybody else'. Six, maybe seven lines, but not a song; nor could he see a way clear to it becoming one. Edwards duly wove them into his bathroom mirror soliloquy, then showed his friend the result. Amazed, Wire made one other contribution. 'Richey didn't have a title and I just felt the propulsive nature of the song, so I said, "Why don't we call it 'Faster'? It seems like everything's speeding up in your head." The acceleration of culture to a point of no return. I remember saying to him, "I can't keep up with you."'

When Edwards handed over the lyrics to 'Faster', James Dean Bradfield became obsessed with writing the music. Although he had two new songs already under his belt – 'Mausoleum' and 'Die In The Summertime' – he still harboured doubts over their quality. Considering 'Faster' the best of the new lyrics he'd been given, he determined that it ought to be a single. Then, having elevated it in his mind, he found himself repeatedly falling short, becoming so annoyed that he started counting the rejected versions. Eighteen, nineteen, twenty . . .

'"Faster" was symbolic. I'd written "Mausoleum" and "Die In the Summertime", but I wasn't sure if they were any good, especially "Mausoleum". And sometimes you've gotta get one really fantastic song to give the others the seal of approval.'

The demo recordings of 'Die In The Summertime' and 'Mausoleum' were the last new Manics songs Philip Hall heard. By now very ill, he was keen to discuss how the next record was shaping up. As his brother Martin, the band's co-manager, recalled: 'Richey said, "We've got one called 'Mausoleum' and one called 'Die In The Summertime'." And Philip said, "Oh, cheery! Thanks for that!"' The ailing Hall's approval emboldened the band to pursue their new direction. As Wire recalled: 'At the end [of listening] he said, "This sounds like you're doing the right thing – this rock 'n' roll has got to stop." That really stayed with me, the idea of inverting rock 'n' roll and getting back to something cold, with a different kind of emotion.'

Dissatisfaction with *Gold Against The Soul*, an expensively recorded empty vessel, curdled into disappointment the longer they promoted it and felt the chill winds of diminishing interest. August 1993 began with a disastrous appearance at a festival in Swansea, where they were pelted with bottles, one of which hit Wire on the head, and continued with a second-tier European festival tour. During a short seaside holiday amid the trudge, James called Nicky from a telephone box in Bishopston on the Gower peninsula. 'I asked him if anything was happening, and he's like,

"Nothing – we're not getting offered anything. No interest from the *NME, Melody Maker* . . . nothing." I remember being a little scared. It had all gone dead.' September's schedule read like a recipe for rock 'n' roll suicide: two weeks in Germany playing small clubs, then opening up for Bon Jovi at Milton Keynes Bowl. Bradfield got home to his parents' house in Blackwood feeling 'bored with *Gold Against The Soul* and the songs we were playing. My memories of the studio were us being pretend rockers. And I wanted to stay away from it. I wanted to be more aggressive. I wanted that opulence to be got rid of. We had a conversation in the rehearsal room about shedding this overblown rockist skin and going back to basics, otherwise the gig is up for us.'

Two days into the German tour, Bradfield learnt that his mother had gone into hospital for an operation to treat cancer. 'I knew something was wrong at home but my parents didn't tell me because they were being good and old-fashioned and didn't want it to get in the way of my life. I thought, "I've really lost sight of something." My mood had darkened. It made me realise that I wanted to try and be like the person I was when I was seventeen. I wanted to be that edgy angst-ridden little prick again. And I wanted that to be reflected in the record.'

As part of his tabula rasa approach, Bradfield sidelined his totemic Les Paul guitars and Marshall amplifiers, in favour of Fender Telecasters, Jaguars and Jazzmasters played through Fender Twin and Vox amps. Pretend rock hardware was out, clean-toned tools of post-punk aggravation were in. Beyond this, however, Bradfield feared his toils over 'Faster' were a manifestation of a deeper malaise: that having drifted so far from his original core principles he could no longer write music that fitted such searing, astringent words. 'It's ridiculous to say, because we were only a couple of years down the line, but I'd already felt that we'd lost it. I thought, "I've gone so far in one direction I can't do this any more. The stuff Richey's given me, it's so important I get this right – why can't I do it?"'

Finally, after three weeks and twenty failed attempts, alone in his parents' house on a Friday night, Bradfield smashed his songwriter's Gordian knot, thanks to darts and a 1944 American novel of existentialist alienation. 'My mum and dad were out – my mum was playing darts. I'm thinking, "I'm going to have to hand this over to Sean completely, let him get on with this one." And then on the twenty-first attempt, I just thought, "Let the lyrics speak to you: what are they trying to say to you?" Not in terms of the message, but I looked at the rhyme and metre of "I am an architect, they call me a butcher" and thought: "It's got to be regimented."'

The decisive move came from Saul Bellow's 1944 novel *Dangling Man*: a meditation by an outsider hero on how to assimilate within a mainstream American society that he abjures. Ultimately, he admits defeat and lines up to join the army, declaring: 'Hurray for regular hours! And for the supervision of the spirit! Long live regimentation!'

'That quote from *Dangling Man* came into my head,' says Bradfield. 'And I thought, "Yes! We can do this!" The secret was I just had to make it like a straight line and make it combative. I remember seeing the title and thinking, "I want it to be vicious but with an amoral singing voice." That's when I thought I was doing something good. "Long live regimentation!" All the songs were marching towards something, and it just became more aggressive. Straighter. Strychnined. Angular. Colder.'

For the recording of 'Faster', a template already existed, in 'Comfort Comes', the B-side of 'Life Becoming A Landslide', recorded at Soundspace with Alex Silva to test the efficacy of both the studio and Bradfield's proposed soul-purifying post-punk aesthetic. 'Faster' essentially conflated the earlier song's desiccated take on the sound of Wire circa *154* with the heroic uplift of 'Hong Kong Garden' by Siouxsie and The Banshees, which inspired the sampled xylophone in 'Faster's chorus. '*154* has that perfect melding of brutal but cerebral. There's a sense of space in "Faster" – there's not many chords, it's not as dense as you think. I came to the chorus, and I wanted something to lift it . . . and then I had that guitar part: "'Hong Kong Garden', we're there! I've done it!" I didn't write "Faster" by understanding the lyric more, I wrote it just by working hard and finding the right answer. It's nice singing lines like, "I am idiot drug hive, the virgin, the tattered and the torn", because it's got really good rhythm.'

The song had two masterstrokes of arrangement. In the first verse, the position of the vocal shifts in the stereo image, an effect that evokes the narrator's self-analysis; Bradfield sounds like dual personalities holding forth with each other. James credits Alex Silva with this call-and-response idea: 'But Mark Freegard did it of his own volition anyway in the mix, so it was obviously in the song's DNA.' Then, to amplify the second verse's move from first- to second-person narrative, thereby opening out the song's scope from the solipsistic gaze ('Self-disgust is self-obsession, honey, and I do as I please') to the universal ('The first time you see yourself naked you cry'), Bradfield doubled his guitar line at a higher pitch. There was also room for serendipity: the siren that wraps around the John Hurt sample came from Bradfield putting down his guitar and forgetting to mute his FX pedal. 'I came back and Alex Silva, who's a little bit wantonly pretentious sometimes, in a brilliant way, had recorded it. A nice little happy accident.'

All these flourishes built upon the 'Comfort Comes' framework, but 'Faster' still kept faith with that earlier song's puritan scheme, which all four band members enthusiastically bought into: Edwards and Wire's spartan lyrical economy; Wire with his high-end bass line in the chorus, suggestive of Joy Division's Peter Hook. As for Sean Moore, 'Comfort Comes' had seen the drummer deny himself the catharsis of cymbals. Now, in line with 'Faster's declamatory posture, he allowed himself a degree of flamboyance: inspiration for his precision thrashing came via Faith No More's 1989 single 'From Out Of Nowhere', and especially Pearl Jam's 'Rearviewmirror', from 1993's *Vs.*, an album with a deeply embedded siege mentality the Manics could relate to. Also, in Mike McCready, Pearl Jam had a guitarist given to fits of caustic virtuosity, very much like Bradfield's climactic solo on 'Faster'.

'It was a particularly hard part for Sean,' says James. 'His bass drum is basically being his hi-hat all the way through the song. Four takes, and he was like, "I'm fucked – if I haven't got it, I'll do it again tomorrow." But he did get it on the first day. Alex Silva provided backing vocals on the "Man kills everything" chant at the end – Sean refused to. "I've done most of the work on this, if you want your yob chorus on, go ahead . . ." I was worried we weren't going to nail the drum take, because it is fucking hard. But Sean did it.'

For all its various root sources, however, 'Faster' presented a band reaching way beyond imitation, emulation, pastiche or homage. The song was torn from an instinctual reservoir of belief – a collective commitment to make a record that would be, as Nicky Wire reflected, 'the truest essence of us. I think "Faster" was important because we felt like we were starting to make a different kind of music – different to anyone.'

High-fiving himself in his parents' house on the Friday night when he finally got its measure, James Dean Bradfield concurred. 'I thought, "We're going to break the Top 10 with this!" Ha! Oh no you're not!'

The Manics knew their stock with Sony in early 1994 was low, though not precisely how low. In the wake of the expensively made *Gold Against The Soul*'s poor performance, some of the record label's top brass wanted to drop the band. Only Rob Stringer's passionate advocacy and casting vote saved them.

'His exact words were, "These boys are gonna sell a million records one day,"' says Wire. 'We didn't think we were in a great position but we weren't aware things were so finely balanced. That's why *The Holy Bible* was done on the cheap.'

'The bottom line is,' Bradfield adds, 'if we realised we were in such a precarious position, we perhaps wouldn't have made a record like *The Holy Bible*. And to be actually thinking of "Faster" as the first single was strange. By the time it came to mix it with Mark Freegard, I'd actually convinced myself there was a "bit of a Blondie vibe" in there . . .'

In fact, 'Faster' entered the 5 June UK singles chart at Number 16. It was the week's fourth highest new entry – below Ace Of Base, Dawn Penn and a Pet Shop Boys collaboration with BBC sitcom *Absolutely Fabulous* for Comic Relief – and seven places above 'To The End', the second single released from Blur's *Parklife*. The reward was an instantly notorious *Top of the Pops* appearance, where the combination of incendiary song and Bradfield wearing a black balaclava emblazoned with the word 'James' somehow provoked a record number of complaints to the BBC. The following week the song fell twenty places. (Bradfield subsequently wondered whether the balaclava was a 'subconscious daubing of actor's paint . . . perhaps hiding behind the balaclava when I knew I was inhabiting somebody else's mindset'.)[1]

For a song that presents humanity in such baleful terms, 'Faster' has a strangely jubilant air. Its live performances always seem shot through with a heightened synergist energy; never more so than at Glastonbury in 1994, when the Manics took the stage for this key *Holy Bible* preliminary campaign wearing military garb, amid air-raid sirens and darkening skies strafed with searchlights, then after a five-second introductory sound-check, with Bradfield barking 'Public Image's 'Hello, hello, hello', 'Faster' crashed over the audience like an acid hailstorm.

But its weight can't be lightly worn. During the 2014/15 twentieth-anniversary tour, where the album was played in its entirety, Nicky Wire delivered the opening Winston Smith speech in tones closer to deathly than deadpan, and the band didn't collectively perform 'Faster' or any other *Holy Bible* songs for another eight years. 'You can't fake them,' Wire reasoned in 2019. 'They are not entertainment, they are a state of mind. A brutal poetry of disgust.'

'Faster' did, however, still occasionally feature during James Dean Bradfield's solo spots, in an acoustic arrangement perhaps most memorably captured on 30 September 2011. *Songwriters' Circle* was a BBC series where three singer-songwriters share a stage at the intimate Bush Hall in London and take turns to perform and discuss the mechanics of their craft. Bradfield lined up alongside John Grant, a near contemporary, and the legendary 73-year-old New Orleans soul and R&B producer-composer-pianist Allen Toussaint. The show ended with the trio uniting for an ensemble parlay of Toussaint's classic 'Yes We Can Can', with James doing well to keep in vocal sync with the master.

Bradfield chose 'Faster' as the last of his solo performances. Introducing the song, he regretfully noted that Richey Edwards was no longer around to explain his lyrics, and spoke fondly and eloquently of his co-author. 'I remember Richey giving me this lyric and it felt like a set of sarcastic commandments for the modern age. I think this lyric is way ahead of its time, in terms of . . . well, just showing the onset of brutality.'

There can surely have been few greater benedictions bestowed upon Manic Street Preachers than their musical linchpin singing one of their greatest songs as the man who wrote 'Yes We Can Can' watched on rapt, gently shaking his head in admiration at 'I spat out Plath and Pinter'. Negaholia in excelsis: at that moment, we were all Allen Toussaint.

30.
P.C.P.

Recorded: Soundspace Studios, Cardiff
Engineer: Alex Silva
Released: 6 June 1994 ('Faster' AA-side, Epic); 30 August
    1994 (*The Holy Bible*, Epic)

'All we have left is the English language. Can it be
salvaged? That is the question.'

               – Spooner in *No Man's Land*, Harold Pinter

If 'Faster's martial tempo and staccato metre offered a foretaste
of *The Holy Bible*'s austere musical discipline, its double A-side
trailed another of the album's defining characteristics: a song
where the message is more important than ever, yet rendered
almost incidental by the music's elemental force, sung in a voice
stretching words and meaning to a point that almost defies logic.
The voice of a preacher, no less.

    'P.C.P.' is all about language, its ownership and deployment.
According to Richey Edwards in an interview published around
the song's release as a single: 'In principle I think the idea of PC
[political correctness] is actually OK. But where it might be good
at qualifying the big things – racism is bad, prejudice of any kind
is despicable – the so-called minorities it's supposed to protect
end up being victimised by these restraints to the point where
they have no identity left at all.'[1] He went on to paraphrase in
the explanatory 'Pass Notes' distributed to journalists ahead of
the album's release, and also featured in the Holy Bible tour
programme: the song 'Links PC + PCP + New Moral Certainty'.[2]
Figuring out this equation of political correctness with a warped
puritanical thought control assumes the knowledge that 'PCP' is

short for phencyclidine, the powerful dissociative anaesthetic drug known also as 'angel dust'. Which was news to Nicky Wire when Edwards sat him down to explain his latest lyric.

'I didn't know PCP was a drug,' Wire says. 'I thought it was the Portuguese Communist Party, because when we had been to Portugal I bought one of their badges, but he said it's got fuck all to do with that. I remember looking at it on paper when he did one of the original drafts and it just seemed like millions of interesting words. Maybe too many words. At the time Richey was reading the magazine *Living Marxism* a lot. I wouldn't even know where he bought it from, but he was big on it because it broke a lot of taboos. *Living Marxism* was actually more 'Living Libertarianism', before the contamination of libertarianism became so apparent.'

Living Marxism was in fact the monthly journal of the Revolutionary Communist Party, a Trotskyist far-left sub-splinter with a disproportionately noisy presence on UK university campuses during the 1980s, which is possibly where Richey Edwards became aware of it. More traditional leftist groups scoffed that the RCP was neither revolutionary nor communist, while enviously noting the conspicuously high production values of its weekly tabloid *The Next Step*, out of which evolved *Living Marxism*, published monthly from 1988 onwards as a brash rival to the Communist Party's classier – in every sense – *Marxism Today*.

December 1993's *Living Marxism* was a special issue dedicated to 'the perils of Political Correctness', with a main feature by RCP founder Frank Füredi bemoaning how 'the PC celebration of identity means emphasising who you are rather than what you can be'[3] – a sentiment that was worthy of Margaret Thatcher's favourite bootboy Norman 'on your bike' Tebbit and could have sat comfortably in any Conservative election manifesto from 1979 onwards.[4] The RCP line on free speech ran counter to contemporary left orthodoxy – it was relaxed about offering platforms to racists, for example – but in some details feels congruent with the permissive edicts of 'P.C.P.'. Indeed, as pointed out by Yusef Syed's

Holy Bible-centric blog A Manic Body Politic, the lyric 'PC caresses bigots and big brother' was almost certainly adapted from *Living Marxism*'s declaration on 'The Right To Be Offensive', published in the February 1994 edition, which drew equivalence between 'the traditional puritans of the back-to-basics right and the new puritans of the politically correct left . . . Whether to combat racism, to protect children or to safeguard our privacy, censorship is an authoritarian infringement of our rights. It should always be opposed. Bans are for bigots and Big Brother.'[5]

In that same issue's editorial, meanwhile, the magazine's editor Mick Hume characterised Conservative PM John Major's 'back to basics' campaign as the 'right-wing version of Political Correctness . . . associated with feminists and social workers. The Tories seek to restrict what we might do and say in the name of traditional decency and family values, while the PC professionals want to lay down their petty law in the name of mutual respect and non-sexism'.[6]

Presumably this was the sort of PC cadre Edwards had in his sights with the song's opening couplet: 'Teacher starve your child PC approved/As long as the right words are used.' But there was more to 'P.C.P.' than merely taboo-breaking or liberal-baiting. The spectre of George Orwell and *Nineteen Eighty-Four* is summoned by the 'Ten foot sign in Oxford Street' – not far from the BBC's Broadcasting House where Orwell worked during the Second World War and conceived his classic dystopian novel – and its baleful exhortation, 'Be pure! Be vigilant! Behave!' This phrase, redolent of *Nineteen Eighty-Four*'s Newspeak, was in fact the motto of Torquemada, the fascist-religious über-villain from one of Edwards's favourite *2000 AD* comic strips, *Nemesis the Warlock*. In *Nineteen Eighty-Four*, Orwell's disillusioned socialist warned against the manipulation and censorship of language by tyrant regimes. Similarly, this aspect of 'P.C.P.' is consistent with the Manics' autodidactic ethos. The couplet 'PC, she says inoculate, hallucinate/Beware Shakespeare, bring fresh air' evokes expunging texts of language deemed offensive regardless of cultural or historic context – a process equally applicable to the Bard as the hip-hop artists whose records routinely carried 'Explicit Content' stickers following the campaign by the Parents Music Resource Center (PMRC), a US lobby group whose membership, like PC itself, united elements of the liberal left and conservative right.

Shakespeare also appends the song, in a sample from Peter Yates's 1983 film of Robert Harwood's play *The Dresser*, with Albert Finney's bewildered fading thespian declaring: '227 Lears, and I can't remember the first line.' To ears still ringing from Bradfield's valedictory Sten-gun punchline 'Pass the Prozac, designer am-nes-i-*a-a-a-a-a-a-ac*', this evoked an Orwellian scenario where *King Lear* has been proscribed for excessive violence and the works of England's greatest playwright are disappearing from memory. The implicit warning is that banning words leads to banning songs, or books – perhaps even the most sacred book of all. Not for the first or last time, the Manics were following McCarthy, whose 1988 single 'Should The Bible Be Banned' satirised PC's erasure of language by envisaging a scenario where a man kills his brother after reading the Book of Genesis parable of Cain and Abel. Yet in also referencing the Old Testament text notorious for prohibiting homosexuality under holy law – 'Read Leviticus, learnt censor-ship/Pro-life equals anti-choice' – 'P.C.P.' ultimately calls out the language police on both sides of the political spectrum.

For all the lyric's contradictory twists and arcane detours, its relentless musical context bestows 'P.C.P.' with a cogent rationale. Bradfield's precise diction is driven forward on a platform of hammered downstrokes, as inspired by the metal-adjacent punk guitar playing of Andy Cairns from Therapy?, the County Antrim trio whose subversive take on post-hardcore grind suddenly accrued commercial bite on 1993's *Shortsharpshock E.P.* and landed them a UK Top 10 hit, ironically by paying homage to the same amphet-amined punkstompf for which the early Manics were pilloried. Indeed, Nicky Wire recalls initial doubts about 'P.C.P.' for that very reason: 'We were a little reticent when we recorded it. There was a debate about whether it was almost *too* punk.'

'I was a bit jealous of Therapy?'s success at that point,' says James. 'I liked the way Andy played on songs like "Screamager" and "Going Nowhere" – it was sharp and tight, and had a nice pop sensibility. I loved how he wasn't scared of going down that road, and moulding all that ambition into a pop single. I felt I'd lost that kind of edge, so that encouraged me to put it back into one song. The intro is Joy Division touched with a bit of Skids' "Scared To Dance". And the drums are amazing, "P.C.P." has my favourite drum sound on the record. It's all in there, like a spindly Argonaut coming towards you.'

Bradfield asked Edwards to explain the Shakespeare reference, but freely admits to not understanding the answer. 'It's the one lyric I couldn't get an angle on,' he says. 'It's schizophrenic. Some of Richey's best lines: "Doctors arrested for euthanasia". "If you're fat don't get ill". And there's quite a few bits of "P.C.P." where I don't know if I quite sit with it . . . But it's sometimes nice doing that on behalf of somebody, and not one hundred per cent agree with them but still agree to sing it. I just loved being among its flow.'

In bringing order to Edwards's lexical maelstrom, Bradfield's design for 'P.C.P.' evolved its own kind of hybrid dialect; very apt for a song about the policing of language, one aspect of which was particularly close to home and addressed directly in 'P.C.P.'s first verse. In 1993 the Welsh Language Act passed into law, establishing the principle of equality for Welsh and English in public services and justice in Wales. The act received its Royal Assent almost exactly thirty years after Cymdeithas yr Iaith Gymraeg – the Welsh Language Society – began a campaign for the right of equal status, featuring direct actions like the defacement or destruction of road signs not displaying place names in Welsh as well as English. In this context, the line 'Systemised atrocity ignored/As long as bilingual signs on view' would have been guaranteed to grab attention.

'I think what he was trying to say was that we were persecuted as a Welsh nation, but were more interested in the language,' says Wire. 'So rather than real rage, we had this faux rage. I *think*. I never quite got it. And I never asked him.'

Hitherto, Cymraeg had been emblematic of divisions in Wales, both geographical and party political. Growing up in the industrial south, dominated by a Labour Party that regarded linguistic equal rights as a frivolous – and nationalist – distraction from more fundamental issues of class and economic power, the Manics were less likely to have felt a connection with the Welsh language beyond singing in church choirs, as James did, or renditions of 'Hen Wlad Fy Nhadau' ('Land Of My Fathers') before rugby internationals. In this instance, Edwards's stance on PC reflected a traditional socialist perspective. His antipathy coincided with the emergence of a new wave of bands, most notably Gorky's Zygotic Mynci and Super Furry Animals, for whom singing in Welsh was not incompatible with reaching a wider audience, nor singing in English a repudiation of their national culture. In *Brittle With Relics*, Richard King's oral history of Wales, SFA singer Gruff Rhys recalled an interview Edwards gave to a Welsh-language pop magazine. 'They asked, "What do you think of the Welsh language?" And he said, "The Welsh language is for people who eat coal."'[7] Although it has the hallmark of classic Richey contrarianism, the statement chimes with others Edwards made on the subject, to the effect that Welsh was a dying language and should be allowed to pass away peacefully, in the name of evolution. 'I don't think you can ever reinvent something that is failing, especially with the language or culture,' he said in a 1992 interview. 'If people always try to cling onto something, nothing would ever change.'[8]

Evidently, Richey did not regard extinguishing a key element in a nation's cultural identity as consistent with 'systemised atrocity'. His attitude was particularly striking given how much casual racism was still aimed at Welsh people under the guise of what would now be called 'banter', and at the Manics in particular from the UK music press, where PC values in 1993 were only selectively applied. Typical headlines of the period included 'Meek Leek Manifesto' (from *NME*'s review of *Gold Against The Soul*), 'The Boyos Are Back In Town' (on the front cover of Tower Records' in-store magazine *Top*), and 'Academic Sheep Teachers' (*NME* again, from an interview with Richey about his time at university). Although stung by such playground-level taunts – 'Would "Potato-Eating Paddy" get a Therapy? cover line?' Richey asked *Melody Maker*[9] – it's interesting how Manic Street Preachers' relationship with Wales and Welshness emerged as a theme in their work only once Edwards's voice was lost.

'Richey's quotes about the Welsh language never sat easy with me,' says Bradfield. 'I was the typical South Walian boy who sang Welsh in the choir but didn't speak it. "Oh so beautiful to hear the language sung but never dare it be uttered" is the old saying that describes what the South Wales Valleys' relationship with the Welsh language was. It's improved now. The Welsh Language Act was about inclusivity, not censorship. The "bilingual signs" line doesn't add up for me. The rest of the lyric would involve itself in today's climate brilliantly, I think.'

In the twenty-first century, the era of cancel culture, unregulated online hate speech and a primal strain of identity politics, 'P.C.P.' feels like a song whose time has come: what is social media if not the new designer amnesiac? At least the PC police have prevailed to the extent that Cymru-phobic headlines are thankfully a thing of the past. Overshadowed by 'Faster' on their twin-pronged single, 'P.C.P.' took on heightened potency when released as the finale of *The Holy Bible*, its delinquent pummelling possibly the only way to follow 'The Intense Humming Of Evil's dread clangour, ending an album mired in hopelessness on an improbably euphoric note. Ultimately, all of its contentious details are rendered moot by the cumulative force of sonic will. Which is a quality *The Holy Bible* shares with spiritual music of every kind.

31.
Revol

Recorded: Soundspace Studios, Cardiff
Engineer: Alex Silva
Released: 1 August 1994 (single, Epic); 30 August 1994
(*The Holy Bible*, Epic)

'Watch out Europe, we're going on tour.'
— Mel Brooks, 'Springtime For Hitler', from *The Producers*

In April 1989, Sonic Youth were photographed in the middle of Moscow's Red Square for a cover feature by UK music weekly *Sounds*. To the band's left, on the western side of the vast plaza, was Lenin's Tomb, a granite and marble mausoleum built next to the Kremlin walls. To their right, on the eastern side, the towering arches and pillars of GUM, the Soviet Union's version of Harrods or Bloomingdales. For Sonic Youth, on the final leg of a tour in support of their 1988 album *Daydream Nation*, the location offered a useful perspective on the distance between theory and practice, or the dimensions of myth and reality. Lenin led a socialist revolution in the name of creating an egalitarian society, which within a few years of his death had come to define totalitarian brutality. Now the tomb was the epicentre of a quasi-religious personality cult, his embalmed corpse a physical manifestation of his very unequal posthumous status, maintained for public viewing by a lab team of 200 people without whose literally face-saving efforts Lenin would crumble and collapse, just like his vision of a communist utopia.

Meanwhile, across the square, GUM's vast ornate arcades were open for business but mostly devoid of actual goods. That evening, Sonic Youth played their hardly conventional version of

rock music to an audience of curious, bewildered locals in a conference hall at Moscow's Orlyonok Hotel, watched nervously by
young soldiers doubtless wondering where the tentative process
of *glasnost* (openness) instigated in 1986 by Soviet head of state
Mikhail Gorbachev would lead next. The following morning, after
a long overnight train journey, glasnost deposited Sonic Youth
in Kyiv, notionally in the same daydreaming nation as Moscow,
but in reality another country and a different world entirely. In
Russia, Lenin gazed down from walls, stood upon plinths, his
image and name embossed into every possible public space and
artefact. In the capital of Ukraine, he seemed much less present,
or revered. Exploring their quarters at the Kyiv Institute of Civil
Aviation before taking the stage in a lecture theatre crammed
with hundreds of screaming, deliriously happy souls, Sonic Youth
opened a door and were greeted by a three-foot-tall plaster
head, plonked disconsolately in a corner. Three sheets of paper,
some scissors and gaffer tape later, the man born Vladimir Ilyich
Ulyanov and since canonised as Comrade Lenin has gained a six-
inch-high mohawk and wears Black Flag's flying bars logo across
his forehead. This is what anarchy in the Ukraine looks like.

'Revol' would reunite Sonic Youth and Lenin. The former gave
the song a title; the latter's preserved body was the song's visual
cue in the *Holy Bible* album artwork. Lenin is also the first Soviet
leader cited in the song's first verse, heading a list that moved
forward chronologically through 'Mr Stalin', then plain old
Khrushchev, Brezhnev and Gorbachev, ending with Yeltsin, the
Russian president who dismantled the USSR and oversaw the
plundering of its assets by privateers, oligarchs and gangsters.
Richey Edwards's lyric, however, did not address any of these
heads of state's public activities, alluding instead in a succession of
opaque epigrams to imagined personal behaviour of a more or less
sexual nature. Thus, Nikita Khrushchev's legacy was 'self-love in
his mirrors', while his successor Leonid Brezhnev, whose lengthy

physical decline came to embody Soviet economic stagnation, had apparently 'married into group sex'. Gorbachev represented 'celibate self-importance' and Stalin a 'bi-sexual epoch' (despite his regime criminalising homosexuality). As for 'Mr Lenin, awaken the boy', this lyric might equally suggest Lenin was a champion of LGBT rights, or a paedophile. Or both . . . or neither. An early lyric draft offered 'descent of arousal' instead, which was possibly too close to Yeltsin's 'failure in his own impotence'.

Only one thing is certain about 'Revol': this is a very strange song. Its title adapted Sonic Youth's dark-eyed 1986 album *EVOL* ('love' spelt backwards), an evisceration of sixties American socio-cultural themes that had featured a string of Manic-approved icons: Marilyn Monroe, Tom Verlaine, Greil Marcus, plus The Beach Boys, whose 'California Girls' are condemned to death in the album's climactic 'Expressway To Yr. Skull', a sequel to Sonic Youth's earlier Charles Manson-inspired doom anthem 'Death Valley '69'. *EVOL* in turn was named after multimedia artist Tony Oursler's *EVOL*, a short video piece depicting 'a psychodrama of compulsion, romance and tragedy [describing] a deadly black hole that attracts and mirrors our deepest fears'.[1]

There's certainly a lot of mirroring going on in 'Revol'. Originally titled 'Revol/Lover', lest anyone fail to get the gist, its second verse lists another six controversial leaders, broadening the scope beyond Soviet Russia but still finding room for Trotsky alongside French emperor Napoleon, tainted Second World War British PM Neville Chamberlain, photogenic revolutionary Che Guevara, murderous Cambodian dictator Pol Pot and Nation of Islam leader Louis Farrakhan. This time the aphorisms are no less enigmatic – the notoriously sexist Farrakhan's was 'alimony, alimony'; for Chamberlain, an avowed agnostic, 'you see God in you' – yet the cumulative impact was clearly felt: highlighting the disconnect between high ideals and mundane reality, just as the distance between Lenin's tomb on Red Square's eastern side and the empty shopping arcade on the opposite west equated to the contrasting performance of the sleek Zil limousines reserved for high-ranking communist officials, and the clapped-out Ladas driven by the proles.

With its use of hammer and sickle imagery and German artist Martin Kippenberger's 1983 painting *Sympathische Kommunistin* (Likeable Communist Woman), the 'Revol' single's cover art reinforced this sense of unfulfilled ideals – the disparity between communism's utopian iconography and the system's banal outcomes – with the added sleeve quotation of the denouement to Orwell's *Animal Farm*. In his *Holy Bible* Pass Notes, Edwards paralleled the metaphor with his pessimistic view of human relationships, bitterly referencing The Who for good measure: 'All adolescent leaders of men FAILED. All love FAILS. If men of the calibre of Lenin and Trotsky failed then how can anyone expect anything to change. Won't get fooled again.'[2]

Significantly, 'Revol' was written and recorded almost three months after the rest of the album, amid Edwards's unravelling mood spiral and a realisation that *The Holy Bible* was light on material that might play well on radio. Following the ill-fated expedition to Bangkok, in May the Manics played a festival in Braga, Portugal – that country again – where Edwards presented the lyric, much to Nicky Wire's bewilderment.

'I just went, "Yeah?!" "Revol" is truly mental. Basically Rob Stringer was saying we need another single. Or we need *a* single. And "Revol" is what we came up with. Which is pretty mad, that we thought this could be a single. I don't know what it's about. Even Richey could never explain that one when we were doing interviews.'

If *EVOL* was Sonic Youth's 'faux goth' album, as bassist Kim Gordon once described it,[3] 'Revol' is the Manics' goth folly, a teetering tower of racked ruin. Its middle-eight breakdown section even resembles Sonic Youth – as Wire says, 'It has that Kim Gordon out-of-tune bass sound, which actually is in tune . . .' – while the introduction suggests a vaporous union of Joy Division and the Banshees, before tumbling into hysteria on the back of a galloping rhythm and Bradfeld's affected evil-guy vocalese. Bizarrely, the sonic reference point was 'Heaven Sent', a 1992 single by INXS.

'Michael Hutchence put a little telephone effect on his voice – he sounds like Iggy Pop,' Bradfield says. 'But it didn't really come out in the wash. In the choruses I reached straight for [Skids' guitarist] Stuart Adamson again, one of many times in my life. "Revol" was just slammed down quickly, but I did connect with it. Nick and Richey were always going on about hypocrisy, so having a lyric which was almost like a satirical vision of the interior lives of historical political leaders, their sexual peccadilloes, kind of made sense. Like a gothic new wave step on from *Spitting Image* – it just seemed like a bit of fun.'

The song's pantomime qualities come to the fore most strongly in the chorus, when Bradfield barks out 'Lebensraum!', 'Kulturkampf!', 'Raus raus!', and 'Fila fila!', like Eddie Tenpole as the camp commandant in a musical comedy version of *Escape From Colditz*. Indeed, for all its bleakly melancholic subtext, 'Revol' has an inescapable whiff of 'Springtime For Hitler' from Mel Brooks's 1967 film *The Producers*. Brooks, who served with the US army in Germany during the Second World War, never objected to his work being accused of bad taste – he regarded that as a weapon against dictators and tyrants. 'Get on a soapbox with Hitler, you're going to lose,' he said. 'But if you can make fun of him, if you can have people laugh at him, you win.'[4]

For Nicky Wire, 'Revol' represents 'the fabulous disaster' aspect of *The Holy Bible*, without which the record would be simply too forbidding. And the disaster could have been yet more fabulous still. *The Holy Bible*'s twentieth-anniversary edition features a previously unreleased version of 'Revol', in which the climactic harpy flight from the 'Sonic Youth breakdown' featured Bradfield reading a passage from *The Torture Garden*, Octave Mirbeau's 1898 satire on sex, sadism and political corruption, which was printed on the album's back cover. He sounds like Richard Burton in *Under Milk Wood* gone to hell. Vetoed at the time on grounds of silliness, in 2014 its place in 'Revol's theatre of the absurd now seemed perfectly apt. Amid the new world disorder of Putin, Trump, Johnson, Modi, Orban et al., 'Revol' was resurgent. Meet the new boss, same as the old . . . and all that jazz.

'It is a strange song,' considers James. 'And one of those that fans seem to love, for some reason. I always thought of it as throwaway, and the metaphor of how sexual proclivities can transfer into lust for power is a well-worn road. But that comedic element has been borne out. You can't read about the white Y-fronts of John Major without knowing that "Revol" had something going on.'

32.
Yes

Recorded: Soundspace Studios, Cardiff
Engineer: Alex Silva
Released: 30 August 1994 (*The Holy Bible*, Epic)

'Existence, well what does it matter?'
— Joy Division, 'Heart Ard Soul'

While the *Torture Garden* quotation on the back cover was illustrative of *The Holy Bible*'s generally bleak view of humanity, the album's opening song focused on the passage's specific theme of lives dehumanised by venal social behaviour – what Mirbeau called 'the poisoned and mortal wound of the civilised world'.[1] 'Yes' begins with an audio clip from *Hookers, Hustlers, Pimps and Their Johns*, a documentary by British director Beeban Kidron about the New York sex industry, which Richey Edwards taped when the film was screened by Channel 4 on 29 December 1993. The sample featured Junior, a peep show pimp using a copy of *Screw* magazine to indicate what he had available 'for sale' – his final words echoed in the lyric, which then flips the scenario from the sex worker's perspective, voicing her disdain for her clients ('Dumb cunts, same dumb questions . . .') and the misery of life on 'these plagued streets of pity'. It then proceeded to describe the contents of a snuff video.

Upon reading Edwards's lyric, Bradfield recognised something beyond the itemised hurt and horror: empathy.

'Of course there was anger there, but there was also a pity felt for the subject. And there was some of Richey there as well. So I wanted the music to be empathetic too. Because it felt like the margins of cruelty in life were being scrutinised and stretched a bit too far. It's heavy – really heavy.'

Having elected not to follow the lyric's downward spiral around 'purgatory's circle', he built an ineffably jaunty guitar motif, inspired by 'Music For A Found Harmonium', a 1981 piece by Brian Eno protégés the Penguin Cafe Orchestra. 'I always had a fascination for that song, the melody would take me out of myself. So with the verse I wanted some kind of almost absent-minded, staring-into-the distance quality. Which was a bit of a trick – me not doing my job properly, just trying to lighten it a bit. It's not ethical when you make things lighter than they should be. Trent Reznor wouldn't do it. He'd go darker, the full-on bloody opera.'

'Yes' was one of the first songs written after 'Faster' had assuaged any doubts about the harsh new aesthetic the Manics were creating for themselves. It's accordingly bold in its modesty, with an affectless sonic vérité that permits the listener to discern the spaces between the ensemble players: Moore and Wire fashioning an off-beat motorik groove that carries Bradfield's incremental build-up to the brief but blessed cathartic burst of the chorus.

'Musically, "Yes" really excited me,' says Wire. 'Everyone's doing a different thing – the drums, the bass, and the guitar are locked in, yet they're all over the shop as well. We felt we'd hit our stride. And the lyric is a perfect piece of prose.'

Just as the arrangement smudged the angular contours of the post-punk template, Edwards blurs his authorial perspective between subject, participant and reporter from the psychic frontline. Each verse ends with a rhetorical punch through a mirror: 'Nothing turns out like you want it to'; 'Just an ambulance at the bottom of a cliff'; 'Everyone I've loved or hated always seems to leave.'

The understated arrangement gave his self-analysis a resonance that the flash and bluster of previous albums had sometimes obscured. Sean Moore was not sat behind a massive kit surrounded by twenty microphones, and felt more comfortable for it. 'We just needed to get back to our roots, where *we* came from,' Moore said. Likewise, the lyric's more autobiographical references – to Edwards cutting himself; his anorexia; that morbid image of the ambulance – offset the sense that writing a song about exploitation was itself exploitative. 'I'm so naive,' says Bradfield. 'I asked Richey, "What does 'I "t" them 24-7' mean?" He's like, "I toss them . . ." So many words, so much effort went into this depiction of how miserable life can be and how frequent victimhood is in society. I don't think Richey was ever being cold in writing about this – I just kept thinking, "How can you keep doing it?"'

Aside from his thoughtfully discursive bass part, Nicky Wire contributed just a single word to what he considered Edwards's 'perfect piece of prose': the title, which mockingly referenced the Manics' acquiescence to the demands of the music industry machine, as per the Trustees Savings Bank's famous marketing slogan, 'the bank [band] that likes to say yes'. Edwards's working title had been the rather more transparent 'Use Me', while his tour programme pass note for 'Yes' stated: 'Prostitution of the Self. The majority of your time is spent doing something you hate to get something you don't need. Everyone has a price to buy themselves out of freedom. Say Yes to Everything.'[2]

'Yes' had been considered for release as a single – the mooted sleeve design featured a pastiche of the TSB logo and the sales pitch: '100% Artificial Insincere Hypocritical Guarantee' – although the band were reluctant to record a 'clean' version, and with one cunt and three fucks to deal with, any radio edit would have been significantly compromised. The song's grim view of human responses to inhuman situations became uncomfortably real soon enough. At the end of April 1994's ill-starred Bangkok trip, Edwards confessed to having said 'yes' to a sex worker during a visit to the city's red light district. As Nicky Wire said a few months later: 'You might think ['Yes'] reads about prostitution, but it's the prostitution of what we've felt over the last three years. It catches up with you . . . It caught up with Richey.'

'Yes' ends on a fade-out, the only song on *The Holy Bible* to do so: the final iteration of the recurrent bridge section, with its lulling melody vaguely reminiscent of Wire's 'Outdoor Miner', is lashed to the insistent snare drumbeat and driven by a four-note guitar siren until it slowly disappears, via another New York pimp audio sample, into its own purgatory circle. In the context of 1994, with Britpop spreading like cultural knotweed, the Manics were reading from an entirely different map.

33.

Ifwhiteamericatoldthe truthforonedayit'sworld wouldfallapart

Recorded: Soundspace Studios, Cardiff
Engineer: Alex Silva
Released: 30 August 1994 (*The Holy Bible*, Epic)

'Free to do anything you choose
Free to wait tables and shine shoes.'
> – 'America' from *West Side Story*; music by
> Leonard Bernstein, lyrics by Stephen Sondheim

Just as their heroes The Clash proclaimed themselves 'so bored with the USA' in spite of an evident deep fascination with the country and its culture, so too the Manics' relationship with America has been both conflicted and contradictory. Belatedly recorded in 1992 with Alex Silva and released as a B-side to 'Little Baby Nothing', the clumpy 1989-vintage 'Dead Yankee Drawl' bemoaned a vapid US consumerism which served as a smokescreen for the country's intrinsic racism, citing Rodney King (or 'King, Rodney') and Mike Tyson as victims of white privilege. 'Ifwhiteamerica' came from a similar premise but far more skilfully, testimony to the intense levels of compositional and performative rigour that characterised *The Holy Bible*.

Atypically for the album as a whole, the lyric was a collaboration between Nicky Wire and Richey Edwards, with much of the initial draft written by Wire, who also supplied the title – often attributed to Lenny Bruce, but also, suggests Yusef Sayed, a possible nod to 'Antiamericancretin', a 1987 McCarthy song with a typically unorthodox critique of the UK left's default position on the US. Hypocrisy, once again, was the overarching theme, specifically the yawning disconnect between rhetoric and actions, with Wire's initial lyric draft setting the tone, equating golden smiles and suntans with proxy wars, then ladling on petty cultural jibes about coffee and smiling. 'Mine was more a nasty anti-American rant,' Wire says. 'And then Richey globalised it into something much better.'

The song's remit duly broadened to address the racist under-pinning of Britain as well as America, a point anticipated by the opening sample of a GOP TV advertisement for a gala dinner tribute to Ronald Reagan on the occasion of the former President's eighty-third birthday, where the guest of honour was 'Lady Margaret Thatcher'. The chorus quoted the seventies England football chant 'There ain't no black in the Union Jack', prefaced by Nicky Wire's 'Conservative say', then its American equivalent 'There ain't enough white in the Stars and Stripes', with the attribution 'Democrat say' imputing equal culpability upon the US's two main political parties for the ongoing inner-city race war. Edwards also added the reference to Abraham Zapruder ('the first to masturbate'), the man who unwittingly filmed the JFK assassination and became 'the world's first taste of crucified grace'. In other words, says Wire, 'Death as porn. Richey's phenomenal lyrics made the song more massive. When he showed it to me, I thought, "How is James going to sing this?"'

Whereas previously he might have striven to mould lyrics with awkward metre and little or no rhyme structure into a harmonious musical setting – as on 'Motown Junk', for example – now Bradfield took the astringent logic of *The Holy Bible* and ran with it, powered by Sean Moore's gymnastic drum part, constructing a bizarre jazz-hardcore ziggurat of clashing rhythms and competing voices, heightened by Nicky Wire's 'Conserva-tive'/'Democrat' asides which are later superseded by the band's own stance – 'And *we* say, there's not enough black in the Union Jack . . .' – proclaimed in Bradfield's best upper-register scream. Compositionally, his source was the musical number 'America', from Leonard Bernstein and Stephen Sondheim's *West Side Story*, itself a sardonic swipe at US race relations. Like its *Holy Bible* counterpart, 'America' deployed multiple voices singing over and across each other, while 'Ifwhiteamerica's choruses conspicuously used vocal harmonies to sweeten its bitter message. 'I saw the adversarial nature of the lyric – Democrats versus Republicans, hawks versus doves,' says Bradfield. 'Then I just thought, "Jets versus Sharks! I'm going to design it as a demented version of *West Side Story*!" It's the American musical gone wrong.'

'Ifwhiteamerica's lurching dynamic and air of hysteria also suggested a less improbable if still unexpected antecedent: San Francisco's hardcore punk pioneers Dead Kennedys, famed for such howling satirical takedowns as 'Holiday In Cambodia' and 'Kill The Poor'. The connection wasn't actually such a stretch: the Manics were fans, dropping an excerpt of DKs' greatest liberal-baiting philippic 'California Über Alles' into live versions of 'Repeat', and had even received a letter plus cheque from DKs' singer Jello Biafra requesting a copy of 'Suicide Alley' after he had read the single's positive review in the May 1989 issue of San Francisco punk 'zine *Maximum Rocknroll*. Meanwhile, Moore's tom-to-snare-switchbacks evoked the taut energy of SoCal avant-hardcore pioneers the Minutemen, or even Nomeansno, a Canadian trio who released several records of politically wry, dyspeptic jazz-punk fusion on Biafra's Alternative Tentacles label.

Jello Biafra would have doubtless appreciated 'Ifwhiteamerica's references to the Moral Majority – the namesake of a 1981 DKs song – and Tipper Gore, the wife of then US Vice-President Al Gore and co-founder of the PMRC in 1985, the year before Biafra and Alternative Tentacles went on trial in California charged with distributing harmful material to a minor when a fourteen-year-old girl bought a copy of Dead Kennedys' *Frankenchrist* album containing a poster of Swiss artist H.R. Giger's painting *Penis Landscape*. The PMRC's so-called Parent Advisory 'Tipper stickers' ensured Mrs Gore remained a hate figure for musicians regardless of genre for many years and forged some unlikely alliances: in 1989, Ice-T opened his new album *The Iceberg/Freedom Of Speech. . . Just Watch What You Say!* with a track titled 'Shut Up, Be Happy', which featured Jello Biafra in the guise of a demagogic US leader proclaiming martial law over a Black Sabbath sample. In a 1991 *NME* piece, Sean Moore cited *The Iceberg* as his favourite rap album.

The Manics' fascination with hip-hop and militant black politics was deep-seated by this point, be it the Bobby Seale sample on 'Spectators Of Suicide' or getting Public Enemy's tech team the Bomb Squad to remix 'Repeat', right the way back to Bradfield in his bedroom at Sir Ivor's Road teaching himself to rap word-perfect to the entirety of Public Enemy's fiercely articulate tour de force *It Takes A Nation Of Millions To Hold Us Back*, much as he would essay *Appetite For Destruction* or *Exile On Main St.* on guitar. With hindsight, Wire believes this perfectionist verbal discipline was a training-ground exercise for turning *The Holy Bible*'s dense, arrhythmic tracts into digestible songs. 'Public Enemy changed James's life; you'd go into his room and he'd be mimicking Chuck D. You realised then that with the scope of our lyrics we could throw anything at him. By the time you get to a track like "Yes", we knew he could do it.'

The closest the Manics ever got to their own version of rap, 'Ifwhiteamerica' obediently follows its own hysterical design, until the coda, when it locks into a reprise of the song's ascending intro like a stuck water cannon, repeatedly hosing the words 'Fuck the Brady bill' into the faces of a doubtless mostly uncomprehending audience.

Named after James Brady, the White House press secretary shot in the head during John Hinkley's failed attempted assassination of President Reagan in 1981, the Brady Handgun Violence

Nicky Wire's Hohner TE Telecaster copy, played at the first Manic Street Preachers gig: umlin Railway Hotel, 5 February 1986. Wire later switched to bass when original bassist Miles icker' Woodward left. 'New Art Riot' stencil made by Nicky's father. **2.** Pete Brown's Gibson s Paul Standard, played by James Dean Bradfield on 'Motown Junk'. **3.** Aria guitar smashed the end of 'You Love Us' (Heavenly version). **4.** Wire's main work typewriter, 1986–99. Sean Moore's bass drum, used on 'Stay Beautiful' and *Gold Against The Soul*. **6.** Richey wards's Fender Telecaster Thinline, used on 'Motorcycle Emptiness' and every MSP um. **7.** Bradfield's 'Faithful' white Gibson Les Paul.

8. Moore's Alesis SR-16 drum machine, used on some of *Generation Terrorists*. **9.** Bradfield Boss Hyper Fuzz pedal, used on every record from 1993 onwards. **10.** Edwards's Sega Mega Drive console and rucksack, used during *Generation Terrorists* sessions.

. The Gibson used by Edwards for his 'La Tristesse Durera' barre chord, subsequently
ashed onstage. **12.** Bradfield's main Vox amp on *The Holy Bible*. **13.** Alex Silva's
ckenbacker amp, used on '4st 7lb' and 'Mausoleum'. **14.** Wire's Rickenbacker bass,
ed on 'Motown Junk', 'Archives Of Pain' and '4st 7lb'.

15. The Allen & Heath desk used for *The Holy Bible*; also 'Suicide Is Painless', 'Sepia' and most demos until *Know Your Enemy*. **16.** Vintage Fender Twin amp, used on 'A Design For Life' and 'Kevin Carter'. **17.** Dave Eringa's Korg MS-20, used on 'If You Tolerate This Your Children Will Be Next'.

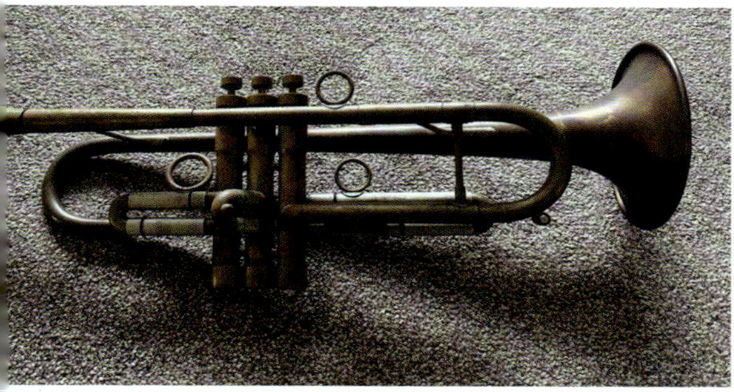

. Moore's Slingerland snare drum, used on *The Holy Bible*. **19.** Moore's trumpet, used on 'cean Spray'. **20.** Bradfield's Gibson J-45, his main recording acoustic guitar, also used to ite 'If You Tolerate This . . .' and 'The Masses Against The Classes'. **21.** Nick Nasmyth's urlitzer piano, used on 'If You Tolerate This . . .'.

22. Bradfield's twelve-string Rickenbacker, won from Mike Hedges in a bet, used on 'If You Tolerate This . . .'. **23.** Bradfield's harmonica, used on 'Cardiff Afterlife'. **24.** Moore's Slingerland snare, used on *Know Your Enemy* and *Send Away The Tigers*. **25.** Wire's Burns bass, used on 'Autumnsong'. **26.** Eringa's 1959 Gibson Les Paul Special, used on 'Autumnsong'. **27.** Bradfield's Gretsch Country Gentleman, used on 'Enola/Alone', 'Ready For Drowning', 'Still Snowing In Sapporo', et al.

29

31

32

8. Wire's Yamaha writing and recording acoustic guitar, used on 'Your Love Alone Is Not Enough', et al. **29.** Suzuki QChord, used on 'Send Away The Tigers'. **30.** Wire's Italia Maranello bass, used on *Send Away The Tigers* and *Postcards From A Young Man*. **.** Bradfield's Fret-King Ventura, used on *Futurology*. **32.** Wire's Guild bass, used *Futurology*.

33. Sequential Circuits Drumtraks drum machine, used on *Futurology*. **34.** 1970s vintage Tri TSM desk, formerly at Rockfield Studios and used for Rush's *A Farewell To Kings*, The Teard Explodes's *Kilimanjaro*, et al., now at Door To The River Studios.

Prevention Act was a gun control law passed by President Bill Clinton on 30 November 1993, after a six-year battle to get the bill through US Congress against opposition from the National Rifle Association, which successfully lobbied to dilute the requirement for background checks on firearms sales to anyone with previous criminal convictions. 'Richey thought that restricting gun ownership was racist, because it was denying the underclass the right to own guns,' says Wire. 'When he finished the lyric, he said, "Charlton Heston'll like this one!"'

As per 'P.C.P.', this was another case of Edwards locating the dogma interzone where communism becomes indistinguishable from fascism, via an article in *Living Marxism*. Indeed, the song's final lyrics were lifted almost verbatim from the headline of a piece in the magazine's November 1993 issue, which paraphrased a slogan coined by the inventor of the revolver to market his weapon to 1850s western settlers – 'God made men, Samuel Colt made them equal' – and argued that gun control was a white middle-class tactic to strengthen 'the authorities' monopoly on the legitimate use of force'.[1]

One of *The Holy Bible*'s great attributes is the power to command total engagement without necessarily endorsing its every edict. Just as he had reservations with 'P.C.P.', so Bradfield didn't agree with every line of 'Ifwhiteamerica'.

'But of course, I still went with it,' he says. 'I'm really proud of every part of this song. Everything interweaves. And I remember thinking it was the best thing Sean had ever done. He did the drum part in two takes and we'd hardly rehearsed it. This was one week in, and I knew then we were going to create a masterpiece, because most of the focus comes from the way the drummer interprets the most difficult song. "Ifwhiteamerica" was the most difficult song to play and he'd just come up with the perfect answer for it.'

The United States didn't get to hear the Manics' state of the nation address and its declaration that there was 'too much white in the Stars and Stripes', because *The Holy Bible* did not receive a contemporaneous American release. It was due to have coincided with a six-week US tour in February–April 1995, but that tour was cancelled when Richey Edwards disappeared, and so too the album, which had been remixed in the hope of aligning more closely with the sensibilities of American listeners. 'To our ears [the remix] was brilliant,' Bradfield reflected. 'For once, we were excited about the American record company's involvement, because the mixes sounded even more powerful. A bit more radio-friendly, but powerful still. Suddenly the record company were saying positive things, for the first time. "We could get on college radio with this! It's not soft rock, it's not metal, it's not indie rock, it's college rock! *This is it*!"'

Consequently, the US mix, by Tom Lord-Alge, remained unheard until its inclusion with the tenth anniversary reissue in 2004. Not every song benefited equally from Lord-Alge's treatment, which essentially bulked up the components' rock credentials and blew away some of the more oppressively fetid ambience, without which the likes of 'Faster' and 'Archives Of Pain' felt oddly inauthentic – but 'Ifwhiteamerica' undoubtedly marched several inches taller as a result, thanks mostly to Moore's head-spinning polyrhythmic pans and rolls and martial cross-beats now occupying stage-front and centre, taking their rightful place at the insurrectionary vanguard. Bradfield recalled Rob Stringer, the band's eternal champion at Sony, lobbying for it to be released ahead of the album. 'He said it was the best thing anybody had done since The Clash had split up. So he wanted it as a single but we resisted. We wanted it to be a great album, we wanted people to discover it as an album.'

The song is certainly strong enough to have stood alone. And while some of *The Holy Bible* is synonymous with the internal politics of Richey Edwards, none of its component parts has a more enduring global resonance than 'Ifwhiteamericatoldthetruth-foronedayit'sworldwouldfallapart' (erroneous apostrophe and all).

'I think it represents a tension which will never go away,' says Bradfield. 'I think just Sean's drumming in itself represents American society – there's absolutely no middle ground, left and right gunning for each other. Musically, that song almost becomes anthropomorphic of what American society is.'

34.

Of Walking Abortion

Recorded: Soundspace Studios, Cardiff
Engineer: Alex Silva
Released: 30 August 1994 (*The Holy Bible*, Epic)

'Capitalism is the most barbaric of all religions.'
– The Pop Group, 'We Are All Prostitutes'

While the first two tracks on *The Holy Bible* were more or less specific case studies of the human condition, 'Of Walking Abortion' offered the macro view. This was a soundtrack to a trial: in the dock, an entire species, indicted for crimes against itself. In the course of four minutes, humanity is found guilty without hope of redemption, but rather, as suggested by the preface audio recording of *Last Exit To Brooklyn* author Hubert Selby Jr, condemned to live life all over again. The final verdict is delivered by James Dean Bradfield repeatedly asking 'Who's responsible?', then immediately answering 'You fucking are', the song ending with his climactic screams as barked through a distorted megaphone.

In between, the irrefutable evidence piles up, once again collated by two writers schooled in political history ('Mussolini hangs from a butcher's hook'). The lyric was a collaborative relay, with Wire's emotive initial draft rewritten by Edwards in a tersely moral tone that's apt for a song which warns that righteousness can corrode civility and how the spectacle of victory, of parades and justice, can duly beget horror with still more horror: 'The massacred innocent blood stains us all'.

Some arcane references leap out from the grim litany, notably 'acedia', from the Greek for lack of care, indifference. The term 'accidie' was widely used up to the Middle Ages in religious contexts to define sloth or spiritual apathy, and was one of the sins that led Dante to hell in the *Divine Comedy*; it was repurposed by twentieth-century writers like Beckett, Camus, Eliot and Huxley to define existential ennui and nihilism. In the context of *The Holy Bible*, 'acedia's blackest hole' implies the all-pervasive apathy that nurtures fanatical right-wing regimes ('Hitler reprised in the worm of your soul').

As well as those aforementioned poster boys of twentieth-century Euro-fascism, 'Of Walking Abortion' has roles for the much less familiar Miklos Horthy and Josef Tiso, antisemitic leaders of Nazi Germany's client regimes in Hungary and Slovakia who collaborated in and facilitated the deportation of their nation's Jews to death camps. 'Horthy's corpse screened to a million' referred to Hungarian TV coverage of Horthy's 1993 state funeral after his body was repatriated from Portugal, where he had died in exile in 1957.

'By this point I was a bit exhausted trying to pretend I had enough intelligence to cope with the subject matter,' Bradfield says. 'So I read the lyric and just tried to write something mean. As soon as I had that in my head I went straight to my memory file and thought, "If I can somehow have a modified version of the riff from 'The Light Pours Out of Me' by Magazine . . ." I just lengthened it, different notes, and that was it. The chorus is just four chords in a row. It's obvious that everything I'm listening to is really feeding through to how I play guitar – a lot more single string riffs, not trying to show off something complicated, but trying for a riff you can sing quite easily, in a post-punk kind of way.'

Once again, Sean Moore was critical to the dynamic momentum, his lockstep verse snare's sudden shift into martial tango rolls for the pre-chorus bridge greatly enriching Bradfield's compositional canvas. The title, meanwhile, saw a return to Valerie Solanas's *SCUM Manifesto*, which defined men as genetically deficient, 'an incomplete female, a walking abortion, aborted at the gene stage'.[1] Tweaking the earlier draft's title 'Walking Abortions' to 'we are all *of* walking abortions' – echoing the Pop Group's similarly vengeful 'We Are All Prostitutes' – extended culpability to every human.

'Grim, isn't it?' says Wire. 'Why would I have come up with a title like that?! Richey must have got to me by this point.'

As the song ploughs towards its screaming denouement, the music hardens into a remorseless rhythm with Bradfield's condemnatory snarl abrading everything before him: 'Little people in little houses/Like maggots, small blind and worthless'. Even by *The Holy Bible*'s unforgiving standards, 'Of Walking Abortion' offers no hope. Edwards had even lost faith in intelligence: 'Modern life makes thought an embarrassment,' he stated in 'Of Walking Abortion's programme note,[2] despairing at capitalism's sedative seep, by then so ubiquitous that in 1991 a Malcolm X-branded basketball shoe was endorsed by Public Enemy's Chuck D.

Thirty years on, badge- (or shoe-) wearing has been digitised as virtue-signalling, and 'Of Walking Abortion's baleful diagnosis feels no less apt. In an age of polarised absolutes it can even read like a hymn to moderation. 'Whether it be the way they consume, or signing a petition, or going on a march, or posting something to acclaim somebody or defame somebody, a lot of people go to bed at night feeling so much warmer about themselves,' says Bradfield. 'Which I understand. But "Of Walking Abortion", a lyric that Richey wrote, says, hold on, you're nowhere near as morally complete as you think. Take a look at yourself. And realise that the answers lie in the compromises that we have to make with each other.'

35.
Archives Of Pain

Recorded: Soundspace Studios, Cardiff
Engineer: Alex Silva
Released: 30 August 1994 (*The Holy Bible*, Epic)

'The advertising quack who wearies
With tales of countless cures,
His teeth, I've enacted,
Shall all be extracted
By terrified amateurs.'

> – 'A More Humane Mikado', AKA 'To Let The Punishment
> Fit The Crime', by W.S. Gilbert, from *The Mikado* by
> W.S. Gilbert and Arthur Sullivan

'Archives Of Pain' has a lot to live up to before even a note is struck. The title comes from a chapter title in David Macey's biography of Michel Foucault, the French philosopher whose celebrated 1975 history of the penal system, *Discipline and Punish*, was a university text for Edwards and Wire. The introductory audio sample features the parched, resolute voice of Irene Mac-Donald from a 1980 BBC *Newsnight* report, where she admonishes the as yet unknown murderer of her daughter Jayne, the fifth woman killed by Peter Sutcliffe AKA the Yorkshire Ripper: 'God give life, God taketh it away, not you. I think you are the Devil itself.'

And then there are the words: shortly before its release, in a bold assertion of the rock album as a work of literature, *The Holy Bible*'s lyrics were printed in full as a double-page advertisement in both *NME* and *Melody Maker*. Amid the dense screed of horror, Holocaust and personal abnegation, one line from 'Archives Of

Pain' cut to the heart of the matter: 'The centre of humanity is cruelty'.

Nicky Wire remembers Richey Edwards smiling as he handed over the finished lyric. 'He said, "I think you'll like this."' In Foucault's grim, fastidiously detailed account of how medieval rituals of public torture evolved into the panopticon prison, Edwards saw an advocacy for what he later approvingly called 'a return to 19th century values of execution and capital punishment.'[1] Foucault himself would have disputed such a prescriptive analysis – 'I'm amused by the diversity of the ways I've been judged and classified,' he once said[2] – but it clearly struck a chord with Wire. 'Richey was obviously appealing to my dodgier side. He said it was a kind of pro-death penalty song. People say the death penalty doesn't work in America, but they always use America as the bad example, rather than somewhere like Japan where it definitely works as a deterrent. But the song's not just about justice, it's about vengeance as well. "Archives Of Pain" is an amazing, complex lyric. An incredibly brave lyric. "Sterilise rapists" – it's what the whole country thinks but is afraid to say. And for James to sing it was an incredible piece of work.'

When he first saw the lyric, Bradfield says he felt something he hadn't felt before, and hasn't since: that being in Manic Street Preachers was hard. He didn't know how to convey the gravity of the subject and not make it seem frivolous. 'I just thought, "This is heavy." It's a pro-capital punishment song, there's no way around that. I remember the conversation: Richey was saying justice is an empty word if you don't serve true justice for the victim. So I had to convey that this band is different, that this song isn't the angle you'd expect from a bunch of Welsh valley left-wingers. And I remember thinking, I don't have to agree with it one hundred per cent but I completely see the argument. So writing music to this, the stakes are high. Whereas with "Yes" I'm trying to lighten the load a bit, with this one I realise there's no hiding place.'

To help him carry the weight, Bradfield went back to first principles, to post-punk's ground zero and the fathoms-deep bass explorations of Public Image Ltd's Jah Wobble and Magazine's Barry Adamson. He wrote a part that first trudges upwards as if to a scaffold or a judge's bench, and then descends, very probably towards hell. The hi-hat cymbals splash like blades being sharpened, while a guitar click-clacks into readiness, until the word 'killer' summons a metallic roar like steel gates slamming down, making the audience captive by walls of conscience. An airy bridge rejects any notion of equivalence between death by hanging and 'Hindley's crochet lectures', then the chorus unleashes an inventory of the damned: a multinational troupe of political bogeymen – Boris Yeltsin (again), Saddam Hussein, Jean-Marie Le Pen, Idi Amin, Slobodan Milošević, Eugene Terre'Blanche among others – are accused alongside various serial killers including the Moors Murderers, Peter Sutcliffe, Beverley Allitt and Dennis Nilsen, plus James Pickles, a UK judge who in the late eighties became notorious for leniency towards sex criminals. All are to receive 'the respect they deserve'.

For some reason, Nicky Wire's bass wouldn't stay in tune amid this frenzy, so in addition to designing a musical platform to accommodate the condemned names and then singing his way through it, Bradfield also had to play the bass during the chorus. 'The bass line that James wrote for "Archives Of Pain" totally defines that song,' says Wire. 'It chills me to the bone.'

One of the serial killers cited was Jeffrey Dahmer, the so-called Milwaukee Monster convicted in 1992 of seventeen murders, whose cannibalistic and necrophiliac modus operandi had generated considerable media notoriety, with books, a feature film and several TV true crime specials already dedicated to his gruesome exploits. Fascination with transgressive nihilist icons had been prevalent in the eighties US post-hardcore scene, where Black Flag, Sonic Youth, Jane's Addiction and others had used the likes of Charles Manson and Ted Bundy as metaphors for a diseased society, sometimes with a relish that felt gratuitous.

Whereas Dahmer's name hummed on the zeitgeist – and still does thirty years on – others on the 'Archives Of Pain' shitlist were more obscure, notably Yoshinori Ueda, a Japanese dog breeder and trainer arrested in January 1994 for killing five people with an overdose of muscle relaxant commonly used to euthanise animals. Perhaps most intriguing was the inclusion of the band itself. The second chorus's substitution of 'Milošević' with 'Manic Street Preachers' is easily missed amid the torrent of words that Bradfield had to accommodate, but confirmed by the twentieth-anniversary edition's reproduction of work-in-progress notes. Implicating the Manics among the guilty feels consistent with the album's core premise as a collective indictment. Those twentieth-anniversary notes also revealed a very significant lyric change, from 'All I preach is execution' amended to 'I am preaching extinction'. This line, the first instance of the word 'preach' in a Manic Street Preachers song, appears to reiterate verse two's assertion, 'If man makes death then death makes man'. In that moment, 'Archives Of Pain' is more than simply a pulpit-pounding demand for Old Testament values, but a reading of the last rites – an immolatory full-stop.

In service of the album's austere design, guitar solos are comparatively rare on *The Holy Bible*. But for most of its final ninety seconds, starting from the last letter of the spelt-out 'd-e-s-e-r-v-e', 'Archives Of Pain' is given over to an infernal James Dean Bradfield mini-concerto. Having already channelled Magazine's bassist, now he evoked that same band's John McGeoch, the most selfless of guitar heroes. Starting with exactitude and successively shedding layers of inhibition as he builds, by its crescendo Bradfield is in full theatrical flow, as if soundtracking the notoriously lengthy and graphic 'horses and chains' execution with which Foucault begins *Discipline and Punish*. In his own estimation, this solo, along with the song's chorus, was the closest Bradfield ever came to Steve Jones's 'serrated power block guitar sound'.[3]

'A guitar solo that long from any band that was vaguely punk-gestated would be questionable,' he says, 'but it just worked. Dare I say it, I'm the guitarist but it didn't feel overblown to have that. It felt like the purest expression at the end of the song. The lyric is weighty enough for me to get away with that moment of moral outrage.'

From Magazine to Michel Foucault and back again – such was the extent of Manic Street Preachers' domain. No one involved with 'Archives Of Pain' puts a foot wrong, even when they do: during that dervish finale, the tempo actually speeds up, yet there was never any debate about fixing it. 'When you're younger you're less aware,' says Wire. 'It sounds like a cliché but you just do what you're doing. In that outro, with that amazing guitar solo, which always reminded me of "Marquee Moon", and the tension of Sean's drums, it just builds and builds.'

It was shortly after completing 'Archives Of Pain' that Bradfield's white Gibson Les Paul, his beloved 'Faithful', was accidentally broken in the studio. His first thought? 'Thank God I did that solo before this happened.'

36.

4st 7lb

Recorded: Soundspace Studios, Cardiff
Engineer: Alex Silva
Released: 30 August 1994 (*The Holy Bible*, Epic)

'I don't know how to live,
I only know how to disappear.'
— Magazine, 'Upside Down'

'4st 7lb' returned to an earlier theme: denialism. Just as the Manics of 'Strip It Down' repudiated decadent behaviour lest they be distracted from pursuing 'pure ideals', so this song's narrator regards abstinence from food as a conduit to a higher spiritual realm. Much like 'Faster's self-harming architect/butcher, while others see a diminished body, she feels empowered by this show of strength, even as it squeezes out the possibility of life: 'This discipline so rare, so please applaud'.

Regardless of his own experience of self-harm, be it cutting or fasting, Richey Edwards's lyric for '4st 7lb' displayed an acutely sensitive awareness of the female anorexic's psychology, one that Nicky Wire freely admitted he couldn't add to. 'His masterpiece – I didn't touch it at all. I thought, "I can't really relate to it." I don't mean that in a bad way, it's just that I've no experience in those feelings.' When presented with an already complete, metrically compact set of words, James Bradfield approached the task of singing them as an actor would prepare for a role. Indeed, he maintains there was still an aspect of reportage to Edwards's perspective.

'There's a certain misconception that it must be hard to sing these lyrics,' he says. 'Obviously, Richey's involved in the subject, but not as much as you think at this point. I knew he was getting a lot of – what would we call it? – the poetry of vanity, I suppose, from people with bulimia, people with anorexia, and he's well into his own personal battle with eating and vanity. But in our perception, he's not anorexic at this point. He's still having a meal in front of us now and again. He's not *as* involved in the subject matter. So singing this, I'm thinking this is a brilliant observation of somebody else. The responsibility is on the person that's written the lyric. So it's not that hard.'

Bradfield spoke with Edwards about designing a musical narrative, identifying several distinct moods – tension, aspiration, defeat, serenity – that shifted in emulation of the narrator's inner conflict. Thus, following an *ur*-post-punk guitar prelude where Bradfield channels Gang Of Four's Andy Gill over the audio sample of an anorexic girl, the verses lurch around a knotted time signature and queasy drones, amplifying a succession of jarring couplets: 'Cheeks sunken and despaired/So gorgeous sunk to six stone'; 'My vision's getting blurred/But I see my ribs and I feel fine'. A sparse bridge sees the protagonist comparing weight notes with her idealised supermodel waif friends Kate Moss, Kristin McMenamy and Emma Balfour, before arpeggiating into the chorus and the song's remarkable beatific punchline: 'I want to walk in the snow and not leave a footprint'. Thenceforth, a slow, halting coda suggests an ebbing away, or an acceptance – 'I long since moved to a higher plateau' – floating down to its gentle conclusion.

Bradfield essayed a couple of heroic notes but was warned off anything flashier when Wire poked an admonishing head around the corner of the control room. 'He said, "Steady on there, Slash, this is not the record!"' Otherwise, his key guides to achieving what Richey had described as 'the freneticism of vanity' were Edinburgh's avatars of skronked-out Bolan boogie the Fire Engines ('there's a lot of them in the guitar work') and Cleveland, Ohio's avant-industrial shamen Pere Ubu. 'I remember going straight to *The Modern Dance* and listening to how everything was somehow pulling apart but also so interlocked together.'

'4st 7lb' has an elusive, opalescent quality that's quite distinct from the rest of *The Holy Bible* with its brittle slate rendering and acute angles. Clearly, the subject matter dictated a specific approach, but another factor could simply have been it was the first song recorded for the album, and the most difficult. 'The transitions are hard,' Bradfield says. 'It's a little bit prog, and only a good band can make sense of that kind of writing. I was at my parents' house, thinking, "Yeah, that'll work," and Sean was a bit like Harrison Ford saying to George Lucas: "It's fucking easy to write this shit, George, but not so easy to say it . . ."'

Nicky Wire, meanwhile, was not only confronted with the most complex bass part of any *Holy Bible* song – and one that during initial rehearsals bore a disconcerting resemblance to The Jam's 'The Eton Rifles' – but Bradfield also insisted he play it on the notoriously unwieldy Rickenbacker, which required constant retuning.

'I didn't have much sympathy for the world at that point,' Bradfield admits. 'It was Valentine's Day, and I'd bumped into my ex-girlfriend who had dumped me a few days before – rightly, because I was a dickhead – and I looked a mess. So we were doing "4st 7lb" because I'm in a bad mood. "Can we do this? Yes we fucking can . . ." And we could! It was amazing. Everybody blended in unison. I think it is really a band just completely on fire, heading in the same direction, who all understand each other. It just wasn't that hard. The biggest step was we couldn't get that Rickenbacker in tune. So we had to keep retuning it all the time. But it was a bit edgy, and that's what made it good. Lots of fun. It was a tough one but it was tough love.'

'James really made me and Sean knuckle down,' concurs Wire. 'Everything was dictated by the staccato nature of the arrangement, and by his desire. He was unbelievably focused. The reaching of the sublime in the outro is one of my favourite things we've ever done.'

*

The Holy Bible was released three days after Manic Street Preachers had played the Reading Festival as a trio; Richey Edwards was in the midst of a rehab programme at The Priory, a private mental health clinic in south-west London, following a severe self-harm incident in July at his Cardiff flat that was very likely an attempted suicide. The band regarded playing the show – and three other festivals before it – as 'a betrayal', and did so only in order to pay for Richey's treatment at the expensive establishment, where Sinéad O'Connor was among the fellow patients and The Priory's patron Eric Clapton a regular visitor. Dropped into this context, *The Holy Bible* was immediately inextricable from Edwards's physical and mental state; in particular '4st 7lb', proclaiming 'such beautiful dignity in self-abuse' and 'I don't mind the horror that surrounds me', lost any credible biographical distance between its author and subject. This judgement only intensified with Edwards's subsequent disappearance in February 1995, after which the album as a whole became synonymous with the forbidding associations of this song in particular.

Yet just as *The Holy Bible* was never an unlistenable grimoire, '4st 7lb' wasn't always necessarily a self-fulfilling prophecy. It had such impact precisely because its author's malaise was conveyed so elegantly by a sublime juxtaposition of tones and emotions, designed and executed from within the Soundspace safe space. If this is Edwards's greatest self-portrait, it received a frame to match. 'People forget *The Holy Bible* wasn't always associated with Richey's disappearance,' said Bradfield. 'It was associated with his being as creatively heightened as you could be. It was associated with some kind of strange euphoria.'

37.

Mausoleum

Recorded: Soundspace Studios, Cardiff
Engineer: Alex Silva
Released: 30 August 1994 (*The Holy Bible*, Epic)

'Now I am become death, the destroyer of worlds.'
  – J. Robert Oppenheimer, quoting the *Bhagavad Gita*

It was Sean Moore's idea.

On 7 September 1993, three dates into a two-week tour of Germany to promote *Gold Against The Soul*, the Manic Street Preachers and their crew spent their rest day visiting the concentration camp at Dachau.

'Sean had always wanted to go,' says Wire. 'It had a genuinely big impact on us. I remember specifically walking around and thinking there's just no wildlife. Not even an insect. We can be incredibly blasé as people, or *I* certainly can, but it did chill you to the bone going there. It was weird – we were still dressed a bit rock 'n' roll then, and there were all these tourists from America and Canada just looking at us. We were very respectful, don't get me wrong, but when you get to the gas chambers . . . You'd then go back on the bus and drive to some dreadful place in Germany to do a gig the next night.'

Four days after Dachau, the tour's one remaining day off saw them eschew the bars of Hamburg for a trip to Belsen.

Wire describes the two-week German tour as 'horrendous'. Edwards was drinking heavily – Johnnie Walker whisky, during the day, 'which he never used to do'. The gigs were in middling clubs, to modest audiences, and the two-week itinerary had been prefaced by some second-tier festivals with ill-assorted line-ups, typically featuring eighties bands looking to revive waning fortunes, or contemporaries struggling to kickstart stalled momentum. 'Sometimes we were next to Bad Brains,' remembers James. 'I was a bit rude to the Afghan Whigs. We were just at the end of our tether, it didn't feel like we'd do another sold-out gig ever again. Everything about that tour was really bad. Even the sandwiches were really bad.'

Shortly after Germany came a two-week tour of Japan. In Hiroshima, before the soundcheck at the Nakimi Junction gig venue, the band went to the Peace Memorial Park and Museum, built just across the river from the skeletal domed ruins of the Prefectural Industrial Promotional Hall, the only building to remain standing after the US atomic bomb destroyed the city on 6 August 1945. They saw the Children's Peace Monument, built in honour of Sadako Sasaki, a young girl who survived the explosion but was caught in the radioactive black rain which fell in the immediate aftermath of the firestorm that swept the city, and ten years later died of leukaemia. While in hospital, Sadako was told the legend that if a sick person makes enough paper models of the crane, Japan's sacred bird, and prays to recover, they will get better. When twelve-year-old Sadako died in October 1955, she had folded more than a thousand paper cranes, which became a symbol of peace, with children across the world sending paper cranes to be placed beneath Sadako's monument.

Moved by what he saw, read and heard at the peace memorial, Richey Edwards immediately sought out a copy of *Black Rain*, a novel about Hiroshima by Masuje Ibuse. He was also upset by the insensitivity of tourists disrespecting the museum's requests that people refrain from taking photographs. 'The people of Hiroshima faced such suffering only fifty years ago,' Edwards reflected to Japanese magazine *Music Life*. 'It's so sad we're unable to learn anything from history.'[1]

The Manics' successive visits to sites of minutely planned, industrially orchestrated mass murder went beyond mere tourism:

they were a kind of spiritual penitence, a cleansing of the collective soul in search of fresh purpose, which directly fed into
two *Holy Bible* songs – 'Mausoleum' and 'The Intense Humming
Of Evil' – and more generally characterised the repudiation of
Gold Against The Soul's 'hollow arena'. As Wire noted, 'Everything
was coming together. The telepathic mission we were on was
happening.'

While 'The Intense Humming Of Evil' would explicitly address
the Holocaust, 'Mausoleum' was a more abstract composite of
the band's experiences in Germany and Japan. Dachau's lifeless
air inspired its original title 'No Birds' – subsequently changed
when Nicky and Richey remembered the Public Image Ltd song
of the same name – while 'The sky is swollen black' connoted
both Hiroshima's inferno and its slow-death rain. The lyric was
another Wire draft amended and augmented by Edwards, their
unison voice an omniscient guide through the horrors of history
('Come and walk down memory lane'), humbled by 'the victims
who have no speech'.

For his main musical cue Bradfield went to a linchpin of his
post-punk firmament: the cold geometric repetition of 'Thirty
Frames A Second' from Simple Minds' 1980 album *Empires And
Dance* – as referenced on *The Holy Bible*'s sleeve art typeface – onto
whose rhythm he doubled down with heavier guitar. 'It cuts to
the chase, keeps your attention.' For the voice, he heard the
sinister dissociation of Scott McCloud from Girls Against Boys,
whose album *Venus Luxure No.1 Baby* appeared in autumn 1993.
'If you're given a lyric which has a bit of history in it, you don't
want to be too overwrought because the words say it already. If
you add to that, you're just doing an opera. So I liked how Scott
McCloud's vocal was right in the middle of depicting something
terrible that had happened. I liked how he brings brevity.'

While the verses adhere to this blueprint, the bridges turn
the lyric's perspective inwards ('Regained your self-control . . .
Analyse, despise and scrutinise/Never knowing what you hoped

for'), with Bradfield slamming into syllables for emphasis until he locks onto the phrase 'Obliterates your meaning', repeated in heraldic equipoise between darkness and light, before the chorus explodes upwards seeking release, but finds only a death cloud.

Dense and thrilling, but abstaining from standard rock heroics such as guitar solos, 'Mausoleum' suggests a misplaced deep cut from Skids' *Days In Europa*, another album that marched in the war-weary footsteps of twentieth-century ghosts. That telepathic mission again: 'I started writing "No Birds" very soon after that terrible German tour,' says Wire. 'I'd bought my house in Wattsville, I'd got married, and I particularly remember playing *Fanfare*, the Skids compilation, non-stop, thinking about [*Days In Europa*'s opening song] "Animation", the way Richard Jobson sings it. So I wrote the original "No Birds" and it ended up a sixty–forty Richey lyric. He did all the "Regain your self-control" stuff, the chorus was mine, as was the first bit of the outro, "And life can be as important as death". I'd been reading Simone de Beauvoir, the idea of the freedom of the existentialist, that you're free even when you're in the firing squad, all that shite, which I love. When we did the *Holy Bible* anniversary tour [December 2014], playing the whole album in sequence, "Mausoleum" was the peak, I thought . . . the best song we did live.'

Both the tenth- and twentieth-anniversary editions of *The Holy Bible* featured the demo recording of 'Mausoleum', recorded at Soundspace with Alex Silva in November, revealing how well formed the song was even then, and emphasising its evolution into something far more powerful when recorded again several months later, midway through the album sessions when the band's internal combustion was truly firing. On this final version, the audio sample atypically appears not at the beginning or the end but after the second iteration of the chorus, the point at which the demo stops. From within an etheric cloud of feedback – Silva and Bradfield recreating their happy accidental noise intro from 'Faster' – we hear J.G. Ballard explaining his motivation for writing *Crash* and inadvertently delivering as concise a summation of *The Holy Bible* as any: 'I wanted to rub the human face in its own vomit, and force it to look in the mirror.'

Then the serrated guitars tear forward, momentum accelerating until Bradfield somehow hangs on to retch out some final lines – 'Prejudice burns brighter when it's all we have to burn'. At that moment, 'Mausoleum's desperate logic becomes clear: these memorials of the past are warnings from history to the future.

38.

This Is Yesterday

Recorded: Soundspace Studios, Cardiff
Engineer: Alex Silva
Released: 30 August 1994 (*The Holy Bible*, Epic)

> 'I've stopped my dreaming
> I won't do much scheming these days.'
> — Nico, 'These Days'

Like 'Revol', 'This Is Yesterday's writing and recording post-dates the rest of *The Holy Bible* by almost three months, after Rob Stringer requested they come up with something that might be a viable single. Upon hearing the Manics' offerings, the Epic MD's response was typically forthright. 'He made a joke,' recalls James Dean Bradfield. '"Fucking hell — one good song, one bad song. That was worth it!"'

Although the 'bad' song of the two, Stringer still considered 'Revol' to have greater standalone commercial potential. In terms of the album, however, 'This Is Yesterday' would prove the pivotal addition. It's an interlude of peace between the storm clouds, giving the listener a moment's respite after the onslaughts of 'Mausoleum' and 'Faster' on one side and before the dire intimations of 'Die In The Summertime' and 'The Intense Humming Of Evil' on the other. Bradfield had been carrying the tune around for a couple of weeks before receiving the lyric, at which point he decided it could fit on the record. 'I thought there's not one moment of oxygen, where people can actually just sit back and realise there is a basic humanity there. Just connecting with the basic premise of if you can flourish in this calm moment, you can flourish in this boredom, you can flourish in this regret . . .

our basic melancholia default position. It just needs to be there.'

Musically, 'This Is Yesterday's gentle descending melody and walking tempo respectively derived from two songs by The Jam: 'In The Crowd', a peak moment on 1978's *All Mod Cons* hymning the individual's embrace by the mass, and the oft-overlooked 'Ghosts' from 1982's *The Gift*, essentially the former song's inversion, a lament for the alienated. Unlike every other song on *The Holy Bible*, it was written in an open G tuning – Bradfield: 'It's like a little John Squire riff' – and eschewed strident drumming patterns for a steady backbeat. Even the guitar solo, Bradfield aiming for a 'Bob Mould-direct-into-the-desk kind of sound', is clear-toned and yearning, respectful of the bucolic mood. 'It felt so different to all the others, lyrically, and so the music's different,' he says. 'But it's in the same sonic palette as everything else, so it fits in.'

'This Is Yesterday' is the only *Holy Bible* lyric predominantly written by Nicky Wire. With the opening line, 'Do not listen to a word I say', and a slightly phased, dissembling effect on Bradfield's vocal, it seems to introduce a dissenting voice to that which has characterised the album thus far, as if the narrator of 'Faster' has emerged from behind his wall of moral certainty and suddenly feels vulnerable. In other aspects, as well as recalling *Gold Against The Soul*'s rueful remembrance of childhood, the song reiterates themes already embedded within *The Holy Bible*, most obviously a pessimistic framing of the present and future relative to the past. Any comfort offered by the childhood homily 'Someone somewhere soon will take care of you' is undercut by its follow-up, 'I repent, I'm sorry, everything is falling apart.'

Significantly, 'This Is Yesterday' was written following the traumatic trip to Bangkok in April, and feels inescapably haunted by what Wire later termed the 'cracked mirror' impact that experience had on Edwards as an individual and the band's collective psyche. When the song's narrator looks to the sky, possibly for inspiration, whether cosmic or divine, it merely 'leaves me blind'.

'Those lines are quite emotional,' says Wire. 'Even though this song sounds soft and gentle, the lyric wasn't trying to lighten things up or anything. And although it's seventy to eighty per cent mine, there's definitely a couple of great lines from Richey. "Houses as ruins and gardens as weeds" was mine, and he added, "Why do anything when you can forget everything". A brilliant line. I think this song has one of the greatest guitar solos as well.'

The 'houses are ruins' line was inspired by *Grey Gardens,* a celebrated albeit controversial 1975 documentary by Albert and David Maysles about two upper-class women living in a dilapidated mansion in East Hampton, New York. The film depicts a mother and daughter, 'Big Edie' and 'Little Edie' Bouvier Beale – the aunt and cousin of Jacqueline Kennedy Onassis – as they potter eccentrically around the infestation and squalor of a once-grand home that they now share with feral cats, seemingly content in their eternal yesterday. 'I'd been watching it on video,' says Wire. 'Quite exploitative, but really good. It's not like I was trying to say anything particularly profound with the lyric of "This Is Yesterday". It was done really quick. But it certainly has its merits.'

While it's possible to imagine *The Holy Bible* without 'Revol', take away 'This Is Yesterday' and the edifice crumbles under the sheer burden of its own gravity. The final key to the album's hall of mirrors, the song even offers an alternative future path, almost daring the band to accept it. 'Thank God it's on there,' says Bradfield, 'because it's so many people's favourite song off the *Bible*. It just goes to show, you have those little moments of serendipity. Perhaps it is a bridge between some fans being able to follow us from *The Holy Bible* to *Everything Must Go*.'

39.
Die In The Summertime

Recorded: Soundspace Studios, Cardiff
Engineer: Alex Silva
Released: 30 August 1994 (*The Holy Bible*, Epic)

'Don't confuse the stage with the dressing room.'
            – Yukio Mishima, *Forbidden Colors*

Richey Edwards described 'Mausoleum' and 'The Intense Humming Of Evil' as 'brother/sister songs'.[1] The same could also apply to 'This Is Yesterday' and 'Die In The Summertime', both of which offer melancholy reflection on youth from the perspective of an older person. In case of 'Die In The Summertime', wholly written by Edwards, the song's author stressed on more than one occasion that this perspective was not necessarily his. 'OAP wants to die with favourite memory month in mind,' stated Edwards's Holy Bible tour programme notes for 'Die In The Summertime'. 'Adult memories tawdry, of little value.'[2] In interviews around the album's release he reiterated the premise that he was the song's narrator, as opposed to its subject. '"Die in The Summertime" [. . .] was basically an old man looking back over his life, over his favourite period of youth,' Edwards explained to *NME*'s Stuart Bailie in September 1994. 'His childhood basically. Everybody's got a perfect mental time of their life, and that's what that song is about. And it was written last summer.'[3]

Inevitably, however, the events of summer 1994 and beyond make it hard to dissociate 'Die In The Summertime's authorial point of view from Richey Edwards's own. When Richey spoke to Stuart Bailie it was shortly after leaving The Priory psychiatric clinic, where he'd undergone treatment following an initial stay at Cardiff's Whitchurch psychiatric hospital in mid-July, having either lost or relinquished control of his cutting habit over a period of two days. 'My mind subjected my body to things that it couldn't cope with,' he said. In this context, twelve months after it was written, a song called 'Die In The Summertime', with the opening lyric 'Scratch my leg with a rusty nail, sadly it heals', and the subsequent 'My heart shrinks to barely a pulse', felt horribly prescient.

The line that particularly spooked Nicky Wire was verse three's 'A tiny animal curled into a quarter circle'. This depiction of a living creature in full regression, whether towards a defensive foetal state or preparing to sleep no more, he found 'genuinely frightening'. When James Dean Bradfield first saw the song's title, he sensed 'the tension of opposites, innocence versus the reality of the world' – and felt scared. 'If you're singing "Die In The Summertime", you are kind of aware that you're intruding upon somebody else's life,' he says. 'Like Richey's memories or something. I don't even want to say any more than that. You don't want to ask, "Why do you feel like this, where's this memory from?" You don't ask.'

However disturbing the imagery, the metrical precision of 'Die In The Summertime's structure indicates a mind very much in command. Two verses of three brief lines juxtapose the depredations of age – dyed hair that grows out; the inability to 'stay a fixed ideal' – with pictures of childhood, when the narrator could 'see myself without ruining lines'. An equally succinct chorus begins with the striking vision, 'I have crawled so far sideways, I recognise dim traces of creation', followed by the title's death wish, a baleful tone maintained into the third verse, which ends on a biblical admonition for anyone considering the song's protagonist worthy of pity: 'If you really care wash the feet of a beggar.'

As the November 1993 Soundspace demo recording shows, the band immediately assimilated their dramatic new post-punk scheme. Seeing an 'almost David Lynchian' quality to the lyric,

James Dean Bradfield's primary musical hook was the curdled eldritch grandeur of *A Kiss In The Dreamhouse*-era Siouxsie and The Banshees – 'I thought that shard of beauty that can almost be shattered with one gust of wind is perfect for this' – with Moore's tom-tom beats advancing with the clanging guitar in a close formation of mutual unease. The sickly mood was heightened by Bradfield's high-pitched wordless keen at the first two verses' end. These were musical cues baked into the band's subconscious, as opposed to the two previous albums' somewhat expedient designs.

'You can tell this song is so good because it doesn't change much from the demo,' says Bradfield. 'It was in our bones to play this. We all knew the reference points, we're all pointing in the same direction, it's all quite fleet of foot. It all made sense to us.'

For such a concise lyric, 'Die In The Summertime' is replete with arresting images, which compel and haunt the Manics to this day. Nicky Wire hears something of T.S. Eliot in the desperate 'I have crawled so far sideways . . .' line, which could actually be a conflation of 'The Love Song of J. Alfred Prufrock's 'pair of ragged claws scuttling across the floors of silent seas'[4] with *The Waste Land*'s grotesque vision of baby-faced bats crawling down a wall. That particular lyric also ventures knowledge of Daniel Day-Lewis's fateful 1989 stage portrayal of Hamlet at the National Theatre, where the actor adopted a bizarre crab-like crouch to denote the 'antic disposition' of a Prince so conflicted by inner demons that he feels himself 'crawling between heaven and earth'.[5] Such is this song's suggestive power.

'This idea of him "ruining lines",' says Wire. 'I'd look at Richey and think he's just brilliant and amazing and handsome, androgynous . . . you name it. But it finally hit me that some people will never see themselves like they are. They'll always pick the fault. Why? After talking to him so many times, all of us, he just couldn't get over those things. On a big scale but also on a minute scale. Having acne when you're fourteen, and shit like that. Made me realise that everyone has that thing – there's always one thing which *could* destroy you.'

In 2023, when songs from *The Holy Bible* made a surprise but welcome return to the band's live performances, it would be 'Die In The Summertime' that got played first. In a concession to more peaceful times, Bradfield omitted the final 'I wanna die' in the choruses. Introducing the song at the Glastonbury Festival, Nicky Wire dedicated it to Richey Edwards, and remembered the four-strong Manics' appearance on exactly the same stage twenty-nine years earlier. 'Everything that could go wrong, did go wrong,' he said. 'But it was fucking fun.'

40.

The Intense Humming
Of Evil

Recorded: Soundspace Studios, Cardiff
Engineer: Alex Silva
Released: 30 August 1994 (*The Holy Bible*, Epic)

> 'Hope is for the loser.'
>
> – Killing Joke, 'Chapter III'

According to Nicky Wire, the Manics considered the Sex Pistols and Joy Division beyond emulation, however much they may have wanted to. 'It's impossible to actually sound like them,' he says. 'They are the two bands you can never touch.' Joy Division had been part of the initial rationale for glamming up into cartoon peacock rockers circa *Generation Terrorists*, inasmuch as people were unlikely to notice yet another *C86*-damaged indie band trying to inhabit the post-punk grey zone. Hence also 'From Despair To Where', where Richey Edwards's infatuation with a JD song was wrapped in patchouli-soaked Faces silk and swagger. As Wire reasoned: 'I don't think we could have been the band that made *The Holy Bible* earlier. I think it would have slipped by.'

By the time it came to record 'The Intense Humming Of Evil', however, Manic Street Preachers were so deep in the grey zone they could capably approximate elements of Joy Division's sonic vocabulary. The song begins with a looped rhythmic pattern that Sean Moore made from a drum machine fed back through an amplifier, reminiscent of the industrial ambience producer Martin Hannett brought to Joy Division records, most notably 1979's *Unknown Pleasures*. When Moore's actual drums finally enter amid feedback peals, soon followed by Wire's deep-hanging bass notes, the mood is strongly reminiscent of the *Unknown Pleasures* outtake 'Exercise One'.

Thematically, too, there was linkage. As well as naming themselves after the section in a Nazi concentration camp where women were forced into sex slavery, Joy Division had a fascination with totalitarian iconography and process, particularly that of the Third Reich. The audio sample that plays out during the first minute of 'The Intense Humming Of Evil' came from an English language version of a 1947 Soviet documentary about the Nuremberg Trials, with sombre orchestral music and a voice summoning 'the martyrs of Oswíeçim' – the Polish name for Auschwitz – to 'rise from the graves' and 'judge the butchers'. The song's title was a phrase Wire wrote down after experiencing the eerie stillness of Dachau. 'The silence was like an incredibly oppressive soundtrack,' he says. 'Back at the hotel I wrote down the title and some other words: "six million screaming souls", "maybe nothing at all". Then Richey took it and ran away with it.'

Edwards's lyric drew on his detailed knowledge of the Holocaust, which he had studied at university. Although the phrase *Arbeit macht frei* ('work makes you free') was notorious from its display on gates at the entrances to Auschwitz, Dachau and several other Nazi concentration camps, some references were much more obscure. 'Transports of invalids/Hartheim Castle breathes us in' refers to a Nazi extermination facility in Austria, initially used to kill German citizens deemed mentally or physically unfit, and later to gas concentration-camp inmates. Also cited was the medical experimentation programme at Dachau under the auspices of SS doctor Sigmund Rascher, and the camp's policy of exposing priests to fatal disease ('In block 5, we worship malaria').

'I remember struggling with it,' says Bradfield. 'You can tell I'm a bit knackered out with just writing stuff by this point. It was the only time I went to Sean: "Mooro, can you just come up with a verse on this one, give me something in two days?" And he did.

He gave me something really clever.' The only musically trained member of the band, Moore surprised Bradfield by eschewing the lyric's grand guignol possibilities, instead delivering a creeping atonal guitar fugue that accentuated the horror by simply letting the silence speak. 'I thought he was going to come up with something more florid. And he gave me a funny look, like – "Well, no, that wouldn't make sense." He started saying something about Penderecki and John Cage and minimalist delineation of modern song structures, to make more out of less. Of course, it made complete sense. The understatement of the chords – of there not being much detail in the chord itself – did work. Then we just needed a chorus.'

With Bradfield's vocal descending from its highest pitch, the chorus provides the song's emotional wellspring – a considerable feat, given that here, as elsewhere, the lyric's moral tone is strikingly conflicted, even somewhat ambivalent. The '6 million screaming souls' were 'lives that wouldn't have changed a thing'. Whereas verse two sympathetically evokes the perspective of camp inmates ('Beauty lost, dignity gone'), in its first verse the song's narrative voice belongs to the oppressor, effectively implicating his victims as agents of their own demise: 'You were what you were . . . You always mistook fists for flowers'.

This is troubling, deliberately contentious territory. The lyric overplays its hand in the third verse when asserting equivalence between the Nazis' genocide and then-Home Secretary Winston Churchill's violent suppression of striking miners at Tonypandy in November 1910, an outrage that still prompts anger in Wales several generations later. But Edwards was writing to shock, to confront an audience with the reality that, barely fifty years on, the Holocaust as a matter of historic fact was being challenged by the Hitler apologist author David Irving. 'That's being debated in universities right now, and I find that really really frightening,' he said.[1]

Testing the efficacy and resilience of one's ethical precepts is part of the deal with *The Holy Bible*, a challenge never more daunting than on 'The Intense Humming Of Evil'. Unlike the album's other heavyweights, the music offers no easy catharsis or euphoric counterpoint to the words, although Bradfield's guitar solo does possess a certain war requiem quality. Yet there is a dreadful drama to the denouement, where the sampled industrial gasps gradually slow to a wheeze, Moore's drum pattern suddenly morphs into the freeform Can motorik of Joy Division's 'Atrocity Exhibition', and the realisation dawns: this is the sound of a train arriving at its final destination.

'I demurred from that,' says Bradfield. 'Feels a bit graphic novel. When you're trying to personify guitar or drum sounds into real things, I always feel we're into slightly dodgy territory. I remember Silva saying to me, "Perhaps there shouldn't be a guitar solo on this, on a death camp song . . ." Because there's no solo on "Mausoleum". But there was nothing else to go there, so . . .'

Although *The Holy Bible* has become intrinsically associated with Richey Edwards's philosophical vision, James Dean Bradfield was every bit as much its architect. Newly single, he instigated a monomaniacal work schedule over the six weeks of recording at Soundspace. He and engineer Silva were typically in the studio for fourteen hours a day, seven days a week. Silva recalled the experience as 'exhausting' – and not just physically. 'The nature of that record, you can tell by listening to it, it wasn't a picnic to make,' he says. 'For that length of time, it was very hard. And James was obsessed. The last day was a thirty-six-hour day. We were finishing the backing vocals – me and James started at ten in the morning and finished at five o'clock the next afternoon. The mind was on its own trajectory at that point. I remember going home with a bottle of champagne, a present from the band, and thinking, "Thank fuck that's over." And then my girlfriend said, "I'm leaving you. I can't stand it any more . . ."'

Everything leads to something. Although not the last song on *The Holy Bible*, 'The Intense Humming Of Evil' feels like a point of terminus, beyond which lay . . . what, exactly? The Manics' response to their prolonged and intense immersion in the annals of human suffering would have repercussions, both good and bad.

'It is a grim song,' says Wire. 'I always remember playing it at Manchester Academy on the first *Holy Bible* tour in the UK. Which, bizarrely, was doing well. We were finally a genuine cult band, like The Cure or the Bunnymen had been before they got really big. But when we played that song in Manchester, people were flooding away. I could see them all, just going to the bar. Don't forget, our contemporaries were talking about cigarettes, alcohol and going to Greece for a holiday. So although that tour was tough we knew we were getting something across. But then we toured Europe with Therapy? for weeks, and that was terrible. Then Suede, and that was even worse. It felt like everything was unravelling with what we were singing every night.'

41.

A Design For Life

Recorded: Chateau de la Rouge Motte, France; Abbey
  Road, London
Producer: Mike Hedges
Released: 15 April 1996 (single, Epic); 20 May 1996
  (*Everything Must Go*, Epic)

'Hope lies with the proles.'

– George Orwell, *Nineteen Eighty-Four*

The *Holy Bible* era concluded, like its scriptural namesake, in
Armageddon. Just as in the *Book of Revelations* a wrathful God
destroyed his enemies, so the Manic Street Preachers destroyed
their equipment – along with lighting equipment that wasn't
theirs – on 21 December 1994, the culmination of a three-night
residency at the London Astoria. Although well versed in the art
of instrument smashing, there was a heightened level of intent
to this display, evidenced in the participation of Sean Moore,
normally very protective of his kit. The drummer later suggested
it was merely a pragmatic response to the band's battered mindset
at the end of a tough year; a week before the Astoria gigs, they
took what for them was the unusual decision to cancel the final
three dates of a gruelling European tour supporting Suede. 'We'd
reached rock bottom,' Moore said. 'We pretty much thought [the
Astoria] was going to be it – that those would be the last gigs
we'd ever do. So we trashed the gear, thinking, "We don't need
this any more."'

The Astoria was indeed the last gig Richey Edwards ever played.
Early on the morning of 1 February 1995, he drove away from
the Embassy Hotel in Bayswater, west London, and was never

seen again. But nothing about the Manics' behaviour during the six intervening weeks suggested a band throwing in the towel. Upon arriving in Cardiff immediately after the last Astoria gig, James Dean Bradfield went to Soundspace Studios to drop off some equipment, and plugged into an amp at the band's rehearsal space, where he wrote two sections of what later became the song 'Kevin Carter'. After sleeping overnight at the studio – 'it was freezing cold' – the next day he went to Blackwood to spend Christmas at home with his parents.

In early January, the band reconvened at House In The Woods in Surrey, where they completed demos of three songs – the Nicky Wire-written 'Further Away' and 'No Surface All Feeling', plus Edwards's 'Small Black Flowers That Grow In The Sky' – and worked on two more. 'I played acoustic versions of "Elvis Impersonator" and "Kevin Carter" to Richey in the kitchen,' says Bradfield. Moore later recalled Edwards's mood was 'unusually upbeat'.[1]

Towards the end of that same month, they were back at House In The Woods, where Edwards presented each of his bandmates with a file of new lyrics. This time they were rehearsing for an upcoming US tour to promote the belated release of *The Holy Bible*; the day Edwards disappeared he had been due to fly to America with Bradfield for an advance round of media interviews. On 30 January, Moore and Wire returned home. The following day, Edwards drove himself and Bradfield from Surrey to London. On the journey, the pair listened to the new demos.

'I asked, "Which is your favourite?" and he said, "Small Black Flowers",' says Bradfield. 'I knew he'd say that, because it was something that could have been on *The Holy Bible* if done a bit differently. I could tell he didn't like "Further Away". He'd given us a kind of mission statement: "next record to be a mix between Nine Inch Nails and *Screamadelica* and Pantera". And there had been conversations between us – nothing like a board meeting, but conversations – saying that wasn't a direction that myself,

Nick or Sean wanted to take. I remember in the car, going, "Well, I don't know, Rich, 'cos I've got this thing called 'Kevin Carter', which you've obviously written the lyrics to, and it's got a bossa nova vibe. I like 'Small Black Flowers', but I feel a bit more splendour coming into my soul at the moment." And he was like, [*airily*] "Yeah, fair enough, but that's my favourite . . ." We were trying to find a new direction, and he discarded everything except a caricature version of what might come after *The Holy Bible*, lyrically.

'It's a bittersweet memory. It is also bittersweet that perhaps – and this is conjecture – but perhaps in his mind he couldn't envisage his lyrics in the frame of what *Everything Must Go* was obviously taking shape to be. And it's a shame that he couldn't have actually seen that, yeah, it can work.'

With Richey Edwards's disappearance, the Manic Street Preachers entered a phase of agonised stasis. The obvious perspective, especially from thirty years' hindsight, is to pin this traumatic moment as the turning point in the band's history, but a better analogy might be the stylus locking into the run-out groove of a record, where it remains stuck until removed, whether by external forces or unforeseeable events. Or perhaps even a new song.

'After three or four months of things not getting any better in regards to finding Richey or getting an answer, we kind of knew we were gonna be left in some kind of situational purgatory,' says Bradfield. 'So anything that presented itself that would give us a sense of relief, I think we were always going to fall into the arms of.'

During this time, Nicky Wire barely went outside other than to walk his dog on the mountain beyond his back garden in the village of Wattsville. His early twentieth-century terraced cottage originally existed to house miners from the nearby pits in Cwmfelinfach and Risca, both of which closed in the 1960s, just a few years before Nicky was born. 'The house would never have been built if there hadn't been a colliery,' he says.

Wire hadn't strayed far from his childhood home. Blackwood was a mere five miles away, albeit a lengthy hike over Mynydd Islwyn, or alternatively a ten-minute drive up the Sirhowy Valley, where towns constructed by the coal mining industry were now crumbling in its absence. Most of the dozen or so remaining collieries around Blackwood and nearby Newbridge closed in the aftermath of the 1984–85 miners' strike, leaving behind physical memorials of their integral function in people's lives. The Manics were among these people. For several years James Dean Bradfield had worked at the bar in the Newbridge Institute and Memorial Hall, built in 1908 by miners from the Celynen collieries to provide their community with cultural and educational facilities: a cinema, a dance hall, meeting rooms, a library. Sean Moore played trumpet in the Oakdale Colliery Silver Band – miners literally taught him about jazz – whose tunes took on an extra melancholy timbre in 1987 when the Oakdale Workmen's Institute shut its doors and was subsequently demolished and rebuilt brick by brick at the Welsh Folk Museum in St Fagans. The colliery itself finally closed in 1989, by which time the Manic Street Preachers had released their first single, 'Suicide Alley', recorded in what had been the swimming pool of the miners' institute in Cwmfelinfach.

Come summer 1995, there were suicide alleys in former mining towns all across South Wales. Hard drug dependency filled the holes in the region's social fabric. Meanwhile, in his hillside miner's cottage, Nicky Wire wrote, attempting to make sense of his situation, both in terms of the band and the world beyond, and plot a way forward. He'd been reading George Orwell, and introduced himself to the bleak, often pitiless poetry of militant Welsh nationalist cleric R.S. Thomas, as well as rediscovering Thomas's more famous, lubriciously lyrical namesake Dylan. Wire also kept an eye on the television and the music press, grinding his teeth at the celebratory tone of the unfurling Britpop banner, a media and music industry-confected Union Jacked flag of convenience beneath which many of the Manics' erstwhile contemporaries were happy to march.

'It completely dominated my thoughts,' he says. 'Some of the lyrics I'd been writing were truly ill focused and internalised, and just not good enough. There was a lot of doubt and a lot of dangling. But I could feel a social history avenue opening up. The anger was starting to come back – the nudge-nudge wink-wink archness of Britpop, turning the working class into something silly, was starting to really annoy me. I can't deny it, I couldn't relate to the knowing irony of Pulp, and Blur's middle-class patronising view of the working class left me cold and angry. I couldn't stand the silliness. Richey used to say, "It's just bouncy music!" The endless irony. There's no fucking irony in working down a pit, no irony in the working-class culture we came from. It's just hard, it wasn't about fucking art school. *Greyhound racing!* I've actually been greyhound racing, at fucking Bedwellty, and it's shit. It was all just too much for me.'

On the evening of 16 August, BBC2 screened *Britpop Now*, showcasing 'the best of British pop'. The programme featured thirteen live studio performances, starting with Blur playing 'Country House', closing with Pulp's 'Common People', and hosted by Damon Albarn himself, whose casually triumphalist introductory address framed this latest new wave as dear old Blighty's plucky riposte to US musical hegemony. 'British bands are no longer embarrassed to sing about where they come from,' Albarn declared, reclining in a green leather armchair. 'They've found their voice.'[2]

That same month, Manic Street Preachers were evolving a new voice of their own. Infusing his disgruntlement at 'Parklife Britain' with reflections on the painful tenth anniversary of the miners' strike, Nicky Wire posted James Dean Bradfield two lyrics: 'The Pure Motive' and 'A Design For Life'. At that point Bradfield was living in west London with Terri Hall and her sister Liz:

'A nice place with nice people,' he says, 'but a bit frozen in time, because of what happened with Richey. And then Nick sent me the lyrics. The pressure was on Nick, rather than me or Sean, because everything else comes after the words. We're all waiting for the words to be right – and they were immediately. Nick says I edited the two lyrics together but it was obvious, they weren't that far from each other. I just smashed them together.'

Smash or edit, Bradfield removed a great many lines from the original drafts, which rambled across several A4 pages. 'The Pure Motive' was an angry interior monologue part-inspired by Jimmy McGovern's writing for the TV drama series *Cracker*, while 'A Design For Life' was more measured and didactic, an elegy for the working class with a title adapted from Joy Division's debut EP *An Ideal For Living*. Some of the rejected lyrics are eye-opening – 'So how can we judge or privatise/Millions and millions of people's lives/As the state abandons responsibility/Why not leave it to the charities (lottery)' – but Bradfield unerringly found the best ones and resisted any temptation to add more. His instincts highlighted one line in particular as capable of heralding the band's return with a new voice: 'Libraries gave us power.'

'My wife was working in the library in Pill, the roughest part of Newport,' says Wire. 'And on the front of that library is the inscription, "Knowledge is power". My brain works like a collage sometimes, so [with] that and the R.S. Thomas, everything else, it all came together. I just felt like I was "for real" – if you want someone to talk about a true working-class essence rather than be told what it is. Whereas Richey was more into *Living Marxism*, where everything's a question, I thought I'd found some answers in the past. So when James phoned me up from London and said, "R.E.M., Ennio Morricone, with some Tamla – I think I've got it," then played me "A Design For Life" on the guitar – that was the turning point, James singing down the phone to me. We might never have continued as a band without "A Design For Life".'

The trio met at Soundspace in Cardiff to work out the song

along the lines of Bradfield's concept. As previously noted, the ruminative chord progression was the same as 'Roses In The Hospital's B-side 'Donkeys'. Sean Moore suggested a 6/8 waltz time signature, envisaging a sweeping grandeur akin to David McAlmont and Bernard Butler's debut single 'Yes', a May 1995 UK Top 10 and the record that had lifted the drummer out of a self-imposed music blackout. Within ten minutes of playing the song together, it was apparent they were onto something. 'It gave me real hope straight away,' says Bradfield. 'I've had that feeling with other songs too, but this one was special.'

McAlmont & Butler's 'Yes' had been produced by Mike Hedges, a name imprinted in the band's collective memory by his eighties recordings with The Cure, Siouxsie and The Banshees, The Associates and Wah!, lending a cinemascopic veneer to each of those bands' post-punk designs. The Manics had actually approached Hedges to produce *The Holy Bible* but his calendar was full. This time, however, he arrived in Cardiff to watch a rehearsal and immediately picked out 'A Design For Life' as 'a jukebox song. I heard it as a hit.'[3]

A few weeks later, the Manics were in Chateau de la Rouge Motte, the producer's grand residential studio in the Normandy countryside. On day one, they recorded a version of Bacharach & David's 'Raindrops Keep Fallin' On My Head', with Moore on trumpet, for the War Child charity compilation *Help* (subsequently released on the *Lipstick Traces* compilation). On day two they moved on to the rhythm track for 'A Design For Life', recording on the same EMI TG12345 Mark IV desk that Pink Floyd used for *The Dark Side Of The Moon*, salvaged from the Abbey Road store room by Mike Hedges.

'We were nervous,' says Bradfield. 'The studio is a vault underneath the ground, we're in a different world. But Mike settled us in straight away. Sean and Nick put the drum and bass down live – we didn't overdo it, the sound was wide and nice already. I was impressed that Mike recognised what our best performances were. Sometimes you go in with a new producer and they'll go, "That's great", and you know it's nowhere near. But he knew. He got the best out of us.'

Hedges didn't suggest any changes to the arrangement. Possibly his most significant intervention was to request Bradfield play his guitars through either a Vox or a Fender amplifier, rather than his favoured Marshall. 'I chose the Fender Twin, but he made me do it. I felt strange, like I'd been denuded of my power!' says Bradfield. 'The guitar sounds quite scratchy in a way. But it was obviously because it would have taken up so much space if it had been a Marshall.'

The producer had recognised the song demanded room to breathe, that this was not the Manic Street Preachers of *The Holy Bible*, where the music had to boil and spit in service of the words. The only embellishment came with session musician John Green adding keyboards as a guide for the strings which were recorded the following spring at Abbey Road.

'It couldn't have gone any better,' says Bradfield. 'I remember playing it to Rob Stringer in his car and he's like, "Best thing you've ever fucking done, by fucking miles." There was no drama. We wrote it, we thought it was amazing. We played for Mike, he thought it was amazing. We recorded it, Rob thought it was amazing. Apart from the expectation, it was probably the most stress-free recording ever.'

Scratchy guitars. Room to breathe. A lyric comprising two verses of four lines, a four-line bridge and a chorus that's simply the title repeated four times. Thanks to the strings and the Mike Hedges magic, 'A Design For Life' sounded massive, but had a minimalist aesthetic. It's also a song that, for all its celebratory garnish, comes steeped in anger and spite. That opening line's affirmation of the working-class autodidactic tradition is immediately undercut by 'Then work came and made us free', repurposing the Nazi death camp motto *Arbeit macht frei* to bitterly lament the shackled indignity of labour. Alternatively, as James Dean Bradfield has suggested, the line's literal meaning is equally valid: 'I always took it in the positive sense,' he told Simon Price. 'South Wales was like the Klondike: yes it was hard, yes it was tough, but . . . it shaped an identity and gave people pride. And in the end, miners were some of the best-paid workers in Britain.'[4] (Bradfield himself wasn't necessarily averse to provocation or ambiguity: in Portsmouth during the Holy Bible tour he introduced 'The Intense Humming Of Evil' with the words: 'Work is good for the soul, you know.')

Likewise, the bridge's three-pints-full bacchanal, 'We don't talk about love, we only want to get drunk', was both a riposte to caricatured depictions of the working class and a defiant exhortation to reclaim and wear them with pride. The waspish tone intensifies with Bradfield's vehemently enunciated 'And we are not allowed to spend/As we are told that this is the end', contrasting the reality of free market capitalism with its espousal as the culmination of human progress by American philosopher Francis Fukuyama in his 1992 book *The End of History and the Last Man*. Fukuyama's cuddly liberalism captured a celebratory post-Cold War mood, into which Tony Blair removing 'common ownership of the means of production, distribution and exchange' from Clause IV of the Labour Party constitution in spring 1995 felt insidiously logical.

Once again, and notwithstanding the fact that McCarthy got there first with their 1988 B-side 'We Are All Bourgeois Now', this was hardly the lingua franca of mid-nineties rock music, especially for a song about getting drunk. 'The lines were perfect,' says Bradfield. 'The subject matter dovetailed into what Britpop was, and what we didn't want it to be.'

Sometimes the most successful political songs are the most enigmatic. 'A Design For Life' entered the UK singles chart at Number 2, having sold 92,000 copies in its first week of release, and was only narrowly beaten to Number 1 by Leicester R&B singer Mark Morrison's 'Return Of The Mack'.[5] Propelled by its emotional swirls and born aloft on carousing swells, like a colliery band marching indomitably uphill into a gale, the song immediately redefined the Manics without sacrificing a grain of authenticity. 'It felt seditious,' says Wire. 'It felt like entryism. This was a song that everyone was singing, with a deeper backstory to it. So I felt really happy about that. And I didn't give a shit there was a load of football fans just thinking it was about drinking. I like the fact that it doesn't trade on any sense of loss we might have been suffering post-Philip and Richey. We did four albums in four years, one of them a double album, our manager died, Richey went missing . . . Just keep fucking going. I was really proud about that attitude.'

Such an attitude dictates repercussions, and entails casualties. The single's sleeve design acknowledged as much: plain embossed silver – and subsequently gold – cardboard, featuring just the band name and song title, a conscious reference to New Order's 'Ceremony'. Like Joy Division, the Manics had lost a member on the eve of a US tour. Unlike New Order, they had kept the band name, but 'A Design For Life' still represented a new beginning. It was difficult to imagine the Richey Edwards-version Manic Street Preachers writing a hit song inspired by a library, or at least one with so few words and so profoundly connected to Wales.

'If you look at the whole package you can tell this is reduced to one vision now, there's a new identity there,' says James. 'Things had to come into focus, post-Richey. When he saw the band drifting geographically and spiritually, perhaps Nick felt a centrifugal force, some sort of lifeblood that he came back to. While we were on tour, one of four books would always be a Welsh book for Nick. He was always deep in that world, but it never found its way into the work. Perhaps the drift of the band, and what happened to Richey, affected Nick. It's another one of those bittersweet serendipitous things – it really dragged us back to where we should be.'

'A Design For Life' was first played live on 29 December 1995, at the Manics' version of a low-key return to the public stage, supporting The Stone Roses at Wembley Arena, and then at every gig since. Its most unusual staging may have been during *The Passion of Port Talbot*, an audacious seventy-two-hour version of the greatest story ever told staged over Easter Weekend in 2011, starring and co-directed by Michael Sheen, the South Wales steel town's latest thespian messiah after Richard Burton and Anthony Hopkins. Sheen sang along lustily as the Manics provided entertainment on his Saturday night Last Supper, until they were 'arrested' at gunpoint by security services.

The song's most apt performance, however, came on 18 June 2009, when the band officially opened Cardiff's new £15 million Central Library. After pulling the ceremonial cord to reveal a plaque inscribed with the opening four words from the song that saved them, the three Manics watched the Cardiff Arms Park Male Voice Choir sing 'A Design For Life' as it was surely always destined to be sung. Libraries gave them power – so it was only right that Manic Street Preachers should give some back.

42.

Mr Carbohydrate

Recorded: Chateau de la Rouge Motte, France; Abbey
    Road, London; Big Noise Recorders, Cardiff
Producers: Dave Eringa and Mike Hedges
Released: 15 April 1996 ('A Design For Life' B-side, Epic);
    14 July 2003 (*Lipstick Traces*, Epic)

'L'existence précède l'essence.'

– Jean-Paul Sartre

Recorded during the second session with Mike Hedges at Chateau
de la Rouge Motte, 'Mr Carbohydrate' reveals the Manics blos-
soming with enthusiasm for their new situation, introducing
what for them was a very different type of song. 'It felt like we
were writing about a personality within the band,' says James.
'It's obviously Nick asserting his identity, the process of living a
humdrum life and getting as much out of it as you can. It felt
like a new direction, so I enjoyed writing it.'

In late 1995, it was hard to remember there had ever been a
period when favourably citing The Beatles seemed unusual, but
thus far the only overt Manics reference to the band was the one
about laughing when Lennon got shot. Now, emboldened by the
sense they were free to reinvent themselves, and smitten with the
songwriting of The Boo Radleys' Martin Carr, the Britpop era's
most obsessive and adventurous Fabs disciple, they gratefully
embraced what might once have felt like forbidden pleasures,
right down to a George Harrison guitar vamp near the end.

'Just sometimes making do with a G and a C and a D and an
E minor and A minor,' says James. 'You know, if it was good
enough for Bob Dylan, why wouldn't it be good enough for the

rest of us? So that song felt like a chance to just strum and see what Sean put around it. And Sean was brilliant. Mike really liked "Mr Carbohydrate" but he was more focused on other songs. He bought into our aesthetic of things being of a slightly higher purpose and thought it was a bit too characterful.'

There was certainly a lot of the title character to go round. AKA 'Mr Inadequate', 'Mr Paranoia' and 'Mr Hypochondria', he represented the precise point where Nicholas Jones met Nicky Wire and settled down for a lengthy moan. Any journalist who had spent time with Wire in off-the-record mode would have recognised Mr Carbohydrate, but this was his gleeful public unveiling, an unapologetic 'boring fuckhead' whose best friend is the TV, and who proudly declares 'Cynicism is the only thing that keeps me sane.' The song even provided the answer to every Manics fan's hottest topic of debate. Nicky Wire's favourite cricketer? Of course, it was Glamorgan's long-handled larrikin Matthew Maynard, whose career was already synonymous with gloriously stylish underachievement and would only become more so as the years progressed, parallel to Nicky Wire's evolution into a curmudgeonly peacock-ish household-cleaning-wipe aficionado.

'"I would rather watch him play than pick up my guitar" – I was proud of that lyric!' says Nicky. 'It was a mode of separation for me as well. Which sort of culminated in wearing a home-made "I Love Hoovering" T-shirt at the Brits. It helped me feel completely different to what in my warped mind I think of as my competition.'

A classic B-side from the last gasp of the era when such things mattered or existed, 'Mr Carbohydrate's original lyric draft included several more verses about sport, one of them hymning the beauty of Welsh golfer Ian Woosnam's swing. Wire thought better of showing it to his bandmates. Even the man who considered a day without crisps as a day wasted knew there was such a thing as too many carbs.

43.

Elvis Impersonator: Blackpool Pier

Recorded: Chateau de la Rouge Motte, France; Abbey
    Road, London
Producer: Mike Hedges
Released: 20 May 1996 (*Everything Must Go*, Epic)

'Every revolutionary ends as an oppressor or a heretic.'
                                    – Albert Camus, 'The Rebel'

Aside from being a pivotal composition – the first Manics song written after Richey Edwards went missing, and the song that came to define the band more than any other – 'A Design For Life' validated new material that had already been written. No one came away from January 1995's House Of The Woods sessions convinced that they had the basis of a new album. '"No Surface All Feeling" was in the bag, "Small Black Flowers" was in the bag, but those songs didn't make sense until we had "A Design For Life",' says Nicky Wire. 'Richey had heard "No Surface", he'd heard a sketch of "Kevin Carter" and he'd heard "Small Black Flowers", but we didn't know if they were ever going to mean anything.'

'Elvis Impersonator: Blackpool Pier' was another case in point. On the day before leaving House In The Woods for the last time, Edwards gave James Dean Bradfield a short lyric – a miniature character study of a pitiable person or thing: 'Fake royalty' . . . 'sequin facade' . . . 'dyed black quiff' . . . 'Overweight and out of date'; essentially the first two verses of what became the album's opening song. Bradfield worked out an unusual chord sequence on acoustic guitar and played it to Richey in the studio kitchen. So this was another future *Everything Must Go* song Edwards had heard, although what Bradfield played was fast, choppy and frenetic, with little resemblance to the finished version. 'I did it in the style of "12XU" by Wire – really fast and frenetic,' he says. 'It would have been awful!'

Bradfield was subsequently dissuaded from this approach by Mike Hedges during an initial survey of the material, and by the time the band rehearsed in Cardiff before returning to France in January 1996 for the second session at the chateau, 'Elvis Impersonator' was recognisably taking shape. 'Rob Stringer came to the second batch of rehearsals and he said it was a bit like Queen,' says James. 'I couldn't quite figure out what he meant but he's kind of nearly a bit right. There is something first-album-Queen to it, without the histrionics.'

That being said, deploying a harp as the first instrument to appear on your long-awaited comeback album, rippling across an opening soundtrack of waves against a shore, could still count as histrionic. Amid the suggestible mood of anticipation around *Everything Must Go*, some listeners aware that Richey Edwards's car was found by the Severn Bridge unsurprisingly assumed those waves were meant to evoke his final act, instead of an audio cue suggested by the song's title. 'We weren't trying to contextualise stuff, it wasn't like, "Richey's walking into the sea,"' says Wire. 'I really didn't mean that at all, and I felt pretty bad about that at the time.'

The eerie atmospherics along with obfuscatory lyrical content – whatever's 'Twenty foot high on Blackpool promenade' is never actually made clear – and the episodic song structure collectively made for a highly effective exercise in dislocation. Did Edwards see himself in the 'overweight and out of date' fake Elvis Presley? The lyrics added by Nicky Wire ('All American trilogy in used up cars and bottled beer' etc.) only amplified the intrigue. Wire hadn't seen the original verses at House In The Woods, as he and Sean

Moore left the studio a day before the others. And then there was the ghostly outro refrain of 'Dixie', from Mickey Newberry's 'An American Trilogy', adopted by Elvis Presley in 1972 and synonymous with the beginning of the King's long fade. 'I can't remember what, when and who made that decision,' says James. 'But I do remember doing it on Mike's organ.'

The song's least ambiguous element is Bradfield's guitar solo, a grateful grasp for glory on a twelve-string Rickenbacker. '[That was the] first time I'd done a twelve-string solo on a Manics record. Mike Hedges handed me this beautiful blue Rickenbacker and said, "Mick Head played that." I was such a massive Pale Fountains fan, so I was bang into the idea. And then Mike said, "But he won't remember playing it . . ."'

The only thing certain about 'Elvis Impersonator: Blackpool Pier' is the subtext: no easy answers here.

'The lyric just evoked a tattered shit flag on a crap beach somewhere,' says Nicky, 'and I really don't know what Richey was trying to say other than literally the sadness of decay. Of a place and a person, and a culture.'

The song was recorded in a wintry Normandy with the first anniversary of Edwards's disappearance approaching. In Kieran Evans's film *Escape From Memory*, Mike Hedges recalls how the band 'didn't mope. They didn't seem to be grieving at that point. I suppose there was a tiny bit of anger actually: "Let's bloody do this despite what's happened."'[1]

In the same film, Bradfield admits that, in contrast to Moore and Wire, he felt scared at completely breaking from the frenetic *Holy Bible* template, out of respect for Richey's feelings. Hence his clinging to the '12XU' arrangement of 'Elvis Impersonator' long past his better judgement, and reconsidering only when Hedges gently urged him to leave the trauma at the door; to 'be who you are now'.[2] Of all the producer's contributions to *Everything Must Go*, none would be more significant.

'With Elvis Impersonator,' says Bradfield, 'I thought it was about how our best memories or ambitions will always be trapped in time, or trapped in one moment. They can't go forward or backwards. I think Richey would have liked this song. Richey liked listening to soppy music, but he didn't actually want to make soppy music. I think he got to a point where he didn't want to be part of that.'

44.

Kevin Carter

Recorded: Chateau de la Rouge Motte, France; Abbey
   Road, London
Producer: Mike Hedges
Released: 20 May 1996 (*Everything Must Go*, Epic);
   30 September 1996 (single, Epic)

'Good pictures. Tragedy and violence certainly make
powerful images. It is what we get paid for. But there is a
price extracted with every such frame.'
   – Greg Marinovich & Joao Silva, 'The Bang-Bang Club'

On 26 March 1993, the *New York Times* illustrated an article
about the south Sudanese famine with a photograph of a starving
child being watched by a vulture. On 12 April 1994, the picture
won 33-year-old South African photojournalist Kevin Carter
the Pulitzer Prize. Already respected for his fearless coverage of
post-Apartheid South Africa's township civil war alongside fellow
members of the so-called 'Bang-Bang Club', Carter would now
experience a new measure of celebrity. Receiving his award in
May at Columbia University in New York, he was courted by
magazines and agencies, and used his prize money to buy new
camera equipment, as well as enjoying a better class of cocaine
than he was used to in Johannesburg. 'I swear I got the most
applause of anybody,' he wrote to his mother. 'I can't wait to
show you the trophy.'[1]

Two and half months later, Kevin Carter killed himself near
his childhood home in a northern Johannesburg suburb. His
heightened public profile had brought tough questions about
the ethics of the vulture photograph – essentially: what had

he done to help the child? – and the scrutiny combined with an already problematic drug habit to fatally contaminate his mood. There had also been the death of his friend and fellow Bang-Bang Club member Ken Oosterbroek, shot in Tokoza township on 18 April, six days after Carter won the Pulitzer. In a note found on the passenger seat of the pickup truck where he had gassed himself, Carter wrote: 'I have got to a point where the pain of life overrides the joy to the point that joy does not exist . . . I am haunted by the vivid memories of killings & corpses & anger & pain . . . and I am haunted by the loss of my friend Ken.'[2]

It's no stretch to imagine how Richey Edwards might have been haunted by the story of Kevin Carter, a charismatic young man who earned money and a measure of fame from documenting human suffering. Although Edwards hadn't witnessed death first-hand, as Carter repeatedly had, or been forced to deal with the same moral dilemmas, his intense study of *The Holy Bible*'s archives of pain had clearly taken a toll, mentally and physically.

The lyric he presented to James Dean Bradfield 'on a scrappy piece of paper' towards the end of 1994, however, proved that his creative muscles remained strong. This was a new type of Edwards lyric, for the first time detailing a real public figure's life, in a taut masterclass of exposition: just three short four-line verses and a chorus that was simply the subject's name. Specific phraseology revealed the extent of Edwards's research into his subject. 'Tribal scars' referenced the wounds inflicted often by knives or machetes in the brutal hand-to-hand fighting between the ANC, whose leadership cadres were typically members of the Xhosa tribe, and their Zulu political rivals Inkatha. The 'Bang-Bang Club' was born out of this specific situation: as four white photojournalists, it made sense for Carter, Oosterbroek, Greg Marinovich and Joao Silva to work as a mutually supportive team when entering the townships during times of peak violence. 'Vulture stalked white piped lie for ever' combined the photograph that made Carter famous, and the subsequent whispers that he had somehow set it up, with the photographer's addiction to 'white pipe': a potent mixture of marijuana (or 'dagga') and Mandrax, smoked through a broken bottleneck. 'Kevin Carter Kaffir lover' was the taunt aimed at the teenage Carter as a young conscript in the South African army when he defended a black mess-hall waiter from a group of Afrikaans-speaking soldiers, who then beat him up. The only faintly oblique reference is the eerie invocation of the elephant ('he sleeps his head/Machetes his bed'), likely a metaphor for the dreams that troubled Carter and his other Club members. The handwritten lyric sheet Edwards handed to Bradfield also featured a photocopy of the vulture picture, and a portrait of Carter himself, with camera, looking gaunt amid the chaos of the frontline.

Bradfield began working on the music at Soundspace immediately upon arriving back at Cardiff after the final London Astoria gig in December 1994, then finished it at House In The Woods in January, where he played the song acoustically to Edwards. The lyric's minimalist shape on the paper suggested the initial musical approach, with clipped rhythmic guitar somewhat reminiscent of 'Comfort Comes', but Bradfield soon elected to move the mood on to somewhere less overtly Wire-ish. It was after playing it to Mike Hedges at the Soundspace rehearsal in August 1995 that the final arrangement took shape and was completed in quick order during the first recording session at Chateau de la Rouge Motte.

'After "Raindrops" and "A Design For Life" we did "Kevin Carter",' says Bradfield. 'Sean was unbelievable, he had the drum part nailed so tight.' Impressive though his drumming was – matched by Wire's quintessential display of bass pocket playing – Moore's standout contribution was a trumpet solo during the instrumental break following the second chorus, exactly where a guitar solo would have been expected. Moore practised diligently and gave a sublime performance, helped by having recently played 'Raindrops Keep Fallin' On My Head' in a similar idiom, so his embouchure was in good shape.

'Usually if you said to Sean, "Do a trumpet solo," he'd have been an arse,' says Wire. 'So perhaps it was better with Mike there.' Bradfield agrees: 'Mike was just like, "This can be really good, Sean, let's work on this." Somebody with a bit of authority and a legacy, being able to convince him to do it. That's what a producer is sometimes, a buffer zone.'

Having a solo played on trumpet rather than guitar better suited Bradfield's vision for the song, which he'd explained to Hedges and engineer Ian Grimble as: 'A hint of the *Sweeney* theme tune with a hint of Gang Of Four playing bossa nova.' The music for tough seventies British television cop drama *The Sweeney* was written by Harry South, a mainstay of the fifties and sixties London jazz scene, thus fitting the TV genre template by utilising the predominant hip sound of a previous era. The pièce de resistance was a sighing harmony vocal chorale, pure Burt Bacharach, which bridged Moore's solo and the final verse, once again obviating the need for a guitar solo. Such was the quality of this unassuming song, elevated by selfless ensemble contributions, where everything falls into place like a dream.

One of *The Sweeney*'s two main characters was named George Carter. Now the Manics' 'Kevin Carter' would perfectly evoke nostalgia for so much that had been lost, be it watching ITV on a Thursday evening, a troubled South African war photographer, or the writer of the song's lyric.

45.

Enola/Alone

Recorded: Chateau de la Rouge Motte, France; Abbey
  Road, London
Producer: Mike Hedges
Released: 20 May 1996 (*Everything Must Go*, Epic)

> 'Every time I see your face, it reminds me of
> the places we used to go.'
>
> – Ringo Starr, 'Photograph'

One evening in his room at Chateau de la Rouge Motte, Nicky Wire picked up a photograph he had brought with him to France. Among its group of smiling faces were Richey Edwards and Philip Hall. The following morning, as he was getting ready for the day's work, the television was showing Blondie's 'Union City Blue' video. Nicky looked up just as an aerial panoramic shot of the New York skyline passed by the Statue of Liberty. From those two moments came 'Enola/Alone', one of *Everything Must Go*'s most extraordinary songs.

'I wrote the lyric in half an hour,' says Wire. 'Easy peasy. Like Lennon said: "Tell the truth and make it rhyme." Three years previously I'd got married. And that great picture has all of us on there, with Richey and Philip and Martin. And it just poured out of me – the sense that within three years two of them have gone. "Enola/Alone" is more of an invocation than a literal song. The line about the Statue of Liberty looking solemn, it doesn't mean anything. But there's a sense of freedom and sadness. It's not a deep song . . . but it kind of is. James sang it exactly how I thought it would be sung – not the tune but the feeling. We were in the chateau, he played it on acoustic and it sounded unbelievable.'

By now comfortable in his surroundings and confident about the path the band were taking, Bradfield's reaction to the lyric was equally spontaneous – and unusual. Whereas he typically looked at a lyric with an analytic eye to structural options, here he simply started strumming and singing.

'It was carefree, felt like I was writing by a campfire,' he says. 'It did come really quickly.'

The recording followed a similar path. 'Enola/Alone' is the one Manics song where their deep affinity with Oasis's *Definitely Maybe* is made apparent: the warm tactile tones of the opening guitar chords, the faintly laggardly drumming, the ascendant melodic trajectory unable to escape the melancholia of gravity's pull, and a raw production palette. That latter quality would get overlooked as the album's signature songs' impact was blunted by familiarity and *Everything Must Go* became a Manics sonic shorthand: the 'orchestral anthemic one'. Yet although some subsequent albums finessed its constituent parts into a template, none had its bare analogue foundations. There are no strings on 'Enola/Alone', just amplified layers of grainy electric signals fizzing into beautiful slow decay.

'At the outset, Mike said this album's got to be "produced trashiness",' says Bradfield. 'And "Enola/Alone" epitomised his idea of what "produced trashiness" was.'

The song broke new ground for the Manics. A lyric as straightforwardly emotional as 'I'll take a picture of you/To remember how good you looked' would never have got past the *ancien régime*'s denialist star chamber. Likewise, Bradfield's impromptu '*Ahh*' as he wound up to deliver the choruses, recalling Liam Gallagher's similar euphoric exclamation during *Definitely Maybe*'s 'Slide Away' (a rejected verse from 'Enola/Alone' had the lyric 'Sing to me some love forever', which could as easily have been 'Live Forever'). The only residual traces of the old ways lay in the title: a palindrome, as per 'Revol/Lover', it also nodded back to 'Motown Junk's sleeve image and the atomic bomb cropped on Hiroshima by the B-29 'Enola Gay'. After the darkness, finally here was some light.

'I can't tell you how excited I was by the title, when I realised that "Enola" was "alone" backwards,' says Wire. 'It's one of our most natural songs, on every level. It's the most sentimental song on the album, undoubtedly. I still love playing it live, I'm always trying to get it into the set. For me, the key line on *Everything Must Go*, unfortunately, is not "Libraries gave us power", it's "All I want to do is live/No matter how miserable it is". Just thinking the moments of terrible isolation will pass. Because they do.'

46.
Everything Must Go

Recorded: Chateau de la Rouge Motte, France; Abbey
  Road, London
Producer: Mike Hedges
Released: 20 May 1996 (*Everything Must Go*, Epic); 22 July
  1996 (single, Epic)

'We all reinvent ourselves.'
  – R.E.M., 'Crush With Eyeliner'

There was a touch of bathos to the creation of the song that
became *Everything Must Go*'s title track and its second Top 5 single.
With the first Chateau de la Rouge Motte session completed,
the band returned home for three weeks, where James Dean
Bradfield sat down with a lyric Nicky Wire had been drafting in
France. By this point it was clear the Manics were going to return
with such a dramatically different sound in response to their
traumatically changed circumstances that Wire felt the situation
required some form of direct address to their fans.

'I could see there was a hole in the album,' he says. 'The idea
of saying "The New Manics" – that we can't be the band that we
were, that we're going to have to junk the last few years just to
be at ease with ourselves. In a nice, concise, almost apologetic
way: "I hope you can forgive us, but everything must go."'

The title was taken from an as yet unperformed play written
by Patrick Jones, who himself saw it on the window of a soon-
to-close shop in Newport. The music, meanwhile, came from the
coincidence of Bradfield being in the living room at his parents'
house at the very moment BBC Radio 2's venerable morning
presenter Jimmy Young played The Crystals' 'Be My Baby'. 'My

mum always listened to Radio 2, either Terry Wogan or Jimmy Young, or she listened to plays on Radio 4. So I was looking at the lyric when "Be My Baby" came on. I had this little chord sequence where I'd suspend that weird A, whatever that chord is, and I just played the opening notes of "Everything Must Go" over the top of the radio. As simple as that. It was like, "Fuck me, it's gonna work!" So then I switched off the radio and wrote the rest of it.'

Before returning to Chateau de la Rouge Motte, there was an abortive session with producer Stephen Hague at Real World Studios near Bath ('Bradfield: 'The place didn't suit us'). On the first day there, Bradfield played the song on an acoustic guitar in the studio's live room for Rob Stringer, by way of previewing material they intended working on at the next session in France. The consensus was that in contrast to Real World's clinical atmosphere, the chateau would better suit the power the Phil Spector-inspired vision required.

'We didn't want it to be like one of those really bad eighties records that does a tame facsimile of a Phil Spector vibe,' says Bradfield. 'If that's where the inspiration is from then it's got to be full throttle. Don't do a bad wedding reception version, have some grit and dirt in it. So we recorded it in France, and it was OK, the raw sounds were good, but we were just trying to push Ian Grimble to put more echo plate on it – more BOOM BOOM-BOOM TSSSCH! And we didn't really get that until we mixed it.'

For a song conceived upon hearing a girl-group pop song as background accompaniment to a mid-morning cuppa, the finished version is counter-intuitively extreme: far from lush and decorous, the strings are left to fend for themselves amid Moore's relentless rolling tympani thunder. Bradfield asked the string arranger Martin Greene to make them 'more Stalingrad', possibly thinking of Shostakovich's Seventh Symphony, which premiered in Leningrad during the Nazi siege of 1942. Although not quite the sound of world war, the recording was a mini-masterpiece, a textbook example of how opposing aesthetics can co-exist, provided all participants understand the strategy and the goal.

'Ian Grimble mixed it and he's a man of small moves – very tasteful, very ex-Abbey Road kind of thing,' says James. 'So it's good when you get somebody of his sensibility meeting ours, where he can mitigate the crassness in me and we can mitigate the slightly conservative nature of some of his moves in the studio. It's a good mixture.'

Whether this most self-aware of bands truly believed they could 'escape from our history', or actually sought forgiveness, was moot: after all, the Manics began using their work as a direct dialogue with their audience as early as 'You Love Us', and would subsequently do so again. Yet its vivid execution affirmed 'Everything Must Go' as an authentic moment, a song that transcended any hint of expediency in the moment of Bradfield's screaming the words 'Just need to be happy'. Its accompanying video cleverly suggested the past and present could co-exist, indulging familiar symbols – its sepia tints and giant clocks were in homage to Coppola's *Rumble Fish* – alongside fetishising the new model band's wilfully understated wardrobe aesthetic. 'It's my Manics at C&A period, definitely,' says James. 'Soon after this I was so happy I started wearing a denim jacket. Never worn one before, ever.'

47.

Small Black Flowers That Grow In The Sky

Recorded: Chateau de la Rouge Motte, France; Abbey
    Road, London
Producer: Mike Hedges
Released: 20 May 1996 (*Everything Must Go*, Epic)

'Choo-choo train, a-chuggin' down the track
Gotta travel on, never comin' back
Wooh-ooh, got a one-way ticket to the blues.'
            – Neil Sedaka, 'One-Way Ticket', RCA, 1959

The initial lyric draft had the title 'Stalemates', and featured a chorus ('Self mutilate self dictate self hate you're stale mate') that could have suggested a more caustic musical approach. Of the three songs on *Everything Must Go* with lyrics wholly written by Richey Edwards, 'Small Black Flowers That Grow In The Sky' was the only one Edwards heard in completed demo form, following the January 1995 House In The Woods session: a solo James Dean Bradfield singing high over desolate twelve-string acoustic guitar in the style of Jackson C. Frank or Nick Drake, an arrangement adhered to by the finished album version.

'It's the last song that me and him listened to, in the underground car park at the Embassy Hotel,' says Bradfield. 'It was written around the same time as "Kevin Carter" – it was part of the book of lyrics he gave Nick and Sean the day before he went missing, but I'd been fed a couple of lyrics in that book before he gave them to all of us, so this would have been two or three months before he left. And it was the last song of ours he ever said that he liked.'

While 'Kevin Carter' presented a character with whom Edwards empathised, 'Small Black Flowers' depicted listless caged animals in a way that was both less specific and also more clearly analogous with his own diminished self-perception: 'Once you roared now you just grunt lame'. Sparked by a television documentary about zoos, the lyric's stark representation of the oppressive treatment meted out by an ostensibly benign power system suggested obvious parallels with Edwards's recent experience of psychiatric hospitals – 'They drag sticks along your walls . . . Here comes warden, Christ, temple, elders' – yet much of its detail was so specific to the self-abusive behaviour of incarcerated animals that a literal reading was equally valid. 'But I don't know if it even is an analogy,' says Wire. 'I actually think it is more about the tragedy of zoos. Obviously it's him built into it, but Richey was capable of distancing himself while writing, sometimes. He wasn't in every single song.'

When he first read the lyric, Bradfield made a connection with *The Woman In The Dunes*, a 1962 Japanese novel by Kōbō Abe about a disappeared man who is trapped with the title character in a deep sandpit by a seaside village's population. After several failed escape attempts, the man gradually acquiesces to his situation, eventually becoming so institutionalised that he spurns the opportunity to leave. The book ends with official documents about his status as a missing person, who after seven years is presumed dead.

'I knew Richey had read *The Woman In The Dunes*,' says Bradfield. 'I talked to him about it, and asked if the lyric was anything to do with that. He went, "Of course not". So that was my attempt at critical analysis shot down in flames. But I loved the lyric and wanted the song to be a little bit like The Rolling Stones' "Spider And The Fly" or maybe "Lady Jane".'

Mike Hedges also rated the song, identifying it as a perfect track five or six – the end of side one, in old parlance, which is exactly where it sits on the finished album sequence. After Wire suggested accompanying Bradfield with a harp, the producer duly obliged. 'He said, "Oh, I know Frank Sinatra's harpist",' says Bradfield. 'Typical Mike, he always tossed stuff like that off. I'd say, "Where's that compressor from?" "Oh, I bought that in a fire sale from John Lennon's home studio." Always a good answer. Might be bullshit, but it's a good answer.'

Julie Allis was indeed Frank Sinatra's harpist – Hedges had previously worked with her on Marc Almond's 1985 album *Stories Of Johnny* – and it's her delicate flourishes that linger over the bleak closing line: 'Here chewing your tail is joy'. As well as also playing on 'Elvis Impersonator', she would subsequently perform 'Small Black Flowers' on *Later . . . With Jools Holland* and at Brixton Academy. 'She was infinitely more rock 'n' roll than us,' says James. 'She loved the song, really engaged with it: "Love the tone of that chord there and the descending semitone there – did you study music?!"'

While the album version features Bradfield playing the same Lakewood acoustic guitar previously heard on 'Little Baby Nothing', his vocal traversed various levels of anguish, from beseeching in the verses to grave in the chorus. It also prompted his 'first proper argument' with Mike Hedges, who after five takes suggested the singer 'wasn't quite there yet' and could he have another five. 'So I told him to fuck off, and he told me to fuck off,' says Bradfield. 'I came back two hours later and started doing the vocal in a very passive-aggressive way. After four takes, I went on the intercom: "Is that all right?" And he went, "Yes, very sensitive." So we didn't talk for about half a day. But we sorted it out that evening in the bar in the village. No argument lasted long enough for us not to go out and get drunk.'

Despite Edwards's refuting any link, the band would subsequently perform the song onstage accompanied by projections of the 1964 Academy Award-nominated film version of *The Woman In The Dunes*, for which they had to pay the rights owner £500 for three years, a period during which the band transitioned from playing halls to playing arenas. In the pantheon of existentialist mainstream infiltration, it must rank pretty high.

'You'd see couples in the audience swaying along to "harvest your ovaries, dead mothers crawl",' says Wire. 'To have a line like that in a pop lyric, so stark and miserable, is genius.'

48.

The Girl Who Wanted To Be God

Recorded: Chateau de la Rouge Motte, France; Abbey
    Road, London
Producer: Mike Hedges
Released: 20 May 1996 (*Everything Must Go*, Epic)

'The pendulum of the mind oscillates between sense
and nonsense, not between right and wrong.'

– Carl Jung

'The Girl Who Wanted To Be God' was salvaged with Mike
Hedges at the early 1996 return to Normandy, following its initial
recording alongside 'Australia' at the late 1995 Real World session
with Stephen Hague. Hague was noted for his production work
with Pet Shop Boys and New Order, and teaming him with the
Manics seems to have been a textbook misalignment of skills and
intent, with each party seeking what the other sought to escape.

'This song is one of our first attempts at trying to write something a bit like Abba,' says James. 'Probably for a bit of light
relief, sometimes you just want to do something different. So
we wanted a bit more shininess, like "Regret" by New Order,
which he [Hague] did and is obviously an amazing record. But
he's like, "No, I need a bit more punk energy from you guys." It's
like, "D'you think we came to you for that? Stop. We're here for
different reasons." Mike knew our best performances. Stephen
didn't. He was making Nick do run after run on the bass, long
after he'd nailed it. Not Stephen's fault or our fault, it just didn't
work.'

Then there was the cultural disconnect. Feathers already ruffled by Real World's communal dining arrangements (Bradfield: 'We barely had dinner with each other, let alone other bands – after the first night they moved our table under the stairs'), the Manics stumbled upon a language gap between themselves and their American producer.

'Stephen Hague loves basketball,' says Wire. 'I think a sport where you score 200 points in an hour is just not a proper sport. He actually got the hump with me because I complained about the squeaky floors and how it's all in gyms and stuff. He was nice, but he'd sit there playing a fucking accordion all the time . . . Uncomfortable. We were pushing for something more disco, and he just turned us into a tiny boxy rock band.'

Keeping some of the Hague session's bass, drums and the scratchy eighties white-funk guitar, the track was loosened up and rebuilt by Hedges into the exultant, panoramic relaunch of the album's second half, with Sally Herbert's Abbey Road string arrangement offering a fuller-bodied reprise of the 'Dancing Queen' flurry from 'Motorcycle Emptiness'. As Bradfield says, 'This is meant to be that moment on the album where there's not much to decode – it's just open and free.'

The lyric was an Edwards/Wire collaboration, Nicky subsequently augmenting a very brief set of lines included in the file Richey presented to the others at House In The Woods in late January. Thus, Edwards's 'You could see that she was true and faithless' and 'Black out the words for the blind have eyes' were bisected by Wire's 'But see through the future and forget all the lies'. In all, the lyric divided roughly fifty-fifty, with the title a quotation from a letter written by the seventeen-year-old Sylvia Plath.

'I added, "Hold me she said, love me to death",' says Wire. 'Which is not a great line, but I have no idea what his original lyric was about. But I really like it, and I love the guitar solo, which is really just rhythm, like a Nile Rodgers part with strings. This could have been a single.'

49.

Australia

Recorded: Chateau de la Rouge Motte, France; Abbey
  Road, London
Producer: Mike Hedges
Released: 20 May 1996 (*Everything Must Go*, Epic);
  2 December 1996 (single, Epic)

> 'We are healed of a suffering only by
> experiencing it to the full.'
>
> – Marcel Proust, *Albertine disparue*

Whereas the album's title track's aspiration to 'escape from our history' implied the opening of a fresh chapter, 'Australia' was far more apocalyptic, a door-slamming piece of exit music, from its first revved-up cadence to the closing mantric invocation of the furthest away retreat possible. 'Nick gave me the lyric and said, "Here's my version of 'Life On Mars'",' says Bradfield. 'It's all his ideas of escape, of another life.'

Also written at Chateau de la Rouge Motte, it mapped the same brittle emotional landscape as 'Enola/Alone', and was inevitably read by some as a rumination on Richey's possible whereabouts. The catalyst this time, however, was literally Nicky's inner malaise. In 1994, after his latest bout of food poisoning while on tour in Germany, he was diagnosed with Gilbert's syndrome, a lifelong genetic condition that impairs the liver's ability to stop the build-up of bilirubin in the blood and leads to jaundice. On the only occasion during the *Everything Must Go* sessions that Wire joined the others for supper in the local restaurant, he took one bite of a galette and had to leave. 'Australia's first verse is a literal account of the episode.

'Because the galette was cooked in butter, my Gilbert's kicked in,' says Wire. 'So "Australia" is probably the only lyric ever in music history to reference Gilbert's syndrome – "my cheeks are turning yellow" is what happens when my bilurubin levels go wrong, and hence "take another pill". It's a sickly song.'

Wire's initial draft was sicklier. 'Phone calls and letters, the future's no better', declared a rejected bridge section. While its fevered disposition was therefore very real, 'Australia' transcended its author's specific circumstances and became one of the Manics' most malleable and universal songs, thanks to its receiving such a dynamic musical vehicle. 'It came really quickly,' says Bradfield. 'The guitar break was courtesy of Ian Broudie – I copied the guitar sound from a Lightning Seeds record. And I think the discussion about getting Stephen Hague was around 'Australia' – it had a New Order vibe. So we did a version with Stephen, and it wasn't great. Too clinical, too clean. There's even a bit of Sean's drumming that was really bad late-era Who . . .'

As bravely revealed on the album's tenth-anniversary edition, the Stephen Hague 'Australia' was even less successful than the original 'The Girl Who Wanted To Be God'. Come the guitar break before the second verse, the band have apparently morphed into mid-eighties Squeeze with synthetic horns. Starting again in France, however, the song still proved troublesome, with the final version emerging only after Dave Eringa was parachuted in at the mixing stage, powering up the drums and finding the glory amid Mike Hedges' 'produced trash' aesthetic.

'Mike's version was just ragged,' says Wire. 'All over the shop, the bass was terrible . . . And I remember listening after Dave had mixed it, and it blew my mind.'

'Dave used a sample on the drums,' adds Bradfield. 'That's what saved it, because Mike and Ian's drum sound didn't have enough front on it. It was a bit too Oasis, and we wanted this one pointed. I can be completely cynical about it – when we wrote this I just thought, "This is a radio song, this is *Match of the Day* goal of the month music." And then it got used on the Nationwide League goals round-up for five or six years. Which is what it was written for.'

For such a spectacular rock song, 'Australia' surprisingly never became a setlist fixture. 'It's probably the one song I don't think we've ever really done properly live,' says Wire. 'If it goes too fast it falls apart, but it has to be on the edge to fly. It's such a hard one.' Proof of that lies in a stunning performance from the Christmas 1996 edition of *Later . . . With Jools Holland*, filmed at the end of three months touring, where the still-young and now road-sharp Manics only just manage to keep control of its volatile energy. The band's fourth successive Top 10 single, 'Australia' proved that however much the tone and presentation had changed, the substance was still down to this same intense, complicated, often contradictory group of people.

50.

Interiors (Song For Willem De Kooning)

Recorded: Chateau de la Rouge Motte, France; Abbey
 Road, London
Producer: Mike Hedges
Released: 20 May 1996 (*Everything Must Go*, Epic)

'Memory . . . is the diary we all carry about with us.'
— Oscar Wilde, *The Importance of Being Earnest*

An earlier mooted title for *Everything Must Go* was 'Sounds In The Grass', after a series of paintings by Jackson Pollock. Ultimately, it would be Pollock's fellow giant of abstract expressionism, Willem de Kooning, who was paid tribute on the album. 'Interiors' is significant for being the first Manics song where the subject is an artist (as opposed to 'La Tristesse Durera', which quoted but wasn't actually *about* Van Gogh), a songwriting device that Nicky Wire would employ regularly from there on. In this instance, his lyric uses De Kooning – who died in 1997 aged ninety-two, having suffered from Alzheimer's since the mid-eighties – as a means to explore the album's wider theme of memory, its capacity to both torment and comfort and how it impacts on creativity.

'I was really into the abstract expressionists at this time,' says Wire. 'Pollock, Rothko but especially De Kooning. There's a great controversy over the last period of De Kooning's life. Did he know what he was painting? Because I personally think the quality does drastically reduce. There was a *South Bank Show* with Melvyn Bragg which was trying to figure this out – are these paintings any good any more? And it was quite ambiguous in terms of maybe De Kooning wasn't aware of what he was doing. So the lyric is about dementia. It's an interesting area about memory and capability. Was he being pressured into moving his arm? Because he wasn't aware of much [by that point] in his normal life. Artists are all so fucked-up and interesting.'

Of course, by using a famous artist as a vessel to explore human psychology, Wire obviated the more painful alternative of analysing himself. This strategy spoke to a possibly limited public appetite for the further adventures of 'Mr Carbohydrate', as well as revealing an understandable instinct for self-protection. 'Interiors' functioned beyond any prior knowledge of what 'young Willem' may or may not have seen, thanks to its clipped melancholic character sketch – 'Your beautiful triangle of distortion/ Now you forget it' – receiving an edgily elegiac soundtrack. The rhythmic template was substantially derived from Saint Etienne's 'Nothing Can Stop Us' – 'I wrote different chords, a different vocal line, but it's definitely that feel,' says Bradfield – and worked into a Northern soul variant that recalled Joy Division's 'Interzone', itself an adaptation of Nolan Porter's R&B floor-filler 'Keep On Keeping On'.

Fittingly for a song about what the mind remembers and what it forgets, and whether it really matters either way, Bradfield sang his vocals into a binaural stereo microphone shaped like a head. 'As in a dummy's head. It was Mike's idea. He also wanted me to use it for ["Everything Must Go" B-side] "No One Knows What It's Like To Be Me" and walk around it on gravel. Rubbish. I think he was just taking the piss out of me.' He laughs. 'I didn't know much about De Kooning at all, beyond his name. So I just got stuck into the song.'

Nicky Wire is far from alone in regarding Willem De Kooning's eighties output as inferior to the tempestuous 'action paintings' that made him famous. Others, however, commend the work from his final creative years for its playful vibrancy. 'His talent survived his own wits,' wrote Peter Schjeldahl, *The New Yorker*'s art critic, in 1997. 'After 1980 . . . the consequences for his painting included unprecedented ease and fluency, the death of his famous dissatisfaction and of his compensating wilfulness. He had forgotten to be anxious.'[1] Perhaps the later De Kooning had simply been 'freed from memory', to quote 'Everything Must Go', and did what young Willem once did, just differently. Similarly, these later Manic Street Preachers were different – certainly more easeful and fluent, less anxious – and yet still sounded like no one else but themselves.

51.
Further Away

Recorded: Chateau de la Rouge Motte, France; Abbey
    Road, London
Producer: Mike Hedges
Released: 20 May 1996 (*Everything Must Go*, Epic)

'In a world that's ugly and a lie
It's hard to even want to try.'
                 – Matthew Sweet, 'Sick of Myself'

As heard on the *Everything Must Go* tenth-anniversary edition, the House In The Woods demo of 'Further Away' is striking for two reasons. First, it shows how fully formed the Manics' future direction was even before Richey Edwards's departure. It also illustrates the extent to which Mike Hedges' 'produced trash' aesthetic would impact upon the band's overall sonic mood: the guitars on the finished version are fresh and bright, and on the demo they're saturnine, with a whiff of Stygian grind in the chorus. Whereas Bradfield's brief bridge solo had a rawness at House In The Woods, on the album it's subsumed by the pervasive effervescence, and bedded down by Hammond organ. Although a subtle contrast, it suggests that *Everything Must Go* could readily have transmitted a much gloomier outlook had its tonal palette more closely followed the lyrics' cue.

Certainly, 'Further Away' came from a low point. Having missed his first wedding anniversary in September 1994 because the band were on tour in France supporting Therapy?, Nicky Wire woke up in Italy two months later midway through the second European *Holy Bible* tour in which the band played second fiddle to Suede and discovered that his suitcase had been left outside the bus at the previous night's venue.

'I never got it back,' he says. 'It had all my brilliant *Holy Bible* clothes and my toiletry bag. That was the tipping point for me.' Wire took advantage of a two-day gap in the schedule and flew to London to see a Harley Street specialist about the chronic stomach problems he had been been suffering during both European tours. He was by now refusing to eat anything from tour catering, subsisting instead entirely on personal stocks of Crunchy Nut Cornflakes, which he kept under his bunk on the tour bus, and the occasional McDonald's apple pie. In London, the private doctor incorrectly diagnosed Crohn's disease and advised washing fruit when overseas. Malnourished, homesick and even more freaked out than before, Wire duly rejoined the band deep in their individual private hells – Richey grappling with post-rehab sobriety; James drinking himself in the opposite direction – to play the life-affirming likes of 'Revol' to at best semi-interested Italian audiences awaiting the evening's main attraction. And there were still another three weeks and ten countries to go.

In this context, 'Further Away' poured out, a straightforwardly touching expression of longing to be elsewhere with someone else. 'We'd done so many gigs that year, despite everything, especially from August onwards,' says Wire. 'Bear in mind there weren't any mobile phones, trying to call home from a hotel and it's costing a fortune and never getting hold of anyone . . . I think my brother had come back from America as well, so my mam and dad were constantly having to deal with him – the prodigal son had returned! It's a proper moaning song.'

Although the 'L' word wasn't actually mentioned, 'Further Away' came as close as any Manics song had to contravening one of the original edicts, as itemised on *Snub TV* in 1991, that they would never write a love song. Bradfield immediately raised an eyebrow, and possibly two, when he saw what Wire had written. 'It was a big thing. I was just like, "We don't write lyrics like this."' Yet for a love song, 'Further Away' is unusually selfless, as Wire rues how his loneliness affects others ('The harder it gets for everyone else'), and acutely descriptive of how long-distance communication can actually exacerbate physical absence ('the circular landscape comes back only with regret').

On the finished album, 'Further Away's plangent modesty doesn't immediately command attention, which is possibly why it wasn't released as a single (although it was in Japan, and Radio 1 DJ Jo Whiley loved it, so perhaps it should have been). Yet it's sequenced perfectly amid *Everything Must Go*'s final third, a pool of bittersweet reflection before the record's purging finale, a consummate piece of team connectivity – a piece of home away from home.

'There was a tricky moment post-Richey,' says Bradfield. 'Because, you know, it was about survival. And it was trying to become a different band and different people, without trying too hard. So, it literally was time to be more natural. Playing the ideas and not worrying about your own rules so much. So, a song about wanting to be at home? For a lot of musicians, that's the great part of the job – being away from home. But actually, you should prefer being at home.'

52.

No Surface All Feeling

Recorded: House In The Woods, Surrey; Big Noise
    Recorders, Cardiff
Producer: Dave Eringa
Released: 20 May 1996 (*Everything Must Go*, Epic)

'There's only one corner of the universe you can be
certain of improving, and that's your own self.'

– Aldous Huxley, *Time Must Have A Stop*

The album that heralded a new Manic Street Preachers ended with
a requiem mass for the old. 'What's the point in always looking
back,' wondered 'No Surface All Feeling's key lyric, 'when all you
see is more and more junk?' This acute slap of self-appraisal owed
its brutality for being written amid the *ancien régime*'s unravelling:
on the band's tour bus as they returned home after cancelling
the final three dates of the four-week European tour supporting
Suede in November/December 1994. The crisis point came when
Nicky found Richey outside the hotel in Munich hitting his head
against the wall and repeating the words: 'I want to go home.'

'We used Richey as an excuse,' says Wire, 'but we all had to get
home. It was a fucking terrible tour.' In Montpelier, a week after
his expensive and futile doctor's appointment in London, Wire
sat down with Bradfield and announced that he was seriously
considering leaving the band.

'James is going, "Hmm, yes." Then he went and got smashed
out of his skull and didn't remember the conversation the next
day. I felt, "Oh well, fair enough." The record was dead. Richey
was obviously fucked up out of his mind. Sean had an absolute
nightmare couple of days in Spain, where he nearly died choking

on a piece of bread in a service station and Brian the lighting guy had to do the Heimlich manoeuvre. Then James and Sean nearly died by carbon monoxide poisoning because the generator in the bus had been left on. And then we stopped at these other services and there was a lorry, absolutely rammed full of pigs going to slaughter, which Richey was taking pictures of, doing his Dennis Hopper [as a war photographer] in *Apocalypse Now* thing. That image was very him, in a very grotesque way. Poor Richey. It was an awful tour.'

As their bus headed home, Bradfield remembers pulling a crumpled piece of paper from his pocket and reading Wire's lyric. 'Me and Sean are just sitting there, so I say, "Come on, Sean, you start the verse off, I'll try and finish it". Which when we used to write stuff together was my favourite way of doing things with him. Sean came up with the verse quite quickly.'

As Moore later recalled: 'I wrote it on the tour bus . . . Richey was always trying to get me to teach him "Come As You Are". But in the meantime that song came about. At the time, we were listening to the Smashing Pumpkins. We were big Hüsker Dü fans too – *Candy Apple Grey*, all that.'[1]

It speaks to the group's reflexive work ethic, and quasi-journalistic instincts, that even when torn and frayed their first recourse was to document and create. Playing the basic idea to Wire and Edwards for the first time, Bradfield indicated space for the twinkling guitar riff which would oscillate throughout the intro and the chorus. 'I think Nick got it straight away, he thought it was pure *Siamese Dream* [-period] Smashing Pumpkins, which all of us loved, including Richey. But Richey was a bit reticent about it. Anyway, we just thought, "OK, well that's one nailed down, we could give it a go in the studio."'

The demo version of 'No Surface All Feeling' recorded the following month at House In The Woods came with a jokey acknowledgment of debt: 'Hello,' Bradfield mugs over the opening riff, à la Lennon spoofing Dylan, 'my name is Billy Coogan.' The mood in the studio was upbeat, despite Edwards's indifference to the new material aside from 'Small Black Flowers That Grow In The Sky'. 'He didn't mind "No Surface All Feeling",' says Bradfield. 'But I couldn't believe how good it was sounding. I remember Dave Eringa miking up the drums, and I did the guitar on the house amps, a Vox and a Marshall. Everything just sat perfectly. When we left with that we knew it was a great song.'

'Richey was reachable and happy,' adds Wire. 'I don't know if he *was* happy, but he was buying me the *Daily Telegraph* every morning for the sport and going into town for photocopying. It was the best we'd all got on since we recorded *The Holy Bible*. And the version of "No Surface All Feeling" sounded so great, we ended up using most of it for *Everything Must Go*.'

Bluntly effective as the music's molten quiet/loud scheme was, 'No Surface All Feeling' really hit a nerve with the lyric's sickly pallor – 'Nothing here but the stains on my teeth' – and dread intimations. There's even a Biblical whiff of reckoning and judgement that's oddly suggestive of Nick Cave's 'The Mercy Seat': the last word in the first verse is 'lies', in the last verse it's 'truth', while the final chorus has the admonitory, 'Feel the guilt of a sinner'.

'The "No Surface All Feeling" lyric is a bit of a pre-emptive strike, it does feel like it's talking about the end,' says Wire. 'There was nothing good about those European tours. The only vaguely nice memory I've got is watching a box set of G.B.H.[2] on the bus, when Richey used to stand under the bunks smoking non-stop. I wasn't even giving these lyrics to Richey at this point, we were writing independently.'

Compounding the song's content was the context of its release into the public domain as the finale on an album called *Everything Must Go*: it felt like a retrospective farewell, regardless of the fact that Richey Edwards was still present when it was created. Nicky even described it as a 'tribute' to Richey,[3] rather fuelling the popular misconception that because the House In The Woods demo had been used, Richey must be playing on it. It's difficult now to imagine the album ending with another song, yet that's nearly what happened: for a long time, Bradfield resisted 'No Surface All Feeling's inclusion at all.

'I had a real bug in my head because I didn't think it fitted *Everything Must Go*, I didn't think it fitted the MO of what Mike had done: it was too chunky, a bit *too* Pumpkins. It didn't have the "produced trashiness". And Nick and Sean had a campaign going that it would eventually find its way onto the album.'

Having wrapped up everything with Mike Hedges, the band booked a session in Cardiff at Soundspace, which was by now renamed Big Noise. There they completed 'Mr Carbohydrate' in readiness for its imminent release as the B-side to 'A Design For Life'. At the behest of Moore and Wire, they also had Dave Eringa get to work on 'No Surface All Feeling'. 'We just asked him to tart it up, chop out any bits that had dodgy tuning, and we'd try to put a guitar solo on the end,' says Bradfield. 'Which we did. The main body of recording at House In The Woods was so good that it barely needed anything done to it at all, I just had to re-sing some of it. So the end section is completely done at Soundspace and ninety per cent of the track before the solo at the end is done in House In The Woods. We kept some of the old vocal, most of the old guitar and all of the old drums. And right until the end I didn't think it should go on, and everybody else did. Obviously, I was wrong. It would be a lesser album without it, definitely.'

Ushered in by Sean Moore's stentorian snare battery, the guitar solo coda section is soaked in heavy flange effect, with additional phased delay for heightened discombobulation. The rationale for this was purely pragmatic: because Moore no longer had the snare drum he'd used at House In The Woods and was hitting harder to compensate, it proved impossible to exactly replicate the drum sound of the demo and thereby make a seamless segue from the earlier recording. Covering the new section in sonic swoosh would theoretically persuade the listener that here was a climactic piece of *Sturm und Drang* rather than a botched union of two separate pieces. This minor subterfuge had the unintended consequence of fuelling the rumour that Richey was bashing away somewhere in the midst of it all, because credulous listeners reasonably assumed that the demo must be the messy end part, when in fact it was the more obviously 'produced' main section.

The other oddity that slipped by relatively unnoticed at the time was that Mike Hedges hadn't produced the grand finale of an album which in large measure he had designed. The last act on the Manics' brave new dawn was to acknowledge the weight of the past – with all that entailed for the future.

'There's nothing of Mike on "No Surface" at all,' confirms Nicky. 'And unfortunately, despite the lovely mythology, there's nothing of Richey. He said to me once, he felt "No Surface All Feeling" was "too optimistic" . . . What?! Is that the level we've got to now? "No Surface All Feeling" is dark – because it felt like everything was falling apart.'

53.

Sepia

Recorded: Big Noise Recorders, Cardiff
Producer: Alex Silva
Released: 30 September 1996 ('Kevin Carter' B-side,
    Epic); 14 July 2003 (*Lipstick Traces*, Epic)

'Most of what follows is true.'
    – *Butch Cassidy and the Sundance Kid*; Dir: George Roy Hill

'Sepia' was written and recorded several months after the release of *Everything Must Go*, under what were then novel circumstances for the Manics: writing a B-side for a third single tasked with boosting a hit record's ongoing success instead of kicking life into something that's gone. Perhaps as a result, there's a weightlessness to the song: its spirit feels bright, despite the evident anguish of its protagonist, who admits to being 'perpetually stuck in a sepia film/But bleeding inside I manage to keep it all in.'

The film in question was *Butch Cassidy and the Sundance Kid*, George Roy Hill's comedic yet sombre 1969 western about two Wyoming train robbers who flee to Bolivia, where they enjoy brief notoriety as 'Los Bandidos Yanquis' but are eventually fatally ambushed. Their final exit is freeze-framed, in a slow fade from bloodied colour into sepia. Shortly before that last charge, Butch suggests to Sundance that once out of their current predicament they run away to Australia ('they got thousands of miles we could hide out in'). A sentimental ode to glorious failure, the film's resonance with the Manics had already been established by Bradfield's solo performances of its featured song 'Raindrops Keep Fallin' On My Head' during the Holy Bible tour and its subsequent recording for the War Child charity album. Composer

Burt Bacharach's bleached jazz-lite sophistication is sublimated through 'Sepia' via Bradfield's high-register backing vocals ('my best impersonation of the Fabulous Wealthy Tarts from Paul Young's backing band') and the arrangement's emulation of eighties Liverpool cosmic soul visionaries the Pale Fountains, a band whose early inventory of cover versions featured both Love's 'Maybe The People Would Be The Times' and John Barry's 'We Have All The Time In The World'. With Nick Nasmyth's surging Rhodes piano underlay and the fractal arpeggiated guitar break completing the picture, 'Sepia' revealed a new side to the Manics (further explored on its companion B-side 'Horses Under Starlight', another spruce Bacharach homage recorded at the same session, with Sean Moore's trumpet taking the melodic lead).

'I just loved the title, loved the lyric,' says Bradfield. 'It was kind of a minor chord song. But with a really wistful air to it – I'm channelling a bit of Bob Mould [Hüsker Dü] in the guitar solo. I think we barely played it two or three times in our life, and I remember thinking, "Oh, we can just do something in literally in half an hour. Play something first time, play it a second time. Rehearse it once more then do it in one take." After the forensic nature of writing songs and demoing some of them and going through it all with Mike, it was nice just being free and easy with "Sepia".'

Equally unguarded was the lyric, its recriminatory flashes directed externally ('No you never kissed me, never felt anything for me') but mostly within ('Experience is lost on me . . . I still smile so stupidly . . . I've spoken so much rubbish'). The extent of the narrator's malaise is such that, 'For the first time ever/I don't understand my television'.

'I wonder what that was about!' says Wire. 'I guess that with the TV being such an important pillar of my life, going off it has obviously wrecked me. "Sepia" is a precursor of what's to come lyrically; there's an overhang of disenchantment. And all of a sudden the suppressed pain is leaking out, definitely. So much springs from a title with us, it's one of my great obsessions in life.

As soon as I've got the title, I let everything flow from there. But "Sepia" is a lovely song, a lovely invocation – you can hear the colour in the song.'

54.

If You Tolerate This Your Children Will Be Next

Recorded: Rockfield Studios, Monmouthshire; AIR
    Studios, London
Producer: Dave Eringa
Released: 24 August 1998 (single, Epic); 14 September
    1998 (*This Is My Truth Tell Me Yours*, Epic)

> 'Art is not made to decorate rooms. It is an
> offensive weapon in the defence against the enemy.'
> – Pablo Picasso

Butch and Sundance went out in a blaze of glory. Richey Edwards disappeared into the realm of myth. Meanwhile, over in the real world, Manic Street Preachers kept on living. Which for them essentially meant working. Fifteen months after *Everything Must Go* was released, on 23 August 1997 the Manics headlined Reading Festival for the first time, the culmination of a relentless touring and promotional campaign that had yielded one million album sales, four Top 10 singles, Brit awards for Best Band and Best Album, and the prestigious Ivor Novello Best Contemporary Song Award for 'A Design For Life'. The band were sitting at the top table at last, but with an empty chair – suspended between euphoria, hope and sadness.

Richey had been very much present on *Everything Must Go*. He was at the initial preparatory recording session, and five of the album's songs featured his lyrics. So its successor would be made under very different circumstances: the first Manics record made from a position of commercial strength, and the first with lyrics solely written by Nicky Wire, who realised that an entire album of sepia songs about how much he missed his friend would not necessarily be the most edifying prospect. The Manics knew they needed to find a new story to tell.

Although largely the same core material the band had been plugging for more than a year, the Reading '97 setlist did feature a new song, 'Ready For Drowning', which had been played the previous night at a warm-up gig in Newport Centre alongside James Dean Bradfield's solo acoustic performance of another new song, 'Born A Girl'. One of these would prove emblematic of the next Manic Street Preachers album, the other an anomaly. At this stage the thematic path ahead was yet to reveal itself – but the catalytic event had already happened.

In late 1996, on a rare evening away from the *Everything Must Go* bandwagon, Nicky Wire was 'freezing my bollocks off' on Tredegar mountain at an event to celebrate Aneurin Bevan, the MP for Ebbw Vale and Minister of Health in the post-war Labour government, on the fiftieth anniversary of the National Health Service, which Bevan had been instrumental in creating. The inclement spot was where Bevan used to address public meetings of his constituents in the three surrounding towns, a place now marked by the Aneurin Bevan Commemorative Stones. Nicky and his brother Patrick were straining to hear the vintage recordings of Bevan's speeches crackling through a Tannoy system under siege from the elements, when suddenly one line leapt out at them with perfect clarity. 'He said, "This is my truth, tell me yours,"' says Wire. 'And that just stuck with me. My only night out for the year was spent on a mountain in winter. That made me feel good actually. Because we're incredibly decadent at this point. Bands were making so much money, it was good times. So now I knew I was about to cocoon myself in something incredibly drab – like my version of Morrissey's Manchester.'

Hunkered down in Wattsville, where he was now getting doorstepped by sightseeing fans, and journalists looking for an angle on why a rock star with a platinum record was living in a miner's terraced house, Wire simmered the ingredients for the Manics' next chapter. Thanks to Nye Bevan he already had an album title, to which he added Welsh history books by Gwyn A. Williams and Hywel Francis, and the poetry of R.S. Thomas. The songs began to flow. 'Ready For Drowning' drew on both history and poetry for its invocation of 1965's Tryweryn flooding, where a North Wales village was wiped out to create a reservoir to supply water to English towns. The lyric to 'You Stole The Sun From My Heart', Wire's latest anthem of existential malaise, directly quoted R.S. Thomas. By April 1998, after preliminary sessions at Whitfield Street in London, Big Noise in Cardiff, two sessions with Mike Hedges at Chateau de la Rouge Motte, and sessions with Dave Eringa at Monnow Valley and its more storied neighbour Rockfield in Monmouthshire, the record was approaching completion, albeit with the nagging sense it lacked an all-important vanguard single – the song which would announce this now hugely successful band's much-anticipated return.

Sony's Rob Stringer favoured 'Tsunami', although even with three separate versions on tape there was no consensus that it had been definitively recorded. The other contender was 'You Stole The Sun', which, according to Wire, 'always felt like an amazing single, but an amazing second single. Not a first. So Rob was still pushing us for something.'

'Truth be told,' adds Bradfield, 'if "You Stole The Sun" was gonna be the first single, then we could just hear the *NME* and *Melody Maker* saying, "Well, there's not much of a narrative here." It felt like we needed the Manics song that hadn't been written.'

Whatever that song might sound like, no one thought 'If You Tolerate This Your Children Will Be Next' was it. Wire began the lyric during a January 1998 holiday to Barcelona, where his idea of carefree reading was *Homage to Catalonia*, George Orwell's 1938 account of his experiences fighting for a Marxist militia during the Spanish Civil War. After more than four years of marriage,

239

this was a first trip abroad for Nicky and his wife Rachel.

'We were sitting in Gaudi's park and I actually said, "I gotta go back to the hotel, I've got sunstroke,"' recalls Wire. 'She pissed herself laughing – "It's eight degrees!" I was so paranoid about my health at this point. I didn't eat much, other than cake for breakfast. I found *Homage to Catalonia* hard to read, but I dug in. We'd eaten in a café on the Ramblas where Orwell had been, and outside there was an old bloke playing keep-up with a football and he'd obviously been a good footballer. Everything just came together. As I often do, I wrote it on the hotel stationery. Then I filled it out later on – the line "The future teaches you to be alone, the present to be afraid and cold", that came after. I'm glad it did, because it's my favourite opening line I've ever done.'

As with other lyrics he'd written for the new album, 'If You Tolerate This' revealed Wire applying a conspicuously higher level of craft than before. Every line had a lulling precision, albeit two of the best were co-opted from *Miners Against Fascism*, Hywel Francis's history of the Welsh presence in the International Brigades fighting for the Spanish Republic against General Franco. 'If I can shoot rabbits, then I can shoot fascists,' was the reply given by Tom Thomas, an unemployed miner from the village of Bedlinog, when asked why he had gone to Spain. The song's title, meanwhile, came from a Republican propaganda poster featuring the photograph of a dead girl superimposed on a squadron of Franco's bombers.

But rather than simply celebrating the bravery of the volunteers and the virtue of their cause, the lyric was far more a critique of Wire himself – and, by implication, his audience – for sins of complacency and hypocrisy, pinned with unflinching candour: 'Gravity keeps my head down, or is it maybe shame/At being so young and being so vain'. In essence, this was 'Repeat's 'useless generation' revisited, older and more eloquent but no less spoilt. '"I've walked La Ramblas but not with real intent" was one of the lines written while I was there,' says Wire. 'I was being a political tourist. It did make me think – would my generation fight against fascism? Well, I wouldn't! Overall, I couldn't be happier with the lyric. The best ones I've written up to this point have been less thought out, but on this album they're more considered. I ended up enjoying the process. Because I'm completely on my own. *Everything Must Go* was much easier because there's still Richey there.'

For all the lyric's accomplishment, when Bradfield finally received the finished draft he mentally filed it on the pile of material destined for bonus tracks and B-sides, merely essaying a quick acoustic sketch, which piqued Mike Hedges' interest. 'He was nagging me to let him do it,' says Bradfield. 'But I thought we needed stuff to do with Dave Eringa. I just tossed it off. I didn't actually think it was that brilliant.'

'None of us did,' says Wire. 'The understanding was this was a B-side. We thought the album was done, bar Rob still saying we need a single. It's not like we were looking for an album track.'

As the band set up at length with Eringa at Rockfield's Quadrangle Studio in April 1998 to record this putative B-side, there were grumblings in the ranks. 'Me and Sean, we're both in a bad mood,' says Wire. 'Because it just felt like, "Why are we doing this?"' Moore's humour had not recovered from an incident earlier in the day when he gave Wire a lift to nearby Monmouth in his brand-new Porsche 911. 'I wanted to go to Woolworths,' says Wire. 'On the pavement outside Woolworths were these massive stone pillars, and I opened the door straight into one and put a massive dent in his £90,000 car.' After playing four live takes with Wire locking straight into the tricky rhythm patterns and Bradfield playing the same Gibson J-45 acoustic guitar he'd used to write the tune, Moore simply got up and left. 'We heard his car zooming off,' says Wire.

With the core song laid down to the satisfaction of all present, Bradfield and Eringa spent five hours compiling the best take, which Moore duly approved the next day. As yet unsure what role electric guitar might play, thoughts turned to keyboards and the band's now regular keysman Nick 'Lord' Nasmyth.

'Lord is our Billy Preston,' says Wire. 'We get him in, number one because he's amazing. But also, he does make everyone behave. He's calming. Just such an old chap.'

Beyond a knack for sensing exactly the right moment to make a cup of tea, Nasmyth's presence in tandem with Eringa would be particularly crucial. Bradfield had a grand concept for a sound that would elevate the song. 'I was saying to Lord and Dave, "You know, it's gotta be like a comet that regularly comes back to the Earth, and it's come back from the distant future to see what a mess we've made of everything, and you can feel its fiery disappointment." That's what I wanted. And they went for it.'

The sound, prominent on the intro and in each verse, and which many listeners took to be a treated electric guitar, was in fact the signal from Nasmyth's electric piano being filtered through a chain of Eringa's battered old Korg MS-20, then one of Bradfield's Hyper Fuzz pedals and a Boss digital delay. As Nasmyth played a chord, Eringa turned the knobs 'It was nice to watch, it was pretty organic,' says Bradfield. 'That's when I started thinking, "This has a chance of being on the album". It sounds great. It's got a great title – long, it stands out, it scans, it's great to sing, I'd done a good guide vocal. But suddenly I had that problem where the keyboard player is at the front and the guitarist's got to find a new place to be. I was having to complement the keyboards, like Charlie Burchill does with Mick MacNeil [Simple Minds], or to a lesser degree Ritchie Blackmore with Jon Lord [Deep Purple]. Finding that space around the vocal, because you've got to stay out of the way of the words.'

There's actually no electric guitar on 'Tolerate' until the bridge section, when Bradfield picked up a blue twelve-string Rickenbacker he'd won from Mike Hedges in a bet, and gave lustre to the song's overwhelming disconsolation. Nor are there any real strings, but rather a Solina String Ensemble synth, its retro-futurist chill balanced out by Nasmyth's Hammond. The pastoral tones and modest performances were in marked contrast to *Everything Must Go*'s 'produced trash' ethic, and though no one yet imagined this could be a single, a consensus emerged that the Manics had gifted themselves a viable album track. Consequently, recording Bradfield's final vocals became a higher-stakes endeavour. Wire began obsessing about the enunciation of the 't's in certain words ('bu*t* not with real in*t*en*t*') and technical glitches at Rockfield didn't help. Yet perhaps the most critical factor in the recording's success was Bradfield's realisation that standing up and singing into a fixed microphone through a pop shield would yield too confrontational a performance for a song which was ultimately defined by its sense of dignity, be it in the voice of the anti-fascist Welsh miner or Wire's vision of the old man playing football on La Ramblas. 'I said to Dave, "I just want to feel like I'm a singer." So it's the first time I ever sang with a Shure SM 58 – I just sat down, like a lounge singer, holding this microphone. I loved doing that.'

When Martin Hall and Rob Stringer came to hear a playback, Eringa had only moments earlier finished a monitor mix. 'Rob Stringer was waiting in the living room at Rockfield and they told him they had this magnificent new thing,' Eringa later recalled. 'We had five minutes to do a monitor mix, and just fluked a good one.'

After settling his band's record company boss on the sofa in Rockfield's Quadrangle studio, James Dean Bradfield hit 'play'. Four and a bit minutes later, Stringer turned to Bradfield. 'He said, "*It's fucking amazing*". Quite violently. I was really shocked. A pure *Rock Follies* moment.'

At the eleventh hour, thanks to A&R genius or pure luck, most likely both, Rob Stringer had the flagship single he'd been holding out for. It would still take a painstakingly constructed radio edit, over which Stringer obsessed much more than the band, and a prolonged mix session at AIR studios, where an extra chorus was added, before the job was done, but eventually 'If You Tolerate This Your Children Will Be Next' completed its transition from tossed-off B-side to Number 1 single. 'At the end there was just me, James and Dave in the studio,' says Wire. 'Everything was perfect, ethereal . . . the way all the backing vocals and everything else merged on the long outro, it was gorgeous. So I'm glad we did go that extra mile.'

Given the almighty muscle that Sony was bound to flex on its behalf, whatever song chosen to herald the Manics' follow-up to a triple-platinum album would have been almost predestined to be a hit. Whereas the promotional campaign for *Everything Must Go* was a reaction to success, 'Tolerate' arrived with the machine already revved up and ready to rage. The sci-fi dystopia video, directed by Andrew 'WIZ' Whiston, had a budget of £200,000 (Wire: 'I said to him I wanted it to look like Stanley Kubrick, and he's like, "I will need a bit of money"') and the single became a hit across Europe, in Australia and New Zealand, even Canada.

Yet 'Tolerate' reached way beyond the crude economics of supply and demand. It's a nineties record that sounds like a seventies vision of the future – the sound of a future that never arrived. A lot of credit there goes, mundanely enough, to each component part's restraint, in particular the drums, which are emollient in contrast with the era's prevailing noise. Another reason for its timelessness is the ongoing currency. 'Tolerate' was written to the backdrop of the Kosovo war, while in 2022, the Manics performed the song at a benefit concert for Ukraine.

One measure of a great political song is its appropriation by the other side. In 2009, 'If You Tolerate This Your Children Will Be Next' soundtracked a diatribe against multiculturalism posted on the website of the far-right British National Party, who presumably didn't listen to the bit about shooting fascists. This only happens when art embeds in the cultural fabric, as per Bruce Springsteen's 'Born In The USA' and Neil Young's 'Rockin' In The Free World', in part because of a certain ambiguity beneath the banner slogans. 'Tolerate' was inspired by a famous episode of heroic failure, but it's equally about the moral and emotional conflicts that everyone faces. Sometimes we are all that old man on La Ramblas playing with memories of the past. And if history teaches us anything, it is that the same questions keep recurring, rarely with any easy answers.

55.
Prologue To History

Recorded: Whitfield Street, London
Producers: Howard Gray and Dave Eringa
Released: 24 August 1998 ('If You Tolerate This Your
    Children Will Be Next' B-side, Epic); 14 July 2003
    (*Lipstick Traces*, Epic); 7 December 2018 (*This Is My
    Truth Tell Me Yours* (20 Years Collectors' Edition), Epic)

'Politics is the art of the possible, the attainable –
the art of the next best.'

– Otto von Bismarck

In a life of public service spanning six decades, Neil Kinnock has
been a member of parliament, the leader of the Labour Party,
a vice-president of the European Commission, and latterly a
member of the House of Lords as Baron Kinnock of Bedwellty.
He also helped inspire the greatest Manic Street Preachers song
most people have never heard.

Kinnock shared bonds of class and geography with the Manics.
Born in Tredegar, the son of a miner, from 1983 he was MP for
Islwyn, the constituency containing Blackwood and its adjacent
communities. His constituency house was on Sir Ivor's Road in
Pontllanfraith, four doors up from the Bradfield family, whose
youngest member he would warmly greet as 'Jimmy'. 'He was a
really nice man,' says James. 'I liked him. He always remembered
my dad's name – which is always a benchmark, isn't it? But not
all of Wales was in love with him.'

The young Nicky Wire met Kinnock during a school trip to
the House of Commons, and left frustrated at the Labour leader's
equivocal response to Wire's question about banning fox-hunting.

But it was the miners' strike of 1984–5 that strained Kinnock's relationship with Wales. Kinnock supported the strike and the miners: along with his wife Glenys, he sent regular secret donations to Dot Phillips at the Newbridge Women's Support Group, as well as another local group and to various individuals. Yet as Labour leader he felt unable to officially endorse the strike so long as NUM leader Arthur Scargill refused to hold a national ballot. As an industrial dispute became a quasi-civil war, with government-directed brigades of riot police battling strikers, Kinnock was stuck in the middle, assailed by ideological foes on the left as well as the right. The issue drained him of authority and energy, and although he successfully faced down the Trotskyite Militant faction in his own party, defeat to Margaret Thatcher in the 1987 general election appeared to puncture his natural good cheer and oratorical vigour. Throughout his tenure as leader of the opposition he was personally abused by the Tory press, which mocked his speeches' alliterative rhythms, dubbing him the 'Welsh Windbag'; on the eve of 1992's general election defeat, the *Sun* stuck Kinnock's face in a lightbulb with the wraparound headline: 'If Kinnock wins today will the last person to leave Britain please turn out the lights'.

Kinnock's treatment by Fleet Street was strikingly similar to the UK music press's contemporaneous lampooning of the Manics in search of a cheap laugh or a punning headline. Because Kinnock had never held ministerial office during Labour's previous spell in government, a presumption grew that his career was based on nothing but a stereotypically Welsh gift of the gab. The Manics were likewise condescended to for being better at interviews than they were at music. Far from evincing a spirit of Welsh kinship, however, during this period the band rarely mentioned their nationality, and Richey Edwards in particular seemed to despise Kinnock. 'He's such a tosser,' he said of his MP in 1991. 'Party politics always seemed irrelevant to us.'[1] In early 1994, his opinion had hardened. 'The Labour Party are the biggest bunch of cunts on the planet. They're selling everybody out, including themselves . . . [Kinnock's successor] John Smith is a coward and a fraud, and deserves execution . . . Neil Kinnock wasn't any better.'[2] As Nicky Wire subsequently noted in a *Melody Maker* interview with Simon Price conducted near the end of 1996, 'Richey was really paranoid about ever coming across as Welsh. He always called it "the Neil Kinnock Factor". I've become more conscious of it lately.'[3]

Written and recorded during the summer of 1997, when Britpop's imperial phase coincided with the Tony Blair-rebranded 'New' Labour Party's general election landslide, 'Prologue To History' opened with the line, 'Were we the Kinnock factor?', an oblique comment on the Manics' perceived footnote status in the nineties cultural timeline. 'The chips were on my shoulder at this point,' Wire says. 'Undoubtedly, Tony Blair would never have won without Neil Kinnock doing all the donkey work to make Labour electable. He was probably the one leader of an opposition that faced more crises than the prime minister at the time. Crisis of conscience, of situation, thinking, "How can I ever win?" And especially on his last election campaign, people from Peter Mandelson downwards were starting to grow under him, whatever you think about that. Personally, I think principles without power don't mean anything. And I kind of felt we were a bit like that – in 1992, we were completely out of time, with baggy and grunge. We were fighting a corner that didn't exist, which then did exist. So that's what I meant by "the Kinnock factor".'

Disgruntlement with the triumphalist Britpop consensus was so ingrained that Wire fused it with his watching a documentary about the Highland Clearances to create another of 'Prologue's zinging couplets: 'Remember ethnic cleansing in the Highlands/No one says a thing in the middle of England', pronounced 'In-ger-land' in the style familiar to all lad-mag-reading *Parklife*-guzzling fans of 'the footy'.

While the *Melody Maker* interview had revealed creative uncertainty and inertia following *Everything Must Go*'s success, this
song's psychological heat map of Nicky Wire suggested a breakthrough, even as it laid bare his conflicted internal dialogue over
whether to embrace his new status, or retreat: 'Do I think I'm
Shaun William Ryder/Or my former friend who's now under-
cover'. As well as the Happy Mondays frontman and Richey, the
lyric went on to cite Britain's maverick middle-distance runner
Steve Ovett – the Soviet vest-wearing rival of future Tory MP
Sebastian Coe – and the quicksilver seventies Wales rugby icon
Phil Bennett. These nostalgic TV sporting heroes mingled with the
domestic neuroses of our old friend 'Mr Carbohydrate', bullishly
fronting-out those who might accuse him of bourgeois tendencies ('So I water my plants with Evian/A brand new Dyson, that
is decadent'; the subsequently released 'Live Rehearsal Demo'
reveals that 'Dyson' was originally the rather less decadent
'Hoover'). Lest anyone query his logic, Wire remembered to insert
the ultimate disclaimer: 'I'm talking rubbish, to cover up the
cracks/An empty vessel who can't make contact'.

When he received the lyric, Bradfield's mind suddenly flashed
back to late-seventies US TV drama *Lou Grant*, starring Ed Asner
as the editor of the fictional *Los Angeles Tribune*. 'I used to love
watching that with my mum,' he says. 'The lyric just felt like a
newsroom to me. I had the image of the opening sequence to
Lou Grant in my head.'

In an instance of musical free association from the lyric, 'Shaun
William Ryder' inspired the pumped-up Italo house piano motif
which drives the song (there might also be a trace of 'Touch Me'
by The Doors). Indeed, producer Howard Gray actually suggested
the band warm up by jamming Happy Mondays' 'Step On', not
realising the Manics were, in Wire's words, 'the least jammy band
of all time. We did try it, and it collapsed after a minute. But the
song was fully formed anyway, he was just trying to add loops
and stuff.'

The leader of electro-rock band and remix crew Apollo 440, Howard Gray's lengthy recording CV had favourable MSP points of contact – producer of the first Pale Fountains album, engineer on Simple Minds' *Sparkle In The Rain*, sessions with Richard Jobson and John McGeoch's mid-eighties group The Armoury Show – and his approach yielded powerful results. 'He got a good percussion backing track and a good bass performance, he really got Nick rumbling,' says Bradfield.

'I love the way James spits out "Shaun William Ryder" – some of the vocals are rhythmically very important,' Wire adds. 'It's our amped-up version of the Mondays but much more disciplined and tight. Lord really hurt his hands playing that piano. I always wanted to get "epilogue" or "prologue" into a title. So I was really pleased with that.'[4]

The first song from the *This Is My Truth* era to be recorded, 'Prologue To History' was set aside as an anomaly when work on the album proper began, revisited only when Dave Eringa rode in on his white horse during the final mixing session at Abbey Road. 'It all became apparent then,' says Bradfield. 'The mix was pretty awful by the time we left the studio with Howard. It was obviously a good recording, but we'd managed to hide the fact that it was a good recording. I can remember Rob saying, "So close . . ." I didn't know whether he meant it could have been on the album or a single. It should have been on there. Didn't need to not be on there. And it's interesting, because we probably could have had a good relationship with Howard if we had done more tracks with him and just got a better understanding.'

This Is My Truth went to Number 1, so omitting 'Prologue To History' had little obvious material impact. Yet the album could have comfortably handled the song's vital spark, particularly during a congealed final third. Tellingly, when the time came for a twentieth-anniversary reissue, 'Prologue' was finally instated at the expense of the original penultimate track 'Nobody Loved You', an eleventh-hour Richey tribute that felt like a third-generation retread of 'No Surface All Feeling'. '"Nobody Loved You" shouldn't have been on there,' says Wire. 'I don't know why it was, apart from sentimentality. Not having "Prologue To History" on the album is one of the worst decisions we ever made.'

The Kinnock Factor continues to manifest at the unlikeliest moments. Some years ago, James Dean Bradfield and his wife were viewing new houses in Chiswick. Entering one, they were almost immediately confronted by the infamous 9 April 1992 'Turn Out The Lights' front cover of the *Sun*. Potential future home or not, that was enough for James.

'It was in the hallway, framed, proudly,' he says. 'I was like, "We're not seeing another fucking room in this house." I couldn't have lived with the ghosts.'

56.

The Everlasting

Recorded: Chateau de la Rouge Motte, France; Abbey
   Road, London
Producer: Mike Hedges
Released: 14 September 1998 (*This Is My Truth Tell Me
   Yours*, Epic); 30 November 1998 (single, Epic)

'My life's a masquerade.'
                    – The Isley Brothers, 'Behind A Painted Smile'

As the opening track on what would be Manic Street Preachers'
first Number 1 album, 'The Everlasting' is perfectly cast: the
moment of walking through an open door, beyond which nothing will ever be the same, and taking one last look back before
bowing to the inevitable forward motion of time and events. It's
a conversation of two selves caught between nostalgia for youth
('In the beginning, when we were winning') and a sense that the
good old days weren't actually all that ('Pathetic acts for a worthless cause'). The music, exquisitely played and beautifully sung,
frames this dialectic between a morning-dew acoustic reveille
and a sunset elegy for strings, projecting an overwhelming celebratory sadness.

   Hitherto, Manic Street Preachers albums had begun with a fanfare ('Sleepflower'; 'Elvis Impersonator') or an exhortation ('Slash
'N' Burn'; 'Yes'). From the introductory taps of a vintage Mini
Pops 35 drum machine, 'The Everlasting's downbeat mapping of
life's grey areas was possibly not what its audience was hoping
for or expecting, especially from a record titled after a speech by
a firebrand Welsh working-class hero.

   'When James first played it to me I was blown away,' says

Nicky. 'It was a lot perkier, it had such an acoustic flow, I thought it was amazing, this cascade of chords folding into each other. A bit of that got lost for the sake of grandeur in the final version. The sedateness went too far. It's probably the first time lyrically where we're referencing the "glory days", so to speak. Maybe we were missing them. Fifth album kicks in, domesticity kicks in, and you slow down.'

The chorus ruefully contrasted this new reality with the band's younger selves, 'when our smiles were genuine' – an update on The Smiths' 'We may be hidden by rags but we have something they'll never have'. At least 'Motorcycle Emptiness' had offered promise in negation's 'everlasting nothingness'. Here, successful yet bereft, the 'unforgiven' faced only 'the everlasting', ebbing away on the tick of an antique drum machine.

'Mike Hedges had massive hopes for "The Everlasting",' says Bradfield. 'He thought it was "the one". And we probably recorded it too slow. Just two BPM sometimes makes all the difference, the notes smash together a bit more, you'd get nice echoes and it gives a bit of magic. The drums are lovely, the orchestration's lovely, the gated guitar is kind of the right move, but it's just a little bit ponderous. Whereas [The Verve's] "The Drugs Don't Work" doesn't need the speed, it just has its own grace. "The Everlasting" doesn't quite have its own grace.'

Bradfield had Hedges to thank for his guitar solo, the first of several immaculately languid Floydian cameos on the record. 'I had this Telecaster custom, called my "bones guitar" [after the sticker his mother sent him as a gift from the family dog], and it just wouldn't work. Three hours of trying to form some kind of solo and nothing was coming. Mike was like, "Why are you fucking around with that guitar, get Faithful out" – which was my Les Paul – and the shape of it came in one take. He was like, "Yayyyy! See? Listen to the producer."'

It's a song the band have fallen out and then back in love with. For a while, Wire so hated the lyric 'The world is full of refugees, just like you and just like me' that he stopped Bradfield from singing it – 'It's like Phil Collins from "Another Day In Paradise",' he laughs – while Bradfield remembers being startled by the same lines, albeit for a different reason. 'Nick had recently been referencing what he saw in the mirror. So, reaching out to the audience felt strange. It is an album called *This Is My Truth Tell Me Yours* – I shouldn't have been that shocked.'

57.

You Stole The Sun From My Heart

Recorded: Chateau de la Rouge Motte, France; Abbey
   Road, London
Producer: Mike Hedges
Released: 14 September 1998 (*This Is My Truth Tell Me
   Yours*, Epic); 8 March 1999 (single, Epic)

'Just like Pagliacci did, I try to keep my sadness hid.'
   – Smokey Robinson & The Miracles, 'Tears Of A Clown'

How odd that a lyric scribbled by Nicky Wire on 'a shitty piece
of paper' during a long flight, the gist being 'I don't care if
the plane goes down', should join the likes of The La's' 'There
She Goes' and The Stranglers' 'Golden Brown' in the direc-
tory of inappropriate wedding playlist hits. Or indeed, that a
song citing R.S. Thomas, the misanthropic grey eminence of
modern Welsh poetry, would become the party-hearty occasion during a Manics gig for James Dean Bradfield to summon
his inner Jim Kerr and whip up a mass clap-along. 'That
line at the end, "I've got to stop smiling, it leaves the wrong
impression" – I always feel it's funny when people sing along
to that,' Bradfield says. 'Why do people empathise with that
so much?'

Well, we've all been there. Grinning and bearing whatever
'it' may be is a universal trait. And almost uniquely on *This Is
My Truth*, 'You Stole The Sun From My Heart' is a place of easy
catharsis, offering straightforward access to the album's recurring
themes of dislocation and ennui, which needed neither decoding,

nor prior knowledge of its author losing the plot mid-tour, to enjoy its escapist thunder.

'The initial lyric was really dark,' says Wire. 'And yet it's such a euphoric song. "I love you all the same" – there was always the sense that I'm gonna get on with things, I'm not going to retreat into a total abyss. That's why, when I got home, I added the "no truce with my fury" line, to show the light was still in me.' Wire's adaptation of a line from the R.S. Thomas poem 'Reflections' was a more positive spin on the original's scenario of co-existence with one's demons as the least bad option. Likewise, Bradfield's route to musical inspiration pointed him towards the warm spot in a cold climate: 'Who Loves The Sun' by The Velvet Underground, an incongruously happy heartbreak song about hating the sun.

'A sweet incantation to let misery roll over you – like, I don't care that the world's gonna end, fuck it, I'm gonna have a good day. So that's the feel I took. We were rehearsing it in the downstairs room in Big Noise Recorders and initially it was in D. Then I changed the chords, and kept the breezy feel, but it was a bit jangly, too wishy washy for me, so I toughened it up.'

The rehearsal demo released on *This Is My Truth*'s twentieth-anniversary edition reveals the band reflexively tweaking the verses' initial Velvets angle nearer to McCarthy's 'Red Sleeping Beauty', an appealing contrast with the chorus's power chordage. But the efficacy of Bradfield's stylistic shift became apparent during the sessions at Chateau de la Rouge Motte. A sample of the studio's pinball machine – a 1986 Gottlieb Genesis, it lived in Mike Hedges' greenhouse; Bradfield eventually beat the previous top score set by the band Travis – through an Akai XR10 drum machine formed a mechanical accompaniment for Sean Moore in the style of New Order's Stephen Morris, while slightly slowing the verse tempo yielded added grit. When it came to the chorus and its riotous invocation, however, nothing could beat the drums and guitars recorded at Big Noise. 'Mike Hedges just found eight or ten bars of drums and tightened them up,' says Bradfield. 'And I added some guitar, using my vintage Tube Screamer pedal. Worth about a thousand quid then and it got stolen on the road . . . Again, Nick Nasmyth's glorious mid-sixties Rhodes is really important. And Ian Grimble mixed it – as with "A Design For Life", we're thinking it's not getting there, then suddenly he just turned one guitar up in the chorus and it exploded.'

A Top 5 hit single, and still liable to randomly appear on radio, 'You Stole The Sun From My Heart' has been maligned down the years by some truculent elements of the band's fan community, who don't seem to jive with its solid gold easy action, or possibly the fact that Nicky Wire plays just one note throughout the entirety of the first verse (Wire: 'Happy days!'). There have been times too when it felt like the band appeared resentful of keeping it around, as one might an embarrassing but benevolent relative.

'We're not the sort of band who can say "fuck off",' says Wire, possibly ironically. 'I mean, it's become a bit of an irritant. But when the crowd loves a song that much it's pretty much impossible not to play it. You can't deny its force.'

Arguably the song's most undeniable element, given how often it's repeated, is the title. It derived from Wire's occasional technique of writing down favourite titles by other artists and then repurposing them to inspire a new design, in this case two songs which together contain the polarities of human emotion: 'You Shook Me All Night Long' by AC/DC and Nirvana's 'Heart-Shaped Box'.

'I didn't know that,' laughs Bradfield. 'Between the VU and AC/DC and Nirvana, we got there!'

58.
Ready For Drowning

Recorded: Chateau de la Rouge Motte, France; Abbey
    Road, London
Producer: Mike Hedges
Released: 14 September 1998 (*This Is My Truth Tell Me
    Yours*, Epic)

> 'Where can I go, then, from the smell
> of decay, from the putrefying of a dead
> Nation?'
>
> – R.S. Thomas, 'Reservoirs'

In Wales, the words 'Remember Tryweryn' carry much political, cultural and emotional weight. The 1965 flooding of Capel Celyn, a small village in the Tryweryn valley of north-west Wales, to create a reservoir to provide water for Liverpool and the Wirral, became symbolic of Wales's impotence under England's dominion. Mandated by an act of parliament in 1962 despite the opposition of all but one Welsh MP, the drowning led to direct action by campaigners for the Welsh language – the slogan *Cofiwch Dryweryn* ('Remember Tryweryn')[1] was originally painted on a wall near Aberystwyth by Meic Stephens, a young journalist and teacher, in the early sixties. This gave new impetus to the Welsh nationalist movement, with ultimately far-reaching consequences for everyone in Wales.

In the rest of the UK, however, the event was obscure. It would take until 2005 before Liverpool City Council issued an official apology for flooding the valley. Even in Wales, Tryweryn had been sliding into the margins of history books for some time, particularly in the anglophone south. Beyond the typically brutal

R.S. Thomas poem 'Reservoirs', or folk singer Meic Stevens's song 'Tryweryn', both from 1968, the scandal of Capel Celyn was barely registering on the cultural radar in 1997, when Nicky Wire handed James Dean Bradfield a lyric titled 'Ready For Drowning'.

'I knew about Tryweryn,' says Bradfield. 'Though not so much from schools. You knew of the gripes about how people from Liverpool were "no friends of ours" and all that kind of stuff. But people were much more aware of it in Gwynedd, in North Wales.'

What impressed Bradfield most about the lyric was its sublimation of both Tryweryn and the Manics' own traumatic loss into a broader canvas of the Welsh psyche. 'It felt spooky,' he says, 'all the echoes of what people were saying about "that boy that you knew". I felt a bit of pressure. There's a chord shape in the verse, going from C minor sharp into C major, which is the same as "Australia". I did it by accident, but it worked, it didn't sound like "Australia". Nick was saying it was a bit like Oasis in the chorus, but that didn't bother me, because I was listening to *Meddle* by Pink Floyd, and Badfinger, so much at this point, and was obsessed with getting that brown sound on the drums, big and spacious, that upfront earthiness. I knew that would take it somewhere else.'

The foundation of the first verse was, as its opening line says, 'a true story': on 21 February 1995, three weeks after Richey Edwards's disappearance, Nicky was the captive audience for a taxi driver chatting about the cover story of that day's *South Wales Argus* – headline: 'ROCK STAR IN BRIDGE PLUNGE?', next to pictures of the Severn Bridge and Richey circa 1992 – oblivious to his passenger's identity. In the space of two lines, the mood shifts from conversational to pitiful ('Drown that poor thing, put it out of its misery') and thence bitterly apocalyptic: 'Condemn it to its future, deny its history'. The chorus balanced the verses' woebegone mood with a refusal to submit to the dying of the light: 'we are *not* ready for drowning'.

'It's not like as a band we were up against it at this point,' says

Wire, 'but I was living in my lovely old colliery terraced house right up in the Valleys, and I kept getting doorstepped more and more. I wouldn't say I felt under siege, but if my dad had been there he would have fucking chucked a bucket of water and then hit them with a shovel. I wish I was capable of his physical rage, this sudden volcanic Welsh rage, which Richard Burton had always talked about, and Anthony Hopkins, this mixture of self-destruction and bitterness and hate. I thought, "Oh – that's me. Let's try and do it more poetically." Like R.S. Thomas would do. There's a particular poem of his called "Reservoirs", which is symbolically about Tryweryn, and it really brought it home. The sickness in the soul. When James first played this to me, I thought it was amazing.'

With R.S. Thomas a spirit guide through this austere terrain, Wire effectively transmuted his inner fury into the hurt of a nation, then heard his friends deliver music that summoned the requisite depth. From the opening sonar pings – a hat-tip to 'Echoes' from *Meddle* – plus Nick Nasmyth's vintage Rhodes and Bradfield's flickering Omnichord, through verse two's citing the nineteenth-century Welsh migration to Patagonia and 'dusting the past off my mind', right to the final line's Stevie Smith tremor ('We are not waving we're drowning'), this is one of the greatest Manics creations, holding an entire universe within its modest yet immaculate design. Sensitive to the chapel aura, Bradfield essays more of a digression than a guitar solo per se, then steps back as a sample of Richard Burton in 1978 supernatural thriller *The Medusa Touch* ('I will bring the whole edifice down on their unworthy heads') chills the song to its bones.

'When we flowed Dicko's voice in, I was a bit spooked out,' says James. 'It was February at Chateau de la Rouge Motte, everything was dark and damp and cold, there was always soup in the kitchen, rotten apples still in the vineyard, everything was a bit J.B. Priestley. When there's snow around, it always feels like good things happen.'

One of 'Ready For Drowning's most notable performances came when James Dean Bradfield paired up with John Cale for *Beautiful Mistake*, a 2000 film by Marc Evans, the premise of which had The Velvet Underground's co-founder returning to South Wales and collaborating with the 'Cool Cymru' generation of musicians, Gorky's Zygotic Mynci, Catatonia, Super Furry Animals et al. The session began inauspiciously: Bradfield arrived at the studio working a coffee and cigarette combo, whereupon the reformed drug monster Cale demanded, 'Get that away from me.' Soon, however, Bradfield found a way through the great man's defences.

'I wore him down with my minutiae of detailed knowledge,' he laughs. 'The first thing he said was, "This song is very special. The words and music are very special." I was like, wow, that's nice, coming from him. "Where did you get the idea of this chord from?" I said, "It just kind of came to me." He said, "It can't all be about ability, can it?" So that made me laugh and it broke the ice. The fact that he was so complimentary was really cool. He got the reference to Tryweryn, he loved "Drown that poor thing, put it out of its misery" – that's his kind of line!'

The film shows Cale on piano accompanying Bradfield on acoustic guitar, delicate vocals, and whistling. During the middle-eight, the erstwhile dark lord of the New York avant-garde offers his own sotto voce commentary, in Welsh, on the flooding of Capel Celyn. It's a worthy addition to a song which, perhaps better than any other in the Manics' canon, carries the burden of history with its own special grace.

59.

Tsunami

Recorded: Chateau de la Rouge Motte, France; Abbey
    Road, London
Producer: Mike Hedges
Released: 14 September 1998 (*This Is My Truth Tell Me
    Yours*, Epic); 5 July 1999 (single, Epic)

'We tell ourselves stories in order to live.'
                                  – Joan Didion, *The White Album*

Although its subjects were Welsh, and thereby somewhat congruent to *This Is My Truth*'s wider scheme, in other respects 'Tsunami'
was thematically closer to *The Holy Bible*. Its lyric gave voice to the
disturbing, tragic story of June and Jennifer Gibbons, the so-called
'Silent Twins' from West Wales who for many years spoke only
to each other in a private language, and in 1982 were detained
indefinitely at Broadmoor high-security psychiatric hospital for a
series of minor arson attacks. At Broadmoor their fellow inmates
included East End gangster Ronnie Kray – who introduced himself to the girls at lunchtime one day – and serial killer Peter
Sutcliffe AKA the Yorkshire Ripper, while now-notorious BBC
presenter and hiding-in-plain-sight sexual predator Jimmy Savile
was a regular visitor. Jennifer died on 9 March 1993, the day of
the twins' transfer from Broadmoor to a less prohibitive clinic in
Bridgend; shortly afterwards, June declared that her sister had
given up living so she could be free, and said she felt 'a sweet
release', a washing away of sins – a tsunami.

'I feel conflicted about the lyric now,' says Wire. 'It feels slightly
voyeuristic. I was trying to write about someone else – well, two
human beings – on a more personal level than, say, an artist. I'd

seen a TV documentary and I'd read the book about the Silent Twins,[1] so it had been percolating for quite a while. Apparently there were discos at Broadmoor – hence, "Disco dancing with the rapists/Your only crime is silence". It was an empathetic lyric.'

Well intentioned it may have been, but the saga of its recording does rather suggest 'Tsunami' was cursed. Three versions were recorded at the chateau: the first, 'punchy and crunchy', Rob Stringer didn't like. The second slowed down the verse and upped the spooky atmospherics, which the band hated (Wire: 'It sounded like [U2's] "With Or Without You", fucking awful'). And the third upped the tempo of the second but was still slower than the first, and became the final released version, albeit only after some additional augmentation at Abbey Road from a Sally Herbert string arrangement and a sitar part by Craig Pruess (Bradfield also played sitar guitar, inspired by the Box Tops' 'Cry Like A Baby'). Ironically, none of the three succeeded in capturing what Wire calls 'the special magic' of the initial demo at Big Noise. 'It was brilliant,' agrees James. 'Again, my literal mind was thinking, "If it's a tsunami the chorus has got to be *whoosh*, it's gotta come as a wave. . ." And the first version had that. It felt like it had a bit of The Police in there, because of the guitar arpeggio. It had a real rush.'

Once in France, however, the Big Noise demo's guitar arpeggio was replaced by a guzheng, a Chinese zither, which Nick Nasmyth learnt how to play, albeit with much difficulty. In the end everyone settled for a sample, and the die was cast. As if to compensate for its transgressive subject matter, 'Tsunami' became slower, more stolid, more tasteful . . . and lost its edge. Subsequently released on the 2018 twentieth-anniversary edition, the first chateau version offers a tantalising glimpse of what might have been. 'A good team effort,' says Bradfield, 'but it never quite recovered.'

60.

My Little Empire

Recorded: Monnow Valley, Monmouthshire
Producer: Dave Eringa
Released: 14 September 1998 (*This Is My Truth Tell Me Yours*, Epic)

'Nothing, like something, happens anywhere.'
        – Philip Larkin, 'I Remember, I Remember'

Whereas 'Tsunami's early spark was snuffed out by overembellishment, 'My Little Empire' demonstrates the value of restraint. After opening with a creepy-crawl Fender Jazzmaster riff, the critical arrangement decision was to selectively deploy Bradfield's guitar thereafter as a respondent to his vocal. Meanwhile, a single cello sombrely underpinned the sound as Moore's drums tripped and rolled to the rhythms of a troubled mind. This was the bleak, dark side of 'Mr Carbohydrate's hermetic bliss – 'My little empire is as good as it can get', 'All of my sins are attempts to fill the voids' – with Nicky Wire himself duetting ghostly throughout and even occasionally murmuring solo ('happy being sad'), his first proper co-vocal.

'It's about the suffocating beauty of small things,' says Wire. 'There are quite a few health songs on this album, and this is one. The post-Gilbert's malaise. I'd never say I was "addicted" to painkillers but I was taking eight to ten a day Nurofen or paracetamol on tour, suffering really bad headaches and the occasional migraine. And I didn't feel like that when I was at home. So I wanted to make this really deeply personal. There's actually a foreboding ferocity to the song but it never comes out – it's constantly constrained.'

Bradfield has credited John Frusciante for inspiring the guitar riff, although its unusual character is specific to himself and what he terms a 'mad tuning': D up to F, and B and G down to A and E. 'No one's ever used it before or since,' he says. 'No one. I made it up myself. Not even Thurston Moore [Sonic Youth] has played this tuning! I just love this song. As soon as the sounds were right it felt brilliant.'

To honour its narrative voice, Bradfield determined 'My Little Empire' had to feel 'small, closed down'. Which presented a problem, because the session was in Monnow Valley, where Oasis first attempted to record *Definitely Maybe*, a huge room which did not naturally lend itself to 'small'. Enter Dave Eringa wearing his Mr Fixit hat, who built what Bradfield describes as 'a Bedouin tent' around Sean Moore's drum kit to soak up the sound. 'It looked like the mountain in *Close Encounters of the Third Kind*,' says James, 'this massive shape of carpets, towels, towels and more towels. You'd walk in and think, "If this collapses it's gonna kill Mooro." But it was the deadest, this really beautiful dead drum sound. We played it and played it, and it felt so delicate.'

The album's emotional centre, 'My Little Empire's debt to *In Utero*-era Nirvana is quite evident, both from the cello and several lyrical genuflections: 'dumb', 'royalty' and that closing 'happy being sad' incantation. 'I remember Gruff from Super Furries in a radio interview,' says Wire, 'you could tell he was a bit bamboozled by *This Is My Truth*, but he said, "I loved the Nirvana MTV Unplugged vibe to 'My Little Empire'".'

'Which is,' chuckles Bradfield, 'the mark of somebody nice enough to make the effort to find one song they like!'

61.

I'm Not Working

Recorded: Chateau de la Rouge Motte, France; Abbey
    Road, London
Producer: Mike Hedges
Released: 14 September 1998 (*This Is My Truth Tell Me
    Yours*, Epic)

'These things go down!'
> – Jonathan Mardukas in *Midnight Run*; Dir: Martin Brest

What began as a fairly routine articulation of aviophobia – 'It's not much of a lyric,' is Wire's assessment – grew into a near-six-minute slow silent scream, thanks to the obsessive instincts of band and producer. Bradfield's reaction on reading the parodically grim opening line – 'Petrified for the millionth time/Slowly my soul evaporates' – was to respond in kind. 'I thought, "If he's gonna write himself into invisibility, I'm gonna grind this sickness into the fucking dust." So it started out really laboriously, almost like a ghost carrying a soaking wet quilt across a field – a tiny bit "have that, fucker". Quite bloody-minded. But then it started feeling like something good was coming through all that.'

To accompany drums recorded at Big Noise during a 'messing about' session with engineer Greg Haver, Bradfield leant into an agonisingly bleak riff on his sitar guitar, like Tony Iommi covering the Cocteau Twins. With Mike Hedges enthusiastically signed up to the task of lending concrete reality to Wire's existential brace position, the song took on mantric properties. Three days passed as the producer became fixated with a looped noise vaguely suggestive of a small mammal stretching.

'Mike freely admits partaking of the eighties hedonistic lifestyle,' says Bradfield. 'Look at the bands he worked with – Associates, Banshees, he was doing live sound for The Cure . . . You'd walk in and three days he's been working on the track, with this loop going "*nnneeeupp*", and he was just giggling. He said: "It's giving me flashbacks . . . we should go to the pub."'

'It became a running joke,' adds Wire. 'We'd come into the studio each day and he'd just be there listening to the same thing. I didn't play bass on this song, because there's no notes.'

The weird loop became both the opening and closing fades. To embroider the main riff's psychedelic vortex, Nick Nasmyth played a Chinese hammered dulcimer – the yangqin – while Bradfield added Omnichord. The curious whistling noise that occurs just after four minutes is him detuning the sympathetic resonator strings on the sitar guitar. 'And then it just hangs,' says Wire, still bewildered, more than twenty-five years later. 'Literally nothing there apart from the drums.'

An oddity in the Manics' canon, and all the more remarkable for that, 'I'm Not Working' was never performed live until 2019's *This Is My Truth* anniversary tour, where its viscous realisation of 'this fucking space' achieved a certain nobility. 'I enjoyed it more then,' says Wire. 'When we actually played it as a band, it became a more definite thing.'

62.

Black Dog On My Shoulder

Recorded: Chateau de la Rouge Motte, France; Abbey
   Road, London
Producer: Mike Hedges
Released: 14 September 1998 (*This Is My Truth Tell Me
   Yours*, Epic)

'He finds his heaven spewing from the mouth of hell.'
   – Ozzy Osbourne, 'Bark At The Moon'

Featuring possibly the finest string arrangement on any Manics
recording, 'Black Dog On My Shoulder' is a worthy addition to
the lineage of incongruously jaunty songs about depression. It's
also the second Manics song to cite Winston Churchill, following
'The Intense Humming Of Evil'. In stark contrast to that Richey
Edwards lyric, which equated Churchill's treatment of striking
Welsh miners to the Holocaust, Nicky Wire's 'My dilemma but
not my choice/Winston Churchill can you hear my voice' was an
expression of empathy to a fellow human. Churchill referred to
the draining, despondent mood that periodically beset him as the
'black dog', and 'Black Dog On My Shoulder' describes a series of
debilitating physical and psychological symptoms: 'I am numb/My
mouth is so dry . . . Melodrama there in my kitchen sink/Double
vision the way it is'. But just as both historians and mental health
experts debate the clinical nature, if any, of Churchill's depression,
so Wire queries the applicability of the 'd' word in his case.

'There is a celebration of depression going on in this song,'
he says. 'But "depression" is a blanket term, and I don't know
if it's too much. I sometimes think hatred can poison the mind.
I have periods when I just feel really ill – my mum and dad

always called me a sickly boy. I was once due to play football for Wales Under-12s and I sent my mother up to the bus stop to say I couldn't go because I was ill. There's obviously a nervous disposition in there, which manifests itself in just wanting to stay in. Which is not a crime. I remember this song more as a piece of music than a lyric.'

'Black Dog On My Shoulder' is certainly a compositional gem. By this point well attuned to his bandmate's vein of introspective words reaching outwards, Bradfield immediately went to the master template for elevating heartache: the timeless late-sixties songs produced by the Wrecking Crew's Al De Lory for Glen Campbell. 'I wanted it to be like a "Wichita Lineman", or "Galveston",' he says. 'I wanted that kind of wistfulness. I wanted it to be slightly removed from the time it was written in, basically. So that gave birth to that little circular guitar riff, and Sean was bang into playing the hot rods when we rehearsed it. The richness of the sounds in Chateau de la Rouge Motte through the Abbey Road desk, with Ian [Grimble] engineering, was amazing. It sounded like luxurious wood.'

Indeed, so persuasive is the sweeping interconnectivity of the band with Sally Herbert's strings during two lengthy instrumental sections, culminating at 3:28 in the time signature downshift into a beautifully humble extended guitar solo exit-to-fade, that the song's mangy subject matter – its kitchen sink melodrama – feels very far away. Which was maybe the point all along.

63.
S.Y.M.M.

Recorded: Chateau de la Rouge Motte, France; Abbey
    Road, London
Producer: Mike Hedges
Released: 14 September 1998 (*This Is My Truth Tell Me
    Yours*, Epic)

> 'The terrorist and the policeman both come
> from the same basket.'
> — Joseph Conrad, *The Secret Agent*

Mid-afternoon on 10 May 1997, Manic Street Preachers were the unannounced special guests at the Hillsborough Justice Concert, a benefit for the bereaved families of 96 Liverpool FC fans killed in a crush at Sheffield Wednesday's Hillsborough Stadium eight years earlier. Held at Liverpool's Anfield Stadium and hosted by John Peel before an audience of 35,000, the show was both an act of solidarity and an important fund-raiser for the families' ongoing struggle for justice in the face of an establishment cover-up of South Yorkshire Police's culpability for the disaster and its determination to smear the victims. As well as the Manics, other performers included local stars Holly Johnson, The Lightning Seeds and Space plus The Beautiful South and Stereophonics.

'They asked us to co-headline,' says Nicky Wire. 'And we said we're a hundred per cent doing it, but we do think it should be a Liverpool act that closes the show. We didn't want to steal any thunder. It was a great gig. Everything felt really warm and important.'

Along with his bandmates, Wire remembered being trans-fixed by the horror as it unfolded on BBC's Saturday afternoon television coverage of the 14 April 1989 FA Cup semi-final between Liverpool and Nottingham Forest. He'd also publicly praised Jimmy McGovern's docu-drama *Hillsborough*, first shown in December 1996, which won multiple BAFTAs in 1997 and subsequently helped fuel the families' campaign during a succession of inquiries, inquests and criminal cases, throughout which the establishment forces always managed to evade justice, clinging to their abhorrent strategy of blaming the innocents. In a letter written shortly after the McGovern drama's initial screening, Bernard Ingham, who as Margaret Thatcher's press secretary at the time of the disaster had visited Hillsborough with the prime minister the day after, reiterated his belief that responsibility for the deaths lay with 'tanked up yobs' who 'turned up in very large numbers to try to force their way into the ground'.

In this context, then, it was not a massive surprise when advance reports of *This Is My Truth Tell Me Yours* revealed a song about Hillsborough, nor that it would become such a bone of contention especially with the song titled 'South Yorkshire Mass Murderer'.

'I was startled when I first saw the lyric,' says Bradfield. 'I remember panicking – thinking, "I don't know if I can actually write music to this". I wondered if Nick was reacting to himself, after *Everything Must Go*, subconsciously wanting to be a bit more confrontational? So the lyric panicked me, the heaviness of it, the harshness of it, and my ability to write to it. And a couple of times in my life, *Meddle* by Pink Floyd has got me out of trouble. Some people would say it's got me into trouble, because you shouldn't use it as a reference point! But I disagree, I think it's a great record. I listened to it a lot one evening and I thought: I've got to be calm about this. If there's judgement in this song, you've got to be calm about it.'

As he had done with 'Ready For Drowning', Bradfield found solace and inspiration in Pink Floyd's pivotal 1971 album, on which the band located a viable identity post-Syd Barrett that wasn't fumbled abstraction. An apt choice, and not just for its deceptively casual array of hooks and spiritual uplift. 'Fearless', arguably *Meddle*'s greatest song – and unaccountably never performed in public – had specific resonance for Bradfield's quest, by featuring excerpts of the Anfield Kop singing the Liverpool anthem 'You'll Never Walk Alone', which was also the closing song at the 1997 Hillsborough Justice Concert.

'*Meddle* seemed to put me in the right space,' says Bradfield. 'My main panic was having to sing "South Yorkshire mass murderer" – everything either sounds too comic heavy, or it sounds too light. So I thought – it's dark already, why add insult to injury? Why don't you just mix up a minor and major chord and have an indecisive chord? It's major and it's minor at the same time. That's what I did, in my head. And of course, once I laid all the footprints in my quite simple mind, then inevitably they lead you to a Dave Gilmour guitar solo . . .'

With Mike Hedges and Ian Grimble enthusiastically on board – literally, thanks to the chateau recording console's previous life at Abbey Road recording *The Dark Side Of The Moon* – the track unspooled in a miasma of pixellating grind and echoey FX, phased drums and reverberant submarine noise, drifting slowly and sadly onwards to an unreachable conclusion. It's an exquisite, awe-inspiring piece of music – and the exact opposite of how one imagined the Manics might approach a song titled 'South Yorkshire Mass Murderer'.

Of course, when the album was released, its closing track was actually titled 'S.Y.M.M.', which alongside the music's precision-rendered indecision led many to conclude the band had bottled out, or been ordered to call it something less inflammatory. The lyric similarly confounded expectations. Far from the heroic tub-thumping of 'A Design For Life' or a retaliatory 'J'accuse!', this was a sparse, prosaic meta-view of a songwriter overwhelmed by the enormity of his task: 'The ending for this song/Well I haven't really thought of one/There's nothing I could ever say/That could really take the pain away'.

Wire was taken aback by the reactions of fans and the press.

'Obviously, people were disappointed for some reason,' he says. 'Even though the lyric says 'South Yorkshire mass murderer' about twenty times. I'd been obsessed with *The Player* by Robert Altman, the idea of a film about the film, and the industry, all the nuances. So it unfolded as a song about songwriting, about the dilemmas of going to certain places. So I never felt like I was copping out. I probably thought I was being a bit of a smartarse – the lyric was like an exercise. Which is not something I'm prone to.'

Wire says the title change was a homage to Black Sabbath's 'N.I.B.', a song originally called 'Nib' in honour of drummer Bill Ward's pen nib-shaped beard but amended because 'N.I.B.' was more mysterious. 'I really thought "S.Y.M.M." sounded darker and [more] powerful. There was nothing like Sony telling me not to call it "South Yorkshire Mass Murderer". Although, I do look back and feel I'd never do something like that now. I'm old and worry about it all too much. Times felt much more liberated then – the idea that I felt I could write a song like that, without even thinking twice about it. I'm glad I was proved right in the end, but people forgot what a gigantic cover-up it was. A dark, insidious, vile cover-up, and it was exposed by TV drama and documentary at the time, because there was no voice for the families. Just to see people so abandoned . . . It's a really genuine song.'

The Manics were indeed proved right, yet it would be almost another twenty years before the second Hillsborough inquest delivered a verdict of unlawful killing due to gross negligence manslaughter by David Duckenfield, the South Yorkshire chief superintendent in charge of policing Hillsborough Stadium on the day. Despite that, no criminal convictions have since been made. Duckenfield was acquitted of manslaughter after two crown court trials in 2019, while in May 2021 the trial of two former South

Yorkshire police officers and the force's solicitor at the time of the disaster, on charges of perverting the course of public justice, was halted by the judge, and the three men acquitted. Two months later, Andrew Devine, aged fifty-five, became the ninety-seventh victim of the disaster, when a coroner ruled that his death from brain injuries suffered at Hillsborough was unlawful. Truly, 'S.Y.M.M.' is the song that never ends.

64.

Socialist Serenade

Recorded: Rockfield Studios, Monmouthshire
Producer: Dave Eringa
Released: 8 March 1999 ('You Stole The Sun From My
   Heart' B-side, Epic); 14 July 2003 (*Lipstick Traces*, Epic)

> 'Feet off the furniture you Oxbridge twat,
> you're not on a punt now.'
> – Malcolm Tucker in *The Thick Of It*

Recorded towards the end of the *This Is My Truth* album process and never seriously considered for inclusion, 'Socialist Serenade' is a choice example of the different creative energy that flows when a band is off the leash or on the spot, tasked with delivering quick results with little jeopardy. Hence the opening sound of Rockfield's labrador barking. 'We love dogs,' explains Wire. 'It was in homage to Jane's Addiction's "Been Caught Stealing".'

Bradfield immediately saw the lyric's blunt-instrument satire on the first twelve months of Tony Blair's 'New Labour' government – 'Is it all about the politics of celebrity/Or endless days in the sun of Tuscany' – as a chance to take things less seriously. His vision of glam-era Roxy Music tackling The Kinks' 'Where Have All The Good Times Gone' began with some solo after-hours fun on the drums at Big Noise.

'I can absolutely see why this wouldn't make the album – my drums, and they are stuttery as fuck. Once we got to Rockfield, Sean demurred from redoing them. He said, "If you want them to sound like a roadie falling over a load of drum cases, I'm not gonna do it."' In addition to aligning his punchy percussive skills in wobbly-step with Nick Nasmyth's saloon-bar organ, Bradfield delivers a fine sarcastic laugh and a vicious guitar solo on his custom Telecaster 'bones guitar'.

'The song's just riffing,' says Bradfield, 'and perhaps a little bit of a reflection that maybe Labour had gone too far. Perhaps we'd gone a bit too far as well! Perhaps it's a little bit of deflection.'

Acknowledgement that one line had been crossed came with the eleventh-hour removal of most of a third verse, which had speculated on foreign secretary Robin Cook's sexual proclivities and celebrated deputy prime minister John Prescott simply for having been born in Prestatyn. At least the best line survived: 'Change your name to "New"/Forget the fucking "Labour"'.

'I can't quite believe I thought that badly of them at the time,' says Wire. 'They've been in less than a year and they haven't renationalised anything?! The "politics of celebrity" line was undoubtedly about Oasis going to Number 10 and the fact that we would never have gone. Not that we would have got an invite. We only meet communist dictators, really.'[1]

65.

The Masses Against The Classes

Recorded: Rockfield Studios, Monmouthshire
Producer: Dave Eringa
Released: 10 January 2000 (single A-side, Epic);
   9 September 2022 (*Know Your Enemy: Solidarity*,
   Columbia)

> 'The old religion redefined
> For the facile, futile, totally blind.'
>   – The Sisters Of Mercy, 'Floorshow'

On 16 February 1999, Manic Street Preachers became the first artist to twice win the Brit Awards for Best Group and Best Album, repeating their success of 1997. Shortly afterwards, it was announced that they would headline three of the big four UK festivals: Glastonbury, Scotland's T in the Park and the dual V events in Essex and Staffordshire. Then, in March, buoyed by the Top 5 ranking of 'You Stole The Sun From My Heart', *This Is My Truth Tell Me Yours* returned to the UK Top 10. In July, 'Tsunami' became its fourth successive hit single, while in September the album notched up fifty consecutive weeks in the UK Top 50.

Throughout the year, the weekly and monthly music magazines scrambled for angles, spurious or otherwise, to cover the band. Yet although ostensibly flush with success, during this same period the Manics began to exhibit some classic symptoms of imperial entropy. Much of the press coverage was negative, with normally supportive journalists and fans arriving at a consensus that with setlists leaning heavily on *Everything Must Go* and *This Is*

My Truth, the band's live shows had become staid and predictable. The discourse had an implicit 'things were better with Richey' tone, especially from long-serving leopard-print ultras who clearly resented sharing 'their' band with Man at C&A. *Melody Maker* quoted Belinda Seed, who had ceased publishing her Manics fanzine *YPF* ('Young, Pretty and Fucked') in disgruntlement at the band's new respectability: 'Forget Hoovering, I want to read about sex, drugs and rock 'n' roll. I was more interested in the Manics when Richey was going through his troubles – it'd be more compelling to read and I'd get a kick out of it.'[1]

The critique's essential premise was the Manics' wrathful iconoclastic edge had been dulled by popularity. *NME* chuntered that they were playing 'too many festivals' – to which the band responded by selling T-shirts emblazoned with said phrase at said festivals. Glastonbury did see a rekindling of the ire of old, albeit in somewhat farcical circumstances. Five years earlier, on the festival's second stage, Nicky Wire had declared, 'I say build some more bypasses over this shithole.' Now returning to headline the main Pyramid Stage, the band took advantage of their new largesse and status by bringing their own flushable facilities; a note on the door declaring them 'reserved exclusively for the <u>Manic Street Preachers</u>'. Billy Bragg, who had played the Pyramid Stage earlier that day, took upon himself the role of whistleblower, declaring private toilets an affront to the festival's egalitarian spirit. The press gleefully ran with the story for weeks, boosted by Wire's subsequent declaration at T in the Park that Bragg was 'the biggest-nosed twat in the world . . . I wouldn't want his dick pissing in my toilet for all the money in the fucking world . . . Get back in the fucking army, you fuckwit – and stop stealing Woody Guthrie's songs!'

Not all the dissent was external. After their set at Glastonbury, Moore and Wire accused Bradfield of 'acting singing' onstage. 'They said, "you were emoting with your hands . . ." I don't fucking know, I may have gesticulated once or twice, but it seemed like a big gig, headlining Glastonbury. I liked it. Nick hated the success of *This Is My Truth*. He said we were shit – "bloated shit".'

The following weekend, on 4 July, the Manics did not fulfil their scheduled appearance at the Rock Werchter festival near Brussels after Nicky Wire went AWOL on the morning of the gig. 'By this point, the press have turned against us and I just remember feeling fatigue and irritation,' he says. 'I was getting really bored by the end of *This Is My Truth*, moaning all the time, annoying everybody else. It was the classic "we shouldn't be this big". And I was getting loads of headaches and migraines, wolfing down twelve painkillers a day, too many. Going onstage with a headache is really depressing, but I was a miserable fucker. And that all culminated when I walked out of that festival in Belgium and I got on the Eurostar.'

The band regrouped and seven days later played T in the Park – pointedly opening with 'Faster', instead of 'You Stole The Sun From My Heart', by then solidly established as the 'we're too big' era's staple curtain-raiser – before immediately cancelling all further engagements, most notably an imminent three-week American tour, prompting press reports that they were about to split up. Yet amid the melodrama, a real-life tragedy was unfolding. On 27 July, almost six years since her cancer diagnosis, James Dean Bradfield's mother died. During the preceding weeks, back at his childhood home, James had found himself instinctively writing music for a new lyric Nicky had given him.

'The band were cancelling things for me, because they knew things weren't going so well,' he says. 'And I was up in my mum and dad's bedroom, looking for something to take to hospital for her. I felt comfortable being in the room, because I was missing her. So I ended up writing the music in my mum and dad's bedroom in Sir Ivor's Road. The only time I ever did that – I wish I'd written something more beautiful!'

From amid this turbulence emerged 'The Masses Against The Classes': a self-directed booby trap of rage at what the Manics had become, thinly disguised as a political blitzkrieg, plotted as a one-off single dropping in the first days of the new millennium to reassert the band's iconoclastic reputation. With the title quoting a campaign speech delivered by Liberal Prime Minister William Gladstone on 28 June 1886 to an audience in Liverpool, the concept was all Nicky Wire's.

'Everybody else was just like, "Why?"' he says. 'We'd sold three million albums. Nobody could see the wisdom of putting out a standalone single. Rob Stringer wasn't against it as such, but he did say, "Do you *need* to do this?". I said to James, "We need to do something angry." It was, "Let's scare the children", one hundred per cent designed to be nasty. But it didn't take a criminologist to reveal the lyrics were really about us.'

On 29 December 1995, Nicky Wire had opened the post-Richey Manics' return to the public stage, supporting The Stone Roses at Wembley Arena, with the words: 'It's only us!' 'The Masses Against The Classes' announced this latest new chapter in similar fashion ('Hello, it's us again') before sarcastically inverting the fourth-wall-breaking schema of 'You Love Us' ('We're still so in love with you . . .'), then directing a tirade at the faithless in the front rows and the media faint-hearts for literally writing the band off: 'Success is such an ugly word/Especially in your tiny world'.

'I'd love to pretend that we didn't care about the press, but this song proves how much we did,' says Wire. 'We just couldn't shake it off. So I liked the triviality of it, I like bands that write about themselves. The whole package is manufactured in its rage. But I didn't expect James to write a song like that.'

In thirty minutes at west London's Chiswick Reach studio, Bradfield demoed the song out of the 'lower-case Kurt Cobain' mode it had occupied on conception in Sir Ivor's Road, and realised it could work in all-caps. 'I thought this has definitely got legs, it can explode,' he says.

Between Chiswick Reach and the full band recording session

at Rockfield, some of the lyric's more egregious taunts fell by the wayside – 'We are the animals but you are the useless'; 'We're still together but you're no longer dangerous'; 'We're so exceptional and we're so fundamental to so many people's lives, it must kill your empty mind . . .' – replaced by the far more elegant likes of 'We love the winter, it brings us closer together'.

'I think there's a tacit board of inquiry going on sometimes, where you kind of know certain lines are not going to be in the final song,' says Bradfield. 'The lyric does sum up the inner tension of Nick's thinking. He has a lot of tension with himself, let alone other people, and this is him trying to reposition himself and us after the "too much success" that he wanted in the first place! He's a complicated soul.'

With Bradfield grieving and Wire guilt-ridden for him being there, Rockfield was not a happy recording experience. 'It was good because my dad was coming up twice a week,' says James, 'and I was taking him for food and stuff. But it definitely felt strange. Me and Sean had an argument about the drums. I was obsessed with getting the low, powerful Paul Cook thud, so I was tuning his drums down, and of course he took umbrage. Why wouldn't he? He didn't tell me how to tune my guitar. Then me and Dave Eringa went round in circles trying to get that serrated Panzer attack going with the guitars. So it was not the best. Also, I think after *Everything Must Go* and *This Is My Truth*, we were a bit out of practice at doing stuff like that. But it got there in the end.'

Given the distressed circumstances under which it was made, there feels a therapeutic aspect to 'Masses' rage, however manufactured – a fractured team re-bonding under their own motivational headline, 'we're the only thing left to believe in'. Ultimately, 'The Masses Against The Classes' makes a virtue of its contrived design by leaving its workings exposed: referencing the screams from The Beatles' version of 'Twist & Shout', the hyperbolic restatement of Nirvana's quiet-loud dynamics, even the opening and closing quotations, included purely to bulk up the song's bogus political context, and both subsequently proving contentious. Bradfield's theatrical delivery of a line from Albert Camus' *The Rebel* over a mangled reprise of the ending to Skids' 'Charles' was cut when 'Masses' was included on 2022's 'remixed, reconstructed' reissue of *Know Your Enemy*. The opening sample of Noam Chomsky critiquing the US founding fathers' aim 'to protect property from the majority', meanwhile, will be absent from any future performance of the song.

'Camus is still one of my absolute heroes,' says Wire, 'but the quote was just me overdoing it. I thought, "We've got Chomsky at the front, let's have Camus at the end!" – because "Motown Junk" samples Public Enemy at the start and then "Charles" at the end. It was a bit forced, too much. But at this moment in time, I wish I'd never put Noam Chomsky on there because he has turned into a Putin apologist. So we'll never use that live again.'

Ten days after it was performed to an audience of 60,000 at the Manics' Cardiff Millennium Stadium concert on New Year's Eve 1999, 'The Masses Against The Classes' was released as a limited edition single, and deleted wihin twenty-four hours. The sleeve featured a Cuban flag minus the star, plus a quotation from Mao Tse-tung ('We should support whatever the enemy opposes and oppose whatever the enemy supports'). On 22 January 2000, it entered the UK singles chart at Number 1, displacing Westlife's cover of Abba's 'I Have A Dream' from a four-week run at the top. Smart work for a record designed to scare people. The architect of this confluence of music, design and the dark arts of marketing felt suitably vindicated.

'Most people were on holiday when it went to Number 1,' says Nicky Wire. 'I think James had gone to Mexico. Rob was away, Martin was in Barbados. And I was like, "Yes! I've fucking done it!" The limited edition was 72,000 in the first week, so it wasn't that limited. I think we did 130,000, which we sold all of. To quote *The A-Team*, "I love it when a plan comes together", and that was a plan.'

Although both a hardcore fan favourite and a commercial peak, 'Masses' never became a setlist fixture – for the straightforward reason that it's very tough to play. 'It's like a hit session,' says James. 'You've got to go down in intensity then back up again. It feels like the song's telling you to *fucking play it like you mean it* . . . If you don't put everything in, it means nothing. So it can be embarrassing sometimes. But it was designed to do what it did. It completely justifies its unique existence. The artwork is perfect. And whenever we do play "Masses", it gets a big reaction. It bridged more gaps in our audience than we realised.'

66.

Close My Eyes

Recorded: RAK, London
Producer: Dave Eringa
Released: 10 January 2000 ('The Masses Against The
    Classes' B-side, Epic); 14 July 2003 (*Lipstick Traces*,
    Epic)

'Missing the point of our mission.'
> – Echo & The Bunnymen, 'Porcupine'

While 'The Masses Against The Classes' was its own autonomous island, its B-side bridged the albums on either side. The lyric is a pure post-*This Is My Truth* sickly Wire gripe – 'Shake some hands and then I feel ashamed . . . I had a vision but it slipped away . . . Attempt to make up and my skin aches' – which keeps circling back to the core malady: 'It's not about us any more.'

'It's me moaning, "I'm too tired, I want to go home,"' says Nicky. 'And about lying, swallowing my pride . . . A pretty sketchy, throwaway lyric, so I was really impressed when James played it to me.'

Wire didn't hear the song before its completion because he isn't on the recording. While he took care of pre-'Masses' promo duties, Bradfield and Dave Eringa were at RAK building upon a Chiswick Reach demo in which James had sensed a 'bittersweet kind of *White Album* whimsy'. That reference led Eringa to a drum loop popular with producers at the time that was based on the rocking reprise of *Sgt. Pepper's Lonely Hearts Club Band*, and Bradfield did the rest. 'The riff is just one of those you can do at the bottom of an E string,' he says. 'It's one of the pillars of indie.'

Whereas *This Is My Truth*'s cold surfaces entombed the listener,

'Close My Eyes' loosened and reframed its author's familiar complaints amid rust-flaked guitar layers, a textural shift that anticipated the forthcoming *Know Your Enemy*, the basis of which would be recorded at sprawling length amid the heat of southern Spain, as opposed to autumnal north-west London.

'I like "Close My Eyes", it's a really good curio,' says Wire. 'James has a nice effect on his voice. It sounds quite homemade, considering we probably spent about five grand making it! That line "Sign some papers and they are my friends"? Sony gave us a million quid – it might have been more, might have been two million – for a publishing advance. Not that I was resisting this big pile of money! And I think it took us until the end of [2010's] *Postcards* [*From A Young Man*] to recoup and start earning again, but it seemed amazing at the time. And until *Everything Must Go* sold 600,000 we hadn't earned a lot. I always remember my dad's famous quote: "Make sure you put your hand in the till of your merchandise sales, make sure you're getting something out of it." Which in retrospect was sound advice. But from '97 to 2001 there was a lot of money. And this song is me saying: everything's too big.'

67.

Found That Soul

Recorded: El Cortijo, Marbella, Spain
Producer: Dave Eringa
Released: 26 February 2001 (single, Epic); 19 March 2001
   (*Know Your Enemy*, Epic)

'Royalty is the gold filling in a mouthful of decay.'
                                          – John Osborne

A campaign launch in Cuba. Shaking hands with Fidel Castro. Prefacing their sprawling new album with two simultaneously released singles. Such was the noise around the Manics' latest return that in the end it drowned out the music it was supposed to be publicising.

The twin singles were a legacy of Nicky Wire's original concept for *Know Your Enemy* to comprise two separate records, à la Guns N' Roses' *Use Your Illusion*, broadly divided along stylistic lines: the 'communist loud one' *Solidarity*, and the softer, more pastoral *Door To The River*. His grand plan was ultimately vetoed, both by Wire's bandmates ('James was getting very weary with me, saying, "Why are you trying to do all this weird shit all the time?"') and also Rob Stringer. But Stringer did consent to the more modest strategy of paired singles, thereby still honouring the original concept and with less risk. 'Because I had bombarded him with so many ideas – I'd mentioned Cuba early on during the recording, we were in the swimming pool at the studio in Spain when Martin and Rob were there – that I don't think he had the energy to reject the singles,' says Wire. 'And if I'm being honest, I don't think he was confident we had a breakout single anyway, like a "Design" or "Tolerate". So he was fine with it and everything felt all right. Until we released them . . .'

'Found That Soul' represented *Know Your Enemy*'s combat wing, punching home its beleaguered defiance ('Not a subject am I/ Sick and pale but strangely alive') with a terse, torqued blast that impressively wore its Stooges-brand minimalism, right down to the yammering one-note piano.

'I liked the lyric because it was narky, but positive too,' says Bradfield. Faced with Moore and Wire in agreement that the band had become 'too user-friendly', he rationalised the best way to calm the troops was to 'tone myself down', taking cues from the parched dune-buggy motorik of the first Queens of the Stone Age album. 'On "Found That Soul" there's no backing vocals in the chorus. I tried to put it in a range where I can get more snarl in my voice so as not to feel I have to put backing vocals on. For the guitar solo I just plugged straight into the desk – didn't use an amp or a pedal. I went for that old seventies Alice Cooper DI [direct input] shtick, so it's less "produced".'

James remembers suggesting Nicky put his bass through a Pro Co RAT, a distortion pedal favoured by hard rock and grunge bands, and being met with a withering, 'Do you want me to put a flannel shirt on as well?' Wire's core self-image remained that of a reactionary poet who occasionally wore a dress, a vision that 'Found That Soul's low-end power-moves amplified with extreme prejudice. 'I think it stands up really well,' says Wire. 'It's concise, its anti-monarchy line resonates through the decades.'

Compared to its twinkly twin 'So Why So Sad', it also better captured the parent album's truculent mood swings – for good and bad.

68.

Locust Valley

Recorded: AIR, London
Producer: Dave Eringa
Released: 26 February 2001 ('Found That Soul' B-side,
    Epic); 9 September 2022 (*Know Your Enemy: Solidarity*,
    Columbia)

> 'Hey Ray, you're driving me crazy.'
>   – John Cale, 'Hey Ray'

Know Your Enemy was recorded over five months in seven studios, with upwards of thirty lyrics being purposed into songs. At times during the creative ferment, things got confusing. Words and music were transposed to and from different songs, sections got moved in, out and around – with 'Locust Valley' a prime example.

Wire had written a lyric inspired by Ray Johnson, a Detroit-born artist who moved to New York in the late 1940s and became renowned among the city's creative underground for his Pop-Dada techniques, most famously mailing pieces of art to friends and strangers, the so-called New York Correspondence School. 'It felt good doing a song about Ray Johnson, because he was quite hidden away,' says Wire. 'He put collages in the post, which is what me and Richey used to do when we were in Swansea Uni. It felt like a nice lineage.'

Named after the small Long Island town where Johnson settled into an increasingly reclusive life from the late sixties until his suicide in 1995,[1] 'Locust Valley' was originally set to music that subsequently became 'Royal Correspondent', a different song with different lyrics. The finished version of 'Locust Valley', meanwhile, shifted its opening verse's mention of 'correspondence school' from the first to the third line, rendering the already obscure Johnson even more 'Famously unknown/Elusive and dismantled', as the eventual opening lines have it.

'It was tortuous,' says Wire. 'There's so many versions, and I really loved it, the guitar solo's great, there's those weird drones in between the gaps, and it was meant to be uncontrolled, but I don't know if we ever got it right. James certainly never thought we nailed it.'

With its frazzled textures and righteous approximation of Dinosaur Jr. harassing a vacuum cleaner, the avant-rockin' 'Locust Valley' is a strong outside pick for wildest Manics song ever. Yet as the recording caravan moved on to AIR, after eight weeks in Spain were followed by stops in RAK, Rockfield and Monnow Valley, any chance of it making the album's final cut disappeared as the intro section's relationship with 'Regular John', the opening track on the first Queens of the Stone Age album, overstepped the line from 'friendly' to 'explicit'.

'This could have been a really good song, it's definitely got a little bit of that American glide about it,' says James. 'Sometimes you're in thrall to something when you discover it on a record and you end up accidentally doing something that sounds a bit like it, and so it becomes a B-side. The music definitely let the lyric down. Dave Eringa went home to see his wife over the weekend when I did a lot of work on this song, and Lee [Butler], the tape op, recorded a lot of it and distorted things a bit too much.'

In a moment of cosmic coincidence, or karma, or good old-fashioned bad luck, when the Manics performed 'Found That Soul' on *Top of the Pops* they found themselves sharing a green room with Queens of the Stone Age. 'It wasn't a great atmosphere,' says Wire. 'Either I'd said something horrible about them, or Josh Homme didn't know who the fuck we were.'

Bradfield elected not to introduce himself to the man who had written 'Regular John'. 'I thought, "If I stand too close it'll just look like the movie poster for *Twins* . . ."'

69.

Ballad Of The Bangkok Novotel

Recorded: El Cortijo, Marbella, Spain
Producer: Dave Eringa
Released: 26 February 2001 ('Found That Soul' B-side,
 Epic); 9 September 2022 (*Know Your Enemy: Solidarity*,
 Columbia)

> 'Just because you're paranoid, don't mean
> they're not after you.'
> – Nirvana, 'Territorial Pissings'

James Dean Bradfield calls *Know Your Enemy* 'our *Sexy Beast*
period' – three pale Valley Boys slowly broiling in the Andalusian
summer for eight weeks. He laughs at the memory.

'There's a picture of me there that's complete *Sexy Beast*. On
the bed, with just a towel for my modesty, I'm definitely prop
forward weight! Nick had this theory: "We should try recording
in the sunshine, see if that affects our music . . ."'

A lot of the lyrics Nicky Wire brought to El Cortijo came pre-
loaded with heat, thanks to their author's fevered disposition
during the post-*This Is My Truth* era: assailed by migraines, mired
in self-doubt, questioning the band's purpose, and in the case of
'Ballad Of The Bangkok Novotel', haunted by flashbacks to one
of the most harrowing episodes of its existence, specifically the
cursed visit in April 1994 where Richey Edwards slashed his chest
open and Wire angered the authorities by wishing death on the
King of Thailand. This lurid rant's final line, 'Five years later, I'm
still shaking', begged the conclusion that for it to have emerged

now was because, consciously or not, Wire felt parallels with that previous long hot summer.

'Well, definitely 1994 felt too fucking hot,' he says. 'I remember a dangling feeling of indecision, because Richey was on the slide. And Thailand exacerbated that. If there's one trip that's lingered with me in a physical and mental health sense it was that one. There was a seed planted there which overwhelmed us over the next year or two, I've never felt so ill at ease with myself. I'll never go back to Thailand. I can taste that hysterical madness still. So I had probably been storing all this up.'

A litany of complaint ('Egg and chips is all I want'), paranoid visions ('Military Police are after me') and self-abasement ('Masturbation, there's nothing left'), the brief for Bradfield, on what would be Wire's first lead vocal, was 'something gonzo – as in silly mutoid punk'. 'Ballad's booglarised Moog modulator freakout certainly delivered. However much played for fun, it's still an authentic representation of a mind in meltdown. And although he questions whether he actually played on it, Bradfield accords the piece its due significance: 'Countless times Nick would say, "I'm not musical . . ." when obviously he's really musical. It's almost like he's got to tell himself these things to rebel against, to prove otherwise. So this is the start of him opening up and becoming more confident musically.'

70.

So Why So Sad

Recorded: Rockfield Studios, Monmouthshire
Producer: Dave Eringa
Released: 26 February 2001 (single, Epic); 19 March 2001
  (*Know Your Enemy*, Epic)

'They call us lonely when we're really just alone.'
— Aztec Camera, 'Oblivious'

If 'Found That Soul' was the blunt instrument, 'So Why So Sad' was the spoke in the wheel, offering a version of the Manics that perplexed even the band. 'The biggest curveball of all time,' says Wire.

The oft-cited template for its spectral mass of bells, chimes, keys and harmonies is The Beach Boys; Bradfield was 'obsessed' with *Surf's Up*, especially the pulsing dreamscapes of 'Feel Flows', which had recently been featured in *Almost Famous*, Cameron Crowe's semi-autobiographical film about the halcyon seventies era of rock journalism. Perhaps its stoned evocation of time unravelling left the otherwise psychedelically disinclined Bradfield in a suggestible mood. A month before receiving 'So Why So Sad' he had been reading a book called *The Dead Sea Scrolls Deception*, and now here was Wire's lyric citing the same ancient Hebrew scriptures.

'I got really excited by that little bit of serendipity,' he says. Bradfield also noted the words' strikingly desolate mood, seeing beyond any superficial reading of 'My smile as real as a hyena's' as a retread of 'You Stole The Sun's 'I've got to stop smiling', and recognising the key line here as: 'Spirit so low that I no longer pretend.'

'The lyric had an emotional surrender to it. Whenever I see that in Nick's stuff I always get quite intrigued – I always think, "Well this could be different." So that's why I went at it.'

Bradfield recorded his guide vocal with an acoustic guitar, then did all the harmony vocals himself, aside from Nick Nasmyth's repeated 'bu-bah-bahs', the latter providing what Bradfield terms 'a rare moment of Manics comedy in the studio' when Nasmyth revealed he had actually been singing 'big bottoms' and maybe they should scrap the last four takes. With Moore laying loosely martial rolls across this vaporous lake of melancholy, Bradfield ignored an inner voice which sounded very much like his guitar demanding to know why he was making it play 'weedy shit' and forged ahead with his vision for the song's emotional climax. 'The whole thing was a construct,' he says. 'And all the time while we're doing it in Rockfield I could hear this thing which wasn't there but which should be there. I was like . . . "I can hear a Stylophone solo!"' Bradfield duly had Nasmyth play a Stylophone solo, rippling joyously in the currents before plummeting like a mayfly on its final doomed journey.

'Rob Stringer loved it,' says Bradfield. 'Martin really liked it. But then the big moment was sensing that it wasn't quite gonna fly with people.'

It didn't help that one of those people was the song's co-author.

'I just thought, "What the fuck is this?"' says Nicky Wire. 'I really liked the lyric, but it sounds nothing like us in any shape or form. "So Why So Sad" came up and for some reason deluded us into thinking that's the most commercial and catchy thing we had and we all fell for it. And then we spent three hundred thousand pounds on the video, which is absolute tripe.'

In subsequent years, the band appeared better disposed towards the B-side's Avalanches' mix, where whimsical party atmos replaced the harmonies; this version took precedence on 2022's *Know Your Enemy* reassembly, although its chief virtue is merely an absence of complicity in the original's failure (a 'failure' that still got to Number 8 in the UK chart). Brittle and beautiful, 'So Why So Sad' may have been an odd choice for a single – R.E.M. covering kosmische supergroup Harmonia produced by Joe Meek – but that's hardly the song's fault.

'I still think there is something really good in there,' says Bradfield, 'but I don't think we'll ever find it.'

71.

Ocean Spray

Recorded: Rockfield Studios, Monmouthshire
Producer: Dave Eringa
Released: 19 March 2001 (*Know Your Enemy*, Epic);
   4 June 2001 (single, Epic)

'Your heart has been broken again.'

                 – Teenage Fanclub, 'Broken'

Sixteen years separated 'Ocean Spray' from James Dean Bradfield's previous lyric, 'Jackboot Johnny', a cautionary rant about the threat of right-wing street violence, which he wrote aged fifteen. After 'Jackboot Johnny', he considered this a job best left to others.

'"Ocean Spray" was the first time since then that I felt, "I need a piece of paper, I need a pen, I need to get rid of all the rubbish lines and get to the good ones,"' he says. 'I still only came up with a chorus and a verse! It left me more in admiration of lyricists, of librettists, of all authors and poets. To be compelled to do something so mundane, and hope something brilliant comes out of it, is fucking amazing. Because I needed the death of my mother to make me want to do it.'

Like all great songs of love and heartbreak, foreknowledge of 'Ocean Spray's subject matter is not a prerequisite to feeling its emotional pull. The song began with Bradfield's poignant memory of visiting his mother in hospital, where he would bring her cranberry juice for its antioxidant benefits. 'She was obsessively drinking it,' he says, 'because when you're that ill you don't want water infections, and she was battling lots of other stuff already. So whenever I'd go there she would berate me if I didn't bring three bottles of Ocean Spray. It became a running joke, and it was nice.' Hence the song's quietly devastating chorus hook: 'Oh, please stay awake/And then we can drink some Ocean Spray'.

'I'll never get over my mum dying so early,' says James. 'And that's it – *so early*. And I never will. I don't believe in "closure", because it's such a pile of shit – you never get over these things, you learn how to deal with pain. Millions of people go through it. That was my experience. And it forced me to do something to deal with it, and I was lucky to have the process of going through that.'

There was no rule prohibiting Bradfield from writing Manics lyrics, or Wire from singing lead vocals. Established custom rather than statute shaped the band's divisions of labour, and it had served them well enough thus far. So it's telling that Bradfield felt perfectly comfortable bringing a lyric to the others, especially as he had written about such a personal experience. Tacitly or otherwise, the group's response to the previous summer's internal strife had been to loosen up and expand the parameters of what constituted a Manic Street Preachers record.

Both Moore and Wire enthusiastically embraced the novel situation. Late one evening Bradfield sat down at Rockfield with his lucky J-45 acoustic guitar and did what he always did with a new lyric: try to let the words inspire music. 'And they did – it came to me that night,' he says. 'I used an open G tuning for some reason, I was probably playing along to a record, trying to sound like "Thorn In My Pride" by Black Crowes or something. But that good luck showed it to be the tuning to write the song in, because it made E minor and A minor sound a bit different, these little overtones were there and suddenly the chord became new to me again.'

The next morning, Moore added some drums in about ten minutes. 'Loose as hell,' says Bradfield, 'but it worked straight away. It was so good that those drums and some of the acoustic guitar are used on the master.' The musicians' simple onward groove responded in kind to the lyric's calm evocation of grief: 'It's easy to feel, it's easy to feel/But it's not good enough, even though it's real'.

Sean too had lost a close relative: Sue Bradfield was his aunt, who had welcomed her sister's son into the family home following the break-up of his parents' marriage. His contributions to 'Ocean Spray' tap a deep well of feeling, particularly the trumpet solo, a desolate masterclass of phrasing and technique.

'He really took his time coming up with the part,' says James. 'And it's brilliant because all his phrases start way after the beat – he starts just at the end of the bar, right at the point where the next bar starts and this one is finishing, he's right in between it all. It is so relaxed, so classy, so restrained, so fucking *Sinatra* . . . I can always tell when something really comes from inside him because I find it hard to replicate when I have to play it live on the guitar.'

Nicky likewise went beyond simply playing his part, when he helped Bradfield complete the lyric, adding a second verse that tapped perfectly into the numbed mood, just as Moore had. Wire plays down his contribution – 'I just finished a bit at the end' – but Bradfield insists he dug him out of a hole. 'Every time I tried to write beyond what I'd written, it felt like I was reaching for something which wasn't there,' says James. 'Everything had been easy up until then. I just thought, "If I'm pushing, it is not right." Nick did it brilliantly, and made it better than anything else I'd come up with. So it's a perfect band song. Started out as my song, and it's probably the purest thing I'll ever write myself – though that doesn't mean that it's the best. But it is a perfect band song.'

'Ocean Spray's impeccably compact design even accommodated some brief cathartic guitar blasts and one very apt quirky detail: the Japanese dialogue prefacing the intro, courtesy of photographer Mitch Ikeda, which translates as 'You have very beautiful eyes . . . such beautiful eyes'. Released as a single just as *Know*

Your Enemy completed its glum three-month slide out of the Top 100, how ironic that this one unassuming yet uniquely powerful song was a far more persuasive advocate for the album than 'So Why So Sad' and 'Found That Soul' combined.

'It should have been the first single,' says Wire. 'It's a really controlled vocal, beautiful guitar sounds, I remember the *taste* of it. It doesn't get enough love, because we've played it a lot live and it's on an album that people weren't that fussed about, but it's up there with our best stuff.'

72.

Intravenous Agnostic

Recorded: Monnow Valley, Monmouthshire
Producer: Dave Eringa
Released: 19 March 2001 (*Know Your Enemy*, Epic)

'If there's a way I wish we'd see it.'

– Dinosaur Jr., 'Freak Scene'

Nicky Wire characterises *Know Your Enemy* as 'the ultimate reaction album – the ultimate vote *against* rather than vote *for* album.' On the premise that the Manics' principal enemy was themselves, or the band they had become, with 'Intravenous Agnostic' they wrote a campaign theme tune, a kind of hymn to this new model 'destructive aesthetic', as the chorus has it. Recorded in three takes after less than an hour's rehearsal during the album sessions' home stretch, its evocation of being spun around in a washing machine – quite possibly Sonic Youth's 'Washing Machine' – demonstrates how deeply the band acquiesced to their mission.

'The idea of non-belief in anything at this point pervades quite a bit of the record,' says Wire, as concise an explanation as any of what 'Intravenous Agnostic' is, or isn't, about. Its seemingly random cut-up slogans tumble forth like negationist bingo: 'Secular mosaic distracted at birth . . .'; 'Brutality is needed in capitalist society . . .'; 'We all pray for pluralist babies . . .'; 'Life becomes Calvinist . . .'

'I was going through a bit of associative lyric writing that is not all literal, based on things that give you joy simply because they do – walking, the sea – without an ideology or religion behind them. Hence "agnostic". The "Calvinist" line, though, I have no idea. Maybe I'd been watching a documentary about Scotland?'

Once again Bradfield wrote the tune in an open G tuning, and for the live band studio takes he used a black Telecaster custom, 'which you can switch between G and standard tuning'. An acknowledgement of the song's primary inspiration came mid-hurtle, when Wire drawled 'What a mess!' through the studio talkback mike, quoting Dinosaur Jr.'s signature fuzz anthem 'Freak Scene'. 'Dinosaur Jr. were gigantic for us in terms of music we listened to,' says Wire. 'Richey was obsessed with *Where You Been*, James too – we were searching for that guitar sound in the verse, which glides without overpowering until the chorus.'[1]

This Manic-scented take on ugly American overkill is toasted through the floor by Sean Moore's spectacular drum-rolling feats. 'I still think it's one of the best, most natural things we've ever done,' says Bradfield. 'Absolutely love everything about it. The sound of three people so tuned in to each other you wouldn't believe.'

'Intravenous Agnostic' would have made a better flagship for *Know Your Enemy*'s militant fleet than 'Found That Soul', which feels more stodgy than Stoogey in comparison. Yet its lightning-bolt energy was too unstable to sustain beyond the precise moment of its creation. Bradfield left Monnow Valley convinced they had just nailed their new album's first single. 'I remember being so excited . . . and then nobody really seemed to get excited about it ever again.'

'Intravenous Agnostic' made its live debut on 20 August 2001, boldly cast as set opener at the North Wales Theatre and Conference Centre in Llandudno – whereupon its middle section didn't just break down, it completely fell apart. The song has never been played since.

73.

Let Robeson Sing

Recorded: Monnow Valley, Monmouthshire; AIR, London
Producers: Dave Eringa and Mike Hedges
Released: 19 March 2001 (*Know Your Enemy*, Epic);
    10 September 2001 (single, Epic)

'He is convinced that he has a mission to lead oppressed
negroes and colonial peoples everywhere. He is a fanatical
communist and intensely ambitious.'
    – MI5 internal memo on Paul Robeson, 13 July 1951

Given its musically low-key tribute to a famous anti-fascist campaigner who had deep bonds to Wales and working-class struggle,
'Let Robeson Sing' could be an exile from *This Is My Truth*, rather
than a member of *Know Your Enemy*'s fevered reaction pact. Yet
Paul Robeson, renowned African-American singer, actor, civil
rights activist and socialist, was an outsider himself. The man who
famously joined a London march of Welsh miners who had been
blacklisted following the 1926 General Strike, was himself blacklisted, and his passport revoked, in 1950 amid the McCarthyite
red scare. Persecuted by the security services in both his homeland
and the UK, where he lived and worked for several periods of his
life, Paul Robeson knew very well who his enemies were.

One of the song's most intriguing lyrics is 'MK ULTRA turned
you paranoid', referencing the theory that Robeson was poisoned
by the CIA as part of MK ULTRA, a covert mind-control and
chemical research programme tested on US citizens with a view to
subsequently targeting foreign leaders. One such was Fidel Castro,
whom Robeson was en route to meet in Havana in March 1961,
when he was apparently drugged at a party in his Moscow hotel

room, and attempted suicide by slashing his wrists. Three weeks later, the CIA staged its abortive Bay of Pigs invasion of Cuba. In September that same year, Robeson left Moscow for London, where he was subjected to heavy doses of barbiturates and ECT at The Priory hospital (the same institution that three decades later treated Richey Edwards) before eventually returning to the US in December 1963, quietly living out his final twelve years in New York then Philadelphia, in the care of his son Paul Robeson Jr. With 'Let Robeson Sing' – titled after the international campaign to have his passport restored, which culminated in 1958 with the US Supreme Court – the Manics covered the expanse of one man and his place in history in a straightforward, concise lyric and music that evoked the folk spiritual idiom, all to celebrate 'his voice so pure, a vision so clear'.

'I think this song falls into the category of "under-appreciated",' says Wire, a status owing as much to his band's then-saturated public profile as Robeson's relative lack of one. Yet in Wales, at least, Robeson's legacy was stirring, and Wire was paying heed: 1999 saw the foundation of the Paul Robeson Wales Trust, prompted by the sixtieth anniversary of the singer's December 1938 appearance at a concert in the Cynon Valley town of Mountain Ash to honour the thirty-three Welsh International Brigadiers killed in the Spanish Civil War. 'I am here tonight because I feel that in the struggle we are waging for a better life, an artist must do his part,' Robeson told the 7,000-strong audience.[1] The following year, he would be in the Rhondda, making his film *The Proud Valley*, where he played an American sailor who jumps ship in Cardiff then takes a train to a nearby town where he finds song and solidarity among the mineworkers.

'I was aware of Paul Robeson,' says Bradfield. 'I knew there was a civil rights background but didn't really know about his connection to Wales so much. Nick gave me the lyric and I thought it was probably his most concise history lesson ever. Of course, you can't encapsulate a life in two verses and a chorus, but it does a pretty good job. I wanted it to be gentle, because you never want to be outraged on behalf of somebody else, you just want to sing for them. And that leads you to a good place.'

Bradfield's arrangement decisions were partly dictated by the plan to include the voice of Paul Robeson himself, recorded on 5 October 1957 when he sang for the Welsh Miners' Eisteddfod in Porthcawl, despite being unable to accept the invitation to attend in person because of his blacklisting. Thanks to the new transatlantic telephone cable, that pure voice and vision reached out from New York to Wales; similarly on 'Let Robeson Sing', where Bradfield recorded his acoustic guitar through the vintage Amstrad cassette recorder he'd used at his parents' house during the band's early years, lending it a weathered timbre that respectfully accommodated the sound of Robeson and the Treorchy Male Voice Choir from over forty years before. 'It worked, because it sounds in places like the guitar in the time of Robeson,' says Bradfield. 'I felt slightly ashamed that there wasn't a key change, or that it didn't have many chords. But I gave in to the simplicity of the lyric when I was writing the music. I love playing it, because it always feels like you're exploring something.'

For all its austere temperament, 'Let Robeson Sing' is rich in overtones, with Bradfield's vocal eerily ghosted by Wire during the verse and Nick Nasmyth adding his best Church of Al Kooper organ accompaniment. The song reached Number 15 when released as a single – its B-side was Bradfield singing the spiritual 'Didn't My Lord Deliver Daniel', which Robeson performed at the 1957 Porthcawl concert – feeding into the narrative of underachievement. But the people who heard, listened. Five days after *Know Your Enemy*'s release, the Let Paul Robeson Sing! exhibition opened at the National Museum Cardiff. When its subsequent tour reached Swansea's Dylan Thomas Centre in January 2002, Patrick Jones and Nicky Wire drove down to see it. There, with the Manics' song playing through the speakers, Paul Robeson

Jr shook Nicky's hand and thanked him for keeping his father's memory alive.

'I look back and I realise we've pretty much only ever written about stuff that has either angered or inspired us,' says Wire. 'And this was a song of aspiration and tribute. So it felt really good.'

74.
The Year Of Purification

Recorded: Abbey Road, London
Producer: Dave Eringa
Released: 19 March 2001 (*Know Your Enemy*, Epic)

'If anyone knows about sullen loneliness, you do.'
— Barry MacSweeney, 'Daft Patter'

In its original CD release *Know Your Enemy* contained a secret cover version – McCarthy's 'We Are All Bourgeois Now', appearing after the five minutes and forty-two seconds of digital silence which follow the ostensible final track 'Freedom Of Speech Won't Feed My Children'. It also features another song that isn't a cover version but which so brazenly walks the tightrope between homage to/imitation of R.E.M. circa *Murmur* – in particular the song 'Shaking Through' – that hiding it in plain sight was probably the only sensible option.

'I heard it straight away when I was writing the music,' says Bradfield. 'Like – oh, God . . . the way I'm riding over the chord changes feels like R.E.M., where Michael Stipe would sing across the bar. I didn't try for it, it was just there. Sometimes you can't deny it.'

Continuing the spirit of full disclosure, when it came to record the song it would have been perverse for Bradfield not to use his blue twelve-string Rickenbacker. 'A great experience,' he says. 'I just wanted it to be good, and be faithful to its inspirations.' An arpeggiated jangle-pop plaint par excellence, 'The Year Of Purification' captured what Bradfield perceptively heard as the 'composed freneticism' of R.E.M.'s formative era too uncannily for comfort, thereby disqualifying it from consideration as a single. 'It really didn't sound like us,' says Nicky Wire, 'so that was never going to happen.'

Written at Bradfield's west London flat then recorded just a mile away at Abbey Road as work on the album neared its conclusion, 'The Year Of Purification' sounded cool and cultured, in contrast to the raw brittle textures they had cooked up in the Andalusian heat. 'By that point we had pushed Dave Eringa to the point of despair,' says Bradfield. 'And him us a bit, too. In El Cortijo, we'd be egging each other on to get a bit more grit out the oyster. So Guy Massey engineered this, he's a good cultured Abbey Road boy. It was nice to have a different take, a different pair of ears.'

Compared to the music, the lyric's catalyst was far less obvious: Barry MacSweeney, an alcoholic poet from Northumberland, inspired by the Beats and Rimbaud, a relentlessly angry writer driven by personal and political struggle, who finally succumbed to the demon drink in 2000 aged fifty-one. 'I didn't know anything about him, he's not on the classic roll call of poets,' says Wire, 'but I had heard something on the radio, how he used to get so hammered he'd crawl into his house through the cat flap, so I found him immediately interesting. Then I got into his poetry. The lyric is about cleansing, I guess, a symbolic cleansing of a lot of things.'

Veering between self-reproach ('What have I said?') and recrimination ('Liberal asinine pricks'), the song offers a window into Wire's mindset as he struggled to reconcile his unreconstructed self-image ('The ravaged corner, cold and embittered') with the popular view of the band post-*TIMT* as representing what he terms 'the acceptable face of socialism'. Of course, shaking hands with Fidel Castro would be one way to dispel that.

Compositionally, 'The Year Of Purification' shows Wire and Bradfield's division of labour evincing a collective consciousness that harmonises their individual parts. In this case, by pinning such a conflicted lyric to music so closely resembling the subject of Wire's most notorious iconoclastic outburst, the song could itself be an act of purification, perhaps even atonement.

'I caused a lot of my own downfalls,' Nicky laughs. 'I m certainly not blaming anyone else.'

75.

Wattsville Blues

Recorded: Rockfield Studios, Monmouthshire
Producer: Dave Eringa
Released: 19 March 2001 (*Know Your Enemy*, Epic)

> 'I do not like your tone, it has an ephemeral,
> whingeing aspect.'
>
> – The Fall, 'It's A Curse'

Popularly mistaken as the first Manics song with a Nicky Wire lead vocal – an honour actually belonging to 'Ballad Of The Bangkok Novotel' – 'Wattsville Blues' also became synonymous with the *Know Your Enemy* era's self-indulgence, on the premise that allowing such a thing to happen was a regrettable byproduct of too much time and money spent in service of an ill-conceived project. If there were any artistic repercussions to the shift in material circumstances 'Close My Eyes' had alluded to, perhaps this was one. 'There was a sense of laziness with that album – a spiteful laziness, I guess,' says Wire. 'I was very ill-disciplined. And I should have put more effort into the singing with this song.'

His voice played the lonesome corncrake to the band's resident choirboy, preposterously so in the verses and a coda where Wire lambasts 'useless fuckers knocking at my door'. Yet for all its wilfulness, 'Wattsville Blues' follows a classic duet template, revealed when Bradfield's harmonies arrive and the chorus takes off: for Nick and James, read Nick and Kylie, or Serge and Jane, or Lee and Nancy, or Shane and Kirsty . . .

'I could definitely hear the duality of him in the verse and me in the chorus,' says Bradfield. 'It was a him and her thing, I could hear us bouncing off each other vocally. The sweetness and the sourness. It came really quickly and I understood it straight away.'

Structurally, the album version stayed faithful to the cassette demo Wire made in the upstairs room at his terraced house in the Valleys, a baleful existential lament in D countered by warm pledges of domestic bliss. Wire's Casio drumbeat and Yamaha acoustic guitar – a birthday present from Bradfield – were retained for the final recording, while Bradfield played bass and Moore added proper drums, lending the whole a downhome funkiness worthy of Ian Dury and The Blockheads, underscored by Nasmyth's Mick Gallagher-esque Hammond organ and in no way undermined by the multiple repetitions of both verse and chorus, a consequence of Wire as sole composer.

'Because I was taken by what melody there was, I wrote less words!' he laughs. 'And there's not much meaning to the words other than I really like being at home – it was the first home I ever bought and I didn't want to leave. Nothing deeper than that. But musically it developed into something really nice, and not particularly down to me.'

The song was debuted live at Havana's Teatro Karl Marx on 17 February 2001 and performed just five times in the UK soon thereafter, bowing to the mid-song verdict of one Brixton Academy attendee who yelled 'Get that cunt away from the microphone!', much to the alarm of Martin Hall who happened to be standing nearby. Yet its benighted status has weathered well down the years – 2022's album remix accentuated the mellow core and removed the grumpy outro – and it prefigured far more significant musical contributions from Wattsville's bluesman. As for his protestations for being 'so happy I know I can never leave', a few months after writing the song Nicky Wire and his wife moved six miles down the road to a much bigger house on a different hill, overlooking the mean streets of Newport. 'Where life blossomed,' he smiles. 'But I felt a lot safer in Wattsville!'

76.

My Guernica

Recorded: El Cortijo, Marbella, Spain
Producer: Dave Eringa
Released: 19 March 2001 (*Know Your Enemy*, Epic)

> 'Art, like morality, consists of drawing the
> line somewhere.'
>
> – G.K. Chesterton

Named after Picasso's anti-war masterpiece, referencing The Human League, misquoting T.S. Eliot, and subsequently despaired of by its authors to the extent it's never been played live, 'My Guernica' is the essence of *Know Your Enemy*'s fever-baked heartland; a wild lab creation that implodes upon contact with reality.

Bradfield's initial idea was a gnarly garage groover tuned in open G, which soon shifted to a gentler template: 'Angels And Devils' by Echo & The Bunnymen, an *Ocean Rain*-era B-side recorded in San Francisco, with Pete de Freitas dum-dumming down to a Moe Tucker nod and Will Sergeant's farther eastern extemporisations on the Vox Mk XII creating one of the great Velvet Underground pastiches. 'But then I played it to Nick and Sean in a dressing room somewhere and it's like, "No, go harder." So we went away from "Angels And Devils", back to a more "White Light/White Heat" kind of vibe. And that was the start of the ruination of quite a good song!'

To amplify the pounding beat, Moore used an upturned bass drum as a floor tom. Meanwhile, El Cortijo's already fuzzy sonics were pushed to extremes by Eringa's use of a seventies-vintage Binson EQ unit. 'It fried everything,' says Bradfield. 'My guitars went through it, my voice was put through it. Nick was just like,

"Make it even more!" I'm saying, "It's gonna sound like you're in a chip shop if we go any more." We pushed it too far.'

Written and recorded early in the album process, the collective appetite for distortion that was applied to 'My Guernica' would define *Know Your Enemy* as a whole. The original mix is demented: crackling wedges of sound at opposing ends of the stereo spectrum in emulation of the lyric's unfolding psychic warfare, with Bradfield in the middle, beseeching 'Keep it together, hold it together'. For better and worse, 2022's 'de-fragged' version recompensed clarity over intensity. It also rectified Bradfield's misreading the title character of T.S. Eliot's poem 'The Love Song of J. Alfred Prufrock' as 'Alfred J. Prufrock', an anomaly that had long vexed Wire, not least when a fan called him out on his knowledge of Eliot. The accusation hurt, as the Prufrock reference was a knowing hat-tip to Lloyd Cole and The Commotions' 'Mister Malcontent', another song in which the narrator dissipates having 'become all I despise' and which featured a lyric – 'Or should I laugh or should I cry/Or should I part my hair behind?' – quoting Eliot's original text.

For this reason, plus its unflattering association with one of the twentieth century's greatest artworks, Wire's relationship with 'My Guernica' remains tarnished.

'*Guernica* made probably the greatest impact any painting's had on me,' he says. 'But I have no idea why I called the song '*My* Guernica'. There's nothing in there that implies being bombed by a fascist dictator! I'm overreaching, I'm being too curious. Also, T.S. Eliot is now quite rightly demonised for his anti-semitism, which I hadn't come across at the time. The one good thing to come from this song is something I didn't do and wish I had – a year or so later, Paul Heaton invited me on a trip to Guernica to write together. I really admire Paul Heaton, but of course, I didn't want to leave the house. So I feel a bit sick about that. There's nothing good for me about this song.'

The pity of 'My Guernica' is it's one of Wire's best-observed

self-portraits, concisely locating the source of his malaise –
'Appearing in more repeats/The mirror man has seen defeat'
– en route to formulating a cure, but only after pouring himself
'another ice-breaker'. The song offers a final sting in the tail:
emerging from studio crackle, a postscript instrumental section
rumbles like Sonic Youth dismantling The Who's 'Baba O'Riley',
eventually fading into its own eternal waste land.

77.
The Convalescent

Recorded: El Cortijo, Marbella, Spain
Producer: Dave Eringa
Released: 19 March 2001 (*Know Your Enemy*, Epic)

'Everybody gets so much information all day long that
they lose their common sense.'
— Gertrude Stein, 'Reflection On The Atomic Bomb'

Around 9 a.m. on Monday 25 October 1999, US Open Champion
golfer Payne Stewart boarded a private plane near his home in
Orlando, Florida bound for Dallas, where he had a business
appointment en route to competing at the Tour Championship in
Houston. Four hours later, the Learjet crashed in a field in South
Dakota, having flown 1,500 miles off-course on autopilot until
running out of fuel then spiralling downwards from an altitude
of 70,000 feet, hitting the ground at near 700mph. Stewart, three
other passengers and two crew members had been unconscious
for almost the entirety of the flight after the plane depressurised
while still on its ascent.

The details of Stewart's death haunted Nicky Wire, who just
one month earlier had been glued to his TV as the 42-year-old
completed Team USA's defeat of Europe in the Ryder Cup at
Brookline, Massachusetts. Fiercely competitive, possessed of a
classically pure playing style as well as a healthy ego and an
occasionally careless tongue, Stewart was a complex individual, whose flamboyant retro apparel could irritate and delight
fellow players and audiences alike. Yet his act of sportsman-
ship in that Ryder Cup victory as he conceded his own match
with Europe's Colin Montgomerie and remonstrated with the

bellicose home crowd was impossible not to admire.

'I really loved Payne Stewart as a golfer,' says Wire. 'He was such a competitor but a real chap as well. One of those people that made the most out of his own talent. And I was struck by the fact that the plane was flying while everyone was dead, but it still flew until it crashed. Flying used to petrify me. By the time you have kids, you're like, "This is good, I get to just sit down." But this was pre-children, and the paranoia used to rage and rage. So the Payne Stewart thing really freaked me out.'

Thus it came to pass that one of the greatest golfers of his generation made the unlikeliest cut of his career and found immortality in a Manic Street Preachers lyric: 'Pity poor Payne Stewart in a death bubble/But what a swing and so much bottle'. With its incongruous juxtapositions of artistic and sporting titans – Goya and Ethiopian distance runner Haile Gebrselassie; Werner Herzog and Cuba's Alberto Juantorena, the only athlete ever to win Olympic gold at both 400 and 800 metres – 'The Convalescent' ostensibly belongs to the same high/low culture-clash tradition as 'Mr Carbohydrate' and 'Prologue To History'. While both those lyrics emerged in a swift unfiltered flow, however, the final version of 'The Convalescent' was delivered to Bradfield only after Wire had sifted and edited down many pages, a rigour evident in the tight metre and clipped consonance of such lines as 'A collage constructed and constantly fed', or the *ur*-Wire couplet 'Kleenex kitchen towels and teletext TV/My favourite inventions of the 20th century'.

'I set out to write a collage that I would have had on my wall, but it was obviously a collage in my mind at this point. I had a song called "The Kleenex Protocol", which fed into "The Convalescent". And "Lovely labradors outnumber musicians" is obviously about Molly, our dog, and the idea of separating myself from other musicians. Let's face it, I'd already done that many times over.'

Titled after one of Welsh artist Gwen John's melancholic

depictions of a lone woman in a domestic setting, the song emulates the fretful surges of its author's migrainous mind from thoughts banal to troubled, while insinuating its own kind of therapeutic process. Amid the doomy invocations ('exit policies'; 'scream until the war is over'), the music's slashing neuroto-motorik groove – suggestive of Stereolab's early Farfisa organ-heavy workouts with Bradfield doing his best Peter Hook impression – suddenly calms itself, trying to 'ease the stress'.

'I understood this was a day in the life of Nicholas Allen Wire,' says Bradfield. 'Haile Gebrselassie and Payne Stewart in one lyric! I was really excited about it. I don't know if the job I did was the best, I remember not being happy with a lot of the sounds. But I wanted it to be like a Wire montage. Sometimes you have a picture which is jarring. And sometimes you get a beautiful one. A post-impressionist postcard of Alfred Sisley next to a picture of Gibby [Haynes] from Butthole Surfers. So I think the song has those peaks and troughs. Still don't quite think we nailed it.'

Bradfield's verdict could be the minority's, albeit he feels happier about the 2022 remix, which broadens the low-end and smooths down the keyboard fuzz while sensibly still shining a spotlight on Moore's propulsive drum detonations. Yet the fact that 'The Convalescent' is another *Know Your Enemy* song bewilderingly never performed live speaks volumes for how awkwardly the album sits with its creators. After 'Ballad Of The Bangkok Novotel's bizarre return to 1994, here were more substantial intimations of darker times: with its references to Dante's inferno, dysmorphia, and the equating of the Bosnian War's Srebrenica massacre with Nazi genocide, the song's final verse could have been lifted from *The Holy Bible*.

'It's awkward and jarring,' agrees Wire. 'Which I guess is symptomatic of that era.' And if destined to remain a period piece, 'The Convalescent' can be relied upon for at least one eternal truth: its repeated declaration 'DNA means does not accept' remains its author's philosophical bedrock.

78.

Epicentre

Recorded: Rockfield Studios, Monmouthshire
Producer: Dave Eringa
Released: 19 March 2001 (*Know Your Enemy*, Epic)

'Oh, isn't life a terrible thing, thank God?'
– Dylan Thomas, Under Milk Wood

There is surely no Manics song more pregnant with foreboding, or so ineluctably drawn to a reckoning with itself, as 'Epicentre'. Everyone plays their part to perfection. Sean Moore's rolling tom-tom interchanges set the tone for its selfless propulsive energy. James Dean Bradfield builds an entire landscape of feeling from an opening guitar motif that's perpetually on the verge of a riff without ever lapsing into easy catharsis. Nick Nasmyth's piano chords are vehement yet simple. Nicky Wire's bass lines are in a state of permanent discovery: a performance heedful of the raised stakes as only the writer of this lyric could be. For 'Epicentre' is where Wire gets uncomfortably deep to the root of his myriad health scourges ('Still clinging to the umbilical cord') and the suggestion it's something intrinsic to him summons words of real power ('I'm sleeping myself away into the half-life of yesterday'), as well as the Manics' greatest baleful animal metaphor: 'Like a stunned fox, with memory loss/A sad numb creature, I worship the painkiller'.

'It became debilitating,' he says, 'and I was just trying to figure out what the epicentre of that was: why? All the fucking time. There were even certain hotels that would trigger headaches. I was thinking: is it pillows? Is it Abbey Road? I used to get fucking terrible migraines at Abbey Road, I didn't know if it was the low lighting or just a phase I was going through. I'd wake up every morning and get a headache within twenty minutes. Was I sleeping too much? So it's all infused in that song. I realised that it was important almost from the start, and I've got nothing bad to say about "Epicentre" at all. James thought his vocal was really nasally, he had a cold at the time, but I kind of think that suits it.'

Bradfield admits it wasn't until years later that he was able to appreciate their achievement with 'Epicentre'. 'I was a bit worried because again, I was trying to be more modest in the writing, there's no backing vocal on the chorus – the chorus isn't quite an anticlimax but it's not really a chorus, it's just part of the song. It doesn't explode into life. Playing twelve-string guitar is like some saint's revenge on guitar players. One string goes out of tune and it's all shit. So I was really concentrating, trying not to sing too loud and trying not to be too expressive in the guitar. And I kept falling out of time with Nick and Sean, who were bang on it. I suppose if we understate things and it works then that's quite a revelation for us.'

The song's atomic bomb moment comes when Bradfield executes a chord change that plunges the pensive verses into that non-chorus and its bitter truth: 'It feels like/There's no escape/Except through/My hate.'

'B minor shifts into the G,' Bradfield explains. 'I remember being worried with that chord change – is it a bit Steve Miller?!'

To Wire, the song's spirit guide is mid-eighties R.E.M., albeit unlike 'The Year Of Purification' this time more in feel than detail. Yet each to their own: in March 2002, with the almost year-old *Know Your Enemy* firmly destined for prodigal status, Greil Marcus reviewed it for *Salon*. His first exposure to a Manics album, he particularly enthused about 'Epicentre' as 'an unbreakably stirring piece of 1970s-style guitar rock that calls back such dead heroes as Paul Kossoff of Free and Rory Gallagher of Taste. One chord after another, the song climbs its own steps, a leap from the top of the tower preordained.'[1]

The erstwhile generation terrorists might not necessarily have aspired to such comparisons from their cultural mentor, but this was sweet vindication regardless.

'I knew that people wouldn't like, or perhaps rate, "Epicentre" at first because they just didn't expect us to have songs like that,' says Wire. 'You know, our songs were *full* of *stuff*. And this one wasn't, so I knew it'd be overlooked. That's why, with the Greil Marcus thing, I felt so over the moon. If there was a Top 10 of my favourite Manics songs, "Epicentre" would definitely be in there.'

'Epicentre' also came with its own epilogue: a ghostly seventy-second intimation of 5th Dimension-style sunshine pop shrouded in the cloudy harmonised mantra 'Happy black days, here's the summer'. This stunned fox was, in fact, a refugee from another song, one we haven't yet met, and its exile status would prove hard to shake off.

79.
Baby Elián

Recorded: Abbey Road, London
Producer: Dave Eringa
Released: 19 March 2001 (*Know Your Enemy*, Epic)

'What we're saying today is that you're either part of the solution or you're part of the problem.'

— Eldridge Cleaver

One member of 'The Convalescent's mind collage became flesh on 17 February 2001 when Alberto Juantorena was presented to the Manic Street Preachers after their gig in Havana, alongside triple Olympic gold medal-winning boxer Félix Savón. Nicky Wire got Juantorena's autograph and talked to Savón about Teofilo Stevenson, the previous generation's great Cuban heavyweight. These men were national heroes not just for their athletic prowess but their loyalty to the Cuban revolution: the boxers, in particular, were offered huge financial inducements to go professional and defect to the US, but always refused. After turning down $5 million to fight Muhammad Ali in 1976, Stevenson famously stated, 'What is one million dollars compared to the love of eight million Cubans?'[1]

The Manics met Juantorena and Savón at a post-show reception in Havana's Nacional Hotel. Earlier that evening, shortly prior to going onstage, they were summoned from their dressing room at the Teatro Karl Marx for an audience with Fidel Castro. Wire said he hoped the music wouldn't be too noisy for him, to which the 74-year-old President replied: 'It cannot be more noisy than war, can it?'[2]

Hindsight suggests that Castro's public image benefited more from this cultural exchange than the Manics'. Upon returning to the UK, rattled by a bruising press conference in Havana where an international posse of journalists picked holes in the band's motives for playing there, Nicky Wire pulled out of a scheduled TV interview with BBC journalist Tim Sebastian on the current affairs show *HARDtalk*. 'It's the only time I've bottled it,' he says. 'I felt like hiding. The press conference had been a feeding frenzy – I just thought, "This is hard work, justifying communist dictatorships!"'

Perhaps the most surreal obligation of the Manics' trip was to meet Elián González, the seven-year-old Cuban child whose rescue from the straits of Florida from a capsized refugee boat in late November 1999 led to a custody dispute involving his estranged family members and the governments of Cuba and the US. 'They took us to a top-secret location,' recalls Wire. 'Well, James didn't come. Martin did and Sean may have. But I was there, Mr Propaganda! It was pretty awkward. He was just a kid being a kid. We met his dad, and the apparatus of the party, so to speak. Obviously the whole Cuba thing is so racked with danger and hypocrisy and exposure to making yourself look a stooge . . . I'd probably lost my mind a bit not to see that.'

The González meeting doubtless appeared on their hosts' schedule as soon as Cuba's Ministry of Culture learnt there would be a song on the new Manics album called 'Baby Elián'. For all Wire's discomfort at how his idle poolside notion for a Cuba album launch had played out, here was proof that the Manics were no Che Guevara T-shirt-wearing dilettantes on a publicity-seeking jolly, but actually au fait with the arcane details of the region's history. The lyric references the 'Cuban adjustment act', a 1966 federal law that incentivised Cuban migration to America – AKA 'the devil's playground' – and 'Operation Peter Pan', a 1960–62 scheme where the US government covertly migrated thousands of Cuban children. But 'Baby Elián' was also a blunt instrument, just like revolutions are prone to be, compounded by its music originally being written for a different lyric altogether. Only when Bradfield reworked 'His Last Painting', and transplanted its original music onto this new lyric that Wire presented him late in the *Know Your Enemy* process, was 'Baby Elián' finally put together at Abbey Road, where thanks to Moore's tumbling drums and a percolating bass figure did this hybrid of McCarthy's 'Red Sleeping Beauty' and New Order finally find its true calling.

'I'm glad "Baby Elián" made the album,' says Bradfield, 'because it definitely is a more sympathetic way of exploring the ambitions, the enmity and the protectionism that exists between America and Cuba. Going to Cuba was the price of an education. We knew we couldn't buy into everything that Castro stands for, just like I can't buy into everything America stands for. We wanted to go outside of ourselves, to go outside the record industry. We wanted to go to a place which had inspired us. And we didn't want to respect that blockade. I found out lots of stuff. Everything comes at a cost.'

80.

Freedom Of Speech Won't Feed My Children

Recorded: Abbey Road, London
Producer: Dave Eringa
Released: 19 March 2001 (*Know Your Enemy*, Epic)

'Apart from the sanitation, medicine, education, wine,
public order, irrigation, roads, the fresh water system and
public health, what have the Romans ever done for us?'
— Reg in *Monty Python's Life of Brian*; Dir: Terry Jones

Liberty, charity, royalty, divinity . . . In its assault upon democracy's hypocrisy, album closer 'Freedom Of Speech Won't Feed
My Children' leaves no stone unhurled, no Western shibboleth
unscathed, no cartoon baddie spared. There's special mention for
the Dalai Lama and his earthly representatives Richard Gere and
the Beastie Boys. And finally, J.S. Pemberton, the Confederate
lieutenant-colonel who formulated the world's biggest-selling
carbonated soft drink. 'I originally had "Coca-Cola" in there,' says
Wire, 'but James changed it. He said you need another syllable
and "Coca-Cola" is too Richey, it sounds like a *Generation Terrorists*
throwback.'

Welcome to a York Notes version of *Know Your Enemy*. While
the title out-Brechts McCarthy and the lyric distils the preceding
seventy-two minutes' accumulated petty bile into a series of
slogans/slurs and two killer couplets ('The pacifism killed us all/
For all the tourists on the Berlin Wall'; 'So we protest about
human rights/Worship obesity as our birthright'), for 'Freedom
Of Speech' to work so well is thanks to Bradfield taking the

high road of elegant satire, while also summarising some of the record's key musical tropes: masterful Krautrock drumming, über-fuzzy distortion, celestial harmonies, and every texture fried to the point of instability, with the near-imperceptible addition of Kevin Shields, brought on board by David Holmes who supplied additional production to this song and 'Dead Martyrs'.

'Kevin wasn't showy,' agrees Bradfield, 'but he does those little fifth notes that hang in the air over the next chord, stuff I was doing on *The Holy Bible* to a degree, and which had washed out of my guitar playing a tiny bit. Almost like gamma rays coming off the sun.'

'Freedom Of Speech' is actually the first song Bradfield wrote without a guitar, having composed the melody in his head during a night on the lash at the Heavenly Social in central London and succeeded in remembering it long enough to make a drunken cassette demo upon arriving home at 2 a.m. He subsequently recorded a demo at Greg Haver and Ceri Collier's relocated Big Noise studio in Alexander Street, north Cardiff, with much of his vocal, the Bontempi keyboard and DI'd guitar surviving onto the master recording.

'It just all came together,' he says. 'It's a militant song. The biggest point of it being we tend to absolve ourselves of any sins just because we are democratic. It doesn't criticise the Dalai Lama per se, but it does say just because somebody is deemed to be a beautiful soul then you never question them at all. You never question their privilege – and that's just not the way to go. That lyric left us somewhere on our own. If we were doing a *Story Of The Clash*-style *Story Of The Manics*, I'd put "Freedom Of Speech" on, definitely.'

Wire felt the visceral approach served his lyric perfectly. 'It was so empowering playing it live, the hatred emanating from it. The complacency of the West felt like it was going to come home to roost at some point, and people didn't want to hear that at all.'

As the dramatic subsequent trajectory in the band's sales

profile would prove, people certainly didn't want to hear it from the Manic Street Preachers, especially not in the gnarly, inchoate context of *Know Your Enemy*. The album cover, with cut-up typography superimposed on an indecipherable layer painting by Port Talbot artist Neale Howells, was the perfect representation for what lay within. Greil Marcus may have finally got on board, but plenty others took this record as their cue to disembark.

'Rob Stringer said that about the album cover as well,' says Wire. 'He said, "You might as well put a sticker on there saying: DON'T BUY ME!"' he laughs. 'It was just me taking things too far.'

81.
Groundhog Days

Recorded: RAK, London
Producer: Dave Eringa
Released: 4 June 2001 ('Ocean Spray' B-side, Epic);
9 September 2022 (*Know Your Enemy: Door To The River*,
Columbia)

'Laughing is easy, I would if I could.'
– Queens of the Stone Age, 'In The Fade'

Incapacitated by routine Wire *This Is My Truth*-era tour ennui
– 'Waking up again/To the same old thing . . . the same old
songs . . . the same old pain' – 'Groundhog Days' came from the
same RAK session where Bradfield and Tom Jones laid down
a Dave Eringa-produced version of Elvis Presley's 1955 hit 'I'm
Left, You're Right, She's Gone' for Jones's 1999 album *Reload*.
'It's a demo, with me playing shitty drums,' says Bradfield.
'We just tarted it up later and decided it was good enough for
a B-side.' The same studio booking yielded a version of Nirvana's 'Been A Son': aptly enough, given the literal and impactful deployment of quiet/loud guitar dynamics in 'Groundhog
Days'.

Wire would be the first to agree the lyric is not his finest. 'It's
me moaning. There is nothing deeper to it. But the guitars are
just so wide and enveloping, I am more than happy to lay down
in the bliss of James being a professional version of J Mascis.'

'Groundhog Days' is otherwise notable for a quintessential Wire
soliloquy ('Wake up feeling like the Messiah/Totally fucked five
minutes later') that opens by quoting dialogue from the song's
1993 film near-namesake starring Andie MacDowell and Bill

Murray, while the version on 2022's reissue gave a new home to the 'Happy black days' stray first encountered in 'Epicentre' – for reasons that elude the individuals concerned.

82.
Masking Tape

Recorded: Rockfield Studios, Monmouthshire
Producer: Dave Eringa
Released: 10 September 2001 ('Let Robeson Sing' B-side,
Epic); 9 September 2022 (*Know Your Enemy: Solidarity*,
Columbia)

> 'I was maimed by rock and roll.'
> – Wilco, 'Sunken Treasure'

That 'Masking Tape' was excluded from *Know Your Enemy* on aesthetic grounds makes some kind of sense – though the same could be said for 'Prologue To History' vis à vis *This Is My Truth*, and few now dispute that was a mistake. This bittersweet saloon bar vamp glows like autumnal ashes in the grate, a memorial to Wilco's *Being There*, itself a double album sprawl inspired by the teenage Jeff Tweedy hearing *London Calling* and realising that punks could have soul too.

'We definitely wanted it as good as something on *Being There*,' says Bradfield. 'And I think we got there. But then we decided that it sounded *too good* . . .! Which is why we left it off. There's a rugby saying – you've got to earn the right to go wide. Well, we haven't earned the right to sound like Wilco, but we have earned the right to sound like debut album Black Crowes.'

The lyric's rueful evocation of the travelling band's life rhythms is amplified by the mostly live ensemble performances, with special mentions for Moore's stoic drumming and Nasmyth's Hammond organ. Yet amid the prevailing millennial angst, no one within the church could see a Manics song like this translating to the world outside. Leaving 'Masking Tape' off the album, however, meant finding a place for what Wire calls its 'fucked up Beach Boys' interlude prior to the exultant final chorus, which it was agreed did have the requisite otherworldliness for *Know Your Enemy*. Thus the refrain 'Happy black days, here's the summer' became an adjunct to 'Epicentre', a role it then mysteriously reprised for the 2022 version of 'Groundhog Days' while happily retaining its original function in 'Masking Tape': the one that never quite stuck, the B-side that was 'too good' for the album, which could have used its steady heart – a song 'for every month of the year' indeed.

'I've always got a roll of masking tape on tour,' says Wire. 'Tippex, pens, stationery . . . Things like that are such a central part of my life. And I've got nothing but fondness for this song.'

83.

There By The Grace Of God

Recorded: Monnow Valley, Monmouthshire; Wessex,
    London
Producers: Greg Haver and Mike Hedges
Released: 14 October 2002 (single, Epic); 28 October
    2002 (*Forever Delayed*, Epic)

'God seems to have left the receiver off the hook, and
time is running out.'

> – Arthur Koestler, *The Ghost in the Machine*

Know Your Enemy was hardly a failure in commercial terms,
achieving sales of around 500,000. As Nicky Wire said in 2021,
'We'd kill for that these days.' But it had been tasked with following a multi-platinum Number 1 record, and its failure to connect
led the band to consolidate with a greatest hits album, named
Forever Delayed – after the 'Roses From The Hospital' lyric – for
which they would record a new single. 'It felt as if we needed
to reset, or be less interested with what we meant to our fans or
other people – just do what came naturally,' says Bradfield. 'But
it didn't quite work out that way.'

There was very little that was natural about 'There By The
Grace Of God'. Amid a lengthy initial writing and recording
session at Monnow Valley trying to dig out a hit, Bradfield's
experimentation with an Electro-Harmonix bass synth pedal saw
a diversion into territory that was, for them, unexplored.

'Dare I say the demo had a sort of Depeche Mode stealthy
majesty,' says Wire. 'Lyrically it's flimsy – I wanted to write
something redemptive. "With grace we will suffer/With grace
we shall recover" – it's defiant. Not a particularly Manics theme,

but it was totally designed as a single off a greatest hits. Then the disaster started.'

After a follow-up session with Mike Hedges, and further tinkering from hot producer du jour Marius de Vries, 'There By The Grace Of God' was placed in a three-way shootout against a *Know Your Enemy*-era relic, 'Door To The River', and the band's clear favourite, '4 Ever Delayed'. Both Martin Hall and Rob Stringer, however, thought 'Grace' was The Hit. And although little of substance lay beneath its swirling clouds of expensively manicured sound, the song went to Number 6 in the singles chart, so perhaps they had a point. 'It wasn't for me,' says Bradfield. 'It's the only time I'll ever say I didn't know if the lyric felt like us. We were still shooting ourselves in the foot at this point.'

84.
Door To The River

Recorded: (v.1) Abbey Road, London; (v.2) Monnow
  Valley, Monmouthshire
Producers: Mike Hedges and Dave Eringa
Released: (v.2) 28 October 2002 (*Forever Delayed*, Epic);
  (v.1) 9 September 2022 (*Know Your Enemy: Door To The
  River*, Columbia)

'All that we can hope for is to put some order into
ourselves.'
  – Willem de Kooning, 'The Renaissance and Order', 1949

The title track of an album that wasn't, 'Door To The River',
named after one of Wire's favourite Willem de Kooning paintings, began its protracted gestation in late 2000, amid mixing and
last-minute recording for *Know Your Enemy*. With the twin-LP
concept now abandoned, a rough demo was made at Abbey Road
and the song parked for a later date. Fifteen months later, the
quest for an advance single to launch the *Forever Delayed* greatest
hits saw 'Door To The River' upgraded with a lavish orchestral
arrangement, the full bells, strings and French horns.

'To hang all that Christmas tree stuff off it, to bring it back in
line with stuff like "A Design For Life",' says Bradfield. 'And just
to have that sense of wonder, a bit more kind of a starry night
kind of vibe. Whereas the version we'd started at Abbey Road
at the back end of *Know Your Enemy* was simpler. I don't really
know what the song was about, I just know that it made me feel
something . . . good.'

Even with Disney stardust flung into its every available crevice,
'Door To The River' was too haunted and fragile a vessel to fit the

musclebound profile of a radio smash in the early twenty-first century. Its anomalous inclusion on a singles compilation vexed Wire, who also remains unconvinced – to put it mildly – by the lyric. 'It's me trying out some pseudo-Bob Dylan religious shit. "The majesty, the majesty . . ." Majesty for me's a chippy and a good bottle of vinegar! The lyric is a lie. But the song has a charm.'

When Bradfield and Dave Eringa went back to the original *Know Your Enemy* multitracks for 2022's reissue, they uncovered 'Door To The River's true character: plain and intimate, a painting patiently awaiting restoration. 'It is arresting to hear now it's just me, Nick and Sean together,' says James. 'It was heartening to hear you can do it on your own.'

The song acquired a tangible legacy in 2017, when the Manics built their own studio in a converted cottage at the head of the Usk valley just outside Newport, and named it Door To The River.

85.

4 Ever Delayed

Recorded: SARM Hook End, Oxfordshire
Producer: Steve Osborne
Released: 14 July 2003 (*Lipstick Traces*, Epic)

> 'The man who removes a mountain begins by
> carrying away small stones.'
>
> – William Faulkner

The phrase 'Forever delayed' was a lyric from 'Roses In The
Hospital', which at the time of its recording in spring 1993 at
Hook End Manor struck Nicky Wire as especially auspicious. 'I
can remember it vividly. I actually said to Richey, "That sounds
like a great title for a greatest hits album."'

To record what was still their putative next single and therefore
the title track of that greatest hits album, the Manics returned
to Hook End, hoping to sprinkle some alchemical good spirits
from a more innocent time onto the song they felt was the pick
of the ten written or demoed at Monnow Valley. By now owned
by producer Trevor Horn, the Elizabethan manor house-cum-
seventies rock folly was even more lavishly appointed than nine
years earlier, with the enormous control room proudly housing a
ninety-six-channel Solid State Logic J Series console, one of the
largest in the UK. The *premier cru* gear, coupled with the opulent
accommodation and recreational facilities, made Hook End, in
Horn's admittedly biased opinion, 'definitely the best residential
recording studio in the world'.[1]

Unfortunately, Bradfield soon discovered the studio's latest
owner had kept possession of its resident ghost ('Still Haunted
– awful'). And there was something of the night about the

atmosphere in the control room too, as producer Steve Osborne's methods landed awkwardly with one band member in particular.

'We're looking for a producer that's going to bring something new to the table,' says Bradfield. 'That U2 philosophy of having somebody shake you up a bit, like [Daniel] Lanois and [Brian] Eno with *Achtung Baby*. On the first day in Hook End Manor, Steve Osborne wanted to change the way we all played. We had signed up to that, but when you're in the room it's suddenly a bit harder. After two days he still hadn't got the drum sound he wanted. So he sat us all down in the control room: "I feel as if we've all bought the ticket, but we're not all on the train yet . . ." I'm looking at Sean's body language, I'm like, "Don't do it, don't do it, *don't* . . . Oh. He's gone." Sean's like, "Steve, you're asking everybody to do things we aren't accustomed to. If that's the way you work, fine. But I've never been more uninspired in my life. And I just don't want to drum for you any more."'

Following a 'clear the air conversation' (Bradfield) or 'a really bad row' (Wire), the session resumed – remarkably, to a positive conclusion. The band loved the alien yet eerily familiar version of themselves that emerged from the Osborne-variant oblique strategies, which however irksome had yielded results: insisting that Moore play different drum fills on each chorus boosted the song's dynamic engine; getting Wire to change one 'delayed' to 'betrayed' intensified the mood of overarching melancholy. Bradfield, meanwhile, was not only forbidden from playing 'like himself' but refused direction as to exactly how he should play. 'I enjoyed it,' he says. 'My old faithful Gibson had an acoustic pickup, and Steve said, "You're not allowed to play anything but that pickup today." Or using a red Mosrite guitar – "I don't want your usual rock guitar, I want something more spindly." So the astral bits in the middle of "4 Ever Delayed" are me denuded of the power of my usual sound, being expressive in a different way.'

Similarly, Bradfield's vocal doesn't attempt to overcompensate for what is a threadbare lyric. Indeed, his tone of stunned understatement makes a virtue of it. But few as they were, the words – part-inspired by Werner Herzog's Amazonian historical epic *Aguirre, The Wrath of God* – held sharp emotional triggers: 'From the city to the sea' invoked one of Nicky Wire's favourite songs by The Family Cat, a London-based indie group who had given the fledgling Manics a support slot at Bristol Fleece & Firkin in May 1990. '4 Ever Delayed's vast yet intimate landscape of lost innocence and wounded experience presented a subtly transformative sonic vision. And then, 'There By The Grace Of God' was released as a single instead.

'We couldn't believe it,' says Wire. '"4 Ever Delayed" just seemed so obvious: it's the title of the album and it's much better . . . So, it was disappointing.'

Annoyed at that decision – and their acquiescence – the band compounded the perceived self-sabotage by vetoing the inclusion of '4 Ever Delayed' on its namesake greatest hits album. It sat on the shelf for over a year until finding a home among the assorted B-sides, off-cuts, covers and live tracks on *Lipstick Traces*, thereby guaranteeing its cult status.

'I still have a residual anger about it,' says Bradfield. 'My first apology goes to Steve Osborne. It's tough being a producer – he wasn't making friends, but he did a great job.'

86.

Judge Yr'self

Recorded: House In The Woods, Surrey; RAK, London;
Monnow Valley, Monmouthshire
Producer: Dave Eringa
Released: 14 July 2003 (*Lipstick Traces*, Epic)

> 'A dog must bark
> So evil calls.'
>
> – The Human League, 'I Am The Law'

Lipstick Traces promised a 'secret history of Manic Street Preachers', its title and subtitle paying homage to Greil Marcus's inspirational *ur*-text, which was also quoted on the album's inner sleeve: 'What appealed to me were its gaps and those moments when the story that has lost its voice somehow recovers it.'[1]

One recovered voice in particular stood out. In 1994, post-*The Holy Bible*, the band accepted a commission to write a song for a Sylvester Stallone-starring film of the 2000AD strip *Judge Dredd* – much to the delight of Richey Edwards, who in the early eighties had had one of his own cartoons printed in the comic. 'Judge Yr'self' was demoed during the January 1995 House In The Woods session, and saw a borderline parody Edwards lyric – allusions to self-harm; directly quoting Nietzsche ('Dionysius against the crucified') – set to a plausible stab at the Nine Inch Nails/Pantera interface he'd proposed as a future artistic direction.

Bradfield was dubious of the terrain. 'Comics aren't my department. And I knew Richey was a big fan of "Walk" by Pantera, which I do think was a quite startling sound, but I remember saying to him it's too male, too blunt for me. But he was bang into the idea straight away, and I'm just thinking, "we'll submit a song, they won't like it and that'll be that."'

Edwards's disappearance ended any immediate prospect of the song's completion (the film ultimately closed with The Cure's 'Dredd Song'). 'At the time I was saying, "There's a bit too much 'you' in there, Rich,"' says Wire. 'But I think it could have been a proper Guns N' Roses moment in the film if we'd pushed on through.'

Subsequently revisited when Bradfield and Eringa were trawling through unfinished tapes, and bolstered with real drums, extra guitar and a proper mix, 'Judge Yr'self' was revealed as both ruthlessly fit for its original purpose and an emphatic dead end.

87.
The Love Of Richard Nixon

Recorded: Stir Studios, Cardiff; Grouse Lodge Studios,
    Ireland; Additional Production: Metropolis Studios,
    London
Producers: Greg Haver and Tom Elmhirst
Released: 18 October 2004 (single, Epic); 1 November
    2004 (*Lifeblood*, Epic)

'I am a lonely visitor
I came too late to cause a stir.'
                                    – Neil Young, 'Campaigner'

In July 1976, Neil Young was watching TV with his son Zeke
when the programme was interrupted by a news bulletin showing disgraced former President Richard Nixon entering a hospital
where his wife Pat had been admitted following a stroke. The
following day, Young wrote a song, 'Campaigner', and subsequently performed it on what proved to be the final night of
his ill-fated tour with erstwhile Buffalo Springfield and Crosby,
Stills, Nash & Young bandmate Stephen Stills.[1]

Young and Nixon had previous: one of CSNY's most famous
songs was the Young-written 'Ohio', which indicted the president by name as responsible for the Ohio National Guard's
fatal shootings of four students during an anti-Vietnam War
demonstration at Kent State University on 4 May 1970, and
became a protest song that transcended its era and specific
circumstances. 'Campaigner' offered a very different verdict on
Richard Nixon. Young now portrayed him not as the Woodstock generation's voodoo doll, but a human being weeping
in a hospital for his beloved. Six years after calling him out

for murder, Neil Young was now feeling sorry for the guy, murmuring in the song's refrain, 'Even Richard Nixon has got soul.'

During subsequent decades, Nixon's demonisation would be cemented in popular culture. He was forever Tricky Dicky, orchestrator of the Watergate cover-up, the political bad seed who begat a litany of Oval Office liars. Film portrayals were typically unflattering, while his name and face became satirical memes everywhere from *The Simpsons* to *Point Break*. In the realm of pop music, 'Campaigner' remained an isolated perspective, typical of its author's famed contrarian urges but echoed by no one else. No one, that is, until the Manic Street Preachers heralded their first album of new material in three years with 'The Love Of Richard Nixon', a song every bit as nuanced as Neil Young's in its sympathetic depiction of a complex man. Richard Milhous Nixon was temperamentally unsuited for public office yet became leader of a superpower through sheer diligence and bloody-minded determination – he once described himself as 'an introvert in an extrovert's business'. Much like Neil Young, then. Or possibly even Nicky Wire.

'I'd had a lingering fascination with Nixon,' says Wire. 'When I watched *All The President's Men* when I was young, it didn't actually make me hate him. But it was the Oliver Stone–Anthony Hopkins biopic that crystallised it, because it felt like Hoppo was playing him almost like Richard III, with a deep sadness. There's a brilliant line in there which stuck with me, when he loses the first election to Kennedy. "Kennedys always win, but I'm gonna get that fucker . . ." You know, Kennedy started Vietnam and Nixon finished it, for all his faults. But it's never written like that.'

Aptly enough, vengeance was the spur to write 'The Love Of Richard Nixon'. In its author's sights? The man who wrote 'Ohio'. 'In a very spiteful way, I was a bit bored of Neil Young,' says Wire. 'He seemed to be on the cover of every other edition of *MOJO* and *Uncut*, so I thought, "Fuck it – because he had a go at Nixon,

I'm going to be the Lynyrd Skynyrd to his 'Southern Man' . . ."
That's the weird process that goes on within me sometimes.'

In 2003 the US was embroiled in the second Gulf War, a deadly
misadventure instigated by George W. Bush, a Republican president far more recklessly doctrinaire than the incumbent of thirty
years earlier. Writing any kind of song about Nixon now would
have felt obtuse, let alone one reappraising his political legacy
('People forget China and your war on cancer') and evoking
pity for the man ('The fear of the future/The best years behind
you'). Wire may have been unaware of the relatively obscure
'Campaigner', but his lyric was no less compassionate.

Heightening the oddity was a musical treatment that divested
the band of so many hallmark features it was barely recognisable
as a Manics song. Bradfield crooned neutrally over an arid jerky
groove built from his own fluid bass playing (Wire: 'I still can't
play it that well now, even after years of practice') with Moore
drumming more clinically than a machine. Even Bradfield's
spectacular 'laser beam' guitar solo had a cryogenic quality. 'The
drama's in the lyric,' says James. 'That's what I took from "Richard
the Third in the White House cowering behind divided curtains".
We're accused of being a bit too operatic sometimes, but with
that lyric it felt like we had to rein it in, we had to express less.
That's why it's so streamlined, it was the only way it worked.'

Pleased as they were with the finished song, the band were
bewildered when Sony's Rob Stringer decided this was the track
to represent their new album to the public. Sonically, 'The Love
Of Richard Nixon' may have been consistent with *Lifeblood*'s overall aesthetic of locating humanity amid cold, precise landscapes,
yet its subject matter felt at odds with commercial sensibilities.
This much would become evident as the band hunkered down
and put their weight behind the promotional campaign: playing
golf in Nixon masks for an ill-judged video that negated the song's
subversive qualities, performing on podiums for *Top of the Pops*,
and pressing the flesh with Ringo Starr on *Later . . . With Jools*

Holland. 'Ringo was lovely, I'd never met him before,' says Wire. 'He came up to me smiling and said, "What's all this Nixon stuff about then?" And I thought, "I can't explain it in this situation – what am I doing?!" Nixon was a tough sell. We thought it was good and interesting, but a classic curveball, weird lyric . . . an album track, nothing more than that. When it all came together I had goosebumps, but I never thought it could be a single – just thought this is us being us, in a mad way.'

Although the song muscle-marketed its way to Number 2, the subsequent chart performance of *Lifeblood* was a more ominous cultural barometer reading – the first new Manics album to land outside the Top 10 since *Generation Terrorists*. Five years on from the heights of *TIMT*, they were still in a process of self-deconstructing, still struggling to rearrange the pieces into a viable new design. Pop feasts on young flesh: the Manics' support act on December 2004's Lifeblood tour were Razorlight, *NME*'s latest post-millennium new wave darlings, a surrogate Libertines whose debut album had gone Top 3 in July and was still a chart fixture five months later. 'It did feel a bit awkward, because they were already big and getting bigger,' says Wire. 'A new generation had come in with their skinny jeans. And we'd just become old.'

Many bands faced with this situation might have acknowledged their best years were indeed behind them, and made a graceful exit. Yet 'The Love Of Richard Nixon' wasn't only about the disgraced 37th President of the United States, the man whose sampled resignation speech brought the song to a close. In his third volume of Nixon history, American academic Stephen Ambrose declared: 'there is no one else like [Nixon] for refusing to quit, for plotting and executing comebacks, for winning redemption, for self-resurrection'.[2] He could just as well have been describing the Manic Street Preachers.

88.

1985

Recorded: Stir Studios, Cardiff; Grouse Lodge Studios,
    Ireland; Additional Production: Metropolis Studios,
    London
Producers: Greg Haver and Tom Elmhirst
Released: 1 November 2004 (*Lifeblood*, Epic)

'Can't remember such a bitter time.'

> – Redskins, 'Keep On Keepin' On'

Nicky Wire first gave James Dean Bradfield a lyric in 1985.

'It was called "Aftermath",' says Bradfield, 'and it was about
the miners' strike.'

For the opening song in their latest act of reinvention, the
Manics returned to the source. The tumultuous 1984–5 strike
and its impact on their teenage selves and their community
already ran like a black vein throughout the band's work, from
early blasts like 'Strip It Down' through 'Gold Against The Soul'
and on to 'A Design For Life'. Now '1985' characterised the
Manics' very existence as a response to that year's political and
cultural landscape.

'It was meant to be a sweeping evocation of the most important year of my life,' Wire says. 'I think 1985 is the best year for
music ever. I could list so many songs – "Marlene On The Wall"
by Suzanne Vega, "Primitive Painters" by Felt, "Makes No Sense
At All" by Hüsker Dü . . . it's all there. Such an important year,
so I tried to put that in social and political context, in a song. I
was aiming for something grand. Even when written down, it
looked different.'

The lyric singled out The Smiths – 'Morrissey and Marr gave

me choice' – for their life-changing properties. The 'bet' placed by the narrator was to form a band of similar importance, albeit he 'lied' by continuing with his education as a failsafe. Almost every other line was haunted by the strike ('the Civil War failed, why?'), its convulsive impact and epochal consequences ('See all the tears for the walking dead'), with some big beasts simmering in the pot – Orwell, Nietzsche, God – alongside ice skaters Torvill and Dean with their 1984 Olympic routine to Ravel's *Boléro* ('redundant as a sad Welsh Chapel') still omnipresent the following year, mysteriously levered into any vacant spaces on the TV schedules apparently as light relief from news bulletins of police baton-charging picket lines. From 1974 until 1980, Christopher Dean was a constable with Nottinghamshire police; had life spun him in a different direction, he could have been grappling with miners instead of going for gold.

'I was so *fucking* bored with Torvill and Dean that year,' says Wire. 'Just the endless fucking *Boléro* . . . Ice skating felt so opulent compared to what was going on right on our doorstep.'

Bradfield's initial reaction to 'Aftermath' wasn't wholly favourable. 'I remember thinking back then, "A bit obvious . . . come on, we're not the Redskins."[1] Which is mad, really. So when he gave me "1985" I thought, "OK, best get on board with it this time . . ." It was brilliant. Things like "circle the wagons" gave you a sense memory, made you feel like you were back there. So many lines tore at my skin. It really did make me feel something.'

The challenge was how to assimilate this brooding text into the Manics' ongoing redesign, itself still not wholly resolved. 'We were messing with our own nature, trying to reform it,' says Bradfield, 'reaching for something more streamlined, something away from the grit, the blood and the bones of that punk philosophy, a bit more grace – looking to co-opt some kind of sheen to replace the blood, I suppose.' An initial arrangement – revealed on 2024's *Lifeblood* twentieth-anniversary edition – had Bradfield hammering away on the piano to a completely different verse melody, redolent of The Waterboys' 'A Girl Called Johnny'. 'Then I realised that with this new way of thinking, I didn't have to write a banger.'

While Nicky hammered New Order's 1985 'cold organic' apex *Low-Life*, James went back to other favourite records from the period: the numbed motorik of David Bowie and the Pat Metheny Group's 'This Is Not America', and 1983's 'The Last Film', a subversively militaristic anti-war song by London band Kissing The Pink produced by Colin Thurston, noted for his work with Bowie and Magazine. Cumulatively, a shift in aesthetic emerged. 'When a pop song comes from the depths of some kind of detachment or coldness, I kinda like it,' says Bradfield, 'because if you find emotion in that there's always something true about it. So I was happy to chase that.'

After a second Cardiff demo had creepily intimated Joy Division's 'Atmosphere' – icy synths and tom-tom rolls – at Grouse Lodge in rural Ireland the song fully bloomed into a definitive example of anthemic understatement, with particular thanks to a pointillist Bradfield solo played on Wire's Burns twelve-string guitar. A final 'couple of glossy New Orderisms' were subsequently added at the mixing stage with Tom Elmhirst. Glacial and dignified, transfusing the past to create a future, '1985' perfectly mapped *Lifeblood*'s DNA.

'I usually run away from the word, but I really am *proud* of "1985",' says Wire. 'Even when we play it now, it still stiffens the back – makes you feel pretty good.'

89.
Empty Souls

Recorded: Stir Studios, Cardiff; Grouse Lodge Studios,
     Ireland
Producer: Greg Haver
Released: 1 November 2004 (*Lifeblood*, Epic); 10 January
     2005 (single, Epic)

'The tongue may hide the truth, but the eyes – never!'
     – Mikhail Bulgakov, *The Master and Margarita*

Among the initial batch of *Lifeblood* lyrics Wire gave to Bradfield
that were then demoed in Cardiff's Stir Studios, 'Empty Souls'
holds the distinction of the first Manics song to be entirely written
on a piano. Hence the prominent figure that drives the melody
over a classic Motown four-to-the-floor rhythm. 'The song was
built around that moment,' says Bradfield. 'I found the riff on
the piano and everything stemmed from there. I couldn't hear
anything but a Tamla backbeat.'

'Empty Souls' reveals the band locking into *Lifeblood*'s processed organic sensibility at an early stage, bringing a chunk of
inspiration from the Associates' Mike Hedges-produced 1982
landmark *Sulk*. The backing tracks are from the demo, all first
or second takes – even the arching fuzz guitar solo, played on
a white Gibson Flying V – with only some of Bradfield's vocal
re-recorded subsequently. Although Wire insists 'the lyric is not
much more than a good title', its formulaic schemes actually suit
the stark emotional landscape. Featuring a return appearance
from some familiar 'black-eyed dogs', the attempted exposition
of 'a truth we don't know' features one faintly jarring image:
'Collapsing like the Twin Towers' was duly amended in a radio

edit. 'I took it as a moment of cataclysm that just hollows life out and you can't make sense of it,' says Bradfield. 'I don't think it was being distasteful at all. But I suppose the song's about hollowness, and it does feel a bit hollow when you play it.'

Like '1985', 'Empty Souls' would have a been a more representative advance taster for *Lifeblood*. The only track mixed by superstar engineer Mark 'Spike' Stent, it was at least eventually accorded a single release, together with one of the great Manics videos: a night-time Berlin odyssey starring Bahnhof Postdamer Platz, the Kreuzberg district and the Grand Hyatt Hotel. Both city and band look the epitome of hi-spec minimalist post-Cold War chic – but a new ice age was assuredly coming.

A few days after *Lifeblood*'s release, Nicky Wire was in the swish Victorian environs of west London's Colonnade Hotel – birthplace of Alan Turing – when Rob Stringer informed him the midweek chart position was 9. Wire knew there was no chance of the album still being Top 10 when the final chart was published.

'I was just staring out of the window in this freezing cold room, thinking, 'That's it. There's nothing left.' I know it sounds trivial, but it was a bleak moment. Two weeks later it was out of the Top 75, absolutely gone. We'd done the "Empty Souls" video upfront, before the album came out, when "Nixon" was still Number 1 in the midweek chart. So that was the one period when I felt good about *Lifeblood* in a commercial sense. Before the dream died at the Colonnade!' he laughs. 'Even when we drive past it now, I think I'm going to be sick.'

90.
A Song For Departure

Recorded: Stir Studios, Cardiff; Grouse Lodge Studios,
    Ireland
Producer: Greg Haver
Released: 1 November 2004 (*Lifeblood*, Epic)

'A way out is a way in.'

         – Patrick Jones, 'You'

Lifeblood's initial Cardiff demo session was followed by a four-week shift at Philip Glass's Looking Glass Studios in downtown New York with producer Tony Visconti, which yielded less than had been hoped. Visconti, on home turf, preferred to work regular hours. 'He'd be gone by five or six o'clock every night,' says Wire. 'I don't blame him, but we were mostly wandering around, buying stuff and eating. It was good fun working with Tony, he'd always have a good story. It just never felt like we were getting anywhere.'

By contrast, moving on to the rustic isolation of Grouse Lodge in County Westmeath sharpened the creative focus. 'We were looking for an angle,' says Bradfield, 'because we realised our own angle wasn't varied enough. What we were doing was quite flat and stainless steel. By then we were trying to pump something different in the record because all our reference points were a bit cold. Going to the middle of Ireland to convince yourself that something's going to seep through from the trees outside.'

A beautifully limpid intimation of how sadness sounds, 'A Song For Departure' vindicated both going those extra miles and following instinct. Almost every element from the demo was re-recorded to template on an austere disco groove that saw

Moore and Wire's rhythmic bond nearing pure symbiosis. No stranger to eighties flash from his role as drummer in Cardiff one-hit wonders Waterfront, producer Greg Haver was fully on board, both with the sonics and how to realise them. Bradfield's vision for the song, meanwhile, occurred as soon as he read the lyric.

'I'm not saying I knew what it meant, but I kind of felt like I knew what it meant, which is important,' he says. 'I connected with it, in other words. I always heard this as our first proper attempt to be a mixture between Fleetwood Mac and Abba. Nick's playing was so on point, half a second behind the bass drum. Him and Greg were obsessing about that.'

Wire's inspiration was in part an almost identically titled 1958 Elizabeth Jennings poem – 'Song for a Departure' – pondering the ineffability of presence and the gravity of absence. With lines like, 'Maybe this strangeness only ever was/To hide ourselves from some kind of happiness', his lyric was no less elusive or affecting. 'The whole album evokes a certain mood,' he says, 'and [in] this song in particular I tried to fit some beautiful phrases together. I don't think we ever had any doubt about any part of it.'

Greg Haver also rolled up his sleeves with Nick ['Lord'] Nasmyth to ensure the piano parts conveyed the requisite clear, precise drama. 'It was a grand piano,' notes Bradfield. 'Probably needed to be. Lord was brilliant. We just said "Rachmaninov", and he did that straight away.'

The only survivor from the original demo was Bradfield's guitar solo, a wild-eyed meld of Lindsey Buckingham fluidity and Billy Duffy twang. 'I did try redoing it and it just sounded too complete, too *right*, it didn't have that devil-may-care vibe.'

The solo was well worth a reprise during the final tearful procession beyond the horizon, where amid the respondent backing vocal fugue there are eerie melodic traces of the outro to ELO's 'Shangri-La', a song written by the broken-hearted, soon-to-be-divorced Jeff Lynne for others to break their hearts to. Such is 'A Song For Departure's modestly monumental scope. 'I don't mind using musical reference points because usually we don't end up sounding like them,' says Bradfield. 'This is one of the only songs where we get close – where the music itself can't escape its inspiration.'

A likely single had the album's promotional cycle not been curtailed, 'A Song For Departure' best exemplifies the prescience of *Lifeblood*'s design. As noted by John Harris in his sleevenotes for 2024's reissue, by recontextualising the cerebral angst of their seventies and eighties pop idols, the Manics effectively anticipated The War On Drugs' shiny-smooth arena rock by at least ten years.

91.

To Repel Ghosts

Recorded: Stir Studios, Cardiff; Grouse Lodge Studios,
    Ireland
Producer: Greg Haver
Released: 1 November 2004 (*Lifeblood*, Epic)

> 'Art is how we decorate space. Music is how
> we decorate time.'
>
>   – Jean-Michel Basquiat

The Manics' version of U2's 'dream it all up again' reset had one obvious casualty: renowned guitar hero James Dean Bradfield. Willingly self-censoring, he sought less traditional modes of expression, spectacularly so on 'To Repel Ghosts', which deployed three separate guitar parts in the introduction alone. Bradfield's approach was suggested by the title, which led him to 'Ghost Dancing', the then-unreleased song with which Simple Minds boldly opened their 1985 Live Aid set. Long-time Minds fans watching that global satellite broadcast saw Charlie Burchill's urgent slashing at a Fender Stratocaster, an unusual guitar choice for him, plus the fact that 'Ghost Dancing' was a stadium-sized re-write of 'I Travel' from the band's art-rock apex *Empires And Dance*, and sensed a change was gonna come. There was nothing oblique about this strategy. With 'To Repel Ghosts', however, the Manics performed an inversion of that same manoeuvre: filleting trademark operatic power structures and rearranging the bones to create a more artful version of themselves, one burnished with synthesiser and delicate guitar latticework, yet still propulsive, and no less heroic.

    'It was the first time I really let a Stratocaster completely take control of the entire track, which was a drastic step for me,' says Bradfield. 'It was quite nerve-racking getting the effect right, so me and Greg spent a lot of time over that and the programming – we had a MIDI fuck-up that lost us a day and a half. But in the end we came up with something big. "To Repel Ghosts" stands for the MO of the record – made me realise that perhaps we could have been another band, more of a stadium band. A bit more of a, dare I say, *Once Upon A Time*-era Simple Minds band, if we'd followed that muse. It was in us, to play like that.'

Bradfield was unfamiliar with Wire's original inspiration for the lyric, a namesake 1985 painting by Jean-Michel Basquiat, the new genius of eighties New York's downtown art scene who died of a heroin overdose in 1988, aged twenty-seven, and was paraphrased in the song lyric. 'He said something very similar to "a soul in pain has no image to reclaim",' says Wire. 'That was the cornerstone. There's lots of ghosts invoked in Basquiat's paintings, metaphorical and real, ghosts in the past, the ghosts of colonialism. This lyric just poured out. Obviously, journalists would ask if there was an overhang of Richey in there, but it didn't feel like it at the time. Perhaps subconsciously.

'To Repel Ghosts' had been performed on just three occasions in almost twenty years when it surprisingly appeared on the setlist at a Bath warm-up for the 2023 Glastonbury Festival. The song then became a regular throughout the band's UK tour the following year, its elegy for 'the disappearing' hitting harder with the passage of time. Meanwhile, Basquiat's *To Repel Ghosts* was sold at auction in 2022 for almost $8 million. Such is the price for reclaiming the image of a soul in pain.

92.

Fragments

Recorded: Stir Studios, Cardiff; Grouse Lodge Studios,
    Ireland
Producer: Greg Haver
Released: 1 November 2004 (*Lifeblood*, Epic)

'Now I'm getting older as I write.'
             – The Comsat Angels, 'Missing In Action'

Nicky Wire credits mix engineer Tom Elmhirst and his sprinkling of electronic 'bits and bobs' – like the programmed drums that emerge almost imperceptibly in this song's chorus – with resolving the only crisis of confidence he had during the making of *Lifeblood*. As Wire saw it, the issue with 'Fragments' was very straightforward.

'"Don't be U2" – it's one of Nick's big things,' says Bradfield. 'He says any band that copies U2, or comes close to accidentally sounding like them, are fucked. And this song comes close. Everybody's playing absolutely together, chasing the truth of the song down. I was surprised, because I thought we were chasing something opposite. "Fragments" is empathetic and soppy – everything that we weren't.'

'Fragments' certainly breaks the cold deconstructionist template: warm ambience, a stealthy floor-tom rhythm, shadowy bass, dobro guitar glissandos, a mournful melodica shouldering the emotional legacy of a lyric that yearns for peace amid a broken world. 'Two minutes silence in a century of screams'? You can see what Wire was getting at . . .

'I thought it was too "With Or Without You",' he says. 'But Tom Elmhirst's little bits and bobs made it less *real*. All of a sudden it had a nice cosmetic edge. But I think this came quite late in the writing process and I'm pretty sure I was looking for something more humane.'

That quest for a different tone saw Wire collaborate with his brother Patrick on the lyric, his first authentic co-write of the post-Richey era (as opposed to 'Ocean Spray', a Bradfield lyric that Wire completed). 'I'm trying to remember if James had started it with a lyric of mine and then I had asked Pat to add some. But it's a fifty-fifty lyric. I love the "two minutes silence in a century of screams" line, that's his. And "Tiny massive hands, emphatic lonely soul, skin against skin" – I would never have written "skin against skin". That's definitely my brother, him having had children. Gives us a warmth. It's funny, because within the dynamic between myself and Richey, often I was the humane voice.'

'I didn't like this song for years,' admits Bradfield. 'I felt awkward doing it, I didn't like it when it was mixed, or even when it was released. And now I love it. That's very rare for me. We can overthink these things.'

93.

Cardiff Afterlife

Recorded: Looking Glass Studios, New York, 2003;
   Additional Production: Metropolis Studios, London
Producers: Tony Visconti and Tom Elmhirst
Released: 1 November 2004 (*Lifeblood*, Epic)

'The days move along with regularity over and over. And suddenly, there is change.'
                    – Travis Bickle in *Taxi Driver*; Dir: Martin Scorsese

During interviews around *Lifeblood*'s release, Nicky Wire was wont to describe the new album as, *'The Holy Bible* for 35-year-olds', or, 'A coffee table version of *The Holy Bible*'. Haunted by empty souls, suppressed trauma and 'the disappearing', *Lifeblood* closed with a tribute to its principal ghost. 'Cardiff Afterlife' was the first Manics song overtly about Richey Edwards; certainly the first to speak specifically to him, in the regretful, respectful voice of someone who perhaps wished they could have kept in touch more. It reclaimed the memory of Edwards the friend from his tragic mythologised media status, and in articulating the remaining band members' painful stasis also honoured his art: 'The paralysed future/The past sideways crawl' directly referenced 'Die In The Summertime'.

'Those are the key lines of the song, really,' says Wire. 'By then it was coming up to nine years since he disappeared, and it was all about perceptions and reinterpretations, what other people thought. I was scratching around for a title and "Cardiff Afterlife" just felt perfect, reminded me of recording *The Holy Bible*, when James and Richey used to go to the pub, Metros . . . It felt like a good time to write about this.'

Bradfield remembers receiving 'Cardiff Afterlife' as a finished article, with no changes required in order for him to sing it (albeit the 'cassette demo' on 2024's reissue revealed some bitter lines about the 'people who think they knew you . . . sad-eyed fuckers with no life' that were never likely to make the final draft).

'It was a very, very, *very* truthful lyric,' he says. 'It just felt really important. We'd been through a lot of stuff with Richey, and this felt like *our* version of events. We were fed up of conspiracies, fed up with us appearing a bit less emotional than other people were being about it, just fed up with all of it.'

There was some internal debate over the line 'I witnessed splendour and evil that no one saw', which Bradfield thought could be misconstrued as saying Richey was evil. 'As opposed to the splendour of our truth and the evil of everybody else weighing in with speculation,' he says. 'It's very poetic, from my point of view. And if you've got to worry about the context because of the way it's written, it becomes an impossible situation.'

To accompany this tribute, Bradfield's musical treatment was likewise a piece of hero worship. 'I wrote it with a capo on the fifth fret, and after I came up with a vocal and the chords, my only direction was: what would Johnny Marr do? That's basically the way I looked at it. I wanted to play like Johnny Marr would play with The The.'

'Cardiff Afterlife' stands apart from the rest of *Lifeblood*: comfortable in its traditional design, content to luxuriate in those waves of sparkling guitar, a palpably warm heart beating beneath the mix's shivery veneer. Significantly, it was the song that benefited most from working with Tony Visconti. He had Wire play the same 1967-purchased Fender Precision bass he'd let Marc Bolan borrow thirty years earlier, and fed the drums through the same Eventide Harmonizer used on Bowie's *Low*, but otherwise there was no Visconti voodoo, just a group of great musicians playing live together in a room under the auspices of a great engineer – as the Manics came to realise a little too late to make the most of the session.

'It was us getting the sums wrong,' says Bradfield. 'We spent so much time as a band digesting all that myth and legend, getting a version of what happens between artists and producer, David Bowie and Tony Visconti, Led Zeppelin and Eddie Kramer, blah blah. You think, "That's how it happens." Then you get there and you realise that with those producers you bring something to them and then they frame it. Their engineering skills are amazing, there are less takes with those guys. They expect you to sing and get it within three takes, because time was money back then. A producer's got to know what the artist's best performance is. Tony didn't quite know what our best performance was, but he expected it. At the end of the session, it clicked in my head that I should have come to him with a few more ideas.'

The recording's most obviously 'produced' moment was also its point of dramatic rupture: the chorus imploding into jazzy dissonance – 'straight from the *Taxi Driver* soundtrack,' Bradfield admits – as Moore's snare tremors trigger a succession of crescendos, like a spirit voice breaching time's fabric. In 2004, Wire described the band since Edwards's disappearance as 'cursed between the idea of hope and closure'. No one song was ever going to make sense of that equation. But in mapping both 'the breaking' and 'the making' of their lives, 'Cardiff Afterlife' show-cased the best of all its participants.

94.
The Soulmates

Recorded: Monnow Valley, Monmouthshire
Producer: Greg Haver
Released: 20 October 2004 (*Lifeblood* [Japan CD only],
  Epic; 12 April 2024, *Lifeblood 20*, Columbia)

> 'Happiness is a warm puppy.'
>
> – Charles M. Schulz

Other songs recorded at Monnow Valley during the speculative 2002 search for a single to trail *Forever Delayed* eventually became B-sides. As a bonus track on the Japanese edition of *Lifeblood*, the eventual destination of 'The Soulmates' was both obscure and anomalous. It deserved so much better. This raggedly glorious bridge between *Know Your Enemy*'s interior aspect and the emotional tundra of *Lifeblood* had its own unique character: curled around Bradfield's latest echoing variation on McCarthy's 'Red Sleeping Beauty', underlain with 'Lord' Nasmyth's best Jon Lord lonesome organ, and with a sparse, heartsore lyric ('The graffiti/ You left on me/Means every part/Is still bleeding'), it felt deeply wrought.

'It's about dogs,' says Bradfield.

'Companionship and dogs,' adds Wire. 'I think James actually suggested writing a song about them.'

'Dogs were a massive common denominator between us,' Bradfield continues. 'Richey, Sean, myself, Nick, our dogs were important parts of our lives. I loved "Soulmates", I thought it was a great tune. I was playing guitar in a slightly different way, not just power chords all the time. We were all locked in, really flying. I was excited. And then, I remember two months later saying to Rob, "What about this song?" And he's like, "Nah." What the fuck?! It wasn't even considered.'

For years, the song's powerful emotional compass and extreme rarity lent it religious status among diehard fans. But really, like all stray dogs, what 'The Soulmates' most wanted was a proper home – which it found at last on *Lifeblood*'s 2024 reissue.

95.

Firefight

Recorded: Stir Studios, Cardiff

Producer: Guy Massey

Released: 19 April 2005 (*God Save The Manics* EP, Sony
  Music)

> 'Now there's revolution, but they don't know
> what they're fighting.'
>
>   – Jethro Tull, 'Living In The Past'

Smaller in venue and cavalier of setlist – opening song at South-ampton Guildhall: 'Of Walking Abortion' – April 2005's Past/Present/Future tour is fondly remembered by MSP devotees, if not necessarily the band itself. 'Remember that mid-era where everybody assumed The Clash were selling out all their concerts, but they weren't?' says Bradfield. 'Suddenly, off the back of *Lifeblood* it was like, *eurrgh.*'

On the drive home from Swansea's 1,200-capacity Brangwyn Hall, Bradfield insisted on diverting through a Bridgend housing estate because the local chip shop had won an award. 'We're in this weird tour bus, which Rod Stewart had just had,' says Wire. 'There was a double bed in the back. Everything was just slightly not right about that tour.'

In an attempt to sell out a second night at Hammersmith Apollo, a new EP was given away to ticket holders, its title and wild stylistic diversity reflecting the ongoing identity crisis. Only one of *God Save The Manics'* three tracks was featured during the tour, but 'Firefight' was played every night, confirming the song had genuine merit: its melancholic guitar figures and swirling piano suggested 'Motorcycle Emptiness' (which it preceded in the tour setlist), as did the lyric's evocation of burning cars and the killer couplet, 'Wake up the past and tell it to stay away/Bad times are here to stay.'

These words were Bradfield's, his second Manics lyric inspired by a visit he and Patrick Jones made to the Aneurin Bevan stones at Tredegar, where they found burnt-out cars at the monument to the great socialist orator. 'I wanted more lyrics off Nick and he didn't have any available, or he wouldn't give me any,' says Bradfield. 'So I just wrote one because I was impatient. "Firefight" was a contender to go on *Lifeblood* but it was too "band-y". We were just all over the place, still looking for angles.'

'The first time James played the song, I really fell for it,' says Wire. 'We had Guy Massey do the Abba thing, recording the piano part twenty times. I thought it was special and we had to save it, I didn't think it was one to chuck away. Then we got to the point where we just chuck it away because we want to sell out Hammersmith Apollo.'

96.

Underdogs

Recorded: Grouse Lodge Studios, Ireland
Producer: Dave Eringa
Released: 19 March 2007 (single, Columbia); 7 May 2007
  (*Send Away The Tigers*, Columbia)

'I got a baby's brain and an old man's heart.'
                              – Alice Cooper, 'I'm Eighteen'

After several years of drift and doubt, the Manics finally figured a way out of their identity crisis. Deconstruction hadn't worked, so how about reconstruction? Especially if it created a version of themselves that was closer to one that people had previously loved – albeit now older, and maybe wiser. 'The whole MO of *Send Away The Tigers* was us trying to reconnect with the band that perhaps we were, that we'd been trying to escape for ages,' says Bradfield.

One of the earliest songs written for the eighth Manics album, 'Underdogs' vaguely suggested 'You Love Us' 2.0, a reminder to the core fan community of what they had been missing – the Grown-Up Generation Terrorists, an us-against-them-anthem 'for the freaks'. The lyric was certainly more Valerie Solanas than Elizabeth Jennings, albeit to a questionable degree when it exhorted 'the lost and weak' to breed their revenge upon the straight world: 'People like you need to fuck/Need to fuck people like me'. Never one to shirk a challenge, upon reading the lyric Bradfield devised what he terms a 'low concept' in the mould of early-seventies Alice Cooper's wry schlock'n'roll, with edgy verses clattering into the chorus like The Who soundtracking a fireworks display.

'We did a demo and it was good,' he says. 'It was tight but rattly and carefree, like Alice Cooper around *Billion Dollar Babies*, quite produced punk in its ethic, with a bit of charm.'

Unfortunately, somewhere in the transition from Cardiff to County Westmeath, the *Billion Dollar Babies* went all *Welcome To My Nightmare* and took 'Underdogs' to another dimension, one reminiscent of mid-nineties Metallica. 'As soon as we got to Grouse Lodge I started hitting the weights in the gym,' says Bradfield. 'I went mad on my 120 kilograms. The next day I couldn't move. My veins were just filled with fire. Then we did "Underdogs" and I got carried away with it. Dave Eringa had a new super-metal amp called a Diezel, and they make you play just one way. I was completely fucking Hetfielded out of my mind. It was too big, too proto-metal, too legs astride. It lost its charm.'

Wire, meanwhile, bewildered at Bradfield's 'mad decision' to start the recording session with this particular song, was now of the opinion that the lyric no longer bore serious scrutiny. 'A mini-manifesto without much intelligence,' he says. 'I loved the title, but really it's just a thirty-five-year-old bloke trying to invoke something, to prove he's still *fucking crazy*!'

The madness continued. 'Underdogs' was not only included on the album but chosen as its outrider, released as a limited edition one-sided 7-inch single and download, with fans invited to make their own videos: a clumsy paradigm of the music industry's struggles to navigate the post-Napster pre-Spotify era. 'For me, it was nearly the end of the album when they released this "soft",' says Wire. 'That was not our decision. It fried my brain for about a week. Me and James had a "Is this going to be all right?" moment.'

Fortunately, the single that ought to have been the first single would soon make everything OK. As for 'Underdogs', it was played live twice prior to *Send Away The Tigers*' release and thence never seen again. The album's tenth-anniversary edition deleted it from the tracklist and replaced it with a B-side. The only proof 'Underdogs' had ever existed was the inclusion of that tight but rattly demo as a bonus CD track. Otherwise the song has been Stalinised as effectively as Leon Trotsky's infamous erasure from a photograph of himself and Lenin in a Moscow crowd celebrating the second anniversary of the October Revolution.

Bradfield takes a philosophical view. '"Underdogs" was like a pre-season friendly – it warmed us up for what we really wanted to do with the record.'

97.

Your Love Alone Is Not Enough

Recorded: Grouse Lodge Studios, Ireland; Eden Studios,
    London
Producer: Dave Eringa
Released: 23 April 2007 (single, Columbia); 7 May 2007
    (*Send Away The Tigers*, Columbia)

'Suicide statements are a measure of the man.'
    – Bill Nelson, 'Do You Dream In Colour?'

Between *Lifeblood* and *Send Away The Tigers*, motivated by a sense
that 'people were sick of the band' (Wire), both James Dean
Bradfield and Nicky Wire made solo albums. This required each to
focus on the discipline normally undertaken by the other. Logic-
ally enough, both Bradfield's *The Great Western* and Wire's *I Killed
The Zeitgeist* felt like unfiltered versions of their band personae:
the former more decorously musical, the latter more astringently
personal. But while Bradfield says he learnt little from the experience beyond a reaffirmation of the band's salience in his life, for
Wire the process was transformative. 'I got quite decent on the
acoustic guitar,' he says. 'In a chordal sense, nothing fancy. But
you do write words in a different way when you're writing the
music yourself – it's much easier to sing, for a start. So when we
came to *Send Away The Tigers* I knew that those words would be
easier for James to sing. Which is not true of *Lifeblood* at all.'

In late summer 2006, Wire took a train from Newport to
London, where he had promo duties for his imminent album to
fulfil. He met Bradfield at Martin Hall's west London office, and

handed over a cassette of a song he'd started, with some extra words to be fitted in. Bradfield took the cassette and the lyrics to his flat in Chiswick, while Wire travelled across London for a photo shoot. Three hours later they reconvened at Hall's office, where Bradfield handed back the cassette, which now contained the completed song: 'Your Love Alone Is Not Enough'.[1]

'I'd basically had a title,' says Wire. 'Tragically, I think it was a suicide note that I'd read about in a newspaper, which ended with "your love alone is not enough". I kept singing those words over and over when I was going around the house – "not enough, not enough, not enough . . ." Then I came up with "trade all your heroes in for ghosts", which is from "Wish You Were Here", by Pink Floyd,[2] and "You said the sky would fall on you, fall on you . . ." So I had done what you'd call the verse and the bridge, and gave James the rest of the words.'

For the line 'But your love alone won't save the world', Bradfield provided an upward counter to Wire's predominantly descendant melody, thereby creating the cross-current of sadness and euphoria that powers the song. It was a melodic nest he'd originally built then set aside while working on *The Great Western*'s closing track 'Which Way To Kyffin'. 'I had it in my head, this little musical picture which I had dumped, but knew was really good,' says Bradfield. 'I realised it fitted what Nick had done already. I knew it would finish it off.'

As Wire listened to the cassette on the train home, he realised this new combination of his and Bradfield's skills had created something special. 'There was such a zing to it, like a classic sixties Who song. It all fitted together so brilliantly. That really was a bit of magic – a pretty magical day.'

One reason 'Your Love Alone' has such impact is its subversion of traditional lyric structure, by opening with the chorus, or a verse that acts as the chorus. Essentially, a song of choruses – which had always been good enough for The Beatles. It also benefited from the different writing energy created by Bradfield having to respond to a piece of music that was already set within the song. 'It was a strange feeling to try and finish something that was so nearly complete anyway. I had to make sure my bit was good.' Bradfield admits to feeling jealous of Wire's repetitive 'not enough' scheme, but resisted the temptation to outdo that quasi-chorus's instant thrill-factor.

'Once you're up against a verse like that, if you try and go farther, then everything falls apart. Because it's gonna be insipidly catchy. You can't compete with that. You've got to come up with something different.' He laughs. 'It felt like a game show – I had three hours to do something, otherwise I would lose the chance to write that bit, because he'd already got so close to it.'

Another factor in the song's appeal is its succinct expression of perhaps life's toughest lesson: bad stuff happens regardless of good acts or intent. The poignancy is magnified when the lyric directly addresses Richey Edwards, the words 'I could have written all your lines' sung pointedly in the final version by Nicky Wire.

'It's a song that's about the empty moral philosophy that love is the answer to everything,' says Wire. 'Which is just a lie. The song is an evocation – there's hints of Richey in there, and there's suicide. I like suicide songs . . . which is probably not a great thing to say. They're kind of inspirational. "Your Love Alone" has got such a flow it leads somewhere quite uplifting.'

Beyond the compositional facets, there's no doubt that its recording as a duet with Nina Persson was a masterstroke. The Swedish singer's strident yet careworn voice proved a perfect female partner to Bradfield's, both in harmony and alternating solo parts: the moment when she takes the lead for 'But your love alone won't save the world' sends the song onto a celestial realm, from where it can credibly reference The Who's 1968 apex 'I Can See For Miles', both in the lyric and Bradfield's iridescent guitar tone.

Conceived from the outset as a piece for two voices – James hoped it might work along the lines of Bryan Adams and Melanie

C's duet 'When You're Gone' – as long-time fans of The Cardigans, the Manics regarded Persson as 'the only option'. At the very end of the Grouse Lodge session, Bradfield flew from Shannon to New York, where Persson's husband Nathan Larson recorded her vocal in their studio. She actually sang the entire lyric, and the lines were attributed subsequently once the band reassembled at Eden Studios in London.

'She had a good eight runs at it, but she had it after the first four,' says Bradfield. 'I was nervous about our voices melding together but we're kind of in the same register. I still didn't know how good it was until we'd finished. Once we got Sean playing on it, it became obvious, probably the closest we'd ever got to Blondie without realising it. "Union City Blue", with a bit of The Who. It made me play guitar differently, more spangled, more clean, more open, less distorted. So easy. It could be seen as the song that saved us.'

Released as a single just over one month after the 'Underdogs' debacle, 'Your Love Alone Is Not Enough' entered the UK chart at Number 26. The following week, it leapt to Number 2, beaten only at the last by the über-pop power coupling of Beyoncé and Shakira. It was still in the Top 75 seven weeks later, when Nina Persson joined the Manics to perform the song at Glastonbury Festival. Sadly, there wasn't time to rehearse her other suggested collaboration: 'Islands In The Stream', the Bee Gees song that Dolly Parton and Kenny Rogers turned into country gold. 'It would have been brilliant,' says Wire. 'It's always been James's dream to be Kenny Rogers.' (Bradfield: 'I've never dreamt of being Kenny Rogers.')

An immediate setlist fixture, in subsequent years Bradfield has sung 'Your Love Alone' with Charlotte Church, Cerys Matthews, himself, and most recently, The Anchoress, whose delivery comes closest to matching Persson's for impact. 'The Anchoress is the best since Nina,' says Wire, 'but obviously Nina is untouchable. I would have loved to have done more with her. We did bags of TV promo with that song – a lot of people thought we were a new band.'

Beyond reaching out to new fans and lighting a fire under the old, 'Your Love Alone' revived the band's battered faith in themselves. After a long period of searching for new directions by going off-grid, they realised the answers lay much closer to home. Amid its debts to classic rock touchstones, this was a song that drew most from the Manic Street Preachers themselves: their work – the lyric quoted from 'You Stole The Sun From My Heart' – and, in the regretful depiction of Richey, the awkward history they had needed to escape. As ever, the answer lies within.

'When we did the track,' says James, 'Nina said – and this is her direct quote – "Yes! I'm so glad that the song's got some joy. I'm so fed up with songs just saying everything is fucked. If you're gonna say things are fucked, do it with a bit of joy."'

98.

Welcome To The Dead Zone

Recorded: Faster Studios, Cardiff
Producer: Dave Eringa
Released: 23 April 2007 ('Your Love Alone Is Not
   Enough' B-side, Columbia); 12 May 2017 (*Send Away
   The Tigers* [10 Year Collectors' Edition], Columbia)

> 'Beautiful! Beautiful! Magnificent desolation.'
>   – Buzz Aldrin

In days of yore, all the very best singles had a B-side that hit the target from a different angle. 'Welcome To The Dead Zone's different angle came from Sean Moore, who conjured this plaintive mid-tempo procession of chiming guitars and teary eyes, like Primal Scream's 'Velocity Girl' nursing her broken heart.

'It's hard to get Sean to write any more,' says Bradfield, 'because, y'know, he's a drummer. But when he does, he comes up with this lovely kind of thing. He had the chords and he sang the verse, then I created a different vocal of the same chords for the chorus. I got my old Fender Jazz out, for that nice crunchy indie sound, the solo's the Strat twelve-string tracked with a Guild twelve-string. We did it one day. Being throwaway's nice sometimes.'

The lyric is boil-in-the-bag lachrymosity – opening line: 'I feel so bad about myself' – with the occasional rogue ingredient. '"Circus full of whores",' Bradfield considers. 'I remember Nick saying, "I can't have that line." And I once had a conversation with Gruff [Rhys] where he just went: "I really hate the word 'harlequin'." "I completely know what you mean Gruff, it's a bad word." And "circus" is one of those. It's a bad word.'

'I'm not embarrassed,' says Wire, 'but the words were totally written for something to write. No deeper meaning. It's a B-side lyric, but a great B-side, which was always something we wanted in the canon when we started.'

Although wholly different in mood, 'Welcome To The Dead Zone' found a higher calling when it replaced 'Underdogs' on *Send Away The Tigers'* tenth-anniversary edition. Only the most tin-eared opponent of historical revisionism could deny it was an improvement.

99.

Send Away The Tigers

Recorded: Grouse Lodge Studios, Ireland
Producer: Dave Eringa
Released: 7 May 2007 (*Send Away The Tigers*, Columbia)

'One by one he shut the door on all the people he knew;
then he shut the door on himself.'

– Spike Milligan, on Tony Hancock

'Send Away The Tigers' was the Manics' first title track since 'Everything Must Go'. Although an album isn't intrinsically stronger for it, having a song deemed worthy of naming an entire record after conveys artistic confidence, however vague or misplaced. Viewed from the other side of that equation, *Send Away The Tigers*' three predecessors were characterised in varying degrees by doubt and/or a lack of cohesion. So for the Manics to open their new album with its title track was a significant statement, even before a note was heard. And once the music did strike up, the statement was pretty clear: *Lifeblood*'s icy millennial version of denialism was gone; bombasticated amps and channelling Slash for breakfast were back.

'Sometimes we get embarrassed by our former selves,' says Wire. "Send Away The Tigers" is just so blaringly loud, and you can say, "Oh, it's so obvious, it's typical Manics . . ." But you can still enjoy how brilliant it sounds. At the time, we were really genuinely enthralled to be ourselves again. We didn't fucking care.'

Bradfield took his cue, as was traditional, from the lyric, and he recognised something he hadn't seen for a while: many words. Ahead of the first chorus stood four verses of four lines, each pristine declamatory phrase rolling into the next, a strikingly glo-balist interior monologue ('There's no hope in the colonies'; 'The zoo's been overrun in Baghdad/Tigers' claws still in my back'), gathering its own catalytic momentum. He heard a familiar voice – demagogue, sermoniser, *preacher* – and the music flowed.

'Something had changed lyrically. If you look at the crib sheet for this, there's barely a line left out. It felt comprehensive – when you're given a lyric that big, you feel like it's important that it's all included. So I went for that sixties thing of singing it in the Dylan sense, keep singing the line and see where it leads you. I was messing on the guitar and thinking, "It's gotta keep going." It's a rhythm and a mind that doesn't want to stop or can't stop. I just followed the chords.'

The lyric linked two men, both haunted by their past and undone by hubris. Nicky Wire had long been fascinated by Tony Hancock, post-war Britain's most famous comedian, whose descent into depression and alcoholism accompanied the progressive alienation of writers, friends, and eventually his wife, ending in a fatal overdose in 1968 while attempting to restart his dwindling career in Australia. Dead at forty-four, Hancock admitted he drank because he thought it would 'send away the tigers'.

Another of the song's lines – 'Things have gone wrong too many times' – was a near verbatim quote from Hancock's suicide note. Wire's lyric drew a parallel with Tony Blair ('Loathsome smile, head full of forevers'), the three-times election winner whose political legacy was trashed by the 2003 Iraq War, a mis-conceived act of liberation symbolised by the plight of animals amid the destruction of Baghdad Zoo.

'I think the line "little things change people's lives" is actually a Tony Blair quote,' says Wire. 'But Hancock's life was really tragic; it sparked something in me. And "send away the tigers", I felt applied to us in terms of, "Just fuck it!" All that reinvention, all the doubt of the previous albums – just fuck it and put it to one side.'

Ultimately, 'Send Away The Tigers' was a cautionary tale of two Tonys and the perils of pride. Whereas Hancock became estranged from the work that had first brought him success, the Manics sought to revive themselves by making peace with their history. And just in case, the song came with its own indemnity clause: 'Look at me, I'm honest and free/I was born to underachieve'.

'You need some muscle to get away with a song like that,' says Bradfield. 'But when we were mixing at Eden Studios there was still one element missing. We knew this was the title track and we knew it could be brilliant, but it needed one more guitar part and I didn't have any of my guitars with me. Somebody said, "The Stereophonics are next door, go and ask them." I'm like, "I'm not playing an SG!" But I knock on the door and end up using Kelly Jones's guitar. It worked straight away.'

The recording also contained a small legacy of the Manics' past: the opening chapel organ atmos came from Chateau de la Rouge Motte's Omnichord, as used on 'Ready For Drowning', and gifted to the band by Mike Hedges.

'Ah, it is a great title track,' says Bradfield, mistily. 'It almost feels like a national anthem, doesn't it?'

On 10 May 2007, three days after *Send Away The Tigers*' release, Tony Blair announced his resignation as UK Prime Minister in a speech at the Trimdon Labour Club in County Durham. History fails to record whether he mentioned the claw marks in his back.

100.

Indian Summer

Recorded: Grouse Lodge Studios, Ireland; Stir Studios, Cardiff
Producer: Dave Eringa; Additional Production: Greg Haver
Released: 7 May 2007 (*Send Away The Tigers*, Columbia); 1 October 2007 (single, Columbia)

> 'Hibernation comes so early this year.'
> – Super Furry Animals, 'Mountain People'

Deploying 'God' as the second word in a song beginning with a conditional sentence ('If God persists, persists in saying yes') indicates either delusion or supreme self-assurance. 'Indian Summer' is guilty only of the latter. Built around a pensive guitar figure, powered by busily rolling drums – a stellar performance by Moore – and augmented by one of Sally Herbert's beautifully circumspect string arrangements, it exemplifies the hopeful mood that took hold early in the album sessions, as the Manics glimpsed a new design for life. It didn't hurt that 'Indian Summer' bore a passing resemblance to 'A Design For Life', most obviously in its accelerated waltz tempo, albeit painting from a very different colour palette, one dictated by the lyric's wistful contemplation of camaraderie amid the quiet thunder of time's perpetual motion.

'It's quite a complicated song because it changes from the minor to the major within the same key,' says Bradfield. 'Whenever you're playing a chord, a note's passing through it. Nothing's lingering. I knew it was gonna be hard for Sean because he is constantly on the move. But I loved the lyric, loved its optimism, and I loved the way it made me feel.'

Wire considers it entirely possible that the chorus's neat metaphysical conundrum – 'Whose crime is eternity when time lost is certainty?' – originated elsewhere. 'Probably Kierkegaard or somebody! The lyric's infused with the whole ethos of the album, going back to source, trying to recapture a former glory – all those things. The late blooming of life. It's saying we're masters of our own destiny, we've got to fucking keep on going. "Persist" is a good word to have in a song.'

Graced by a sweetly homespun Patrick Jones video of the band eating chips and playing football on Penarth beach intercut with archive Super-8 family holiday footage, 'Indian Summer' is a marvel of (mister) blue sky thinking, lower-case joy right to the toe-stub ending. 'Nick plays the wrong note against my chord,' explains Bradfield. 'But it's the right wrong note.'

101.

The Second Great Depression

Recorded: Grouse Lodge Studios, Ireland; Stir Studios,
    Cardiff
Producer: Greg Haver; Additional Production: Dave Eringa
Released: 7 May 2007 (*Send Away The Tigers*, Columbia)

'It is not the consciousness of men that determines
their being, but, on the contrary, their social being that
determines their consciousness.'
    – Karl Marx, *A Contribution to the Critique of Political Economy*

While working with Greg Haver in Cardiff on an accompaniment
to a Wire lyric equating worldwide economic depression to his
own, Bradfield discovered a violin bow left in the studio. One
thing led to another, as it were, and soon Bradfield was getting
all dazed and confused with what he terms 'the shite Jimmy Page
thing' of bowing his electric guitar. 'I wanted to be dramatic and
heavy,' he says. 'I wanted the song to describe everything that
it felt like it had lost. After all the subtleties of *Lifeblood* and my
solo record, it felt nice to be over-the-top-like again. It felt nice
to be histrionic.'

Comparing the demo version to the final master is a case study
in how a great song can become lost in translation. The former
is understated and very moving, as Moore's drums shadow the
humming bowed guitar and Bradfield's vocal locates the hurt
in lines like 'I thought about it a million times/When you and
me did nothing but smile/When forgiveness was the best'. This
could have been a standout track on *This Is My Truth*. But given

the full-vent production, with strings augmenting the guitar and Bradfield off the leash in the chorus, the emotional connection is compressed almost out of existence.

'I was a big proponent of this song,' says Wire. 'The lines have interesting rhymes – "figured/lingered", "withered/mirrored" – and I remember thinking it could have been a single. Perhaps it just got too hot.'

So hot, in fact, that Bradfield couldn't sing it every night without ruining his voice. Although one of those bands for whom more is rarely enough, the Manics oversold even themselves with 'The Second Great Depression'.

'Perhaps it was a bit too histrionic from my part,' agrees Bradfield. 'But it did feel good.'

102.

Autumnsong

Recorded: Grouse Lodge Studios, Ireland; Stir Studios,
    Cardiff
Producer: Dave Eringa; Additional production: Greg Haver
Released: 7 May 2007 (*Send Away The Tigers*, Columbia);
    23 July 2007 (single, Columbia)

'Leaving the things that are real behind.'
                                – Aerosmith, 'Toys In The Attic'

To run with Bradfield's football metaphor, if 'Underdogs' represented the pre-season warm-up version of *Send Away The Tigers*,
then 'Autumnsong' was a team of invincibles cruising their way
to the league title. No lyrical own goals or bludgeoned riffola; the
clarion guitar figure that opens then binds the song together like
a drawer's worth of knotted silk evokes glittery glory days, a time
before Slash became a dirty word. Propelled by a multitracked
simulation of Queen, the chorus soars on air currents generated
by an arena-load of clapping hands. The lyric, meanwhile, deals
in T-shirt slogans tailored to the true believers, the only ones who
know: 'Wear your love like it is made of hate/Born to destroy
and born to create'. Even the *Bible*-bashers get their own slice
of raw meat with the Yes-alluding 'wear your hair in bunches'.

Here was a palpable reconnection of both band and audience
with their former selves and each other, at probably the last time
it would be seemly so to do. 'Seemed like a pop song lyric to me,'
says Bradfield. 'I just got into it. Just wanted to be free.'

But free never comes easy. The string arrangement got rewritten after a Wire meltdown. 'I went a bit over the top,' Bradfield
recalls, 'but it was too obtuse and classical for a song like this.' He

was all for jettisoning the main riff due to its more than passing similarity to 'Sweet Child O' Mine', until dissuaded by Wire, who reminded him that lack of inhibition was the point of the song. Then Moore, having played a double bass drumbeat during the verse on the demo – as with 'The Second Great Depression', a notably restrained early iteration of the song – refused to do so on the master. 'He just dug his heels in,' says Bradfield. 'So Dave went, "Fuck it", and put a delay on it. And Sean didn't notice. I think his problem was perhaps he thought it was too much like a slow version of "Walk This Way".'

A different Aerosmith song was definitely implicated, however: 'Baby, what you done to your hair' is very adjacent to 'Honey, what you done to your head' from 'You See Me Crying', the grandiose piano ballad finale to *Toys In The Attic*, the 1975 album that also features 'Walk This Way'. By Wire's own admission, his lyric is the least effortful thing about 'Autumnsong', where for want of a new verse after the chorus Bradfield repeats the first, but with the stanzas in reverse order. 'I feel a bit bad because James did ask me to write another verse,' says Wire. 'Pure laziness, nothing more. But the meeting of the lyric and the tune is exactly as it should be. A big swoosh of uplifting melancholia.'

A Top 10 hit when released as the album's second 'proper' single, 'Autumnsong' epitomised the band's irrepressible progress through Europe's festival circuit during the summer of 2008. Even one year on, its premise – 'Remember, the best times are yet to come' – felt viable. And as parents of young children, both Wire and Moore were grateful for the weekends away. 'In many ways the most enjoyable period I've ever had in the band,' says Wire. '"Bob Dylan's asked us to support him in a stadium in Croatia?! We'd better go a day early!"'

'In Switzerland, we played on the same bill as Lenny Kravitz,' adds Bradfield. 'His guitar tech came up to me at the end of this song and said, "Good solo, man . . ."'

103.

Imperial Bodybags

Recorded: Grouse Lodge Studios, Ireland; Stir Studios,
    Cardiff, 2006
Producer: Dave Eringa; Additional Production: Greg Haver
Released: 7 May 2007 (*Send Away The Tigers*, Columbia)

'Saw Vietnam as a partisan and wished I'd never been.'
    – Skids, 'Working For The Yankee Dollar'

The vital spark that punches through the accumulated eardrum
buzz towards the end of *Send Away The Tigers*, 'Imperial Bodybags'
has surprises for all. The lyric is an empathetic appraisal of American blue-collar cannon fodder, clearly prompted by the ongoing
post-9/11 wars in Afghanistan and Iraq ('Children wrapped in
home-made flags'), a perspective similar to Skids songs like 'Into
The Valley' and 'Melancholy Soldiers', which lamented how
desperate inhabitants of 1970s de-industrialised Scotland were
recruited into the British army. 'It was actually saying that people
on the right have just as many feelings about dead people coming
home as people on the left, who might protest against it but tend
not to do so much of the fighting,' says Wire.

Upon hearing its rust-bucket white-trash belt-buckle boogie,
however, Sony's Rob Stringer was confused. 'We played him the
demo,' recalls Bradfield, 'and he just said, "It's all a bit fucking
patchouli oil and Status Quo!" I had a crisis of confidence at that
point. When someone says "patchouli oil" you know something's
wrong.'

Luckily, the song made the final cut, with the crucial addition
of Moore's finest Stray Cats rim taps and an extended Bradfield
solo so intense it supplies its own false ending. When the chorus

lets rip ('Prom queen disposable!') it's like The Clash's version of UK rock 'n' roll pioneer Vince Taylor's 'Brand New Cadillac' getting flattened by a tank. On an album where the monolithic sonic design can feel overbearing, 'Imperial Bodybags' is a welcome anomaly.

The subject matter also tweaked the ears of the record's Los Angeles-based mix engineer Chris Lord-Alge.[1] 'We sent him the song,' says Bradfield, 'and he came on the phone: "Oh, so the American eagle is swooping down in your fucking sound now, is it? Are you trash-talking my country, motherfucker?!" "It's a bit more complicated than that." "I'm only kidding . . .!" He did a great mix, not over the top. It's just a heavy song, you know – it's that kind of power we can do sometimes.'

104.
Peeled Apples

Recorded: Rockfield Studios, Monmouthshire
Producer: Steve Albini
Released: 18 May 2009 (*Journal For Plague Lovers*,
   Columbia)

'A film is never really good unless the camera is an
eye in the head of a poet.'
                    – Orson Welles, 'Ribbon Of Dreams', 1958

The Manics chose to follow their biggest hit record for ten years
in typically counter-intuitive fashion: by getting the old gang
back together again. They would create an entire album from the
lyrics Richey Edwards bequeathed them shortly before his exit,
and compound this potentially risky strategy by visiting musical
terrain not dissimilar to *The Holy Bible* in the company of Steve
Albini, the sonic architect whose preferment of audio vérité over
commercial sensibility had earned him much notoriety, not least
in 1993 when Geffen Records' higher-ups briefed to press sources
that he had made Nirvana's *In Utero* 'unreleasable'.

   For once, the in-house saboteur was James Dean Bradfield.
Near the end of the January 1995 House In The Woods session,
Edwards had presented the band with an A4 ring binder bought
from high street stationer Ryman, featuring a cover image of
Bugs Bunny with the word 'Opulence' scratched bloodily into his
cheek. The file contained collage artwork, notes and about thirty
lyrics: five of these, including some already works in progress –
'Kevin Carter', 'Small Black Flowers That Grow In The Sky' et al.
– would eventually feature on *Everything Must Go*. The rest stayed
in the file, which was kept in Nicky Wire's bedroom wardrobe.

Aside from the period immediately after Edwards's disappearance, when he scoured the words for possible clues as to what Richey might have done, Wire didn't read the lyrics at all. But from around 2002, Bradfield began looking at his facsimile copies, with a view to possibly using these words in songs. 'It happened quite a lot,' he says. 'Sometimes when Nick hadn't given me any lyrics and I wanted to write. I playfully toyed with writing tunes to some of them and it came quite easy.'

Fragments of two 'Opulence' lyrics – 'All Is Vanity' and 'Doors Closing Slowly' – were incorporated into 'Picturesque', a *Lifeblood*-era song recorded in 2004 but unreleased until the 2005 *God Save The Manics* EP. Still, Bradfield couldn't envisage making an entire album from Richey's lyrics. 'I'd always close the book – like, "No, don't go there. What's the point of doing it when it may never get done?"'

With the unexpected success of *Send Away The Tigers*, such questions seemed moot. But towards the end of the album's extended touring cycle, thoughts had turned to the next record. Bradfield recalls a discussion in an airport-bound taxi where he and Wire discussed how they might build on *Tigers'* momentum. 'We both wanted to keep going,' says James, 'but what we didn't want to do was a straight follow-up, make the album we knew we could make as quick as we could. It felt like we'd been plastered all over the place with *Send Away The Tigers*, and I felt like we needed a respectful gap. A bit of a nineties way of thinking, perhaps, but it was born out of having fucked up so many times, so let's make sure we do this right. So I was like, "What if we did an experimental album in between, where we keep writing and enjoying ourselves . . .?" Nick's like, "What do you mean?" I said, "Richey's lyrics. I've been looking at them again and I'd like to do something."'

On 23 November 2008, Manics PR Terri Hall confirmed to the media that Richey Edwards's parents had been granted a court order confirming their son as presumed dead. By this point, work on *Journal For Plague Lovers* was well under way. After an initial writing and demo period at the former Stir Studios in Cardiff, where the band were now leaseholders and had renamed the facility Faster Studios, the first few weeks of October were spent recording at Rockfield. Creative decisions were dictated by a desire to honour Richey, and specifically invoked his masterpiece. The album cover would feature a painting by Jenny Saville, the star of 1994's 'Young British Artists III' exhibition whose triptych *Strategy (South Face/Front Face/North Face)* Edwards had chosen as the centrepiece of *The Holy Bible*'s sleeve artwork; as previously, Saville granted permission for the band to use her painting *Stare* on the cover of *Journal For Plague Lovers* free of charge. As on *The Holy Bible*, songs featured voice samples – in the case of 'Peeled Apples', that of Wales-born superstar actor Christian Bale from the film *The Machinist*. Most fundamentally, the album was being made with Steve Albini, iconoclastic frontman of legendary eighties post-hardcore trio Big Black, much of whose subsequent renown as a recording engineer stemmed from his helping Nirvana create their capital 'A' work of art *In Utero*, a record all the Manics loved and to which *The Holy Bible* had become regarded as a UK equivalent in both artistic triumph and personal tragedy.

'We wanted somebody to take Richey's words seriously, and our interpretation of his words seriously,' says Bradfield. 'We just didn't want to sell Richey short in any way. Steve Albini felt like the natural choice.'

Rockfield was one of few studios still offering the capability to record on tape, the infamously digital-averse Albini's preferred way to work. A diligent curator of sound, Albini also abjured the term 'producer', regarding anyone who called themselves such 'in the same way that baseball players regard baseball umpires as a lesser and interfering, meddlesome presence in the game'. Defining his role instead as a pure technician whose role was to remove impediments to the artists sounding like themselves – or, as he sometimes put it, 'a plumber' – he also resisted offering subjective opinions on the music he was helping a band make. Yet his technical skills were framed by such deeply held aesthetic preferences that his recordings had intrinsic qualities that were recognisable whether the artist was P.J. Harvey or Page & Plant, The Jesus Lizard or The Wedding Present, Pixies or Bush, Joanna Newsom or Low or Neurosis, or any of the myriad others that were typically less known but made to the same exacting methods and high standards.

'The choice to have him as the engineer set the tone for everything, somebody who would disentangle us from choosing inappropriate colours for certain songs,' says Bradfield. 'Sometimes I'll make things too melodic, my ELO thing. Steve would say, "No, don't do that. Why the fuck are you doing that?" He had that sensibility, where "don't do it" is really important. I think he was quite disingenuous in putting himself at the back of the room when it comes to creative decisions. He was making decisions for us. I don't know what Steve was if not a producer.'

But as writing progressed, it became clear that this source material would not necessarily dictate a *Holy Bible* sequel, or simply be the new testament to the previous record's old. For all that he unravelled during 1994, amid *The Holy Bible*'s creative cocoon at Soundspace Edwards was in full bloom. By contrast, much of the 'Opulence' material reflected his spells in Cardiff's Whitchurch and Roehampton's The Priory, psychiatric institutions with routines of medication and rehabilitation via the quasi-religious strictures of the Twelve Steps. Whereas *The Holy Bible* placed Edwards's bleak self-analysis amid a broader critique of humanity, and even its overtly autobiographical pieces, like '4st 7lb' and 'Faster', evinced its author's moral and physical authority, reading these 'new' lyrics with a guitar in his hand – 'which is not something I would have ever done before' – Nicky Wire realised the context for these words was very different. 'There are hints of resistance in *The Holy Bible*,' he says. 'Like "Faster": "I am stronger than. . ." But with this it feels that the bodily strength has disappeared and the mind is just in a frenzied state of information and on a road to somewhere bad. Just a road to an end.'

The lyric to 'Peeled Apples', however, with its opaque allusions to 'riderless horses', falcons attacking pigeons, and *Rethinking Camelot*, Noam Chomsky's assessment of US Vietnam policy, defied straightforward analysis. Wire wrote music to the chorus, yet without the option of asking Edwards for clarification he could only speculate at what it might all mean. 'Is it a critique of Chomskyite groupthink or an endorsement of it? I can't say. My chorus sounded very fey, a lot like Heaven 17's "Temptation",' says Wire. 'Which James twisted enough so it just had echoes of it.' Bradfield then wrote the remainder of the song, built upon a menacing bass and drum riff bed that was pure gravy for Albini devotees.

'The music had to be heavy, had to be full of something coming to life, against its own will,' says James. 'I liked perhaps the way those words made me feel uneasy. I liked it, because it inspires you. Even if it's not the most positive feeling.' Bradfield's vocals sound like he's coughing up ash, his words evaporating into miasma on declaring 'the naked light bulb is always *wrong*'. 'We stole that effect from the demo,' Bradfield notes. 'Steve actually made some great decisions on "Peeled Apples". In the middle, where Sean's just riffing and there's a little bit of hum and feedback, I had my Boss Hyper Fuzz pedal on the fuzz setting, whereas I usually use the gain setting. I asked Steve, "Can I do something there?" He's like, "Why? What the fuck?" He played it back . . . "It's great. Leave it." I was like, "No, can I *try* something?" And he went, "Well, you can try something but it's gonna be shit." "*Excuse* me?" "Shit in comparison to that, so just leave it." Uh, OK!' he laughs. 'So it took a lot of getting used to. But I really enjoyed working with Steve.'

In lieu of a single – an old-school gesture towards the integrity of the album form, and congruent with Albini's sensibilities, but also quite likely pragmatic from Sony's point of view – the opening track accrued greater significance. It was honoured with a gargantuan PiL-popping remix by Andrew Weatherall, which the band subsequently used as intro music on tour. And 'Peeled Apples's glowering mid-tempo dollop of dinge certainly fulfilled the elevator-pitch premise of a Manic Street Preachers tribute to Richey Edwards engineered by Steve Albini.

'"Peeled Apples" always felt like the first track on the album,' says Wire. 'It sounds perfect, the way the air moves between the bass and the bass drum, it's like playing live during an amazing gig and you just feel the frequencies move. No one does that like Albini. I think Richey would have loved it. You know, if we used one of his lyrics for "I'm Not Working" he might have thought it was a piece of shit! Or "Black Dog On My Shoulder" probably wouldn't have done it for him. But here, we felt the aesthetics added up. It was a definite experience – feeling like he was back in the room.'

105.

Jackie Collins Existential Question Time

Recorded: Rockfield Studios, Monmouthshire
Producer: Steve Albini
Released: 18 May 2009 (*Journal For Plague Lovers*, Columbia)

'I've met the man in the street and he's a cunt.'

– Sid Vicious

As early as its second track, *Journal For Plague Lovers* served notice that this album was much more than an exercise in nostalgia or role-play. At no point did *The Holy Bible* skip along merrily like 'Jackie Collins Existential Question Time': this batch of Richey Edwards lyrics were of a different temper and pointed the music towards different outcomes. The wry gallows humour that Richey exhibited in personal interactions but only occasionally in his lyrics became more apparent, reflecting his altered circumstances. Thus, a rumination upon sexual morality and religion is couched in a delirious vision of *Hollywood Wives* novelist Jackie Collins appearing on the BBC's current affairs roundtable debate show *Question Time* in a 'Situationist sisterhood' with her elder sister Joan. An imagined scenario, alas, though the naive melody refrain's 'Oh mummy, what's a Sex Pistol?' – a pure *Generation Terrorists* flashback – derived from a punk-era badge.

'I wanted the music, in its own punk way, to be as confused as the lyric,' says Bradfield. 'So there's an element of youth club Van Halen, there's a little Wire in there, little bits of Stuart Adamson. I just wanted a magpie of a song because I felt the lyric was a magpie. I didn't really know what it was about, except for looking at the world through an absurdist set of eyes.'

The song's sprightly gait particularly excited Columbia Records' managing director Mike Smith upon first hearing. 'He thought it was amazing,' recalls Wire. '"So commercial! It's going to be all over Radio 1!" Well, it's absurd enough. I was definitely very enthused too, because we sound a very young band on this.' Reality bit, however, and 'Jackie Collins Existential Question Time' was left to soundtrack the dream Pere Ubu jukebox musical that never quite got written.

106.
Me And Stephen Hawking

Recorded: Rockfield Studios, Monmouthshire
Producer: Steve Albini
Released: 18 May 2009 (*Journal For Plague Lovers*, Columbia)

'See the little nuclei, bursting full of information.'
— The Stranglers, 'Genetix'

Perhaps the oddest thing about a lyric that encompasses a genetically modified sheep named Tracy and the wrestler Giant Haystacks being watched by a crowd of 100,000 in Bombay is its basis in fact. As noted by Yusef Syed in his 227 Lears blog, these and other details from 'Me And Stephen Hawking' were taken from articles in the 30–31 July 1994 editions of the *Independent* and *Independent On Sunday*, demonstrating that even during this post-breakdown recovery period Richey Edwards continued to source material for songs.

'That lyric is the epitome of Richey's mind working in a positive way in terms of artistic creation,' says Wire. 'It felt intrinsically like him. I always thought there was some kind of relatability between him and Stephen Hawking, of somehow being trapped in a mind that can't stop. Richey talked about him quite a bit, as some kind of portal to understanding, which I didn't understand at all. I think Richey thought he was on his level.'

In a mordant evocation of Philip Larkin, here Edwards cited Hawking as a metaphor for his meagre carnal capabilities – 'We missed the sex revolution, when we failed the physical'. It would certainly have been interesting to hear the pre-eminent particle physicist's take on 'Me And Stephen Hawking's version of the big bang. Musically as well as lyrically the song packed a lot of information into a very compact space, with Moore's drums running the emotional gamut from propulsive splutter to slave galley brutish, via the chorus's spacey introspection, revelling in his role at the fulcrum of Albini's soundworld, the sorcerer's apprentice shooting out sparks.

'It was one of the first songs we did and we had a good demo,' says Bradfield. 'Nick said he felt we'd hit on a kind of Minutemen moment, and I felt a bit of Rush. We just met on it. Steve's like, "Hmm, got a bit of prog punk going on here." "We hope so." "Yeah. Well, we'll see how close you can get . . ." I enjoyed little snidey moments like that. Two, three takes, we had it nailed down straight away. It's weird how the drum parts change throughout lots of these songs. Sean loved playing and monitoring to the sound Steve had got. Because Sean always says, "There's not enough power in my earphones", and yet he was immediately quite happy. Very happy actually. What I took from the lyric was that science and snake-oil salesmen will one day meet. That will be the next part of our evolution. Hopefully I'll be dead by then. So let's just make the song absurd.'

The unedited 'Opulence' lyric was prefaced by an excerpt from a speech Hawking gave to a 1994 US computer trade show, stating that computer viruses should be regarded as a man-made life-form: 'I think it says something about human nature that the only form of life we have created is purely destructive. We've created life in our own image.' 'Me And Stephen Hawking' spoke to the moment where J.G. Ballard's once esoteric notions of technology supplanting religion became part of the mainstream conversation. Or, to quote its co-option of a Dutch animal rights group's poster protesting the production of transgenic milk: 'Today it's a cow – tomorrow it's you!'

'I always liked this song,' says Bradfield. 'It doesn't sound like it takes itself too seriously.' He laughs. 'And I don't think we have too many of those moments!'

107.

Journal For Plague Lovers

Recorded: Rockfield Studios, Monmouthshire; Faster
   Studios, Cardiff
Producer: Dave Eringa
Released: 18 May 2009 (*Journal For Plague Lovers*, Columbia)

> 'Too many empty spaces
> I can't seem to fill.'
>
>   – Dumptruck, 'Island'

Instead of the opaque 'Opulence', from the cover of the A4 ring binder Richey Edwards had presented him, Nicky Wire elected to name the record for one of its songs – specifically titled after Daniel Defoe's fictionalised history of London during 1665–6, *A Journal of the Plague Year*. 'It felt like an important song,' says Wire. 'Whereas "Opulence" didn't fit the bill for me. Maybe I was wrong. But it did feel like a fucking year of plague when Richey wrote those words.'

'Journal For Plague Lovers' certainly reads like a dispatch from the frontline. Its words carry the bitter residue of Edwards's treatment at The Priory, under the aegis of the Twelve Steps' submission to a god or equivalent higher entity, and the ambivalent power structures of institutionalised medicine: 'These perfect abattoirs/These perfect actors'; 'Doctor, divinity/So much love this blind affinity'; 'Only a god reserves the right to forgive those that revile him'. The original draft, as printed in the album artwork, was much longer, its language much harsher ('Wake in hell murder one').

'There was a lot of stuff there that I couldn't sing because it didn't feel poetic enough,' says Bradfield. 'Richey was always up for editing, and sometimes I think he's just getting rid of a crap line in his head. Actors do it, painters do it through drafts. Reading it now, it feels like we were struggling to get a lyric. But I just picked out the best lines.'

Bradfield visited Edwards at The Priory every other day for three weeks and saw Richey becoming part of this new community, saying hello to fellow patients. 'This song felt like a participant's observation,' says James. 'But it's also his struggle under diagnosis. I went in one day and he was actively angry. He's like, "If I sat in a bush with 'KILL 'EM ALL' on a helmet and talking about 'VC action', they'd be convinced I was fucking mad. But I tell them how I'm feeling and they say I'm borderline this or that. But I'm not right, there is something inside me which I'm not in control of." That's why he was angry. Because he hadn't gone the full *One Flew Over The Cuckoo's Nest* he thought they weren't taking him seriously. This lyric's obvious when you realise what The Priory is and what the treatment is. "Pretend prayer/Pretend care" – it's questioning the surrender of yourself to the Twelve Steps.'

Musically, 'Journal For Plague Lovers' digs out a path of defiance for its beleaguered subject, built upon a riff not dissimilar to Rush's 'Spirit Of Radio' – another song whose emphatic mood veils a lyric of bitter disillusionment. In acknowledgement of the musical debt, Wire reached for his Rickenbacker, à la Geddy Lee. 'We rehearsed this one hard,' he says. 'It's amazing that James moulded this lyric into a song that just flows so gracefully, as it's a pretty stark and depressing statement.' He sighs. 'You do wonder how much the Whitchurch [hospital] affected Richey, because he was severely sedated in there. It wasn't a great experience visiting him. I'm certainly not blaming anyone for him being there – his personal circumstance at that point couldn't have been any worse.'

Produced by Dave Eringa after a family illness forced Steve Albini to return home to Chicago, the *Journal For Plague Lovers* title track result is a triumph of collective will in the face of adversity (not least Eringa, who performed wonders in ensuring it was compatible with Albini's sound design). Going back to Edwards's spells in hospital was never likely to rekindle happy memories: the finished album booklet features the draft lyric next to an 'Opulence page' with illustrations of the nine circles of hell in Dante's *Inferno*, with added handwritten references to the Nick Cave song 'A Box For Black Paul', a ten-minute dirge about a villainous character who rails at being traduced even in death.

'There's probably a bit of me that just didn't want to hear some of these lyrics,' reflects Nicky. 'I'm less of an artist than James in that respect, I freely admit that. But I'm glad this is in our canon and I'm glad that aesthetically everything works.'

he four of us against the world': Manic Street Preachers' first Mitch Ikeda photo shoot,
ondon, 1992. From left: Nicky Wire, Richey Edwards, James Dean Bradfield, Sean Moore.

Top: Dressing room, Reading Festival, 29 August 1992.
Bottom: 'When our smiles were genuine': backstage at Newport Centre, 10 July 1993.

hollow arena to make arena rock': four-poster comfort at Hook End Manor, *Gold Against the Soul* sessions, spring 1993.

'Be pure – be vigilant – behave': scenes from *The Holy Bible* promo shoot, 1994.

Backstage at Glasgow's Barrowland Ballroom, 5 October 1994.

Top: 'Just need to be happy': *Everything Must Go* promo shoot, 1996.
Bottom left: Dressing room, Reading Festival, 23 August 1997.
Bottom right: 'It gives the wrong impression': *This Is My Truth Tell Me Yours* promo shoot, 199

usting the past off my mind': Japan, February 1999.

Culture. Alienation. Boredom. Despair.

108.

Facing Page: Top Left

Recorded: Rockfield Studios, Monmouthshire
Producer: Steve Albini
Released: 18 May 2009 (*Journal For Plague Lovers*, Columbia)

> 'I'm lost in the dark
> And I feel like a dinosaur.'
>
> – Buffalo Tom, 'Taillights Fade'

'Facing Page: Top Left' was a companion song of sorts to the album's title track, inasmuch as the lyric concerned Edwards's clinical treatment and the disconnect between its surface veneer ('Here is hospitality . . . tinted UV protection') and actual outcomes ('Here is oblivion bathed acid red'). Musically, however, the song took a very different approach. Although saddled with a bellicose reputation, Albini was equally skilled at making quiet, delicate records with the likes of folk singers Nina Nastasia and Bill Callahan, or soprano-voiced harpist Joanna Newsom. Aware of this work, and sensing the album would benefit from a breathing point midway through, the Manics opted for an acoustic arrangement featuring Katherine Thomas, harpist with the Welsh National Opera. The parallels with 'Small Black Flowers That Grow In The Sky' were deliberate.

'Richey loved that song, even though he never heard the final version,' says Wire. 'And he was a real sucker for a soppy, stark number, so we felt very comfortable doing it that way, with James playing the arpeggios on the acoustic, and the harp is a nice symmetry too. It's a beautiful thing – Richey's laying himself completely bare again.'

As indeed was Bradfield the vocalist who broke through an

initial impasse beautifully to capture the lyric's queasy dialogue between hope and fear. 'I thought, "I don't know how to sing it. Why have I written this, why am I trying to fit these words where they don't go? I just hit a brick wall." The lyric, though tightly written, certainly has its blind summits and concealed corners, notably the line 'This beauty here dipping neophobia', which Bradfield made into a refrain.

'I always took that to mean that once you've achieved self-improvement, whether it be your mind, your body, your soul, it's never enough,' he says. 'We're scared of ourselves. We're renewed all the time. We're constantly trying to improve ourselves in this age, and it's never enough.'

109.
Marlon J.D.

Recorded: Rockfield Studios, Monmouthshire; Faster
    Studios, Cardiff
Producer: Dave Eringa
Released: 18 May 2009 (*Journal For Plague Lovers*,
    Columbia)

'Stare at each other and wait 'til we die.'

– Big Black, 'Kerosene'

Ironically for an album predicated upon having Steve Albini's
sonic imprint, the song that could well have been its lead single
– had that concept not been ruled out in part-deference to Albini
– was recorded after his exit from the project. And unlike the title
track, this Dave Eringa production didn't strive to emulate the
great machinist's hallmark, but rather carved out its own unique
space, while still keeping faith with the overall code.

The song also had a distinct character for the very fundamental reason that Nicky Wire wrote the tune – the whole tune, as
opposed to just the chorus (as in 'Peeled Apples'), or just the
verse (as in *JFPL*'s 'She Bathed Herself In A Bath Of Bleach'),
or just one half of the song (as in 'Your Love Alone') . . . or
indeed, 'Wattsville Blues'. His vocals on the demo were so sweet
they were retained to harmonise with Bradfield's for the master-
version chorus.

'I felt really good at this point just playing an acoustic guitar,'
says Wire. 'Because I'd never written much, I could use all these
obvious chord changes James had gotten bored with. The verse
is just two chords, and the chord progression as it goes into the
chorus is really the kind of stuff you write in your twenties. But

because I never had, it somehow felt fresh. James, quite rightly, if he'd written it himself, would have been like, "Oh, I've done that so many times." So it was a nice added texture to the palette that could allow us to be young and naive again, without seeming forced. I was really excited when I presented the song to the boys.'

Who reciprocated in kind, Moore building himself into a percussive iron man to accompany the chattering drum machine pulse, while Bradfield's reptilian guitar abrasions suggested Steve Albini's own in Big Black, a point James himself made to Albini when they listened to the song's demo version. 'Steve said, "Well you think it's 'Kerosene', but it's not as good . . ."!' he laughs.[1] 'Nick writes differently to me, in terms of vocals – it will start in a lower place in the scale to me when he writes music. So my guitar can ride above it, and I loved playing guitar on this. I was trying to do a Bill Nelson kind of thing, where it's rock 'n' roll, but slightly skewed rock 'n' roll. And Sean is so brilliantly linked in when he plays with technology, it doesn't feel like he's trapped by it. He's in control.'

These elements poured into the spectacularly combustible vehicle for a lyric which, although brief, contained multitudes: essentially, Edwards's tight synopsis of the 1967 John Huston film *Reflections In A Golden Eye*, a torrid melodrama about repressed sexuality on a post-war Southern US army base, starring Elizabeth Taylor at her most volcanic and Marlon Brando substituting for the late Montgomery Clift. The lyric's opening line describes the scene where Brando's Major Penderton is whipped across the face by Taylor as his wife Leonora, in like-for-like punishment for whipping her horse.

'I knew how much that film meant to Richey,' says Wire, 'not that I really know in what context, but some sort of complicit witness to persecution or submissive taking of pain. He was obsessed with Elizabeth Taylor and Marlon Brando, beauty and manliness. So there's a lot to unpack in what looks like six lines of words!'

The song and its inspiration progressively meld: the middle-eight section features a sample of Brando from the film wistfully extolling the virtues of an austere barrack-room life ('clean as a rifle'), words already precis'd in the second verse, and his voice reappears at the end, as if to counter Bradfield's brief guitar solo, a rare burst of flamboyance on a record otherwise defined by its own brand of austerity. But if 'Marlon' was readily identifiable, what of 'J.D.'? After all, James Dean Bradfield's namesake was long gone by 1967.

'Obviously Marlon Brando and James Dean are the figurehead bastions of male sexuality in the fifties,' says Bradfield. 'And I remember reading that James Dean was obsessed with Marlon Brando, there were always questions about how fluid their sexuality was. Apparently James Dean was obsessed with Brando, and Brando was a wicked bongo player, so James Dean played bongos too. Probably bullshit, but we'll never know. I just think this song is Richey's fascination with beauty, and how beauty consumes itself, in any kind of form. I felt we constructed the song really well. And it should have been a single.'

110.

Doors Closing Slowly

Recorded: Rockfield Studios, Monmouthshire
Producer: Steve Albini
Released: 18 May 2009 (*Journal For Plague Lovers*, Columbia)

'And heaven I think is too close to hell.'
— The Jesus And Mary Chain, 'Darklands'

Perhaps the purest realisation of the album's mandate to reunite Richey Edwards's words with his band's musicality under the custodianship of Steve Albini, 'Doors Closing Slowly' is a sad masterpiece of restraint and instinct. Albini himself was so taken by the song that his professed neutrality in artistic decisions dropped and he behaved very much as a producer might.

'I wanted to put an overdub in,' says Bradfield, 'and he went, "No. No, this is a modest song. Don't do any more." Which is anti-production – and I really liked his input. It is a modest song. It's resigned, it's limp. "Realise how lonely this is" . . . fucking hell. Every line I read, I just thought there's no way out. "Drowned in love and false kisses, gathering of no meaning" – there's just no point. That's such a theme of Richey's, not trusting any kind of love whatsoever. But I was really happy when I came up with the music for it. Reminded me of those evenings where the trees go still.'

While Edwards's lyric delivers the bleakest appraisal of his rehab regime, the trudging accompaniment evokes an ultimately futile cyclical process. Both words and music are laced with religious tropes – imprecatory piano, martial drums, 'Who threw the first stone, if the stone is you?' – none of which offers much solace. The one flicker of resistance arrives in the final verse, where a peal of guitar feedback rises around the lines 'Listen to the selfish ones/They are the voice of accomplishment', and eventually engulfs the song to its dread conclusion: the sound of a ticking clock, following a piece of sampled dialogue from *The Virgin Suicides*, the Sofia Coppola film adaptation of Jeffrey Eugenides' 1993 novel, one of Edwards's favourites.

'You don't hear the word "accomplishment" much in the rock lexicon, do you? That's a great line,' marvels Wire. '"Doors Closing Slowly" might not jump out but Albini's old-school stuff here is really good, the drums sound amazing. Richey loved the book of *The Virgin Suicides*, because of its ambiguity more than anything. There's no answers in it. Much like Richey himself. A question mark.'

111.
All Is Vanity

Recorded: Rockfield Studios, Monmouthshire
Producer: Steve Albini
Released: 18 May 2009 (*Journal For Plague Lovers*,
  Columbia)

'Infamy, infamy, they've all got it in for me!'
　　　　　– Julius Caesar in *Carry On Cleo*; Dir: Gerald Thomas

On an album with plenty of questions but few answers – and
none of them easy – 'All Is Vanity' heralded a breakthrough of
sorts, both for its lyricist and his interpreters, not least because it
segues directly out of 'Doors Closing Slowly', the *Journal*'s lowest
low in a series of songs charting Edwards's circling quasi-religious
descent. Over a pummelling soundtrack, the narrator asserts
himself, starts asking questions, switches the narrative: 'It's not
"What's wrong?", it's "What's right?"/Makes me feel like I'm
talking a foreign language sometimes . . .'

Edwards's original draft had the 'What's wrong/What's right'
line – repurposed from 'Too Cold Here', an acoustic *Holy Bible*-era
song released on the B-side to 'Revol' – as the bridge, whereas
here it functioned as the chorus, followed by the bitter pay-off,
'It's the facts of life sunshine'.

'I love "All Is Vanity", it feels like we've cleaned the pipes a
bit,' says Bradfield. 'This is the point in Richey's life where he is
writing about himself and how he interacts with therapists, self-
help books, medication, and let's face it, suicidal thoughts. There
are recurring themes. And they all coagulate into one stream of
consciousness. But this lyric stood out – there was more sarcasm
in it. Because the worry with any kind of therapy is it washes out

people's sense of humour. Cynicism is a good filter, and I think this song filters out some of what he's going through in terms of treatment – the sarcasm is back and it makes you think the person is still with us. So that's what the music was about.'

That Bradfield saw something in this lyric is evident from having already used its second verse in the *God Save The Manics* EP track 'Picturesque' (alongside a stanza that became the de facto chorus of 'Doors Closing Slowly'). But whereas 'Picturesque' most closely fitted *Lifeblood*'s frigid pop template, 'All Is Vanity' was a *Holy Bible* update, suggesting the heroic bludgeon of Killing Joke circa the Chris Kimsey-produced *Night Time* as opposed to their earlier claustrophobic Conny Plank-helmed *Revelations*. Moore and Wire fell into lockstep line, tom rolls and bass popping in and around each other in spasmodic rapture, while Bradfield even snuck a few bits of Eddie Van Halen flash past Albini's raised eyebrow. Such were the levels of ensemble engagement by this point.

'We were performing in front of the world's greatest live recorder of sound, so we had to be well on it,' says Wire. 'This one we were recorded as us, together. There was no overdubbing. "All Is Vanity" was perfect for the MO of the album, just an endless power rage. It's the sort of thing we'd be afraid to do now. It would have no meaning.'

112.
Pretension/Repulsion

Recorded: Rockfield Studios, Monmouthshire
Producer: Steve Albini
Released: 18 May 2009 (*Journal For Plague Lovers*,
   Columbia)

'Everything has beauty, but not everyone sees it.'
                                          – Confucius

Although he had no prior knowledge of the band, and despite
their differing cultural backgrounds, Steve Albini found that he
and the Manics shared much in common – not least a staunch
work ethic. Albini subsequently cited *Journal For Plague Lovers* as
a textbook example of an 'easy' record to make, thanks to the
band's attitude and effort. 'The Manic Street Preachers were very
well rehearsed, very good musicians and they were obviously
intimately familiar with each other,' he said in late 2009. 'So
they worked well together and were all very much in control of
what they expected out of that session. It went very smoothly.'

'Pretension/Repulsion' is a case in point: a song so convulsively
driven it could not have been made by a band whose shit was
any less together. 'I can come up with a tune like that but I can't
get the power that Nick and Sean give to it,' says James. 'The
way they play this is part of the writing. It felt like something
being fused, something being cleansed, something happening. I
remember especially thinking Richey would like this song and
"All Is Vanity".'

Certainly, 'Pretension/Repulsion' feels likewise evocative of *The
Holy Bible*, albeit dispatched by a band with more than a decade's
worth of extra experience. The lyrics featured a litany of words

mostly connoting pain, subjugation, and exploitation – 'Sickened and howled, streaked and spurned/Plucked, lived, compelled and called' – with echoes of the animal suffering of 'Small Black Flowers'. 'It's a short song but really detailed, Sean's drums are amazing,' says Wire. 'It's the one where I would let myself go and think almost like Richey was . . . there was some presence there.'

The chorus, meanwhile, referenced Jean-Auguste-Dominique Ingres' painting *La Grande Odalisque*, infamous for its anatomically impossible representation of the female nude. But Bradfield deleted the Edwards draft's mention of Benetton's controversial nineties ad campaign. 'The dying Aids patient – I just didn't want to go there,' notes James. 'I don't know if I want to do it every night, but playing a tune like this with Nick and Sean is just brilliant. The splintered, atomised kind of energy, you can't tell if it's enthusiasm or hatred – it's a great experience.'

113.
William's Last Words

Recorded: Rockfield Studios, Monmouthshire
Producer: Steve Albini
Released: 18 May 2009 (*Journal For Plague Lovers*, Columbia)

'Oh Sleep!, it is a gentle thing,
Beloved from pole to pole.'
        – Samuel Taylor Coleridge, *The Rime of the Ancient Mariner*

If Nicky Wire could almost sense Richey Edwards's presence in 'Pretension/Repulsion', then the ensuing 'William's Last Words' – the closing song of *Journal For Plague Lovers* – had the uncanny aura of a final conversation between the two friends: Nicky singing Richey's words of farewell, poignantly ending on the lines 'I'd love to go to sleep and wake up happy/Wake up happy'. Except, 'William's Last Words' isn't so straightforward. As per the title, these aren't necessarily Richey's words at all. The final lyric was edited from over a page of prose, which reads like the jumbled-up record of a conversation, real or imagined, in which 'William' – or 'Bill', or 'Billy boy', as the text calls him – is just one participant, written in an idiom that suggests post-war reminiscence: the first words on Edwards's draft are 'Gracie Fields, lovely lady, lovely lady'. There are even parenthetical stage directions – 'I'll sing one more song (sings slurred national anthem)'. In its raw version 'William's Last Words' actual last words are the wry 'I've come a long way, really, even for a tone deaf singer, if you want to know.'

'I think Richey might have written this when he was in [the] Whitchurch, because it's like reportage,' says Wire. 'But like everything he did, it's never as plain as that. There's always another element to it. "I'll be watching over you" and 'Good night, my sweetheart" also reminded me of the passages in *The Waste Land* when T.S. Eliot describes the London pub and uses cockney vernacular, which we often talked about. Also, Richey was obsessed with Archie Rice in *The Entertainer*, the Laurence Olivier film [directed by Tony Richardson], about the passage of time and the showman who's on his arse. It obviously sounds like it is some kind of analogy.'

Written by John Osborne in 1957 as a stage play specifically for Olivier in the title role, *The Entertainer* used the dog days of music hall as a metaphor for Britain in decline; while Archie is bitter at the world, his father, whose name is Billy, basks in nostalgic memories of better times. It's not hard to imagine Edwards recognising a parallel with his own diminished circumstances, or those of the Manics. So the popular reading of 'William's Last Words' as a valedictory message from someone who knew they were going away, never to return, is a simplistic hindsight view. But in the context of *Journal For Plague Lovers* as a tribute to Richey Edwards from his bandmates, the song gives the album a satisfying resolution, and its bittersweet farewell – including the Welsh 'nos da', for 'goodnight' – is wholly valid, indeed necessary.

'I felt like the essence of the song was deeply humane,' says Wire. 'A wave goodbye imbued with love and rest in peace – that was the essence of Richey's piece. I didn't necessarily think it was all about him, but it deeply resonated with what happened. The fact that he put "nos da" in is very much, I think, down to his nan, who he was very close to. It's the sort of thing your nan would say, as in the remnants of Welsh language. My mum would still say it to me. It's not necessarily a Welsh speaking thing any more, it's become more prevalent. But I thought that was interesting that he put that in there – it's not exactly "P.C.P."!'

From its opening synthesiser splash to his final wavering chord, Wire's Cardiff demo was of such emotive calibre it left no doubt that he should sing the finished song. 'The start is a sample of Cabaret Voltaire, literally lifted from one of their records,'

Nicky says. 'There's some peaceful resonance to it. You're almost in the dentist's chair going under. And the chords: I was trying to write in a very basic way but they are quite jazzy for me, because there's little fingers left on – like "The Rain Song" by Led Zeppelin. I had a proper moment where I was just looking at those lyrics and I wrote the song on the spot in about twenty minutes.'

Equally adept at tending to the sensitivities of acoustic instruments as channelling electrical fury, Steve Albini again demonstrated his 'anti-production' producer skills during the recording of the string section. Bradfield had asked the Vulcan String Quartet's leader Andrew Walters if he could track the part twice more. Albini demurred. 'He's like, "Why more?" So I ceased and desisted, and of course, he was right.'

Then came Nicky Wire's vocal, for which Bradfield made himself scarce. 'I came back in after half an hour and Nick was listening to three or four takes. "What do you think?" I said, "That line, that line . . . give it four more takes and we'll have it." And Steve was like, "No. This is what it is, I don't think he's gonna get it better. I don't think it *needs* to be better." Steve understood the kind of record we were making, and I wasn't quite buying into it. I just don't think like that. I think I'll get the perfect version of me, the perfect version of all of us. And I've relaxed on that since. Nick wrote a brilliant song and Steve knew when the performance was good enough.'

Wire's vocal was nervous but resolute, like watery early morning sunlight, and the making of the song. Like all great music, 'William's Last Words' transcends foreknowledge of its creative context, a beautiful testimony to the heart and craft of everyone involved. Writing to Richey Edwards's words again had summoned a special power from the band, which as often demonstrated on *Journal For Plague Lovers* could feel forbidding and dangerous. Here, however, was a different kind of special power – and a fitting way to say goodbye.

114.

Bag Lady

Recorded: Rockfield Studios, Monmouthshire
Producer: Dave Eringa
Released: 18 May 2009 (*Journal For Plague Lovers*,
    Columbia)

'To fill the hour – that is happiness.'
    – Ralph Waldo Emerson, *Essays: Second Series*

And then it turns out William's weren't the last words after all. Unlisted on the sleeve, hidden in the digital void long after the basic CD edition of *Journal* had ostensibly finished, not quite an album track, a lost classic B-side to a single that never existed . . . 'Bag Lady' was all this and more: a problem child from the very start.

'We went in with Dave Eringa to mop up the tracks Steve couldn't do because he'd had to go home,' says Wire. 'And for some reason the first track we decided to do was "Bag Lady". It's a difficult song, [an] atonal riff, and Dave just couldn't get the drum sound. We spent two days literally getting nowhere. Then we changed the drum kit into a different room and we got cooking. James had a lot of faith in the song – quite rightly because it turned out to be something blisteringly strange and wonderful.'

After limbering up with the likes of 'All Is Vanity' and 'Pretension/Repulsion', the Manics now ran amok in their own private post-punk gene lab and emerged with this relentless PiL/Magazine *Übermensch* construct, a veritable archive of pain to wrap around another uncomfortable Edwards clinical disquisition: 'You cover illness with flowers/And flowers die'.

'It was a vignette about somebody he had met in the hospital,' says Bradfield. 'Suddenly you think, is this a bit too precarious? Richey wrote it, we don't know who it's about. It's his observation, it's part of his community at this point. Is he being empathetic? Is he being voyeuristic? What are we channelling? In the end you just go "fuck it" and enjoy playing. It's unbelievable, this natural second language we have inherited from our post-punk record collection.'

Ultimately, the song too plausibly resembled *The Holy Bible Part 2*, which despite the surface linkage *Journal For Plague Lovers* assuredly was not. So 'Bag Lady' got buried. 'A perverse decision,' admits Bradfield. 'Good tune. But it's got too much power.'

115.

(It's Not War) Just The End Of Love

Recorded: Faster Studios, Cardiff
Producer: Dave Eringa
Released: 13 September 2010 (single, Columbia);
    20 September 2010 (*Postcards From A Young Man*,
    Columbia)

'Finger on the pin, do you like my grin, huh?'
    – The Teardrop Explodes, 'The Culture Bunker'

In the *Frasier* Season 7 episode 'They're Playing Our Song', the title character is tasked with writing a ten-second jingle for his radio show – a straightforward assignment that inevitably balloons into a Sondheimesque musical theme featuring trumpet fanfares, harp glissandos, an atonal monologue, and a coda proclaiming Dr Frasier Crane 'the man who feels everyone's pain' in the style of 'Supercalifragilisticexpialidocious' from *Mary Poppins*. 'Whatever happened to the concept of "less is more"?' asks Niles, as he watches his brother rehearsing a full orchestra plus choir. 'Ah,' says Frasier, 'but if less is more, just imagine how much more "more" will be.'

James Dean Bradfield enjoys relating this scene, not least as he freely admits to some Frasier tendencies of his own, tendencies that making an album with Steve Albini obliged him to quell. *Journal For Plague Lovers* had always been a tactical detour from the record they were primed to make after *Send Away The Tigers*, the rationale being that more 'more' might actually be too much, too soon. This time, however, the Manics knew 'more' would be back in play. Sensing the shifting topography of music industry business models, as well as taking stock of his situation as any 41-year-old with two young children sensibly might, Nicky Wire declared a mission statement for the new album: 'One last shot at mass communication'.

'I remember Nick coming up with that line and it drove the writing,' says Bradfield. 'What that does is, you try not to write too many album tracks – you're really aiming for a single every time. People hear a sentence like that and they don't think it's an artistic enterprise. But you're trying to create the moments that got you into music. Most of my favourite bands were great singles bands. So *Postcards* was the record that was going to follow *Tigers* – it was supposed to be *Everything Must Go* going into *This Is My Truth*, basically, a little bit of evolution but not much. Just trying to be us and enjoying it.'

Bradfield recalls concurrently writing music for *Journal* and demoing two songs that would go onto *Postcards*, so to pivot back felt straightforward and work proceeded briskly. Having had no requirement to write any new words for the previous album while also being constrained by its unique parameters, Wire now felt creatively off the leash.

'It was a massively productive time,' he says. 'I had loads of lyrics. And James was in the process of moving from Chiswick back to Wales and had sent us quite a lot of demos, so me and Sean had gone to the studio in Cardiff and put bass and drums on. We were working like a peak band, but ten years older – controlled but frantic. I honestly couldn't have done another album like *Journal*. Because obviously you had to be incredibly respectful in everything you said, which is how it should be. But it's quite an ask for me. It was very reverential, rather than irreverential. So, "It's Not War" felt really quite joyous, I guess, after *Journal For Plague Lovers*.'

The first draft for the song that would be the album's advance single and its opening track was written in the Radisson Hotel in

Glasgow on 18 February 2010, following a one-off gig to celebrate the twentieth anniversary of legendary basement club venue King Tut's Wah Wah Hut. The set began with 'Strip It Down', to commemorate the Manics' previous visit, in April 1991. 'It was the first gig we'd ever done where we'd been given hot food,' says Wire. 'So we thought it would be a nice thing to do. Then I went back to the hotel. I'd started drinking again – from *Tigers* to the end of *Postcards*, gig-wise, I was drinking nicely – so I was pretty drunk. Then I woke up in the morning and realised I've written most of the lyrics.'

In its finished state '(It's Not War) Just The End Of Love' was more a collection of snappy aphorisms than an exercise in profundity – 'To feel forgiveness you've got to forgive/It's lost on me, I believe in revenge'. Nonetheless it caught something of the wider landscape's uncertainty, post-2008's global financial crash and a few months' prior to the fateful 2010 UK general election that ushered in fourteen years of Conservative governments.

'I like the lyric because it's not straight-talking,' says Bradfield. 'It weaves its way in and out of reason.'

The musical design was more straightforward: flavours of Rush's 'Closer To The Heart' for the guitar arpeggiation and bellicose tom rolling, a vigorous string arrangement and a guitar solo with a very good reason for sounding windswept.

'Via a contact in Cardiff, I'd been given the little box which facilitates Brian May's sound,' says Bradfield. 'It's dark science – remember, he was an astrophysics student. The sound of Brian May is in the fingers, most of it. But you take two Vox amps, turn down all the tones so it's really flat and muddy, then this box pumps all the tone you took *out* of the amps and puts it back *in* in a different way. I was obsessed. I'd stay behind in the studio at night and play a myriad of Brian May parts and think, "Does that sound more like him with this splitter box? Or less?" That was all over this track. And I used a Brian May copy guitar. It's fun being a musician sometimes.'

Unable to decide whether it should be the first single, the band eventually acquiesced to their brusque booking agent Scott Thomas who stood up at a Sony planning meeting and declared 'It's Not War' the obvious choice. 'And it was the last Top 40 hit single we ever had!' laughs Wire. 'A pretty uplifting record all round. It's rare that I feel grateful for being in a band, but in that period I was thinking we're getting on a bit and all our contemporaries had either split or were about to, and here we are all over radio, we did a brilliant video with Michael Sheen and Anna Friel, we were back on the cover of *NME* . . . The last remnants of a culture that just disappeared.'

116.

Postcards From A Young Man

Recorded: Faster Studios, Cardiff
Producer: Dave Eringa
Released: 20 September 2010 (*Postcards From A Young
Man*, Columbia); 28 February 2011 (single, Columbia)

'Experience is the name everyone gives to their mistakes.'
— Oscar Wilde, *Lady Windermere's Fan*

Ironically for a meditation on how real life greys out the certainties of youth, 'Postcards Of A Young Man' comes in the boldest colours. Bradfield doubts there's a more shocking Manics opening couplet than 'I don't believe the absolutes any more, I'm quite prepared to admit I was wrong', every word landing emphatically as the stadium-glam intro defers to a plaintive piano, drums and vocal.

'For Nick to say that is a big thing. "I don't believe the absolutes any more" – whoah! Because it was a way to live our lives for quite a long time. But everyone comes to that point, don't they? I think absolutes have been proven to be for idiots many, many times. Well, except perhaps being a republican, and not believing in private education . . . and hating the England football team . . . Anyway! It's poetic, but also quite blunt as well. "The postcards from a young man" – everyone from our generation could readily share that sentiment.'

This song, written two years after the birth of his second child, was Nicky Wire's lament both for his former self and that of the band: 'So sad and lonely and so derelict as the optimism that we once shared.' Yet as the title track of an album that triangulated between regret, anger and defiance, a title track every bit as much an emotional fulcrum as Echo & The Bunnymen's 'Ocean Rain' or The Smiths' 'The Queen Is Dead', in spite of everything else 'Postcards From A Young Man' was also an assertion of ongoing viability.

'It was saying, "We are different now,"' says Wire. 'It's the start of the realisation that when you witness personal and national failure, whether in politics or your own career, or anything, when you realise your voice is most of time unnecessary or un-listened to, you start to think that all you can actually control is your own small circumstance. It's not reverting to conservatism with a small *c* or anything, it's just being ravaged with doubt. You know, when we started the band, me and Richey loved using the "we" or the "our". And obviously it's turned into the "me" or the "I". And I don't think certainty has ever returned to us as a band.'

The sending of postcards had always been a big thing in the Manics' world – James was especially prolific on tour – and Wire still maintained the habit, whenever he was holidaying in Tenby or visiting Dylan Thomas's house in Laugharne. Struck by the historic resonance these lyrics held, Bradfield found himself writing in the same time signature as 'A Design For Life' and 'The Second Great Depression'. 'I've done it a few times and I don't know what takes me there,' he says. 'Sean's pointed it out to me; I do like a bit of a waltz. It takes a lot of twists and turns, this song, and there are a lot of caesuric pauses before you go back into the verse again, a pause to give meaning to the next verse.'

James also partly credits this restless energy to tension between himself and Dave Eringa during the recording session. 'I'd just moved house and I wasn't having the easiest time, which I imparted to Dave, but he was not treating me with the kid gloves I demanded at that point. Sometimes Nick had to say to me: "I think you've got to chill the fuck out." But it's a really good record, so sometimes that old traditional tension can make a good rock 'n' roll record. And the ending offers some kind of optimism, offers embrace, offers communion. A bit more Hollywood from us, I think.'

The song's coda doesn't just nod to Queen's 'Somebody To Love', so much as give it a kiss; though the rhythm also resembles Skids' 'Grievance'. Either way, the debt is well paid, as Bradfield emerges likes Martin Sheen from the swamp in *Apocalypse Now* with choir and strings accompaniment, delivering the climactic twist: 'This world will not impose its will/I will not give up and I will not give in'.

'To think I might still have felt like that, that I still had a sense of passion about everything, still gives me a bit of a kick,' Wire reflects. 'This is a proper piece of work.'

117.
Some Kind Of Nothingness

Recorded: Faster Studios, Cardiff
Producer: Dave Eringa
Released: 20 September 2010 (*Postcards From A Young
    Man*, Columbia); 6 December 2010 (single, Columbia)

'He that plants trees loves others beside himself.'
                                    – Thomas Fuller, *Gnomologia*

On 9 October 1984, James Dean Bradfield, Richey Edwards
and Sean Moore, plus their schoolfriend Rowan, travelled from
Blackwood to Bristol to see Echo & The Bunnymen. They arrived
early enough to see the band arrive at the venue and got each
member's autograph as they left after soundcheck: guitarist Will
Sergeant, singer Ian McCulloch, bassist Les Pattinson and drummer Pete de Freitas. 'Will Sergeant said, "Why do you want my
autograph? I'm not God, you know",' Bradfield recalls. 'I saw Pete
ride away on his motorbike. I was utterly starstruck.'

Just over twenty-five years later, Ian McCulloch was sitting
in the Manics' recording studio in Cardiff. 'Doing a Daffy Duck
impersonation down the microphone,' says James. 'It was a genuinely discombobulating weird moment – from young starstruck
kid, to this, and I was still starstruck.'

Other highlights of Mac the Mimic's repertoire included David
Bowie ('perfect') and larrikin Scouse comedian Stan Boardman.
'He turned his back on us and just shrugged his shoulders,' says
Nicky Wire. 'And it did look like Stan Boardman,' he laughs. 'The
Bunnymen was it for James, Sean and Richey, their first gig. So
to have him singing on our song was a massive thrill.'

Ian McCulloch was the wilful genius crooning, shimmying and

roaring at the helm of Echo & The Bunnymen's heroic quest for an indefinable glory, the lippy figurehead of Liverpool's post-punk scene who in 1984 had a new kind of pop stardom bestowed by the single 'The Killing Moon' and its subsequent album *Ocean Rain*. But the band bitterly sundered in the late eighties: Mac left for an underwhelming solo career, de Freitas died in a motorcycle accident, and although a brief reunion the following decade stirred memories of what had been lost, by 2010 McCulloch's star was fading. Such was the pull of Bunnypower, however, that those who remembered still dared to believe in magic. Surely all it needed was the right song – and in 'Some Kind Of Nothingness', Nicky Wire had a song that even Mac considered worthy of his time.

'I had written it as a duet, with him in mind,' he says. 'Which turned into the longest day of Dave Eringa's life, trying to record it. But sometimes you've got to go through the pain to get somewhere. It was all worthwhile.'

Along with its elegiac quality, the song shared subject matter with Wire's previous starry duet, 'Your Love Alone Is Not Enough'.

'There was a suicide close to where I live, near a particular beautiful oak tree,' he says, explaining the otherwise mysterious 'The tree gave more to you than love' lyric. 'This fellow who passed away, I'd see him from my bedroom window, sat in the tree. The song's also an evocation that my dog Molly, our black Labrador, had died. So there's three components: a massive oak tree, a suicide, and my dog. And much like "Your Love Alone", the lyrics came really quickly.'

If Wire's demo, recorded with Loz Williams, had a fuzzy elegance, the band version went the full Burt Bacharach, with Bradfield filling the pocket with crisp Steve Cropper guitar, and strings and a choir piling in as early the first chorus to honour Molly 'stretched out in the sun'. The gospel stylings came from the same seven-piece choir featured on 'Postcards Of A Young Man', authentically hewn from the deep south of Wales by arranger Cat Southall, while it was Wire's turn to butt heads with Dave Eringa over the precise emulation of his demo guitar part by the string section.

'Dave's more Frasier than me sometimes,' says Bradfield, 'and Nick was a bit control freaky over this song, like "No, no . . ." But getting Mac to record his part was the real operation. When he got there, he asked for two packs of Marlboro Red, two pints of milk – "full fat, none of that World War Two shit" – and a bottle of Courvoisier. I just left Dave and Mac with each other for about two hours to do the vocal.'

Aware of McCulloch's mercurial ways, the band had asked Andrew 'Davvo' Davitt, a Liverpudlian Manics roadie whose band Johnny Boy's single Bradfield co-produced, to attend the session as an intermediary ('they were speaking in tongues half the time,' says Wire, 'you had no idea what was going on'). It was Davvo who suggested Mac quote the Bunnymen classic 'Never Stop' during the pre-finale breakdown: the song's *coup de Scouse* moment, it follows Mac repeating his line from the previous verse, 'There's beauty doing nothing at all', as if he's just seen a ghost – or a younger version of himself – and then, over a classic Pete de Freitas tom-tom homage from Sean Moore, he ascends to a new dimension.

'Mac's been a bit lower case up to that point,' says Bradfield. 'Then the cracked mirror revealed itself to be perfect again.'

A euphoric contemplation of death, like many great Manic Street Preachers songs, 'Some Kind Of Nothingness' breaks with structural norms. A pop duet would typically alternate the singers before uniting them in the chorus, whereas here McCulloch takes the second and third line in each of the first two verses with Bradfield on either side, until the third verse mixes things up. It was, says Bradfield, simply a case of having Mac sing the entire song and then picking the lines where the voices worked best.

'It's a mini-masterpiece, I think. And then we played it with Mac on *Later . . . With Jools Holland*. We soundchecked, and Phil

Collins and his manager Tony Smith were watching us. At the end, they just went, "That's a hell of a song." I said to Nick, "That's props, you know!"'

Two days before that *Later* recording, Molly the labrador died. Heartbroken, Nicky skipped the first day's rehearsal. 'Typical Mac, when I finally arrived he said, "Yeah, y'know, I'm not a dog man, I'm a cat man . . ."' He smiles. 'I remember when we got Chris Lord-Alge's mix of this song and Mac sends me a text: "That's the fucking one, it's amazing." And I did have a moment, thinking: "It's Ian McCulloch, he's just sung on our song and he thinks it's fucking brilliant." That was sweet. It just felt like my work here is done.'

118.
Auto-Intoxication

Recorded: Faster Studios, Cardiff
Producer: Dave Eringa
Released: 20 September 2010 (*Postcards From A Young Man*, Columbia)

'The crisis consists precisely in the fact that the old is dying and the new cannot be born.'

— Antonio Gramsci, *The Prison Notebooks*

Whereas 'Postcards From A Young Man's title track mourned a dying culture, other songs warned of oncoming dystopias. 'Auto-Intoxication' was named after a medical theory whereby body and mind are poisoned by toxic substances produced from within the gut. Although no stranger to the general concept thanks to his struggles with Gilbert's syndrome, in this instance Nicky Wire's concern was the psychological impact of digesting the swirl of ideas and thoughts in the new digital age. The lyric mocks the feelgood nostrums of tech giants – 'My work will set me free and fulfils my dreams' – and prefigures what later becomes known as 'doom-scrolling'. As the refrain declares: 'The disaster's not coming/It's already arrived!'

'We'd just come out of the financial crisis, when you realise that basically capitalism is just a mechanism to create debt,' says Wire. 'And the song's about poisoning yourself with your own vitriol. The poison was coming from a place where I had never realised it would come from before – i.e., a digital unifier separated from any forms of prosecutorial judgement, infecting the culture that had been so precious to us. It seems trivial now, being told that we weren't going to have physical singles any more and the idea that I had to say yes and agree that everything was being replaced for the common good, but I was raging.'

Musically, 'Auto-Intoxication' simulates the titular condition, its steady motorik pulse interrupted by a dreamy narcotic interlude ('welcome to the new slave trade') then gleefully embracing chaos via John Cale's sublimated keyboard and Moore's righteous snare swats. 'Really obtuse,' nods Bradfield. 'We asked John Cale specifically because he's really good at jarring bits. I love how Nick and Sean play it like something off *Ziggy Stardust*, rock 'n' roll but in a sardonic fashion. It's a proper album track – you basically look at the lyrics and think this can never be a single, so let's do what the hell I want.'

119.

Golden Platitudes

Recorded: Faster Studios, Cardiff
Producer: Dave Eringa
Released: 20 September 2010 (*Postcards From A Young
Man*, Columbia)

> 'My Shangri-La has gone away,
> faded like The Beatles on "Hey Jude".'
>   – Electric Light Orchestra, 'Shangri-La'

In a quintessentially Manics mangling of intent and outcomes, what began as a Nicky Wire bedtime serenade to his newborn son Stan turned into this arms-aloft lament for the straightforwardly adversarial political ideologies of yore: 'Where did it all go wrong?/Born to be a communist/But then the marriage failed . . .' Perhaps unsurprisingly, Wire says Stan was a good sleeper.

'I used to have him in my study, in his little rocking chair, and I'd be playing him "Golden Platitudes" – my thinking was, "Golden Slumbers" by The Beatles. I can picture him now, he was such an angel. Rachel would feed him and then I'd sing him "The platitudes, they all dissolved . . ." and he'd just nod off and then I put him down to bed. We had four or five weeks of that and the lyric came on and on, I didn't write the words down for a long time, they were embedded in my head.'

That the final version's massed strings and choral la-la-la's somehow don't feel excessive is testament to judicious arranging – 'I had to really concentrate because a lot of the same chords repeated,' says Bradfield – and adherence to the core musical inspiration: thinking Beatles at all times. 'I wanted it to be something off *The White Album* played by Guns N' Roses,' says Wire.

'James was bristling a bit, because I'd been nagging him to play it like George Harrison, but I think he definitely got there, especially on the outro.'

For the audience beyond baby Stan, the key to the success of 'Golden Platitudes' is Bradfield's empathy for the writer, aided by his appreciation that the line 'where did the feeling go' referenced Big Country's wintry tearjerker 'Chance'. He heard a potentially hazardous lyric like 'The liberal left destroyed every bit of our youth' and dug into the source. 'It's an emotional song,' he says, 'because it's about knowing you're never going to live in a political Shangri-La. Life's all about compromise. Admitting defeat gracefully, I think, is quite an important moment. That's what life is about, isn't it? So that's a really sad song.'

120.

A Billion Balconies Facing The Sun

Recorded: Faster Studios, Cardiff
Producer: Dave Eringa
Released: 20 September 2010 (*Postcards From A Young Man*, Columbia)

> 'A world lying on its back is vulnerable to any cunning predator.'
>
> – J.G. Ballard, *Cocaine Nights*

In his novel *Cocaine Nights*, published in the same year the Manics released *Everything Must Go*, J.G. Ballard imagined a future world where rich people retire in their thirties and fester together in private luxury, cocooned in the gated leisure societies of their own minds. 'A Billion Balconies Facing The Sun' took its title from the book (also the source for 'personal gods' from 'Groundhog Days') and suggested that particular Ballard future had arrived, or was at least accelerating towards a screen near you soon, like a reverse vanishing point.

Although self-evidently prescient in its portrayal of hate speech, fake news et al. – 'We've finally found a way/To consume boredom every day'; 'We found expression for our hate/Without any kind of consequence'; 'A billion lies becoming the truth' – the song was derided by some at the time as either reactionary or hysterical. 'There was an element of "What you on about, the internet's amazing!"' says Wire. 'I know, we're all complicit. But I was looking at the long tail.' Beyond dispute was the vehemence of its execution, an adversarial blend of Alice Cooper tuff and

Fleetwood Mac boogie, quite unlike anything else on the record.

'With a lyric like that, as opposed to "Golden Platitudes", you can't make the argument with some solipsistic song that's sad about its potential fate,' says Bradfield. 'You gotta be powerful about it. "A Billion Balconies" is fighting for something which isn't quite set in stone, it requires a completely different emotional angle – needs to be more expressive, more ferocious, more aggressive.'

Extra aggro came from Guns N' Roses bassist Duff McKagan giving the low end a star layer of sinewy threat, thereby completing the album's formidable guest quota and returning the favour Bradfield had paid in October 2009 when he joined McKagan's solo band Loaded at Hammersmith Apollo for an encore of GN'R's 'It's So Easy', after which McKagan declared Bradfield 'an EPIC dude!'. The kinship runs deeper than mere mutual fandom: a working-class product of Seattle's no-shits-taken early eighties punk scene, McKagan's three professed bass idols are Magazine's Barry Adamson, The Clash's Paul Simonon, and Lemmy. 'Duff's always been cool, he bisects a lot of worlds,' says James. 'He's like a Nicky Wire soul twin in terms of the aesthetic of who he is onstage.'

Bisecting worlds? The Manics could relate. As the bridge between J.G. Ballard and Guns N' Roses, 'A Billion Balconies Facing The Sun' speaks eloquently to a very twenty-first-century appetite for (self-)destruction. Curiously, the song has only ever been played twice, on a two-date stand at London's Brixton Academy in January 2011, where the venerable citadel shook with approval.

'We were playing great, with a grateful crowd in the middle of winter,' recalls Wire. 'And this song just felt brilliant in that setting, somewhere real and old. Somewhere built for something that was disappearing.'

121.

All We Make Is Entertainment

Recorded: Faster Studios, Cardiff
Producer: Dave Eringa
Released: 20 September 2010 (*Postcards From A Young Man*, Columbia)

'The moment I was born, I opened my eyes
I reached out for my credit card.'

— Gang Of Four, 'Capital (It Fails Us Now)'

Written in the twilight of New Labour's dance with the free market devil, 'All We Make Is Entertainment' illustrates how within a group dynamic one person's success can be another's failure. Nicky Wire loves that his death notice for British manufacturing industry got soundtracked by such a theatrical manifestation of blue-collar rock. James Dean Bradfield, however, feels that his part of that equation let down the other.

'I thought the lyric was amazing,' he says. 'A song about how the nuts and bolts of our mums and dads were absent in us, perhaps. I grew up with people that dug stuff, that made stuff, that worked their fucking arses off and had lovely retirements and passed it on to another generation. And then we're in this ether world where my grandma said to me, "When I ask people what they do now, they tell me and I don't know what they do!" She didn't recognise jobs any more. So Nick's lyric talked about that hollowed-out service-industry culture, stuff that people would be talking about for a long time. The tune came quickly and I had such faith in it. Then we start recording and the desk broke down for three days. The song was never seen again – it became too big, too widescreen, too unwieldy.'

The counter-argument maintains that the song's ripely turned oratory – 'This country is but an empty shell/A clearing house for heaven, a clearing house for hell' – would have been exposed by a less histrionic treatment, and the guitar solo's parachuting of Stuart Adamson into the E Street Band is wholly justified. But Bradfield isn't having any of it.

'I should have written a different tune, as simple as that. I lost the ability to concentrate and say no, let's re-record the drums, take some guitars away, make it smaller. It just got away from me. Makes me feel sad.'

Wire is relaxed about the song's fate. Its themes, after all, have rumbled on through his writing ever since. 'I know James has a problem with this, but I love how over the top it is. It's like Orwellian patriotism, a sort of *cry* – "we can be better than this!"'

122.
Don't Be Evil

Recorded: Faster Studios, Cardiff, October 2009
Producer: Dave Eringa
Released: 20 September 2010 (*Postcards From A Young Man*, Columbia)

> 'And dogs are dead with broken hearts
> Collapsing by the coffee carts.'
> – Grandaddy, 'The Crystal Lake'

Into the Silicon Valley of death rode Manic Street Preachers for the last time on *Postcards*' closing track, titled after the Google motto that once adorned the tech giant's HQ and was written into the prospectus for its 2004 stock launch. '"Don't be evil" – what a fucking insane thing to say when you're giving people the capacity to promote their evil on your platforms,' says Wire, whose lyric lambasted both the medium and the messenger for enabling 'sickos and bullies', as well as denuding the analogue culture which had inspired and nourished the Manics: 'The music is going . . . The printed word is all done and dusted.'

Just as 'Nat West-Barclays-Midlands-Lloyds' was perceived at the time as lyrically naive, so too 'Don't Be Evil' has subsequently found itself vindicated by events. Although the critique of digital panaceas aligned with 'Auto-Intoxication' and 'A Billion Balconies Facing The Sun', the musical approach here was more playful, less tight-wound. Bradfield apparently saw the title and ran to Television's 'See No Evil', evoked in the opening guitar chimes – placed in the left channel, as per Tom Verlaine's on the original – with Wire's bass notes high up the neck and

Moore's tumbling snare and tom-filled groove also emulating one of the great New York band's signature tunes.

'I don't know if the double downstroke on the D chord was a subconscious tick to Television,' says Bradfield. 'I wouldn't back myself against muscle memory involuntary reflexes. I do remember playing it and knowing that we were in a groove so natural that it would be perverse to pull it apart. There was an easy flow and enjoyment to that day that felt uncoded and warm. A nice antidote to the song's target. I used my touring *Holy Bible* Jazzmaster and *Generation Terrorists* Marshall Shred Master pedal – old friends.'

As close as the Manics have ever come to true garage rock, with its loose improvised guitar solo and gritty sonics, 'Don't Be Evil' has never been performed live. But what a way to close an album conceived as a communication shot: with a display of pure collective engagement.

123.
Rewind The Film

Recorded: Faster Studios, Cardiff
Producers: Manic Street Preachers and Loz Williams
Released: 8 July 2013 (download, Columbia);
   16 September 2013 (*Rewind The Film*, Columbia)

'You know the way it is in life, it's so hard to live up to.'
                              Richard Hawley, 'The Ocean'

As last shots at mass communication go, *Postcards From A Young Man* hit the mark: the album sold around 140,000 copies, the band played large tours in sold-out venues, and a relentless promotion campaign re-established the Manics' status as radio airplay fixtures. Notable television appearances included performing 'Some Kind Of Nothingness' on Saturday-night family favourite *Strictly Come Dancing*, and when biennial golf grudge match the Ryder Cup was staged at Celtic Manor just outside Newport, an astute Sky producer soundtracked celebratory footage of Europe's victory over the US with '(It's Not War) Just The End Of Love'.

All decent work for a 25-year-old band onto its tenth album. Yet even amid this heightened profile, amber signs were flashing. 'Nothingness' failed to make the Top 40. Subsequently released as a single, the album's title track landed outside the Top 50. It would prove an irreversible trend. The confluence of new technology and shifting customer habits meant the era of aggressively marketed multi-format physical product was over. Even as they toured *Postcards*, the Manics could sense the tide was against them.

'We looked at each other and thought, our time to be that band has actually gone for a bit,' says Wire. 'Things got really fractured under the full weight of parenthood for the three of us. Sean had three, I'd had two. James was on his firs-. It was just getting pretty impossible to pretend that we could make the full insane commitment to everything that goes with being in a band.'

The year 2011 was one of consolidation and decks-clearing. Faber published a lavish hardback book of Nicky Wire's Polaroid photographs. At the end of October, Sony released *National Treasures*, a compilation of every Manics single from 'Motown Junk' onwards, and on 17 December the band performed all of its thirty-eight songs in concert at London's O2 Arena.

Beyond this, nothing was certain. In an *Observer* interview to promote the book, album and gig, Nicky Wire suggested the O2 show would be their last 'for a few years . . . If we're going to have one last go as a band, we need to reinvent ourselves. We won't be releasing a record for two or three years but we'll be trying hard to make one. Can we do something good enough so we keep going? We've got to do something gigantic.'[1]

Wire had already talked of making 'a grand folly',[2] titled '70 Songs Of Hatred And Failure' after The Magnetic Fields' *69 Love Songs*. That eventually mutated into the more modest but no less dramatic concept of two albums, recorded more or less concurrently and released less than a year apart: *Rewind The Film* was predominantly acoustic and reflective, *Futurology* electronic and dynamically forward-facing.

'We only took one advance off Sony for the two albums, because we did see it as a project of two records,' says Wire. 'Not that they're similar, but they were from the same mind space.'

When BBC 6 Music premiered *Rewind The Film*'s title track on 8 July 2013, the advance talk of reinvention felt borne out. A six-minute cosmic pastorale, its rheumy melodic path traced by twelve-string acoustic guitar and strings, the song was halfway done before the arrival of the chorus and James Dean Bradfield's voice, the first familiar indicator that this was a Manic Street Preachers song at all. The preceding five verses had been sung by Richard Hawley, Sheffield's master bard of velveteen baritone remorse.

'I think Nick and Sean were getting a little tired of the sound of my voice,' says Bradfield. 'Which is understandable, I really don't take any offence. I gotta push my voice to get the right result out of it. And that gives you a certain restrictive emotional zone, I suppose. This was quite an openly bare emotional lyric from Nick, so having Richard's vocal, we knew it was always going to work. It felt great to play. Ambitious, but somehow homely as well. It was a nice experience.'

The ambition derived partly from the song's unusual composition. Wire had become 'quietly obsessed' with David Axelrod's 1969 album *Songs Of Experience*, the producer-arranger's second set of funky orchestral interpretations of William Blake poems, featuring the elite Los Angeles session players known as the Wrecking Crew. 'My wife really liked this album, we played it in the car a lot, driving around with the kids in the back,' says Wire. 'I started singing along to this particular piece of music, just going, "rewind the film . . .".'

With that touchstone phrase in his head, at the band's studio Wire had engineer Loz Williams sample and loop a section of Axelrod's track 'A Little Girl Lost', then began riffing more lines. 'I didn't write the lyrics down until I had sung them all in some shape or form,' he says. 'We did a pretty good demo of me singing to Axelrod's music. Which I thought we could get away with – but we couldn't.'

Instead, the Manics recreated the Axelrod sample – an 'interpolation', in music publishing jargon – going to great lengths to evoke the original's weathered sonic patina, with Moore sourcing a set of vintage drumheads, Bradfield playing bass (Wire: 'There's no way I could play that pure jazz feel'), and Richard Hawley adding flashes of Hawaiian guitar. For the choruses, Bradfield wrote a folk madrigal figure, contrasting the verses' melancholy escape into 'my childhood dreams' from 'the nothing of the now' with an upward surge of hope – albeit, hope tempered by the sad realisation that experience will always overwhelm innocence eventually.

'I think that song is really a consequence of the fragility of being a parent,' says Wire, 'and relating that to your own parents, seeing them suddenly age. "Rewind The Film" is almost too genuine for me to feel comfortable about, it's a different version of the band, lyrically and musically – the internal strength was verging on a sense of collapse, that we can't be those people any more. I never thought I'd reach that point. But it is a magical piece of work.'

124.
Show Me The Wonder

Recorded: Faster Studios, Cardiff
Producers: Manic Street Preachers and Loz Williams
Released: 9 September 2013 (single, Columbia);
   16 September 2013 (*Rewind The Film*, Columbia)

'I'm home again/But I've been here before, old friends.'
                    – Edwyn Collins, 'Home Again'

The last Manics single to be released as a physical product – albeit a 7-inch vinyl limited edition – 'Show Me The Wonder' is curiously unrepresentative of the album that followed a week later. As Wire notes, 'Sometimes we still think we can dig something commercial out of a non-commercial record.' But don't mistake its easy charm for lack of gravitas, or indeed craft: the horn arrangement by Gavin Fitzjohn is a self-replenishing feast of detail. On seeing the title, Bradfield's writing compass pointed him at Las Vegas-era Elvis Presley ('"The Wonder Of You" was probably my mum's favourite song'), a cue from which he conjured up a rhinestone jukebox beauty, thanks to his trusty Gibson J-45 acoustic and a suggestion from Sean. 'He told me to sing it in D because he could hear me struggling in E when I played it to him first time. So the whole thing is tuned down to make it richer, and to suit my voice more. There's a crystalline reason and honesty in this song I loved. There's something warm about it.'

After the often fractious studio atmosphere of *Postcards*, when Bradfield struggled to assimilate work and domestic routines, the band's musical hub now felt much more harmonious. 'I was relaxed,' says James, 'having fun dragging my old acoustic guitars out of the cupboard. Sean said something like, "It's almost like doing an ambitious B-side record." The typical bluntness of Sean! I tried to set the benchmark a bit higher than that.'

The bar was already set with Wire's lyric, an adroit piece of individual and collective self-awareness that acknowledged the complex layers of a relationship with one's homeland: 'The tapping pain of madness running through the veins/We may write in English, but our truth remains in Wales'. Amid its nostalgic brass-flecked upswing – beautifully amplified in Kieran Evans's video depiction of the band playing a seventies colliery social club – the song provided an alternative perspective to the album's mostly spartan melancholia.

'There's an attempt at some kind of transcendence there,' considers Wire. 'The cover of the single is a view from my back garden. You look out and realise that it's virtually unchanged for four hundred years. I love that other line: "I've seen the birthplace of the universe . . . /I have seen miracles move in reverse". It's not religious per se, but there's something going on. Then again, we're making a cold but quite optimistic European record at the same time. So we are inhabiting different spheres.'

125.

This Sullen Welsh Heart

Recorded: Faster Studios, Cardiff
Producers: Manic Street Preachers and Loz Williams
Released: 16 September 2013 (*Rewind The Film*, Columbia)

'We hate it when our friends become successful
And if they're northern that makes it even worse.'
— Morrissey, 'We Hate It When Our Friends
Become Successful'

There's an arguable case for *Rewind The Film* having the bleakest opening track of any Manic Street Preachers album, even *The Holy Bible*: 'Yes' is a bona fide toe-tapper next to 'This Sullen Welsh Heart', a song devoid of instrumentation beyond acoustic guitar and organ. Not that it requires sound and fury to make its point. As first lines go, 'I don't want my children to grow up like me' is as quietly shattering as they come.

Although plain of speech and attire, there's more to 'This Sullen Welsh Heart' than first impressions suggest. The title was a punning act of theft from Dylan Thomas's poem 'In My Craft or Sullen Art'. If the Manics were finally to invoke Wales in a song title then why not steal from their country's greatest bard, and then create a negationist national anthem? The lyric contained another knowing act of appropriation: 'It's not enough to succeed, others must fail,' a phrase most commonly attributed to Gore Vidal in the mid-seventies though the American literary titan probably took it from elsewhere, perhaps Iris Murdoch's 1973 novel *The Black Prince*, with earlier variations by Somerset Maugham in 1959 ('Now that I've grown old, I realise that for most of us it is not enough to have achieved personal success.

One's best friend must also have failed.')[1] and even a splendidly named seventeenth-century French writer of maxims, François de La Rouchefoucauld. Like all the best word weaponisers, Nicky Wire wears his magpie stripes with pride. Moreover, this lyric's deepest cuts were entirely his and directed inwards ('You can't keep on struggling when you're alone'), both at the band now into its fourth decade ('Time to surrender, time to move on') or a misanthropic middle-aged man ('My unhappy mantra, I wish I could escape').

'At this point there is a lot of self-realisation,' says Wire. 'In the early years, when we were arrogant/confident/delusional, we never cared about what we were saying. When you're older and you have kids, it creeps up on you, because it's there for ever. You think you're quite a reasoned and vaguely decent human being, but you can be decapitated by the things you've said. And that unadulterated pettiness still inhabits the very core of my being. So the title of this song was the crucial thing. It's embarrassing to say but I finished the lyric in a hotel in South Korea then gave it to James. Biting, with a little bit of self-deprecation – I thought it would be a brilliant song.'

Bradfield gave the harsh confessional lyric a soft treatment, muting his natural voice and burnishing the country-folk mood by adding a female duettist. Lucy Rose popped into Faster on 19 May 2013, before playing Cardiff's Glee Club, and received a blue Fender Jazzmaster as a thank you for bringing her quintessentially English voice to the song. 'Three takes and she was there, Lucy made it so painless,' says James. 'I liked how she's saying, "Calm down on the emotional incontinence, dear boy! Wash the melancholia off your Welsh soul!" I wasn't expecting this lyric. It's a lovely place to be in, to still be surprised by someone you've been working with all your life.'

To wit, 'This Sullen Welsh Heart' evinces hope simply by its existence. Amid the litany of harsh home truths, its key line – 'The act of creation saves us from despair' – affirms the simple virtue of keeping on keeping on. 'I remember writing that and thinking, "I'm not saying it does save us from despair,"' says Wire. 'That's just me trying to convince myself – if I jack that in, then we are in a pretty bad state.'

126.
Builder Of Routines

Recorded: Hansa Tonstudio, Berlin
Producer: Alex Silva
Released: 16 September 2013 (*Rewind The Film*, Columbia)

'Get out the crane, construction time again.'

– Depeche Mode, 'Pipeline'

Exemplifying the intertwined genesis of *Rewind The Film* and *Futurology*, it was by no means certain where 'Builder Of Routines' would end up. Indeed, Nicky Wire has to consult the track listings to be sure. 'There might have been a point where it could have fitted on either album,' he says. 'It could have been twisted a bit.'

Built around whirling celeste arpeggios and a boom-thwack rhythm reminiscent of both America's 'Horse With No Name' and Depeche Mode's 'Personal Jesus', the song's eerie suggestion of a band locked inside a musical box is apt given how it was made. Having arranged a much-anticipated two-week recording session at the fabled Hansa Studios in Berlin, staying at the Hyatt on nearby Potsdamer Platz where the 'Empty Souls' video was shot, Nicky Wire had to stay at home when his family were stricken with norovirus. 'To this day, Rachel can't believe I didn't get it,' he says. 'She was in hospital for two days. It was pretty bleak. When they finally got better I could have gone for the second week but we had a massive snowstorm and the airport was closed. So I never went to Hansa, which I was so looking forward to. I love that hotel!'

While on Domestos duty, Nicky got a text from James, saying they had some spare time and did he have any extra lyrics? Wire said he didn't have many, but texted back 'Builder Of Routines'.

Flinching at yet more blunt self-analysis – 'How I hate middle age/In between acceptance and rage' – Bradfield duly went to work with Moore, Loz Williams and producer Alex Silva, now Berlin-resident with his own room in the Hansa studio complex thanks to a long and successful association with German singer Herbert Grönemeyer. Moore spirited up a French horn visitation of The Beach Boys' 'God Only Knows'. Bradfield, meanwhile, perhaps influenced by the building's location at the intersect of European history as well as its storied past as a recording venue for films, David Bowie and U2, found his mind flashing back to Jan Švankmajer's surreal 1988 stop-animation film version of *Alice in Wonderland* as a visual cue. 'I don't know why,' he admits. 'I just had that feeling of spookiness. It was snowing in Berlin and it was perfect. You get a concentration of a kind of forensic intensity when you're there. If you convince yourself you feel something, then you feel something, I suppose.'

Quarantined at home, Nicky Wire settled into a new routine, and saw it evoked in this compact, self-contained vignette. He may not have had many words, but every one was made to count.

127.

4 Lonely Roads

Recorded: Faster Studios, Cardiff
Producers: Manic Street Preachers and Loz Williams
Released: 16 September 2013 (*Rewind The Film*, Columbia)

'It's not that I love myself/I just don't want company.'
— Joan Armatrading, 'Me Myself I'

Nicky Wire's latest solo composition was of a markedly different character to his previous efforts, setting morbid visions on a jazz-curious quest for truth in the naive style of Young Marble Giants or early Everything But The Girl. The demo presents a winning clash of skills, agile bass taunting Wire's heroically basic drums. 'I was obsessed with "The Two Of Us" by The Beatles, lolloping forward in a gentle and sweet way,' he says. 'Some songs unfold into themselves. There's not a huge chorus or a huge bridge or verses, just everything seems to take you somewhere.'

The lyric's feverish poeticism partly derived from A.E. Housman's 'Hell Gate', a fable set on a similar path to Wire's 'darker hell stood up on high' and which likewise concludes with a kind of redemption. Although the title source of '4 Lonely Roads' is lost in the mists of the author's mind, he is convinced it's a metaphorical conduit for people seeking to kill themselves. Yet at its final verse, the roads appear to turn back from the brink: 'And if we can/Then we must/Hold our heads up/Learn to trust'. Having possibly scared even himself with its dread implications — 'I'm trapped inside this skin/Can't let love back in' — Wire invited Welsh singer-songwriter-producer Cate Le Bon to contribute vocals. It soon became obvious her surgical enunciation was so powerful that thoughts of another singer sharing the space were abandoned. Only Loz Williams's fluid keyboards come close to stealing Le Bon's thunder.

'I don't know if she meant to, but at the start you can hear her walking to the mike,' says Wire. 'She did four takes and we just thought, "She needs to sing the whole thing". There's such purity to the vocal. There's a lot of internal conversations going on on this album, isn't there? "Can't let love back in" – I'm glad Cate sang that, and not me.'

Aside from some guitar and a bass part that defines 'tasteful baroque', Bradfield was happy to stand back and enjoy. 'You see Nick flowering into another version of himself, slowly but surely, over these last two records. I barely had anything to do with this. And Cate, the texture of her voice is just unbelievable. Makes everything go to a different place. I think this song's perfect.'

128.
Running Out Of Fantasy

Recorded: Hansa Tonstudio, Berlin
Producer: Alex Silva
Released: 16 September 2013 (*Rewind The Film*, Columbia)

'This old house is falling down around my ears.'
    – Richard and Linda Thompson, 'Dimming Of The Day'

One of the first lyrics Nicky Wire wrote after *Postcards'* last hurrah, 'Running Out Of Fantasy' defined the Manic Street Preachers' version of austerity, the dawning of their new dark age.

'*Postcards* was the last throw of the dice for that version of the band,' he says. 'I remember an *NME* review of that period, where I'm talking to the journalist John Doran and I mention "Running Out Of Fantasy" as a possible album title, saying to him: "We've reached that point." So it was funny that I was thinking this so early. How old were we then, forty-two? Pretty old. The Stones were washed up by then!'

Handed Wire's most fluent confessional lyric, Bradfield settled upon a still, unadorned treatment – the finished recording features just him on an old Gibson acoustic, Loz Williams's keys, and a string arrangement by Hansa's young assistant engineer, Tim Tautorat. 'Nick kept saying, whether it was in the back of a tour bus or in the studio, or if he was having a bad day, he kept saying he was "running out of fantasy". Which was basically code for running out of inspiration and running out of places to go – you know, running out of self-soliloquy'd mission statements. Didn't know what to say or do or think. So I think this was quite an important mantra in his head for a while.'

If you're after a pop song that features the word 'tyranny', look no further. 'I'd always wanted to get that in!' laughs Wire. 'These lyrics are quite exposing, but there wasn't many rewrites. Some of *Futurology* was much harder, more of an academic exercise, whereas this floods out.' No less impressive than Wire's eloquent candour was how tenderly Bradfield accommodated some awkward lines ('Drawn deep into some distant episodes/I don't know whether to laugh or cry') into such an understated scheme. 'I didn't really know what to do with the lyric except for this,' he admits. 'I tried to write something else, but perhaps it wasn't for me to find it.'

The song's coda repeats one line four times: 'The obsession with change has bled me dry'. 'Running Out Of Fantasy' is desolate, yet also signals relief in its acceptance of something that's passed. 'Realising that is really important,' says Wire. 'Because otherwise you can really degrade yourself.' Beyond which, a future beckoned.

129.
30-Year War

Recorded: Faster Studios, Cardiff
Producers: Manic Street Preachers and Loz Williams
Released: 16 September 2013 (*Rewind The Film*, Columbia)

'I could see the faces of those who led
Pissing theirselves laughing.'
— The Jam, 'Funeral Pyre'

But before the future, the past.

One of the most memorable Manic Street Preachers television appearances occurred on 17 September 2013, when James and Nicky were sat on BBC *Breakfast*'s sofa for a playfully combative interview with Susanna Reid and Bill Turnbull. The exchange took on a more militant aspect when the presenters observed that despite *Rewind The Film*'s reflective overall tone, there was one song that indicated the band 'still felt the passion, politically – particularly towards the establishment'.

Possibly attuned to the passing of a 9 a.m. watershed, Wire parked his week-of-release smile and calmly got stuck in: 'Sometimes it just feels like there's been an establishment coup,' he began, voice suddenly modulating closer to that of Nicky Wire, the erstwhile generation terrorist. 'You survey the last thirty years of British politics and the cover-ups, the espionage and where we are now, when I look at the front bench when I'm watching [Prime Minister's] Question Time and I can't relate to a single person on there . . . We're living in a country based on privilege.' He then blamed the New Labour 'shambles' for letting the Tories back into power, and declared Ed Miliband 'the most pitiful opposition leader I can remember in my lifetime, and I've seen some good ones and bad ones.' To Bradfield's evident relief, Bill Turnbull deftly changed the mood – 'Other political opinions are obviously available' – before steering the discussion onto the safer topic of double albums.

'Bill was lovely, he was cool,' says Bradfield. 'When we got sat on the couch he went straight in with, "So this song takes aim at Eton and the BBC – I feel it's a song against me!" I said something like, "Keep it light, stay on message, mate . . ."'

The song in question was '30-Year War', occupying a buffer zone between the contemporaneous twin records, sharing musical kinship with both *Rewind The Film* (horns; acoustic guitar) and *Futurology* (synthesisers; electronic percussion), plus a political perspective closer to the Manics of a previous era: quoting Lenin ('What is to be done'), calling out 'the lies of Hillsborough, the blood of Orgreave, all the evasion at the BBC', alleging that L.S. Lowry's paintings were removed from public display after he turned down a knighthood in 1968, and a chorus weighing in against 'the endless parade of old Etonian scum'. On and on it goes, a five-minute outpouring of class invective from a suddenly roused sleeper cell at the end of a record that otherwise turns its fire inwards.

'It's a bit of a return to form,' says Bradfield. 'I loved it when Nick gave it to me. Like, oof, the BBC, do you really want to go there?! Those are some of the only radio stations I listen to! I ended up making that distinction between something that happened, the remembrance of our wars, and just setting it plain out there. The ramifications are still being felt from that war. It fucking destroyed us. It's amazing the amount of times that song *hasn't* been written.'

The song's impact actually derives less from the lyrics per se as their assimilation with the electro-percussive backdrop. Bradfield originally wrote an acoustic arrangement that all quickly grew bored with. The final version's modernist sensibility begins with Sean Moore's introductory trumpet reveille – a hauntological parade of NUM banners in the valley – being subsumed into waves of synth noir, then drives along via Peter Hook-style bass until erupting into a fist-pumping mechanoid moonstomp. The only prominent acoustic element is Bradfield's brief solo take on 'The Red Flag'. Evoking the band's origins amid the miners' strike and zooming to a future yet to be revealed, here was a full thirty-year sweep of the Manics' life and times.

'Once we released ourselves from the shackles of thinking it has to be completely acoustic and tie in with the rest of the album, I think that helped make it a better song,' says Wire. 'There's a lot of *us* in there – a good Bradfield heart attack lyric!'

130.
Walk Me To The Bridge

Recorded: Faster Studios, Cardiff
Producer: Loz Williams
Released: 28 April 2014 (download, Columbia); 7 July
  2014 (*Futurology*, Columbia)

> 'One must be strong/For without, the weather
> will change.'
>
> – Orange Juice, 'Felicity'

Although deep-rooted in ancient Welsh soil, *Rewind The Film* wasn't the whole truth. Hence *Futurology*, the second part of the Manics' latest exercise in rock cognitive dissonance. Predominantly cold and forward-looking where its decoupled twin was earthy and contemplative, it came together amid the propulsive blur of a European tour in 2012 in support of *National Treasures*. The implicit challenge of that era-ending retrospective – what now? – found its answer on the five-mile-long Øresund Bridge crossing between Sweden and Denmark.

'It was a moment of the world opening up,' says Nicky Wire. 'We'd been doing a festival, it hadn't been a great gig or anything, but that bridge was phenomenal, like seeing the Pyramids or something. And I suddenly thought the capability within this thing can apply to us as a band.'

Wire took his Øresund epiphany as a catalytic affirmation of the band he had seriously begun to doubt. 'On the greatest hits tour I got deeper into the artistic sense of travelling through Europe, where there's an amazing collision of intellectual aesthetics, and wondering if we could get that into a record. I knew about the Futurists, not so much about futurologists, but "futurology" felt like a great word to sum up that optimism. "Walk Me To The Bridge" was a song about possibilities and the world opening up to new adventures. Through art movements and motion we found a way to survive and move on.'

Because of what happened to Richey Edwards, any Manic Street Preachers reference to a bridge is going to trigger certain assumptions. When 'Walk Me To The Bridge' was released as the first taste of *Futurology*, however, its lyric mobilised an especially vehement strain of commentary, apparently unable to reconcile how a song which so clearly honours Richey could also be 'about' something else – let alone an actual bridge. That the band in turn struggled with this reaction was no doubt partly due to Richey's subliminal presence in everything they do anyway.

'There's obviously references to Richey in this song,' says Wire. 'About his intellect, and the "indie disco" line, which was basically Richey and James when we were recording *The Holy Bible*, they'd go to the indie disco at the Central Hotel in Cardiff for a night out. Yes, "curled like an animal lying on the floor" invokes "Die In The Summertime". But they're all metaphors for the band, which obviously he's a big part of, a crucial element of. It was us seeing him and ourselves as the band, nothing outside it. Whereas the previous album is clogged up with all the limitations of 'normal life", this was infused with the sense of the moments you get when it feels right to be in a band again. And that's what the song is about.'

It's telling that Bradfield professes not to have asked Wire specifically about the lyric, though he probably doesn't need to. 'I just took it as one big holistic picture about how this place can transport us to another or to a memory – or makes us feel we're in between two places and that's where we feel happy, because we don't want to be anywhere. Felt like an escapist song to me, while being rooted in a lot of our history as well.'

Likewise for their musical cues, Bradfield and Moore looked to the band's history, not for the first time taking inspiration from

Simple Minds' pomp-art glory days, all percussive musculature and sleek-lined bombast, decorated by glimmering synths and an Ebow guitar solo that suggested both Bowie's 'Heroes' and The Stone Roses' 'She Bangs The Drums'. 'Sean got his old drum machine out, which was nice, and I was definitely trying to channel mid-era Charlie Burchill,' says Bradfield. 'The production should have been shinier, which is probably my fault, I pushed for the low-mid vibe. I think it's a step away from becoming a live classic.'

A little over six months separated the release of *Rewind The Film* and this first blast of *Futurology*. Having travelled to an inner crossroads and staring at the versions of themselves they met there, instead of retreating further the Manics decided to look outwards. With a nod to the fatal friend dancing through its heart, 'Walk Me To The Bridge' jangled the keys for a new phase: 'The roads never end, the motion starts . . .' Momentum was theirs once more.

131.

Europa Geht Durch Mich

Recorded: Faster Studios, Cardiff; Hansa Tonstudio, Berlin
Producers: Loz Williams and Alex Silva
Released: 12 May 2014 (download, Columbia); 7 July
　2014 (*Futurology*, Columbia)

'Tragedies, luxuries, statues, parks, galleries.'

　　　　　　　　　　　　　　　　– Simple Minds, 'I Travel'

On 27 May 2014, UK Prime Minister David Cameron arrived in
Brussels for an informal summit with fellow European heads of
government, just days after EU parliamentary elections had seen
a surge in support for Eurosceptic parties on both the far right
and left of the political spectrum. Cameron, now pledged to a
referendum on the UK's membership once a new EU settlement
had been agreed, was no doubt conscious of the simultaneous
presence in the city of UK Independence Party leader Nigel Farage
when he addressed journalists before sitting down for dinner:
'Europe cannot shrug off these results,' he said. 'Brussels has
got too big, too bossy, too interfering. We need people . . . that
can build a Europe that is about openness, competitiveness and
flexibility, not about the past.'[1]

　　Cameron had been a professed schoolboy fan of punk during
his time at Eton. Were the PM less busy that evening he might
have fancied taking himself along to the famous Ancienne
Belgique concert hall, where the Manic Street Preachers' setlist
featured their new single, 'Europa Geht Durch Mich' – a song
projecting a much grander and more romantic European vision
than his.

　　'David Cameron was in our hotel!' chuckles Nicky Wire. 'John

Harris was doing an interview with us for *The Guardian* and we were in the lobby – I remember John was all excited. Everything was colliding. And this song is a real song of collision. A love letter to a very complicated idea of a continent which has been the bloodiest battleground the world has ever known and yet also produced so much amazing art, great thinking, great people.'

As with so many of the best Manics songs, 'Europa Geht Durch Mich' began with a title. For a long time, Wire had been carrying around a scrap of paper in his work folder with the words 'Europe moves through us', without it ever leading to anything. But one day he looked at the phrase and did a literal translation into German. 'I was trying to learn German at this point,' he says. 'Which didn't stick. But that's how the title came about and then it came together. It's very direct. Really, this song was me trying to evoke prime-time Jim Kerr.'

The sixteen-year-old pre-Simple Minds Jim Kerr's life goals were 'making music and wanting to travel'. A year after leaving Holyrood Secondary school in Glasgow's southside, together with best friend Charlie Burchill he hitch-hiked to London where they planned to see hot new band the Sex Pistols. Instead, the pair got the offer of a lift to France, then just kept going, from Paris to Munich, Milan . . . 'Back then you could get a passport in the Post Office,' said Kerr. 'Every border we crossed just gave us a sense of some sort of emancipation. Within that trip, Charlie and I made this pact that we weren't going to settle for what was on the table in front of us. We had this thing about the road. Between that and the music, some magic could come from it.'

Wire's lyric began with a direct homage to his inspiration: 'Europe had a language problem' differs by just one letter from a line in 'I Travel', Simple Minds' breathless Moroder-beat ode to the joy of trans-Europe expression. The rest of the verse aligned the Manics with a similar faith in the creative synergy of forward movement: 'German roads, they gave me vision . . . This motion makes a modern love song.'

'On the National Treasures tour through the heart of Europe we fell in love again with the idea of motion and European cities and art,' says Wire. 'I remember going to a lot of galleries.'

For tour-bus reading matter, Wire devoured John Gray's *The Immortalization Commission*, a wild *Lipstick Traces*-esque gambol through the parallel manias that simultaneously gripped an English Edwardian elite and Russian Bolshevik 'God builders' in seeking a scientific, as opposed to religious, basis for eternal life; in the case of the Soviets, using the corpse of Lenin as a case study. Such fantastical thinking enhanced the lyric's darker aspect – 'God builders, divine losers/Let's salute eternalism' – providing 'European screams' to counter 'European dreams'.

For Bradfield, a set of words that began with a direct quote from one of his favourite bands really was the stuff of dreams. He and Loz Williams spent two days at Faster making a demo, to which Moore added some drum loops, emerging with a behemoth man-machine beat repeatedly punctuated by a bovine distress horn, effectively crossbreeding PiL's 'This Is Not A Love Song' with another Simple Minds song, '70 Cities As Love Brings The Fall'. Meanwhile, over in Berlin, Alex Silva reckoned it sounded like a car stuck in second gear driving up the motorway.

'Right away I thought that was a great description,' says Bradfield. 'It was one of those strychnined straight-line songs which I like – it had a discipline to it. And then, we have the idea . . .'

Silva's partner happened to be Germany's greatest contemporary actress, Nina Hoss. She agreed to sing 'Europa Geht Durch Mich', in German. Whereupon a car stuck in second gear driving up the motorway found its rightful status: regal, relentless, an autobahn ass-kicker.

'It was unbelievable,' says Bradfield. 'The lyric was perfect for her and her doing it was just perfect. It was grinding. It was portents of doom. It was powerful. It was a vision of the future. It was so many things. And we got that vocal in Hansa too. You gotta believe in happenstance or fate sometimes, her being part of this couple with Silva and she's one of European cinema's biggest stars. For her to say she would do it, and then to do it live with us a couple of times, was amazing.'

A measure of just how much Nina Hoss brought is that the verse she sings in German contains the song's most emotive lyrics: 'Ghosts appear like ruined sleep/Destroyed by time I left behind/ Keep on moving to escape/Keep on running away from life.' Amid these words, 'Europa Geht Durch Mich' clearly impacts beyond whatever political currency it may contain, but has a personal dimension too – one that suggests new beginnings are always possible, so long as we remember the lessons of history.

132.
Futurology

Recorded: Faster Studios, Cardiff; Hansa Tonstudio, Berlin
Producers: Loz Williams and Alex Silva
Released: 7 July 2014 (*Futurology*, Columbia);
  22 September 2014 (download, Columbia)

'Strib nicht im Warteraum der Zukunft.'
['Don't die in the waiting room of the future.']

– DDR punk graffiti

By his own admission, Nicky Wire may not have known much about the vague interdisciplinary means of forecasting events known as futurology, but he was au fait with the early twentieth-century art movement the Futurists, and the latter at least seemed to be onto him. On 2 June 2014 the Manics played the Rock In Idro festival in Bologna. When Wire got to his room in Bologna's Grand Hotel Majestic he looked out of the window to see the Prendiparte Tower, as featured on the Martin Kippenberger painting used on the cover of 1994's 'She Is Suffering' single. Amazed, he rang room service and had his food order taken by a cheery chef from Brecon. Head now whirling with the uncanny sequence of connections, Wire glanced at the bedside table and saw a book about Futurism. 'Neither James nor Sean had been given one of these, only me,' he says. 'The hotel we were in was where the Futurists formed and had their first ever meeting. There was this sense of serendipity going on. Very intriguing. And yet despite all that, I was just annoyed that we were supporting the Pixies at this festival . . .'

None of which has much to do with the song 'Futurology'. Composed wholly by Wire at Faster, its luxuriant motorik urgency punctuated by Moore's tympani dramatics certainly had the aspirational qualities required of an album-opening title track. Indeed, this was a classic Manics address to the church, in the tradition of 'You Love Us' or 'The Masses Against The Classes': its declamatory first line 'Defenders of the faith' and the chorus's Wire-sung 'We'll come back one day, we never really went away' addressing the diehard fans who perhaps had found their own faith tested by what Nicky terms the 'bucolic strangeness' of *Rewind The Film*.

That said, 'Futurology' has some strange undercurrents of its own: notably Super Furry Animal Cian Ciaran's off-kilter keyboards, a lyric inspired by a childhood memory of Wire and his brother killing ants and woodlice with a screwdriver – during which Patrick Jones punctured his younger sibling's fingernail – and a mid-section breakdown where Bradfield conjured some top-grade post-punk *son et lumière* to distract from the sudden absence of melody.

'That lyric about the ants confused me,' says Bradfield, reasonably. 'So I just went with it. Which is the best way sometimes. I had fun, played my Fret King Ventura all over this, one of my favourite guitars, it's sharp and to the point. I really love the song – I just didn't know what it meant.'

133.

The Next Jet To Leave Moscow

Recorded: Hansa Tonstudio, Berlin
Producer: Alex Silva
Released: 7 July 2014 (*Futurology*, Columbia)

'The untenable must be maintained.'
— The Fatima Mansions, 'Blues For Ceausescu'

Words and music by James Dean Bradfield, beautifully balancing detail and concision, 'The Next Jet To Leave Moscow' is a composite of three separate episodes, each of which challenged the Manics to justify their rhetoric in the face of reality. Its first verse splices the occasion of the band's gig at the B1 Maximum Club in Moscow on 23 July 2008 with a prior interview where a British journalist chided Bradfield for having played in Cuba, calling him a 'Rediffusion socialist' – as in the venerable UK television rental company which also supplied cable technology to the Soviet bloc in the 1980s. Thus, Bradfield is the first verse's 'ageing commie walking in Red Square, with Rediffusion eyes . . .'

'I said that I wasn't a "Rediffusion socialist" because I don't think there's a model of communism that works, so I kind of agreed with him,' says James. 'But then I said, "Going to Cuba was an experiment, but there are certain states in America that if I went to you wouldn't reproach me because they don't allow abortion, would you?" He had no answer to that. So it's a song about being slightly misunderstood, about other people's hypocrisy when they want you to be something you're not but still use it as an insult to batter you with.'

Meanwhile on 20 August 2010, Nicky Wire was being interviewed backstage at the Trutnov Festival in the Czech Republic when a hippy veteran of the communist era's dissident underground music scene interrupted and began haranguing him about Cuba. 'All this stuff, "you didn't have to live here", and I was about to try and explain, but he was going on and on and we were due onstage in an hour, and then he called me an "English so and so". So my one riposte was: "We're not fucking English, mate." It's a brilliant song, with a fantastic lyric by James.'

Recorded in Hansa, this is a loving homage to the Bill Nelson-era Skids sound, from its opening sequenced synth flashes to a guitar solo that's brief but full of sublimated force. Once again Sean Moore became at one with the drum machine for the eternal beat, while Alex Silva was an instinctive conduit for the music's liquid possibility – the producer even included field recordings of Cardiff's Tremorfa steelworks that he made during the eighties as a member of experimental theatre company Brith Gof. 'You can hear those noises at the start,' says Bradfield. 'Just to show the industry of where we came from. Alex knew all the references, Bill Nelson and the Skids – I love working with him. It was a fun song.'

And the jet to leave Moscow?

'We had to bribe our way out,' says Wire. 'They basically put a premium on our equipment. Under the mask of officialdom, of course, but our tour manager Angus had to pay something like twelve grand or else we weren't getting on that plane. Our hotel was next to the Kremlin and I never left my room, didn't feel very comfortable the whole time I was there. And I knew I was never going back.'

134.

Dreaming A City (Hughesovka)

Recorded: Faster Studios, Cardiff
Producer: Loz Williams
Released: 7 July 2014 (*Futurology*, Columbia)

'Nearly everyone believed that good would triumph, that honest men who hadn't hesitated to sacrifice their lives, would be able to build a good and just life.'

– Vassily Grossman, *Life And Fate*

James Dean Bradfield is fond of saying each Manics song begins when Nicky Wire gifts him a lyric. The creative spark for 'Dreaming A City' was an actual gift from Wire to Bradfield – a book telling the remarkable story of Merthyr Tydfil engineer and industrialist John Hughes, who in 1869 travelled with a hundred managers and workers from his Newport steel plant to establish a new foundry in the coal-rich Donbas region of Ukraine, then part of Imperial Russia. The city that grew around the Welsh settlement was named Hughesovka.

'Obviously, people have traded geography and skills for centuries, but I found this story particularly inspiring,' says James. 'The pull of industry and what we might call the moral propriety of people travelling long distances to try and make their fortune, and buying into that other place, and staying there. Because Newport was so bound up with that industry at that point, I loved the idea that out of dirt and slag iron a city arose. Hughes had that industrious pompous nature that sometimes serves as a good jet fuel. So I tried to convey that in an instrumental.'

For his template Bradfield looked no further than the acme of industrious instrumental pomp: Simple Minds' 'Theme For Great Cities', from 1981's *Sister Feelings Call*, a thrilling bass-powered synth-sparkled race along the cerebral cortex. Having worked up a demo on his own, Bradfield then handed it over to Sean Moore to fill in drums, Loz Williams helped out with keyboards, and the job was done. It's a challenge for an instrumental to convey its title: both 'Theme For Great Cities' and 'Dreaming A City' do so brilliantly.

'The only thing I did on this song was give James that book,' laughs Wire. 'We've played it live and it was absolutely epic. The true soul of JDB might be Slash at times, but it's equally that period of Simple Minds. I don't think any band's had a bigger influence on him.'

Today Hughesovka is called Donetsk, the fifth largest city in Ukraine. In 2014, it became the focus of an ongoing military assault by Russia that would seek to erase Donetsk's European identity – and with it the legacy of John Hughes.

135.
Black Square

Recorded: Faster Studios, Cardiff; Hansa Tonstudio, Berlin
Producers: Loz Williams and Alex Silva
Released: 7 July 2014 (*Futurology*, Columbia)

'The truth I hear is not what I always see.'
   – China Crisis, 'Some People I Know To Lead Fantastic Lives'

'Black Square' opens with the ghostly echo of Nina Hoss, her now reduced voice intoning: 'Europäische Träume, Europäische Schreien/Europäischer Himmel, Europäische Lust . . .'

This wasn't so much a postscript to 'Europa Geht Durch Mich', but a return to one of its themes: the Bolshevik 'God-Builders', whose cuboid design for Lenin's mausoleum was inspired by *Black Square*, a 1915 painting by Kazimir Malevich, one of the greatest works of twentieth-century abstract art and which, according to the tenets of Malevich's own self-styled Suprematist movement, symbolised the ultimate expression of geometric form. Or, as Nicky Wire's lyric had it: 'Free yourselves from the tyranny of objects/Purged of all colour, the purest abstraction.'

'I'm sure the "tyranny of objects" line is a quote,' he says, 'but I can't remember whose. I treated this song a bit like an exam, there was lots of reading and writing. Malevich stood out, he tried to marry the idea of breaking the constraints of how art had been perceived with freeing man through communism. Which he realised pretty quickly was not compatible.'

The lyric's aphoristic whirl throws up some striking juxtapositions of sources: notably 'Art is never modern for art is eternal' (Egon Schiele), 'Paintings are never finished but merely abandoned' (attributed to everyone from Leonardo Da Vinci to Jean

Cocteau; Wire lifted it from an interview with *Know Your Enemy* sleeve artist Neale Howells), and even a Richey Edwards cameo with the last two words of the chorus's 'Endless endorsements/ Slowly passing always' taken from *Everything Must Go*'s 'Removables'.

'I guess this is all about comparing the hideousness of Damien Hirst and Jeff Koons' awful conceptual art with Malevich, who was striving for the eternal truest sense,' says Wire. 'The main fascination here is that even in a suppressed society, unbelievable talent can flourish – not for long, obviously, before Stalin. But even then, the odd one like Shostakovich could shine a light on the worst of things.'

Presented with an enigmatic lyric about an enigmatic painting, Bradfield and Moore came up with an appropriate musical setting, built around Moore's disconsolate keyboard melody summoning a metaphorical flock of seagulls flying over a black square. 'I wanted it to sound hollow,' says Bradfield. 'Sean walked over to the Mall of Berlin shopping centre and recorded it on his phone. It's not a rich song, I didn't want it to be too powerful. Sometimes, with great art, or books, I don't think there's as much theory behind them as people like to think. People write about something to try and find the truth.'

136.

Between The Clock And
The Bed

Recorded: Faster Studios, Cardiff
Producer: Loz Williams
Released: 7 July 2014 (*Futurology*, Columbia)

'Nestling in sweet sorrow is the saviour of our youth.'
– The Wild Swans, 'Revolutionary Spirit'

Named after an Edvard Munch self-portrait, 'Between The Clock
And The Bed' is a pitiless rumination on the inevitability of death.
Unlike Munch's painting, however, which depicts the artist as a
frazzled living cadaver stood next to a grandfather clock that has
no hands, the song offered a seraphic countenance quite at odds
with its grim admission: 'between the clock and the bed there's
only space and hell'.

Making the blackest thoughts sound shiny and beautiful was
a strategy straight out of the early eighties handbook of those
erstwhile post-punk groups who shifted their energies away from
deconstructing mainstream music to subverting it – using conventional pop modes to advance challenging artistic ideas. James
Dean Bradfield's adolescence coincided with that aspirational
phase of British music, when the likes of The Associates and
Scritti Politti reached for the charts, enabled by John Peel's more
consensually inclined Radio 1 colleagues such as Janice Long
and David 'Kid' Jensen. So having completed a demo treatment
for Nicky Wire's latest report from the existential trenches, he
sought professional help from Scritti Politti's Green Gartside, a

man possessed of a honeycombed voice who just happened to be a local hero.

'There was a very delicate tone to the lyric, really beautiful,' says James. 'And I could hear Green Gartside's voice, I could hear it before it was sung – it was just there. I remembered Scritti Politti's "Wood Beez" and being so confused – he had the chiffon blouse and the *Dynasty* hair and yet he's from Caerphilly! And his voice was absolutely pitch perfect. I wish we'd made more of this song.'

The contrast between Bradfield's solo demo and the finished duet, where he cedes verses to Gartside, is comparable to the aspirational primitivism of Scritti Politti's final Rough Trade releases, like 'The "Sweetest Girl"', and the subsequent high-end dazzle of the Arif Mardin-produced *Cupid & Psyche 85*. Yet in each version the song's structure is almost identical – reeling out 'the struggle of survival' slightly behind a lugubrious contrapuntal bass melody and downstroked guitars – aside from the crucial addition of a coda, hung around Green's celestial stacked vocal mantra: 'Hatred and failure go perfectly together/Like the quick and the sand, beautiful and damned.'

Wire disputes the suggestion that his lyric matches the Munch painting for bleakness, but concedes it's still a troubling self-portrayal. 'I saw that painting in the museum in Oslo. Sometimes you just get little obsessions and this painting is very disturbing, because it's very much based in the symbolism of death, the next phase. What's the line in the chorus, "waiting for the transportation"? OK, perhaps it is bleak.'

For all its doomy portent, however, the lyric also permits self-deprecation – even a joke at the author's expense – in its admission that this 'man of little consequence' is 'still building the bypass in my head'. Bypasses? Nicky Wire? With his reputation?!

'Yes,' laughs Wire. 'Again, the sweetness of Green, his unbelievably precise phraseology, and the tune just takes you away from the hatred. Sometimes a duet works out so well.'

An important song that ought to have been a single, 'Between The Clock And The Bed' is eminently worthy of its eighties fore-bears, gilded of melody and fearless to its cobwebbed heart.

137.

Misguided Missile

Recorded: Faster Studios, Cardiff; Hansa Tonstudio, Berlin
Producers: Loz Williams and Alex Silva
Released: 7 July 2014 (*Futurology*, Columbia)

'In my fucked up gestalt I'm a slug in salt, losing its skin.'
                          – Mudhoney, 'Inside Out Over You'

Any song with the opening lyric 'I am a self-obsessed fool' has to deliver music with presence to match. And while the Cardiff demo, built around a riff played by Bradfield on Wire's string-dampened Ovation bass, certainly had a spooky something, 'Misguided Missile' properly took off once it arrived at Hansa.

'Because Nick wasn't there with us in Berlin, I felt as if me and Sean had to take him some good stuff back,' says Bradfield. 'The Ovation bass put it very much in the Krautrock corner, I thought it sounded a bit like "For The Love Of Money" by The O'Jays. And I love the idea of a misguided missile yet with Sean's really disciplined drumming underneath. The lyric felt like a brilliant fiction, a lovely thumbnail character sketch – I couldn't figure out if it was Nick's perspective or someone else's. When Silva took on the reins of the production in Berlin he really got into the soul of the song. He even got a choir to sing on it.'

Along with the icy string synth, the Berliner Kneipenchor was one of several textural flourishes elevating the final version. That said, upon hearing them sing 'I am the Sturm and Drang, I am the schadenfreude', Wire realised that his mispronounced German had been subtly corrected. 'That aside, I thought it was amazing what they've done to it!' he says. 'And I love the way James sings "tiny piece of *malcontent*", which was a word I'd always tried to get in. There's so much serendipity with this album – especially considering the only reason to go to Berlin was so I could have two weeks in the Hyatt . . . This song really is the sound of Hansa, it reminds me of a Berlin night. So perhaps it's good I wasn't there. I'd have just distracted them with some moaning.'

138.

The View From Stow Hill

Recorded: Faster Studios, Cardiff
Producer: Loz Williams
Released: 7 July 2014 (*Futurology*, Columbia)

'So much sadness between you and me.'
— Graham Nash, 'Military Madness'

Looping from the city's western fringes, at first gently then in a steep descent as it nears the River Usk, Stow Hill is one of the most storied thoroughfares in Newport. At its foot stands the Westgate Hotel, where on the morning of 4 November 1839 the Chartist Rising was bloodily suppressed by the British army, killing up to two dozen in the crowd of several thousand who had marched down Stow Hill in support of the People's Charter for political reform. One day, over 170 years later, instead of the usual walk from his house into the centre of Newport, Nicky Wire elected to take the longer route down Stow Hill. 'I had a mini epiphany,' he says. 'The sky broke apart, I looked up and realised the under-appreciated splendour of the buildings, and felt the history of the Chartists who walked the same street.'

The Westgate Hotel still stands, complete with bullet holes in its pillars, but has been empty for years, a decaying symbol of Newport's struggle to revive in a post-industrial era. Moved by the area's proud aspect even amid the reality of its graffiti-covered walls and litter-strewn streets, Wire wrote a stunned underdog elegy for his adopted home city. 'I was really happy with the line "Always caught between the capital and the other country", as Newport is squeezed by Cardiff and Bristol. I loved the music – it had a three-dimensional quality, and an odd structure, that reminded me of "Games Without Frontiers" by Peter Gabriel.'

Stow Hill held special significance for Bradfield too. On 23 September 1985 he saw Hüsker Dü play at Stow Hill Labour Club, the great Minneapolis power trio's second UK gig and the only time they would ever play in Wales.

'It was an amazing venue, sweaty and grimy,' Bradfield says. 'Newport was such a proud industrial city and you go there now and it seems to have had so much taken from it. To still see the remnants of that fateful order to shoot the Chartists, it's quite spooky, so I wanted to make the song full of portent. I loved the lyric, the theory of being caught between places, certain lines stopping you doing things, certain accents stopping you doing things – all those vagaries of culture that mean so much but never really get talked about. I wanted to do it justice, and Sean and Loz made a brilliant rhythm track from some spindly bits of programming. It was nice and tasteful.'

139.

International Blue

Recorded: Door To The River Studios, Newport
Producer: Dave Eringa
Released: 8 December 2017 (download, Columbia);
    13 April 2018 (*Resistance Is Futile*, Columbia)

'That's the colour of my room.'
                        – David Bowie, 'Sound And Vision'

Resistance Is Futile was an album made out of adversity. Nothing comparable to the extraordinary circumstances of *Everything Must Go*, more the quotidian stuff that comes with age and its accrued responsibilities. There were young children to raise (in James Dean Bradfield's case) and ailing elderly parents to care for (in Nicky Wire's). In October 2016 the band had to leave Faster, their studio-cum-ganghut for more than ten years, when its building and adjacent courtyard was sold by the landlord to a property developer. Relocating their operational HQ to a location on the edge of Newport was a drain on time and money, with the logistical upheaval of moving equipment, including the vintage recording console that was originally housed at Rockfield Studios, further disrupting the process of writing and recording new music. Some songs were demoed at Faster, some at the new Door To The River, and others at Watertown, a studio in Cardiff Bay run by Gavin Fitzjohn. Although everyone strove to power through, the final record showed the strain.

'It's an uneven album,' says Bradfield. 'There were certain points where perhaps we would have pushed ourselves to write more or do things differently but we just didn't have the chance. Just lots of little important decisions that didn't get made because the politburo wasn't quite working. I wilted under the pressure, I think.'

Up until 'International Blue', the penultimate song to be recorded, the album had no obvious single. James kept gently pushing his bandmate for more lyrics. One day, just as he was leaving the studio to visit his mother in hospital, Nicky handed over a sheet of paper. 'He just said, "Here you go, have this,"' says Bradfield. 'I looked at it and thought, "How many good lines can you have in one lyric?" Nearly every one was perfect. We'd always had an aesthetic about the colour blue – whether it be when we started out our little movement was called the Blue Generation, or shiny indie moments like "The Story Of The Blues" [by Wah!] – so that set me off. I was so nervous but looking forward to writing the music to it, I stayed in the studio that night with Dave Eringa.'

The lyric had been patiently awaiting its moment. In 2013, Nicky and his wife Rachel visited Nice for their twentieth wedding anniversary, and at the city's modern art museum were trans-fixed by the monochrome paintings of Yves Klein, the French avant-gardist whose obsession with the colour blue led him to trademark his own formulation: International Klein Blue.

'We hadn't been away together since we'd had children,' says Wire. 'We were in this lovely hotel looking over the bluest of blue sea and the bluest of blue sky. So it started on a piece of hotel paper. I think I used a line or two from a book on Yves Klein, the one about writing an autograph on the far side of the sky is biographical. It's a tribute song, like "Let Robeson Sing", but much better written, I think.'

Klein died of a heart attack in 1962 aged just thirty-four, by which point his short life had also embraced music, photography and even judo, at which he excelled, receiving a 4th dan black belt in Japan. An earlier lyric draft saw Wire awkwardly attempt-ing to reference that particular endeavour. 'Something like, "You lived in Tokyo and marshalled the art . . ." It was not going to work!' he laughs. 'But I really liked the finished lyric, it actually reads like you can sing it.'

As a potted history, the final lyric captured the proto-pop artist's greatest hits in a succinct succession of epigrams – he really did record the rain and paint with fire – while also packing an emotive resonance that obviated specific knowledge of Klein's life and work. The line, 'Here's my gift to you, a soundtrack to the void', for instance, referenced his 1958 exhibition 'La Vide', an empty cabinet in an empty gallery, but could also read as a commentary on the band's relationship with its audience, or even Wire's gift of this lyric to his band – who were, in that moment, very grateful for it.

The real gift came when Bradfield and Eringa emerged from their studio all-nighter. Having built a drum-machine rhythm initially inspired by a discarded sample of the Simple Minds track 'Speed Your Love To Me', the sparks really began to fly with the pealing main riff in place.

'That clarion call was the memory of something more hopeful, of something beautiful being born,' says James. 'It was the colour in my head. And it all just flowed. The verse had a tiny bit of "Dancing In The Dark" and I remember thinking, "I'm excited for the boys to hear this." Then Sean really locked in with that drum machine, like Nigel Preston did with "She Sells Sanctuary" [The Cult], where the drums and the machine are indiscernible from each other. I loved the fills Sean did in the middle of the chorus, where it lets loose. It felt full of hope and full of energy.'

It also felt like they had a single. Better still, they had a bona fide Manics soundtrack to the void, in the tradition of 'Motorcycle Emptiness', 'Faster', 'A Design For Life': the sort of trick bands do well to pull at any time, let alone after twenty-five years and under difficult circumstances.

'Out of a pretty turgid period in my life, we had a glide song,' says Wire. 'Also, it's based around a guitar riff, which not a huge amount of our songs are. Riff songs which don't descend into shite metal, they're really hard to write. The minute we played it to the record company it was getting a thousand plays on radio, it just sounded so good. It cuts through. It cuts through our history too.'

A final positive augury was the video shoot: arriving at their Nice hotel, the band discovered they had been booked into Yves Klein rooms, each with a Klein quote above the mirror, and with views of the international blue sea.

'We kind of knew then that this is gonna be good,' says Nicky. 'Because even at our most confident we weren't quite as sure about the rest of the album. Sometimes you just need one song to coalesce around.'

140.
People Give In

Recorded: Door To The River Studios, Newport
Producer: Dave Eringa
Released: 13 April 2018 (*Resistance Is Futile*, Columbia)

'Tin can at my feet, think I'll kick it down the street.'
— Randy Newman, 'I Think It's Going To Rain Today'

If 'International Blue's levitational properties made it a perfect single, then 'People Give In' better represented the album's over-all pensive mood. Its opening lines thudded down remorselessly, crunching like a cricket ball into the ribs of a batter whose best days were long gone: 'People get tired, people get old/People get forgotten, people get sold.' Anyone placing their hopes in the higher minds of science or religion were flattened by the string-soaked logic of the chorus: 'There is no theory of everything/No immaculate conception, no crime to forgive'. Then a second verse noted that 'people cave inwards', an unexpected echo of 'Faster's 'so damn easy to cave in'. Evidently, this preacher subscribed to the hard truth bible.

'I'm getting to that point where just getting my mum and dad to the hospital was something,' says Wire. 'All I wanted from life was some good news from the leukaemia ward. And obviously when you're close to someone and you know they're probably going to die, you soon realise how worthless religion is. Certainly for me, there's no comfort in any of it. But as I've said before, it's better to realise than to pretend.'

Written at home in Cardiff on his Gibson J-45 acoustic and finished off on piano, Bradfield's response to the lyric was an emollient middle path. His demo, recorded with Gavin Fitzjohn at Watertown, had grace in its verses' ambulatory momentum, while the chorus's ascending release offered comfort. 'It felt lovely, and quite humble in its own way,' he says. 'But then we recorded it here at Door To The River, and it got too big. That's perhaps the failure of all of us – myself, Sean, Dave. Perhaps Nick, if he had been in the studio more – but of course he couldn't be – perhaps he would have said, "Shall we rein in the 'Kashmir' a bit?" If you go too big with a track, it feels like you're making a proclamation. Like a Roman Emperor, you're carving a bit of stone and putting it in the town square. But if you just go a bit smaller, it's a pledge rather than a command. It's a really important line not to go over, and we've gone over it many times!'

In fact, although not disputing that the curiously hollowed-out approach of 'People Give In' went too far, Nicky Wire claims personal credit for its most outlandish detail: the reversed drum breakdown towards the end. 'It's almost Def Leppardesque,' he says, 'which was definitely me telling Dave to just make it bigger and bigger and bigger . . . Y'know, "Let's get the rock outta here!" In retrospect, we were over the top.'

141.

Distant Colours

Recorded: Faster Studios, Cardiff; Door To The River
    Studios, Newport
Producer: Dave Eringa
Released: 13 April 2018 (*Resistance Is Futile*, Columbia)

'Hell, I never vote for anybody. I always vote against.'
                                                – W.C. Fields

In what already threatened to become a theme, 'Distant Colours' saw an affecting lyric – this time Bradfield's – short-changed by an overreaching arrangement. The concept was sharp: a lament for a political tradition that no longer recognisably exists sung from the perspective of a disillusioned lover. 'Four times in a row I went into the polling booth, be it general elections, local elections, or something else, I didn't know what to vote for,' says Bradfield. 'It just feels like a mass of meagreness. That's probably because I don't actually know what I want or feel, and that's all part of living in the digital world. The left feels like it's splintered and arranged itself into many different tents, and they'd rather attack each other than something else. I didn't feel a sense of loyalty. Well, I feel a sense of loyalty to what you might call "post-classic seventies Valleys Labour socialism", but it's quaint to think like that. I actually abstained a couple of votes, which when I was young I was taught was a sin. I never thought that time would come. So "Distant Colours" was about all those things.'

The demo featured Bradfield alone – the verses sad, the choruses angrily sad – and the song's hurt convinced. There was no obvious need for the final version to simulate how U2 might have treated it, amid synthetic whirrs and stagey gestures, but that's what played out. 'I think it still has an emotional pull,' says Wire, 'and what James tried to do with the lyric, about what the left forgot, is very interesting.'

Also interesting is the song was almost overlooked in the scramble to move out of Faster, until Chris Dempsey, from the band's management, asked to listen to all the demos. 'It had fallen down the back of the settee a bit,' says James. 'Chris said, "Why aren't you doing this one?" Lots of times somebody else sees something you don't. But we let it get away from ourselves again. It's too grandiose, too aggressive.'

142.

Dylan & Caitlin

Recorded: Door To The River Studios, Newport
Producer: Dave Eringa
Released: 13 April 2018 (*Resistance Is Futile*, Columbia)

'Maybe the most that you can expect from a relationship
that goes bad is to come out of it with a few good songs.'
— Marianne Faithfull, *Faithfull: An Autobiography*

Beautifully realised in duet form by James Dean Bradfield and
The Anchoress, this Nicky Wire vignette of the co-dependent
abusive relationship between Dylan and Caitlin Thomas – the
Sid and Nancy of twentieth-century literature – reveals an intriguing contrast in perspectives. 'At the time it felt like a lot of
the atmosphere around Dylan Thomas seemed to be airbrushing
the fact that his life had gone so sour,' says Wire. 'There was an
avoidance of the brutal nature of Dylan and Caitlin's relationship,
which could even be physical at times, as much if not more from
her, just because she was stronger. So I was definitely going for
the combustible dark side.'

Bradfield's treatment, however, presents the desperate lovers'
mutually penitent exchange as a courtly dance rather than a slug-
fest, with starring roles for the Vulcan Strings and The Anchoress's
elegant embodiment of regret. After taking a verse each, 'Dylan'
and 'Caitlin' come together in the choruses, and swap lines in a
final doomed valediction: '[C] It's so hard just surviving the truth/
[D] The words don't cover the scars any more'.

All emerge from the experience with their reputations enhanced, none more so than the Thomases.

'When you read Caitlin's memoir, you just think, "You two

deserve each other!"' says Bradfield. 'So with the music I tried to find what you might call the cute melodrama, because I didn't want it to be too grimy. It's a really simple song, almost a tragi-comedy. Me and The Anchoress bounced off each other nicely, but thank God we didn't have to sing onstage and look into each other's eyes and act – it would have been a bit *Rock Follies*.'

Not *Rock Follies*, but the Manics' template for the duet dated from the same year as Bradfield's favourite seventies ITV rock drama: 'Don't Go Breaking My Heart', the Motown pastiche by Elton John and Kiki Dee that was the UK's Number 1 single for six weeks during the hot summer of '76, clearly making a big impact on two seven-year-old boys from Blackwood.

'Their performance was so charming, and me and James used to really fancy Kiki Dee in her dungarees,' says Wire. 'She had amazing hair as well.'

143.
Sequels Of Forgotten Wars

Recorded: Door To The River Studios, Newport
Producer: Dave Eringa
Released: 13 April 2018 (*Resistance Is Futile*, Columbia)

'Hiding out in treetops, shouting out rude names.'
— Peter Gabriel, 'Games Without Frontiers'

James Dean Bradfield vividly recalls the genesis of 'Sequels Of Forgotten Wars' as the moment his wife spat out her tea at what she'd just seen on television. It was August 2008, Russia had invaded Georgia, and on the Sunday evening TV news a distraught Georgian woman was being interviewed, along with her son. 'I was her son,' says Bradfield. 'It was me, *This Is My Truth* era. The only difference was his arms were slightly shorter. Then my phone went, and obviously it's Nick, watching the news. "Are you Georgian?! That's why you got followed around in that shopping centre in Moscow by security guards . . .!" It was really freaky. Then a couple days later there was a story about how the BBC had mistakenly misappropriated footage from another conflict over the top of that one. It got me thinking about that Orwellian prospect of successive wars, all the time . . . This is where we are, these are sequels to forgotten wars, where all footage is interchangeable – and I'm in it!'

Having found himself a title, in due course Bradfield wrote a lyric, which Wire augmented, forming a true hybrid vehicle for bitter celebration of defeat in the old-school MSP mode: first verse Wire ('There will be no parades for the likes of us'), Bradfield the second ('Echo echo in a chamber of purity/To a lip-synced moral maze soliloquy'), and the chorus a bit of both.

'I remember thinking that "moral maze soliloquy" line was James sounding like Richey,' says Wire. 'Bar "International Blue", this is my favourite track on the album, and I didn't have a huge amount to do with it. James played the bass. I tend to think these are backing tracks that only family members can play, because it does seem like James and Sean are trying to make it as difficult as possible for each other!'

The song's musical spark came almost nine years after the Georgian doppelgänger experience. Bradfield arrived at the studio, where his 1962 Stratocaster was still set up between two amps plus various pedals from an earlier attempt to emulate Robin Trower's psych blues guitar sound from a 1974 *Whistle Test* clip. 'I thought, "'Sequels Of Forgotten Wars'? Sounds a bit proggy. I'll go with my Robin Trower sound" . . .!' Cue an uncanny intro evocation of TV screen flicker via the synth pulse of Skids' 'Circus Games' sidling into 'Turn It On Again' by Genesis. Topping off this pipe-smokin' punky-prog soufflé was the fruitiest Nick Nasmyth organ solo this side of The Stranglers' Dave Greenfield. All told, a welcome satirical crunch amid an album where dark clouds were never too far away.

'Definitely a lighter touch,' agrees Bradfield. 'We've never played this live, and I really wish we had.'

144.

Hold Me Like A Heaven

Recorded: Door To The River Studios, Newport
Producer: Dave Eringa
Released: 13 April 2018 (*Resistance Is Futile*, Columbia)

'I never think of the future. It comes soon enough.'

– Albert Einstein

Imprinted with the sadness of Nicky Wire's family situation yet not wholly defined by it, 'Hold Me Like A Heaven' is a meticulous configuration of words and music, yet also deeply moving. This was the final song written for *Resistance Is Futile*, after the 'International Blue' video had been filmed and as winter arrived in the Valleys.

'It was cold, it was wet, it was Wales at its darkest,' says Wire. 'My mum had definitely got iller. She'd had quite a good six months, but there were more blood transfusions and her skin was so thin. And James was looking for one more lyric, which I definitely had in me.'

The title, adapted from one of Philip Larkin's less scathing poems, was the vulnerable pivot around which the chorus wrapped, while the verses dug out the darker stuff: 'I dance around the exit signs/I hate the world more than I hate myself'; 'What is the future of the future/When memory fades and gets boarded up . . .'

'So much time in hospitals, staying at my mum and dad's a lot. There'd been really bad snow and my dad couldn't dig his way out like he usually could. So me and Pat went up there, dug them out, and the dog, Meg, had fallen in the pond. Just domestic shite, and yet there were genius moments of hilarity involved in that. My mum had fallen and some of her skin had come off, and my dad glued it back and put TCP on. He's saying, "TCP is the last resort but I needed to use it this time!" So that immense deepness between people fed into the lyric really easily.'

Inspired by oblique eighties synthesists like China Crisis and Talk Talk, Bradfield and Moore pulled together a riskily time-signatured construct of cross-patterned melodies and false spaces, albeit at the cost of a massive argument: they didn't speak for a week afterwards. 'But a beautiful song came out of it,' says Bradfield. 'Sean came up with something so lovely and simple and sweet for the verse, you wouldn't know there was blood on a track this pretty. I think it would have been a much lesser album without it.'

Wire believes that if 'Hold Me Like A Heaven' had been recorded by Fiction Factory in 1982, it could have been a big hit. The song was certainly too unusual for mainstream pop tastes in 2018. Even Bradfield's avant-curious guitar solo had a transcend-ent scope. The only blemish is the massed 'woah-woahs', which sound parachuted in from a late-night taxi rank.

'We pushed that chorus too far,' says Wire, 'but we thought it's so catchy, this song about a seriously mundane topic. I was really enthralled with it. And the line about me hating the world more than myself is important – because basically for my entire career it's been the other way around!'

145.
A Song For The Sadness

Recorded: Faster Studios, Cardiff; Door To The River
   Studios, Newport
Producer: Guy Massey
Released: 13 April 2018 (*Resistance Is Futile*, Columbia)

'Do you realize, that happiness makes you cry?'
                 – The Flaming Lips, 'Do You Realize??'

'A Song For The Sadness' was the final *Resistance is Futile* track to be finished, yet also one of the oldest, with an early demo recorded before the exit from Faster. 'The demo didn't feel of much consequence,' says Bradfield. 'But Nick reactivated it, after we had done "Hold Me Like A Heaven". He said he felt the album was out of balance.'

On a record not exactly burdened by levity – aside from 'International Blue' the most upbeat selection, 'Liverpool Revisited', was a tribute to the survivors of Hillsborough – the fresh perspective was welcome. Many Manics songs sound like they should be called 'A Song For The Sadness', but the one that actually is upsets preconceptions. The lyric's bittersweet memories – 'Fragments of lost melancholy/Traces of a generation gone' – came dressed up in a carefree orange-sunshine psych-rock air of *carpe diem*, with Moore's processed Thor-hammering heavily suggestive of The Flaming Lips' Steven Drozd and his baby John Bonham routines. There was also a fresh set of hands and ears behind the desk, with Dave Eringa on compassionate leave following the fraught atmosphere of 'Hold Me Like A Heaven'.

'We've got to the point where James was about to kill Dave,' says Wire. 'Definitely the Billy Preston moment. "Calling Guy

Massey! Murder is approaching!" Guy really did bring it together, and James's guitars are really strange and Arcadian. I don't think it's the greatest lyric I've ever written, but it's a series of nice words.'

The lyric does have the distinction of juxtaposing Dolly Parton's 'Islands In The Stream' with The Clash's 'One More Time', thereby mapping the full panoply of the Manics' universe. Bradfield, meanwhile, got to play his faithful white Les Paul though his Creamy Dreamer fuzz pedal and wallow in the luxuriant sustain. 'It gives you the "Motorcycle Emptiness" tone, but more – Kelsey Grammer more!' he laughs. 'This was just a little shiny moment on the record. Nothing too deep.'

If resistance really is futile, you might as well go down smiling.

146.
The Left Behind

Recorded: Faster Studios, Cardiff; Door To The River
    Studios, Newport
Producers: Dave Eringa and Loz Williams
Released: 13 April 2018 (*Resistance Is Futile*, Columbia)

'When an old cricketer leaves the crease, you never know
whether he's gone.'
    – Roy Harper, 'When An Old Cricketer Leaves The Crease'

Even before his parents' health seriously deteriorated, Nicky Wire
found himself making more frequent trips to visit them at the
family home. Between running errands or helping sort out his
father's will, he'd walk the streets of Blackwood, rekindling lots
of happy childhood memories but also noticing a rawness to the
area's countenance and mood. Blackwood, like much of South
Wales, and indeed, similar towns across Britain, had seen nothing
fill the void left by the vanished traces of the heavy industries
that had once made Britain prosperous and given its people
work – a process that began in the immediate post-war years
and intensified from the seventies onwards, an ongoing crisis
that successive governments were either unwilling or unable to
resolve, leading eventually to the traumatic rupture of the 2016
referendum vote to leave the EU.

'You could feel a pre-Brexit "you don't care about us" vibe,'
says Wire. 'Maybe from 2015 onwards, there's something in the
air. You could feel politics becoming more about what you haven't
got, not what you want. So there was definitely an element of
that in "The Left Behind".'

The song began with Wire and Loz Williams at Faster. In the

absence of Bradfield and Moore, they put down two songs that would eventually appear on Wire's 2023 solo album *Intimism*, plus a demo of 'The Left Behind', the latter distinguished by Wire's increasingly comfortable singing voice and Williams's piano vividly evoking hard times in a last chance saloon somewhere on the final frontier: 'From an open book/To a closed shop/Feeling like an animal/The one that time forgot'. The lyric also found room for a painful childhood flashback involving a screwdriver ('My fingernails are getting broken', see 'Futurology', page 457) and ended on a single word utterance of the ultimate enemy: 'Time'.

For all its socio-political subtext, the song was principally the anguished self-representation of its author and his band, struggling to stay upright against the winds of change. 'The squadron never dies,' it insists, a lyric that, Wire admits, reflected his admiration for The Libertines' Pete Doherty, a true believer who continually refused to abort his kamikaze mission, often in defiance of public opinion or common sense. The album's title and its sleeve image of one of Japan's last samurai articulated the same existential malaise.

'Obviously I was feeling like a dying breed,' says Wire. 'So yes, the lyric mixes the metaphor of feeling abandoned politically with the collapse of what was important to us as a band. It's amazing how the music press does feed into a lot of our lyrics. It's a very niche attitude. I doubt any other bands gave a fucking shit about it. But this song feeds into a collapse of how we find a way to justify our existence, the constant yin and yang of commercialism and critical acclaim, and then there's suddenly no way of getting critical acclaim.'

Bradfield's contained blues wail and Moore's spectacular tumbling double rolls combined to amplify the beleaguered mood. 'I just tried to play as if I was a second vocalist,' says James. 'It's a lovely song. Frequently Nick will do a vocal, and I know he doesn't really want me to sing it, because his vocal fits in a perfect place in the track. There's no point me trying to do it. So I knew I was just gonna be the guitarist, and just to be the guitarist is enough.'

Walking slowly yet proudly towards the door, 'The Left Behind's lonesome warrior exits the stage on a suitably heroic note. His fingernails may have been broken and his grip looser, but he's not done just yet.

147.
Concrete Fields

Recorded: Faster Studios, Cardiff; Door To The River
   Studios, Newport
Producer: Guy Massey
Released: 13 April 2018 (*Resistance Is Futile* [Deluxe
   Edition CD bonus track], Columbia)

'Tonight I am playing my three-thirty-five
While gazing at your photograph.'
                    – Dean Wareham, 'The Past Is Our Plaything'

'Concrete Fields' is effectively an appendix to 'The Left Behind'. Its strolling tempo and semi-spoken vocal suggest Nicky Wire dictating the song from the streets of Blackwood while looking after his parents and walking their dog Meg, noting all the things that have changed since his childhood, none of them for the better – starting with the recently closed Oakdale Comprehensive, where Nicky and his brother had been pupils, along with James, Richey and Sean. Wire's grumpily heartfelt appraisal of the locale ('The vaping and the super-schools, the breeding grounds of hate') comes insinuated with a political subtext ('The mountains we climbed are now mountains of debt'; 'Freedom at what cost?') alongside idealised memories of how things used to be. ('Just me and my brother, kicking a ball/The world so close and so beautiful').

'I realised so many of the old rhythms and landmarks of my youth had been obliterated,' says Wire. 'Green spaces no longer existed, makeshift cricket and football pitches were covered in houses and cars. The words came quick, as did the melody.'

Musically, the template appears to have been Primal Scream's

'Velocity Girl' flirting with Terry Jacks's 'Seasons In The Sun', with the latter's chorus incorporated on the heels of a completely unexpected baroque keyboard solo from Loz Williams. 'I was taken back to a vivid memory: listening to Jimmy Young on the radio with my mam, having a day off school, and "Seasons In The Sun" entrancing me with its lyrical flow. The song became an evocation of everything I knew disappearing.'

This quirky outlier was denied classic B-side status due to singles becoming obsolete, undone by the same forces of 'progress' the song bemoaned.

148.
Orwellian

Recorded: Rockfield Studios, Monmouthshire; Door To
    The River Studios, Newport
Producer: Dave Eringa
Released: 14 May 2021 (download/7-inch, Columbia);
    10 September 2021 (*The Ultra Vivid Lament*, Columbia)

> 'The chances of factual truth surviving the
> onslaught of power are very slim indeed.'
>
> – Hannah Arendt

Outside the BBC's Broadcasting House HQ stands a statue of George Orwell, next to an inscription: 'If liberty means anything at all, it means the right to tell people what they do not want to hear.' The words were taken from the original unused preface of Orwell's *Animal Farm*, a book that upon publication in 1945 and over subsequent decades would face opprobrium from both wings of the left/right ideological spectrum, essentially for the same reason: an espousal of democratic socialism.

Either in what they were saying or the way they said it, there have been times when Manic Street Preachers lived by Orwell's definition of liberty. The title of their first Number 1 album quoted Aneurin Bevan, a fellow provocateur who, like Orwell, did not mind upsetting allies with 'his truth'. So there was some irony that the Manics' first release of the Covid age, a period characterised by fractious and polarised digital babble, should be a song called 'Orwellian', where amid images of burning books the lyric's assertion 'It feels impossible to pick a side' ruffled some feathers among those ostensibly on 'their side'.

'"Orwellian" got reproached by the left intelligentsia a little bit,' notes Bradfield, 'saying, "Don't be ridiculous, there's no censorship here . . ." But we're all attacking each other on the same basis, from a different angle; everything has become misappropriated. And "Orwellian" is mostly about appropriation, I think. I loved the lyric because it summed up the way we'd been feeling for years, just that confusion of not knowing who we are or who our side is any more.'

Written shortly before the UK's first pandemic lockdown – Wire remembers playing the demo to Martin Hall on the day they heard Andrew Weatherall had died, 17 February 2020 – then recorded during the periodic easing of restrictions while keeping a nervous eye on the news, and released two months after the third national lockdown had been lifted, 'Orwellian' reflected the uneasy times musically as well as lyrically. Propelled by a series of decaying piano chords, it had a lulling aura, as if in shock or transfixed by a realisation of oncoming events, but with a sing-song melody, particularly in the chorus with its upward chord sequence recalling Abba, who would prove a touchstone influence on the new album as a whole.

'"Orwellian" has a sickliness to it, I don't know if we'd ever really sounded like that before,' says Wire. 'I play bass completely differently on this record, really clipped – the bass sound on Arctic Monkeys' *Tranquility Base* had quite on influence on me. It's a strange sound. But the Abba obsession has always been there, from "Motorcycle Emptiness" all the way through to this. For absolute melody with just that hint of sadness, you can't shake it. I think we found it was really difficult to express anger in songs any more, something we'd been wrestling with for a while. Because there's lots of anger on *The Ultra Vivid Lament*, but it's not manifestly angry.'

A key book on Wire's reading list during this period was Jill Lepore's *If Then*, which traced the roots of the twenty-first century's algorithm-driven data-mined political manipulation to methodologies developed in Cold War-era America by a shadowy outfit called The Simulmatics Corporation, creators of the 'people machine' mentioned in 'Orwellian'. Little wonder that the Manics' instincts were scrambled in the face of such deep systemic forces. Nonetheless, this was a band for whom 'taking sides', however sometimes contradictory, was once its raison d'être.

'I think Richey had found an amazing way to reconcile himself with hypocrisy, which, as you get older, is just a fucking impossible gig, especially if you're trying to vaguely be truthful about yourself,' says Wire. 'That just can't work when you're in your fifties and you've got kids.'

The heightened presence of piano on 'Orwellian' and the subsequent album was down to circumstance as well as aesthetic choice. An elderly friend bequeathed the Bradfield family a piano, named 'Margaret' after its owner. So a combination of having Margaret in the house and James's subsequent confinement there meant he began writing with her much more.

'Piano has a massive place in lots of music I've loved from the eighties,' he says, 'so there's no problem with that. I think "Orwellian" should be bigger, more expansive – not brutal, but it should have been shinier, had more of the Simple Minds widescreen vibe about it. But we kept it smaller and that was on purpose. We wanted it to feel as if you were still trapped in a waking dream, for obvious reasons.'

149.

The Secret He Had Missed

Recorded: Rockfield Studios, Monmouthshire; Door To
    The River Studios, Newport
Producer: Dave Eringa
Released: 16 July 2021 (download, Columbia);
    10 September 2021 (*The Ultra Vivid Lament*, Columbia)

> 'I never see what has been done; I only see
> what remains to be done.'
>
> – Marie Curie

The Ultra Vivid Lament's second advance sortie upped the Abba-esque quotient with a bravura duet between Bradfield and Julia Cumming from New York indie band Sunflower Bean. 'I did feel we were privileged to get somebody that young and cool on our record,' says James. 'I am that generation now where I'm genuinely old to a young musician. Like, "She's agreed? Quick! Get the vocal done before she thinks otherwise!" But Julia was brilliant, as is the lyric. Perhaps Nick should try being a librettist, because his dialoguing between two characters in one song is pretty impressive here.'

Written in late summer 2019, the song imagines an exchange between the sibling artists Gwen and Augustus John, who grew up in the Pembrokeshire seaside town of Tenby and impacted the early twentieth-century international art world in contrasting ways. Wire's lyric paraphrases the famous comment by Augustus – 'In fifty years' time I shall be remembered as the brother of Gwen' – and in specifically citing two of Gwen's most celebrated paintings suggests the reclusive older sibling was unfairly overshadowed by her flamboyant brother ('Bohemian with no

control') amid the sexist attitudes of the time. The title meanwhile, refers to the notion that Augustus John insufficiently cared
for his own talent.

'Augustus was the fêted bad boy of British art,' considers Wire.
'He was almost like a Richard Burton character, in that he did
so much, people thought he had cheapened his legacy – he was
portrait artist for the stars, whereas Gwen John's output was very
small and intimate.'

As well as Cumming's voice modulation, there was a less
obvious but equally apt Abba allusion in the lyric.

'The line "left your heart on the beach in Tenby" was a direct
nod to the line about Glasgow in "Super Trouper",' says Wire.
'When I was young, Terry Wogan on the radio would always go
on about that line. "Why Glasgow?" And then he'd do spoofs
of it, like, "When I called you last night from Scun-thorpe" . . .
I'm lucky to have a flat in Tenby, and to walk the beach where
Gwen walked and painted just gives me a little thrill. And I really
enjoyed writing this lyric. It's a song that moves and flows and
dances to its own tune.'

A tune of its own indebtedness to Abba, Julia Cumming, Terry
Wogan and two great Welsh artists, 'The Secret He Had Missed'
is one of the Manics' great dramatic miniatures; a team effort
too, with Moore's cajoling rhythms and Bradfield's sleek guitar
lines holding steady amid the rollicking 'Waterloo' piano vamps.
'I was trying to make the guitar more subservient to the song,'
says Bradfield. 'As you get older, you realise it's not about being
a guitar band, it's about the song. Nick and Sean have reminded
me about that many times!'

150.

Still Snowing In Sapporo

Recorded: Rockfield Studios, Monmouthshire; Door To
The River Studios, Newport
Producers: Dave Eringa and Gavin Fitzjohn
Released: 10 September 2021 (*The Ultra Vivid Lament*,
Columbia)

> 'Bands, those funny little plans, that never
> work quite right.'
>
> – Mercury Rev, 'Holes'

A quintessential Manics album opener to rank alongside 'Elvis Impersonator: Blackpool Pier' and 'Send Away The Tigers', inasmuch as it's both aspirational and self-referential, has quiet bits and loud bits, feels simultaneously euphoric yet bereft, and sets the emotional thermostat for everything that follows. Moreover, with *The Ultra Vivid Lament* being perhaps the most personal Manic Street Preachers album, indelibly affected by Nicky Wire losing both his parents within twelve months, 'Still Snowing In Sapporo' also happens to be a true story of love and loss.

In October 1993, flying from Tokyo to Sapporo for the final date of a two-week tour of Japan, the band's plane landed in heavy snow. The lyric frames the drama of the event ('Our hands all gripped together holding on so tight') in the wider context of a *Gold Against The Soul*-era state of their nation address, loaded with bittersweet portent ('Those days may never come again/My optimism resembles a dying flame'). On the Manics' next tour of Japan, there would just be three of them against the world.

'It was a bit hairy,' recalls Wire. 'Because at the time, Japanese planes would actually have a TV at the front, which shows the pilot's view – which you don't really want to see when you're coming through a blizzard. It went completely dark, then bumpy. I was wearing a fur coat and had my make-up on. "Make-up running eyes"? True, maybe slightly exaggerated. But it was pretty frightening.'

Wire initially baulked at Bradfield's proposal that the opening verse should feature just his unaccompanied voice until Moore's entrance in the pre-chorus bridge. 'Nick was saying, "There has to be something keeping pace, some pulse . . ." I'm like, "No! The song gets interrupted by Sean bringing us back to reality, but why can't I be floating in time? Because that's what the lyric is doing, floating in time."'

Bradfield's strategy helped the song build the sustained grace periods to carry what for the Manics is an atypically long duration – just over six minutes – without any slack. After demoing with Gavin Fitzjohn at Watertown, the master recording with Dave Eringa proceeded smoothly, with Fitzjohn pointing Bradfield towards another atypical move: a guitar solo that simply echoed the melodic terrain covered thus far. 'He started singing it and I just ran with it,' says James. 'That's my Gretsch Country Gentleman all over this track, my first proper posh guitar purchase. This felt perfect, like one of our classics. A remembrance of something quite important – we'd gone back to Japan for the second time and were reproached by the Japanese journalists because we hadn't killed ourselves.' He laughs. 'Fair point! But it was a great time, because it felt like we were failing by our own standards, falling on our own swords. This felt like a pure memory – conflicted but brilliant. I think we carried it off.'

151.

Quest For Ancient Colour

Recorded: Rockfield Studios, Monmouthshire; Door To
	The River Studios, Newport
Producer: Dave Eringa
Released: 10 September 2021 (*The Ultra Vivid Lament*,
	Columbia)

> 'I kind of wanted to glorify insecurity rather
> than being confident and successful.'
>
> – Anita Lane

Some of Nicky Wire's grouchiest verses set to one of James Dean Bradfield's loveliest musical arrangements, 'Quest For Ancient Colour' amply demonstrates the power of opposite attraction. On the one hand, an ode to 'negative capability', the confessions of a man who 'explored internal galaxies', whose 'scream had lost its source', who 'used to control but now I just feel used', his 'soul a suburban sinkhole'. And on the other, a piano ballad that blooms from dearth into glorious abundance then skips towards better days, complete with a playful variation on the 'Motorcycle Emptiness' guitar solo, only to succumb at the last: 'Modern life was killed and crushed . . .'

'It's a song about Nick's aesthetic, that went through about three or four different tunes, and then I finally rested on this one,' says James. 'Written from start to finish on Margaret, mostly in lockdown, then I would drive into the studio to flesh it out. I felt it was a great track and it never really landed with people, they didn't get it. Which disappointed me.'

Perhaps the worm in the words discouraged some. With a title sourced from a documentary about ancient Japanese dyeing techniques, Wire embarked on his latest design for life, based upon an affirmation of negative thinking. 'I bored James to death with this theory that anti-positivity gets more done,' says Wire. 'Now, I hate Chelsea more than any other football team. All I want them to do is lose – but I will bet on them to win every week, thinking if they are going to win, I want to make some money out of the fuckers. And if I lose that money, I'm even happier. This is like my version of Brian Eno's Oblique Strategies! So that was the genesis of the song. I was blown away with James's Elton John piano-playing, all the flourishes, which seem to have come from nowhere. James can probably play any instrument he wants to, but he really pushed on here.'

To counter the bitterness, Wire referenced both Don Henley's 'Boys Of Summer' and Bruce Springsteen's 'Girls In Their Summer Clothes', two sweet lyrics predicated upon melancholy remembrance of younger days. Ultimately, 'Quest For Ancient Colour's tussle between darkness and light ended in an honourable draw.

152.

Don't Let The Night Divide Us

Recorded: Rockfield Studios, Monmouthshire; Door To
  The River Studios, Newport
Producer: Dave Eringa
Released: 10 September 2021 (*The Ultra Vivid Lament*,
  Columbia)

> 'Kept in line with truncheons, rifle butts
> and truncheons.'
>> – Discharge, 'State Violence/State Control'

The Manics' advance bullet-point précis of *The Ultra Vivid Lament* was '*London Calling*-era Clash playing Abba', and 'Don't Let The Night Divide Us' the song that most closely fitted that brief. Unusually for Nicky Wire, whose instincts veer closer to Sex Pistols negaholia, the lyric was a hopeful exhortation for solidarity against the forces of darkness, in the wake of the latest Conservative election victory: 'Their lies will help unite us, let's make a promise here and now/Don't let those boys from Eton suggest that we are beaten – no no no'.

Even Wire himself sounds surprised at the song's tone.

'Some of those lines are a bit positive,' he laughs. 'But you've got to manipulate your writing technique at times. This was just after Boris Johnson had won, and I was thinking of that brilliant John Le Carré quote about Etonians being a curse on the Earth. This is an angry lyric. James's Abba key change in the chorus is phenomenal. It was quite a seditious way of getting something political into a kind of joyous pop song.'

Wire initially presented Bradfield with a brief, urgently downstroked acoustic home demo of himself singing two verses, the first of which included the 'boys from Eton', at this stage coupled with a threat to 'scale their castle walls'. Bradfield got to work, shifting 'Eton' to the pre-chorus bridge, and delivering the propulsive glissando into the chorus like a catapult between the beastly Bozo's eyes.

'The verse is in A,' says Bradfield, 'and sometimes the chorus just needs to go up. I thought, "I want this to fucking *take off*. I want to go from A to C, a big shift. What's the best way to do it? I'll just do a *rrrrrrrr* on the piano . . ." And lo and behold, it was Abba. I had six hours before I was driving to west Wales with the family, and I came in to the studio and did it. Felt good!'

'Don't Let The Night Divide Us' has a noble quality that once again transcends knowledge of the song's inspiration. For a long time it was in pole position to be the album's first single, only to be passed over for reasons no one seems to recall.

'Perhaps it was a bit authentic?' suggests Wire. '"Orwellian" fits the retro-futurism thing a bit more. Just one of those things. I've got a lot of affection for this song.'

153.

Diapause

Recorded: Rockfield Studios, Monmouthshire; Door To
    The River Studios, Newport
Producer: Dave Eringa
Released: 10 September 2021 (*The Ultra Vivid Lament*,
    Columbia)

'My mind is failing
A sheltering of sorts.'
        – Bill Ryder-Jones, 'A Bad Wind Blows In My Heart Pt. 2'

'Diapause' is *The Ultra Vivid Lament*'s secret weapon: the sleeper
track at the album's centre, titled for a type of animal dormancy
where development is delayed in response to unfavourable environmental conditions, and the song on the record that Nicky Wire
says is most often mentioned to him by fans.

'It seemed to strike a chord. If there is a Covid song on the
album then there's something about this, the languid saturation,
that gets to people. Certainly there's an atmosphere to it.'

That atmosphere was prompted, says Bradfield, in direct
response to the 'ghostly' aura of the words. His solo demo saw
him playing 'amateurish drums', guitar, piano and an old double
bass which he had been learning to play after it was gifted to him
by a friend. 'I knew I wanted it to be fragile and have that nature
of just not knowing whether you can survive this thing,' he says.
'It has a little bit of my Thomas Dolby fascination, a little Talk
Talk, the China Crisis thing. It's really a song that could collapse
under its own flimsy weight.'

Although a quick construction, the demo proved a sturdy
blueprint for a master recording with stellar upgrades from all

concerned. Think jazz fusion Joy Division, and dig the perma-frost Herbie Hancock vibes of Nick Nasmyth's solo, equalled in the cool school stakes by Bradfield 'indulging my mad, tasteful George Benson fantasy'. As for the lyric, Wire admits he feels as pleasantly disturbed by its hypersensitised dramas as anyone. 'I don't really know what it's about,' he says. 'It's easy to say some of it's Richey, but it's not. A lovely language song that doesn't really go anywhere. It takes off and goes places but there's no conclusion, just an ongoing process.'

The song's emotional resonance is undeniable even to its author, however: particularly the chorus's visions of a broken sunken heart, building walls, and the repeated admission 'I've burnt so many bridges but not the one that leads to you'.

'Which is probably the nearest I've got to writing a real, proper love song,' he says. 'Thirty years married, and just being in the house with the kids – that was the only thing that made sense.'

154.

Complicated Illusions

Recorded: Rockfield Studios, Monmouthshire; Door To
    The River Studios, Newport
Producer: Dave Eringa
Released: 10 September 2021 (*The Ultra Vivid Lament*,
    Columbia)

'I was like an industry, depressed and in decline.'
— Scritti Politti, 'Jacques Derrida'

'Complicated Illusions' does well to live up to its vivid opening
dictum: 'On a street of old bones/Dust masquerades as skin'. The
terse punchiness is maintained throughout, remarkably so given
that the lyric was influenced by Nicky Wire reading Jacques Derrida. The notoriously challenging French philosopher's theory of
deconstruction and its application to breaking down notions of
truth became au courant in the age of culture wars, so-called
'fake news' and 'alternative facts', the latter term infamously
deployed in January 2017 by Kellyanne Conway, manager of
Donald Trump's first presidential campaign, in response to alle-
gations that the White House Press Secretary was lying.

'I read a lot of Derrida, which fried my brain, but I thought it
was weird he was being twisted into the rot of Trump's White
House,' says Wire. 'He'd probably have been pretty depressed
with the way his ideas were being used. It sounds unbelievably
pretentious but this song is partly about the battle between struc-
turalism and deconstruction, and how I just think life is much
more complicated. The line "I defend the middle ground", I feel
is where we are as a band. I'm not ashamed of that. Because the
forces on either side seem to be really destructive.'

Rooting through Derrida's 'margins', Wire confronted the awkward realisation that although he no longer necessarily endorsed his younger self's outlook, it still defined him. But the song proved he could at least be philosophical about it. 'If you've been in a band this long, and also if you've talked as much shit as I have over the last thirty years, you're always going to trip yourself up!'

After Bradfield had listened to Wire's voice message demo for the song, he did his own bit of deconstruction, repurposing what were originally verses into a chorus. 'I knew the song could go somewhere else,' he says. Stranded alone one weekend mid-lockdown at Rockfield, Bradfield decided to use a newly delivered bespoke guitar handmade in Abergavenny by Richard Meyrick. 'I had that glorious, cinematic moment in my head. You know, "I'm gonna finish this song off, and it'll be the first song I've written on this guitar." So I wrote the chorus and it flew.' Bradfield recorded a new demo, also featuring the Rockfield piano that Queen famously used on 'Bohemian Rhapsody', from where the song proceeded to its final state of nuanced grace with a full band session at Door To The River: like prime Roxy Music, constructing harmony out of doubt and dislocation.

'It's one of my favourite things we've ever done,' says Bradfield. 'Especially the instrumental section, it feels pure. I think we're all in complete union with each other.'

155.
Blank Diary Entry

Recorded: Rockfield Studios, Monmouthshire; Door To
    The River Studios, Newport
Producers: Dave Eringa and Gavin Fitzjohn
Released: 10 September 2021 (*The Ultra Vivid Lament*,
    Columbia)

'The sound so ominously tearing through the silence.'

– Abba, 'The Visitors'

The first thing Mark Lanegan did when he saw James Dean
Bradfield at London's Royal Festival Hall on 8 October 2008,
where both were singing at a John Cale-curated Nico tribute,
was apologise for the previous time they met. That had been
in September 1996: Manic Street Preachers and Lanegan's band
Screaming Trees were the support acts on the infamous Oasis US
tour that began with Liam Gallagher missing the first show after
claiming he needed to stay in London to buy a house and ended
thirteen days later when Noel Gallagher got fed up and flew home
on Concorde. The Manics enjoyed the novelty of not being the
focus of attention, while Oasis and the Screaming Trees, both
bands built around combustible pairs of siblings, simmered on the
verge of fighting among themselves and each other, with Lanegan
taking exception to the younger Gallagher's wind-up routines.

'A great moment of rock history, on all sides,' says Bradfield.
'Liam was giving it the "who'd you think you are – Barking
Branches, Crazy Conkers?" In between the shows where Mark
was not suffering perception problems because of his drug intake,
I really got on with him. Talked to him a lot. Contrary to popular
belief, he was really calm, and deep thinking, and actually just

liked chatting. I quickly became aware that if I'd met him when I was young, I would have been mates with him. Or, I would have *liked* to be mates with him.'

Upon reuniting in 2008, the now-sober Lanegan gave Bradfield his contact details and they kept in touch. A little over ten years later, Bradfield was at Watertown with Gavin Fitzjohn, working on a musical treatment for 'Blank Diary Entry', the most overtly lockdown-influenced lyric on the new record, and began to envisage it as a duet. 'The demo was effortless. Felt like the song was going to take on a darker Glen Campbell kind of moment. I just thought, "Who does a better darker kind of Glen Campbell than Mark Lanegan?"'

Now resident in Ireland, having decamped from Los Angeles 'with hell-hounds at my back', Lanegan readily agreed and brought his hallmark instrument to the party, singing 'Blank Diary Entry' like the man who swallowed a thundercloud. On paper, 'In a garden full of locusts/Pain was a crying man', reads like a well-wrought fiction; voiced by this infernal amalgam of Ian Curtis and Prince Far I, it feels like a frontline dispatch from Acheron, the mythic Greek river of woe. Next to him, Bradfield plays the Lucy Rose role, shining a brighter light on what nonetheless remains a bleak corner of Nicky Wire's soul, despite him trying on a different narrator's hat.

'There is an almost Southern Gothic accent to some of the words,' says Wire. 'Which was maybe one of the reasons we asked Lanegan. Perhaps I was trying to get outside myself. But the blank diary . . . when you're institutionalised in a band, you always look forward to next year's diary. And obviously, in the Covid world, they were pretty irrelevant. Usually there's gigs in there, there's album releases. If there's nothing, it feels a bit weird. I really enjoyed playing on this, everything felt really important. And Mark Lanegan sounds amazing. When he sings "I must confess", it's a real moment.'

Lanegan's vocal on 'Blank Diary Entry' was his final recording.

Having struggled long and tortuously with Covid, he passed away on 22 February 2022. 'This song always feels pertinent and sad to me,' says James. 'It seriously hit me, because I really liked him. His voice is perfect – that's all I can say. The song brought out the best in everybody.'

156.
Afterending

Recorded: Rockfield Studios, Monmouthshire; Door To
   The River Studios, Newport
Producer: Dave Eringa
Released: 10 September 2021 (*The Ultra Vivid Lament*,
   Columbia)

> 'It was fun for a while.'
>
> — Roxy Music, 'More Than This'

The Covid pandemic's disorientation effect, wherein time seem-ed to simultaneously crawl and disappear, is elegantly simulated by 'Afterending'. Wire's lyric observed how the period's extreme acquiescence ('we clap for a crumbling state') mixed with a loosening of political deference ('the statutes crack and drown'), with the chorus conveying the oddly euphoric mood of perpetual impending doom: 'Sail into the abyss with me . . .'

'There was a sense of playfulness and irony there,' says Wire, 'what with all that catastrophisation we were surrounded with and the endless news cycles. We actually played this live a few times. It turned out quite a singalong.'

Bradfield recalls asking the album's mix engineer David Wrench to 'make this one as smooth as Galaxy chocolate'. Job done, especially when the loping verse swoons up to the beatific refrain with so little fuss, a co-mingling of classy templates. 'I'd say imperial phase Roxy Music, so "More Than This",' says Bradfield. 'That nether-land of not knowing quite what was real. A feeling of stasis, in a waking dream.'

'We must be the only band in the world that prefers Roxy when Eno left,' laughs Wire. 'It's my brother's fault. Every girlfriend he brought home he put on fucking *Avalon* and turn the lights off . . . But for the verse, Sean was totally going for the Abba song "The Name Of The Game". I love this, the way it drifts off into a sense of nothingness. So there's something valedictory, I think, about "Afterending".'

157.
Rosebud

Recorded: Monnow Valley, Monmouthshire; Rockfield
    Studios, Monmouthshire
Producer: Dave Eringa
Released: 22 July 2022 (download, Columbia);
    9 September 2022 (*Know Your Enemy: Door To The River*,
    Columbia)

> 'Did you hear the distant cry
> Calling me back to my sin.'
>
>   – Screaming Trees, 'Nearly Lost You'

While remixing and reconstructing *Know Your Enemy*, a process that involved much time and largely unheralded curatorial energy, there was one massive eureka moment: the discovery of a song originally overlooked amid the fevered writing and recording sessions as the band followed the trail of the album's messy conception through multiple studios, slowly frying its collective brain along the way.

'It is silly,' admits Bradfield. '"Rosebud" could have gone on *Know Your Enemy* in place of others, let's be truthful. I'd written the music to try and please a fascination Nick had with "Soul To Squeeze" by Red Hot Chili Peppers. I wanted a song built round the guitar figure at the start, rather than just have it as an intro, I loved the longing and repetition of the verse over that riff. Nick and Sean are amazing on it, we got Nick Nasmyth into Rockfield to play Hammond, and we all loved it. Then we forgot about it.'

The lyric was consistent with Nicky Wire's post-*TIMT* suspicion that the essence of himself and the band had been 'lost . . . along the way'. Drawing parallels with Orson Welles's *Citizen Kane* might have been a step too far, but even that doesn't explain the song's bewildering disappearance. 'The working title for *Know Your Enemy* at one point was "Masterpiece",' laughs Wire. 'I've got the receipts to prove it! Then we thought, "Fuck, making a masterpiece is hard work . . ." Stuff from that session that felt like they were going to be big songs just drifted away.'

'It was a different way to play, more restrained, more thought-ful,' says James. 'I was like, "Why is it unreleased? I thought it must have at least been a B-side." So thank God it found its way back.'

158.
Decline & Fall

Recorded: Door To The River Studios, Newport; Rockfield
   Studios, Monmouthshire
Producers: Dave Eringa and Loz Williams
Released: 30 August 2024 (download, Columbia);
   14 February 2025 (*Critical Thinking*, Columbia)

> 'Blue is the colour of longing for the distances
> you never arrive in.'
>   – Rebecca Solnit, *A Field Guide To Getting Lost*

Ever since setting an impossibly high bar with the Worldwide
Number 1 Debut Album Then Bust edict, the Manic Street
Preachers have been in the business of managed decline. So
successful have they been that almost thirty-five years later the
band could write a song in celebration, release it as a single, and
enjoy adding a new imprint onto the popular cultural surrounds.
'I know our time has come and gone,' sang James Dean Bradfield, over the sleekly sprung riff of 'Decline & Fall', 'but at least
we blazed a trail and shone.'

For a rock group to accumulate fifteen albums requires abun-
dant reserves of perseverance, ability and luck, and 'Decline &
Fall' harnessed all three in perfect equilibrium. Wire's lyric wove
random inputs – 'Heart Of The Sunrise' by Yes; Australian doom
metal band Divide and Dissolve; a title shared with both an
Evelyn Waugh novel and a song by Bill Nelson; an appreciation
of drystone walls as 'something deep and resonant' – into a taut
state of the nation address. The keystone couplet: 'Society used
to be my worst enemy/Now I want to build a small one for you
and me.'

'It was a post-Brexit comparison of one's own decline and the country's,' he says. 'Which obviously has been going on for a longer time, but seemed to be accelerated from this point. That "society" line is definitely haunted by the ghost of the impossible task of feeling like a unified country. Or unified county, or unified town, or street . . . It felt like that collapsed and the urge to withdraw was getting stronger. And as a band, all you can do, really, is circle the wagons and make the best of it you can.'

When Bradfield received the lyric at the end of January 2023, two months after an invigorating American tour with kindred spirits Suede, his commercial radar crackled in recognition. 'I was like, OK, game on,' he says. 'It's a great lyric, there's no spare meat here, and in my head I'm thinking it's got to be a single. So I did a version. And it was awful. Terrible. Quite twee. I don't want anyone ever to hear it. I'd been through a period where I wasn't sure I was hitting my mark with Nick and Sean, so I really wanted something to hit home with.'

The lucky catalyst came when he heard 'Hymn' by Ultravox on the radio, a 1982 George Martin-produced up-shine of the band's definitive Conny Plank era, and then 1985's 'You've Got The Power' by Win, the high-concept pop strategists formed out of the Fire Engines. Both records had nagging guitar figures and explosive electro-underlay. 'That Win single is a fucking weird song,' says Bradfield. 'I'd already been thinking about it, and then I heard it. That's when it hit me – I come from the eighties. I'm born in '69 but I come from the era where the supreme indie pop single is unassailable, whether it be The Associates' "Those First Impressions", or "Come Back" by The Mighty Wah!, or "You've Got The Power". It restarted the fire in me to carry on in that tradition. So I went back to it, because I thought this lyric was brilliant and it deserved to be a single on the radio.'

In Bradfield's mind, all he needed was a riff to weave around the chorus lines like a call and response. At the band's studio, he had his Les Paul 'Faithful' plugged into a Deacy Amp, a 2010 copy made by one of Brian May's former guitar technicians of an amplifier originally built by Queen bassist John Deacon. In his head, not for the first time, Bradfield was thinking Skids. 'Because the Deacy Amp has a fuzz thing that does a perfect approximation of Stuart Adamson in "Into The Valley". You can still hear detail, but it's fuzz. I thought, "I'll start the song with the chorus". And it happened in a second. I spun off a guitar set-up that I arranged to try and get myself going. It all flowed from there.'

With Moore away for a week, Bradfield needed a percussive element to keep time and create an atmosphere. He made a loop of the middle breakdown in Squeeze's 'Cool For Cats'. 'Slightly menacing. As I built the demo I wrote the verse – there's proclamation in the chorus but the verse is a bit more observant. And sometimes when you want to do that, you just go G to A, you just float around these two chords. I'm not saying it's the greatest thing ever, but it just felt like a good shiny moment.'

Bradfield's demo went to Rockfield, where Wire and Moore added bass and drums. 'We just tarted it up, added flourishes really,' says Nicky. 'From the outset, when we played it together it always felt like a first single. I really like that we can still come up with records like that.'

Sean Moore's splenetic drum fills certainly gave tarty flourishing a good name. 'Yes, he's just brilliant,' says James, 'especially in the middle and where he's really accenting on my vocals. We did have a bit of a to-do, y'know, "put some more toms in there", that kind of thing. I left the room and let him have a grumble at me . . . and then he did it. This got a bit big and powerful in the studio, because Nick and Sean play heavy. When Caesar Edmunds mixed it he brought it back in again, made it sleeker.'

For a final touch, Wire added a sample of the intro to That Petrol Emotion's 1987 crunch-collision album closer 'Creeping To The Cross', which itself was a sample of TPE singer Steve Mack saying 'Ah!', in a register startlingly similar to Bradfield's. This would be the closest the album came to a guest lead vocalist, after a run of five records that made a feature of 'featured' singers, although Bradfield, giddy from having aced a single and thereby clearing the band's onward path, did initially consider offering 'Decline & Fall' to a significant other: Skids' Richard Jobson.

'When I was doing the demo, all I could see was a glitter ball on *Top of the Pops* and Jobbo doing his dance with one of his Captain Kirk tops on. Which, in my head, is completely fucking iconic. But we never quite called him. Because I really wanted to sing this one myself.'

159.

Hiding In Plain Sight

Recorded: Door To The River Studios, Newport; Rockfield
  Studios, Monmouthshire
Producers: Dave Eringa and Loz Williams
Released: 25 October 2024 (download, Columbia);
  14 February 2025 (*Critical Thinking*, Columbia)

'And time has told me, not to ask for more.'
                              – Nick Drake, 'Time Has Told Me'

The bullet-point pitch for 'Hiding In Plain Sight' focused on its
status as the first Manic Street Preachers single with a lead vocal
by Nicky Wire. And while a landmark moment, it wasn't entirely
unexpected. During the summer of 2023, with work proceeding
on the new Manics album, Wire self-released his second solo
album. Named after the art movement whose notables included
Gwen John, *Intimism* was a more welcoming proposition than
2006's *I Killed The Zeitgeist*, partly because he had settled upon an
agreeable singing voice. One song in particular, 'Contact Sheets',
was a classic nugget of Wire melancholy landing in the bittersweet
spot where eighties indie enigmas Felt met Jimmy Webb, and
begged the thought: this could be a Manics song.

'Hiding In Plain Sight' was cut from a similar cloth. 'I've used
those chords before,' says Wire. 'They're my go-to chord sequence
– it's not far from "Your Love Alone". But everything just took
over me, really. I wrote the entire thing in an hour, all the lyrics,
the music, even the bridge. I kind of knew as well – it really did
give me a tingle, when you get a lyrical flow like that, where
everything folds in on itself. I don't even think I wrote it down. I
started off with the initial line "Keep the curtain drawn all day",

which was inspired by Bowie's "Sound And Vision", "Pale blinds drawn all day", which reminded me of him in the hotel in LA coked out of his mind. Whereas I was with my dog in Newport looking at the beautiful view, drinking Ribena.'

There were other noteworthy artistic references: 'The procession is long but the time is very short' is adapted from Tom Stoppard's play *Arcadia*, while 'as I walked the soft parade' nods to The Doors ('who I've been totally converted to by my wife over the last thirty years'). The song's emotional heft is all internally generated, a fifty-five-year-old quite literally reflecting on his younger self, reachable now only in memories and keepsakes: 'I wanna be in love with the man I used to be . . .'

After working on the song in detail and at length, Wire asked Bradfield if he would try a vocal. 'Perhaps he was just being polite, perhaps it was just the chance that it might be good,' says James. 'I was just like, "Well, I don't really see the point, because the vocals are pretty much perfect." I tried it and took an hour over doing it, tracked it, and I don't even think Nick or Sean ever heard it. So there is a version with my vocal, which just isn't that good. It sounds a bit half-hearted, because I knew I was trying to replace something that didn't need to be replaced.'

Musically, the song's onrushing momentum throws up treasure with each breaking wave, especially Lana McDonagh's backing vocals sugarcoating Wire's à la Kirsty MacColl and the hitherto inconceivable sound of Wire and Bradfield trading guitar solos. 'Mine's the first one, the indie one, the really quick one!' laughs Wire. 'I love James's solo, I did ask him to do something arch. It's a bit camp. Steve Harley's "Make Me Smile" had been in my mind.'

Bradfield, ever sensitive to the group's ongoing viability, regards 'Hiding In Plain Sight' as a significant moment.

'The more the band goes on, the more important it becomes for other people to sing your songs, I think. Nick is still a relatively new voice on our tracks, and people are going, "Wow, that's the Manics, that's a different angle." It worked brilliantly. He's got his voice to a place where it feels like he's closer to people like Ian McCulloch, where it's a bit more relaxed in expression, shall we say. Whereas I was in a choir, I've got a voice that *goes* somewhere. I'll try and sing more humbly sometimes and then I forget myself and go back to my choir ways, or punky shouty ways, whatever. His voice takes us somewhere else, and I'm eager to find more of that.'

Wire, however, isn't getting carried away.

'James was asking me to play bass on "Hiding In Plain Sight" when we play live. I said, "I cannot sing and play bass. You've got to get into your head that I'm not like you!" But I was really pretty chuffed with this, I'll be honest. Pretty chuffed. I didn't want to end the song, but I made sure I did. Because I can drone on and on, you know.'

160.
People Ruin Paintings

Recorded: Door To The River Studios, Newport; Rockfield
    Studios, Monmouthshire
Producers: Dave Eringa and Loz Williams
Released: 10 January 2025 (download, Columbia);
    14 February 2025 (*Critical Thinking*, Columbia)

'In the vastness of the cosmos, there must be other
civilisations far older and more advanced than ours.'
                       – Carl Sagan, *Cosmos*

The soundtrack to a morning stroll plausibly plucked from the
Levi 501 arse pocket of a passing eighties indie guitar boy,
'People Ruin Paintings' is that rare thing: a gently misanthropic
eco-protest song framed as art critique.

The lyric had three trigger elements. A photograph, humorous
but troubling, of polar bears living in an abandoned shack on
a Siberian island. 'It sparked something off in me,' says Wire.
Then, a BBC documentary featuring a tribe deep in the Amazon
rainforest. The next week, Wire watched a Channel Five documentary on the same subject. 'I like a travel programme like
everyone else,' says Wire, 'but the idea that they're doing it for
us, when they have some of the biggest carbon footprints known
to man, is so annoying. It's our insatiable appetite to colonise
every fucking thing and everyone.'

Ergo, without people, the world would be better place – as
would paintings, to Wire's eye, hence the song's opening couplet: 'Take the climber out of the mountain/Give me a Pollock,
give me a Rothko.'

'People Ruin Paintings' was one of the earliest songs written for the album and essayed 'live-ish' at Door To The River, and Bradfield had a couple of 'awful, florid' false starts before taking inspiration from Sean Moore's passion for taking photographs without people in them. 'I thought, "I need to empty this out", and it worked,' says Bradfield. 'It's quite an articulate song, a very grown-up song.' The dramatic crux of a luminous ensemble performance comes in the breakdown, where Bradfield starts expressing on his rare Martin EM-18 and is mischievously shadowed by Wire, with Moore's rimshots keeping the party on the righteous path, until one of the singer's exultant 'Ahh's leads us into the final chorus. Typically, James gives most of the credit to the guitar.

'It belonged to Robb Allan, our old sound engineer, and I coveted it for about twenty years. Eventually he found it in his garage, all battered. So the deal was I'd rehabilitate it, and now I've got it, and it transformed this track. I have started believing that gear affects songwriting. Well, where else have you got to go after all your theories have been rubbished when you get to the age of fifty-five?!'

161.
Brushstrokes Of Reunion

Recorded: Door To The River Studios, Newport; Rockfield
　　Studios, Monmouthshire
Producers: Dave Eringa and Loz Williams
Released: 31 January 2025 (download, Columbia);
　　14 February 2025 (*Critical Thinking*, Columbia)

　　'Peace is always beautiful.'
　　　　　　　　　　　　　– Walt Whitman, *Leaves of Grass*

The three Manic Street Preachers still live within thirty minutes
of each other but they're no longer the last gang in town. Real-
life diktats have been messing with Nicky Wire's beloved annual
band diaries at least since the advent of parenthood, and while
having their own studio brings independence it also allows each
member to do their own thing in isolation from the others.
Perhaps, however, loosening the ties that bind has strengthened
the collective. 'Brushstrokes Of Reunion', *Critical Thinking*'s emotional wellspring, doesn't feature Wire at all, while Bradfield
and Moore recorded their parts separately. Indeed, until Moore
arrived at the studio, Bradfield didn't think this was a Manics
song at all, so personal was its subject matter.

　　'There's this little painting in my office that my mum did when
she was having chemotherapy – one of the only ones she let me
keep. She'd destroy a lot of her paintings. There was one she did
of Mynyddislwyn mountain, the view out of the back window
of my parents' house. I loved it, and she ripped it up. Perhaps
it's because she was going through therapy and the painting was
supposed to be something that alleviated the darkness, but this
painting was *of* the darkness. Anyway, if I'm having a tough time

I go and stare at that painting – a daisy on a recrudescent azure background with a hint of something ghostly. It reminds me to realise how fragile everything is. It's the only way I can really connect with my mum, so I wanted the song to be simple and show the accumulation of the effect it had on me.'

Bradfield's template was the The Waterboys circa *A Pagan Place*, songs like 'Rags' and 'Church Not Made With Hands', with piano, guitar and drums clattering onwards in zealous concert to somewhere unspecified but definitely spiritual. Having recorded acoustic and electric guitars, Bradfield also demoed drums – as noted by Moore when he arrived at the studio the next day. The cousins exchanged texts. Bradfield explained the song was likely destined for a future solo record, but to 'feel free' if he wanted to try something. 'I'll have a go,' said Sean.

'I come back the next day and he'd fucking gone ballistic,' says Bradfield. 'His parts were brilliant. And from there, I tried not to put too much on it, just kept it powerful. It felt like blowing through the fuse of sadness. Go for it and make it beautiful, make it how the little painting makes you feel.'

Wire heard the yearning crescendos as Bradfield stretched for joy amid sadness and loss ('I listened to the sound of your singing/Now the pain had reached its final limit') and realised his services were not required. 'What would be the point?' he says. 'I love it. It's got a real crunch from those two trying to outdo each other. I'm looking forward to doing it live, just to see the pain on Sean's face!'

'It was a humble beginning that turned into something bigger,' says Bradfield. 'A good experience. Because there was no pain involved in the process of the recording, no arguments. But Sean's the one who turned it into a Manics song.'

162.
Critical Thinking

Recorded: Door To The River Studios, Newport; Rockfield
    Studios, Monmouthshire
Producers: Dave Eringa and Loz Williams
Released: 14 February 2025 (*Critical Thinking*, Columbia)

'Don't push me, 'cos I'm close to the edge.'
    – Grandmaster Flash and the Furious Five, 'The Message'

Nicky Wire's initial title for the fifteenth Manic Street Preachers album was 'Dialectics' – 'as in the path of opposition, trying to find some resolution'. He thought it applied on various levels, principally as describing how the band continued to function as a creative entity, despite the members' differing perspectives and methods. Wire was also tickled by the notion of having 'ripped off Socrates'. In the end, he dumped the idea. 'Too pretentious. And, everyone kept saying "dialects", as opposed to "dialectics".'

Of course, Socrates was also a big cheese when it came to formulating the philosophical discipline of 'critical thinking': applying rational thought processes to every sphere. In Wire's view, presented in the album's opening title track, the lack of critical thinking was responsible for the malaise of contemporary existence. To wit, this deadpan satire on the 'wellness' guru, reciting the linguistic crud of an industry dismissed for decades as pseudoscience but which by the social media age had become mainstream: 'It's OK not to be OK/Live your best life . . . Be your authentic self . . .' Allied to a percussive dub-industrial soundscape assembled with evident glee by Bradfield, Moore and Loz Williams, 'Critical Thinking' shaped up like the opening dance soundtrack to a J.G. Ballard-themed disco: a bonfire of the banalities.

'I'm into body negativity, not "body positivity",' says Wire. 'Or, "prioritise pleasure"? I prioritise misery. The easy option is to go with the pretence of caring and the kind of safe-space aesthetic of Coldplay. My philosophy has always boiled down to: forget about doing good – if you just don't do the bad, we'll all be in a better place. We wouldn't have to signal our goodness.' He laughs. 'I wrote a whole list of stuff for this song which James said, "I think you should leave that out . . ."'

By the final two verses, Wire has loosened his tie, moved on to bogus digital elixirs ('Net neutrality! Smart meters! Smart water! Smart fucking motorways!') and is metaphorically punching out windows on the upper deck of the Clapham omnibus in time to Bradfield's hacking Andy Gill guitars and Moore's dead-eye beats.

'Nick and Loz had done that in a day,' says Bradfield, 'Loz with his mental programming and Nick's sarky, don't-give-a-fuck voice. I knew what I had to do. I enjoyed just snapping at the heels of everything.'

163.

Dear Stephen

Recorded: Door To The River Studios, Newport; Rockfield
    Studios, Monmouthshire
Producers: Dave Eringa and Loz Williams
Released: 14 February 2025 (*Critical Thinking*, Columbia)

'You call the shots and they follow.'
                – The Pretenders, 'Talk Of The Town'

On 25 September 1984, The Smiths played the University of Cardiff's Great Hall. Nicky Wire did not attend. 'I was ill,' he says. 'And I probably wouldn't have gone anyway, knowing me.'

His mother sent a postcard to the band, via the university, explaining the situation. 'Out of the kindness of her wonderful heart. Lo and behold, a few weeks later, it came back saying, "Get well soon. Morrissey." Andy Rourke had signed it too.'

'Dear Stephen' is Wire's belated reply to the reply, although his message is a subtly different, 'Get well Morrissey'. Over warmhearted guitar twangs and chimes, the song gently pleads, 'Please come back to us/I believe in repentance and forgiveness', even appealing to Morrissey's infamously robust self-opinion by paraphrasing three of his own songs, most pertinently 'I Know It's Over': 'It's so easy to hate, it takes guts to be kind'.

As an articulation of the dilemma felt by fans of any artist revealed to hold objectionable views or behave abhorrently – in Morrissey's case, supporting racist far-right political parties and individuals – the song is hugely impressive. Not least because it's as much a critical examination of the narrator, who instead of excommunicating Morrissey still believes that, as Bradfield says, 'the situation is retrievable'. The lyric also invokes Philip Larkin, a literary hero to both Morrissey and Wire, and another great writer with a contentious legacy.

'It's almost an admission of guilt,' says Wire. 'And I am a hypocrite, because I can't read T.S. Eliot any more. The anti-semitism in his poetry is so nasty and brutal, I find it really distasteful. So obviously, I've made a choice there. But as I say in this song, it's like an addiction and my secret drug. The idea of a tactile object triggering so much and why I've kept something so worthless monetarily, and see it every day.'

No false starts for Bradfield on receiving this lyric. Sidestepping the obvious approach, his guiding light was 'the tenderness of the Pretenders', the band which Johnny Marr joined for a six-month period after The Smiths' 1987 split. 'I was really excited with this song,' he says. 'I felt a sense of responsibility. Like, "This is the good stuff."'

164.
Being Baptised

Recorded: Door To The River Studios, Newport; Rockfield
    Studios, Monmouthshire
Producers: Dave Eringa and Loz Williams
Released: 14 February 2025 (*Critical Thinking*, Columbia)

'Oh, God sent a raven to spread the news.'
                    – Mahalia Jackson, 'Didn't It Rain'

Whenever he encounters his musical heroes, James Dean Bradfield is very much of the *carpe diem* school of thought. 'It just all
comes out,' he says. 'When I met Jim Kerr at Rockfield, after
five minutes of me talking at him I see his eyes glaze over – like,
"get me away from here, I only came up to borrow some salt".'
In 2018, the Manics headlined the Beautiful Days festival, where
James happened upon Richard Jobson. 'Even though he was
freaking me out, by the time I started quoting some Disques du
Crépuscule poetry album back at him I think I'd freaked him
out more.'

One, however, was a more mutually rewarding exchange.
Ahead of meeting Allen Toussaint in 2011 for the BBC's *Songwriters' Circle* show with John Grant (see 'Faster', page 123),
Bradfield repeatedly told himself: 'Be calm, be calm'. On the day,
James bided his time, eventually mentioning that his mum really
liked Toussaint's song 'Holy Cow'. 'Then I asked him what it
was like for him the first time he heard Glen Campbell's version
of "Southern Nights" – because I adore that song. And Allen's
the first person that wanted to answer all my questions. We
got a cup of coffee and just talked. He asked me how I learnt
music, asked about Welsh choirs, it was just lovely. One of those

moments that when you come out the other end you feel you've learnt something. He was so patient, and ever so slightly scary. So I kind of wanted to write about that experience.'

Bradfield's lyric quotes moments from their conversation. For instance, the title. When James asked how it felt to lose his studio in Hurricane Katrina, Toussaint replied: 'It felt like we were drowning – or we were being baptised?' Some lines capture the essence of the great writer-producer's gift: 'Praying like an angel and playing like the devil/I can make you breathe, I can make you cry'.

'The way he spoke was just good,' says James. 'A lifetime of experience speaking. And he paid me a compliment musically in the soundcheck, when I was doing "A Design For Life". He's like, "The fourth and fifth chords in that verse ['What price now/For a shallow piece of dignity'], that was cool, man. I didn't expect it to go there. The first three chords, I thought, OK, here we go, rope-a-dope . . . Oooh! Good!" I was like a puppy dog on the floor.'

The only downer about 'Being Baptised' is Toussaint didn't live to hear it. He'd have checked its vaulting melodies bringing sunshine after the rain, admired the rhythm section's supple movement, and doubtless smiled at the memory of the unquenchable Welshman who asked all the right questions.

'Everything is just so sympathetic to each other on this song,' says Wire. 'And the lyric is pretty special. Possesses a warmth and humanity I don't know if I can get to.'

165.
My Brave Friend

Recorded: Door To The River Studios, Newport; Rockfield
    Studios, Monmouthshire
Producers: Dave Eringa and Loz Williams
Released: 14 February 2025 (*Critical Thinking*, Columbia)

'I was going to drown, then I started swimming.'
                                          – The Sound, 'Winning'

Proof that a great song will wait as long as it takes, 'My Brave
Friend's story begins at the 2002 Monnow Valley session when
the band were writing a potential new single for the *Forever
Delayed* greatest hits. At that point it was called 'The Greatest',
a hopeful case of nominative determinism. 'Mike Hedges and
James had done a version with a beautiful synth sound,' says
Nicky Wire. 'Like the solo in "All My Love" by Led Zeppelin
– cheesy, but good.' Bradfield recalls the Monnow Valley track
'having a Roxy Music vibe. And then it got left behind.'

Several years later, Wire suggested Bradfield offer the song to
Hedges, who was producing the erstwhile Hot Gossip and *Phantom of the Opera* star Sarah Brightman's new album. 'I'd always
thought this song could be a massive *Eurovision* hit,' says Wire.
'Not modern *Eurovision*, but something of the sixties, and sixties
old school. It had a grand sweep, I could hear a Barbara Dixon
and Elaine Paige duet.' Hedges suggested it to Brightman, but it
wasn't used. 'Then,' says James, 'it got reactivated. Nick changed
the lyrics, we worked on it, and it came alive again.'

The circumstances for the song's revival were profoundly sad:
the death in May 2011 of Jim Fletcher, the band's product manager at Sony. 'Sometimes you connect with someone on so many

different levels,' says Wire. 'Jim loved cricket, went to university in Cardiff, he was a big Leicester Tigers fan . . . A quiet, unassuming person, really funny. He did a fantastic job on *Send Away The Tigers*, same on *Postcards*, nothing ever seemed a problem. Then *National Treasures* is when he got ill. He had Crohn's, problems with his immune system. It's an awful death. You can hear it in the lyrics – the last time I spoke to him, he just went, "I'm really tired, not feeling too good." It was two weeks after that.'

Wire wrote a lyric titled 'I Watched As You Sailed Away', which evolved into 'My Brave Friend'. Musically, the latest song is essentially 'The Greatest' – Bradfield: 'Same key, kind of the same feel, just better' – and even retains a few words from 2002. 'The originals weren't great,' says Wire, 'apart from the "Have you ever walked between the raindrops" line which seemed to fit. A couple of lines remain from the lyrics I'd written after Jim passed away. It was really awful, I remember Allegra, his partner, saying to me, "He really fought like a lion." Finally, I put it all into the song and James came and sang it properly. We were thinking Scott Walker's "No Regrets" – Sean did some overdubbed toms which we instantly loved, and Dave Eringa did a lot of good work too.'

Given its deeply personal subject matter, the final version is perhaps most remarkable for its discipline – a beautiful tribute, sailing a dignified course, straight from the heart.

166.
Deleted Scenes

Recorded: Door To The River Studios, Newport; Rockfield
    Studios, Monmouthshire
Producers: Dave Eringa and Loz Williams
Released: 14 February 2025 (*Critical Thinking*, Columbia)

> 'I'm outside in the dark
> Wondering how I got so old.'
>
>   – The Cure, 'Endsong'

Basically a considered appraisal of 'Critical Thinking's primordial splurge, 'Deleted Scenes' turns off the screen and looks to the mirror for its elegant summation of the album's conflict zones, whether psychic or societal: 'The ecstasy of making things worse/ Seems to have become a worldwide curse' is 2025 in digest form.

'That lyric is indicative of where we still are,' says Wire. 'And that's very much reflected in my own disposition at times, the savage pettiness that only silence can control. Some lyrics come off the bat, like "Hiding In Plain Sight", but this was an exercise. "Multiple narrative graphs" is tricky to get in a song! Purely on a vibe sense, the music reminded me of Voice of the Beehive or Strawberry Switchblade, it had a spring to it. Which is such a rare thing as you get older.'

In the music's balance of experience and innocence, Bradfield acknowledges the impact of seeing The Cure play Cardiff's Motorpoint Arena in December 2022. 'It was fucking astounding,' he says. 'So many of the songs were so simple, yet played with such depth. It made me realise the way you play a song is what makes the song sometimes. I think this is the most complete lyric on the album. It is about relevance. It is about how you don't fit in any more. And it is about how your memory does matter.'

Tantalisingly, amid the synthetic sheen of machine-tooled drums, iridescent keyboards and rueful voices, there's also a hint of the brief intersect between Big Country and Abba, when the former recorded 1984's *Steeltown* at the latter's Stockholm studio and Stuart Adamson wrote a song for Anni-Frid Lyngstad's second solo album. 'Well,' says Bradfield, 'Abba's always there, it's not tokenistic. It just seeps through. It's really one of our parents' biggest legacies.'

167.

OneManMilitia

Recorded: Door To The River Studios, Newport; Rockfield
 Studios, Monmouthshire
Producers: Dave Eringa and Loz Williams
Released: 14 February 2025 (*Critical Thinking*, Columbia)

> 'No his mind is not for rent
> To any god or government.'
>
> – Rush, 'Tom Sawyer'

Nicky Wire spent the day of Queen Elizabeth II's funeral in the appropriate manner. He went to the Manics' studio, sampled Paul Cook's introduction to the Sex Pistols' version of The Stooges' 'No Fun', then wrote 'OneManMilitia' on the spot. 'I just wanted to hide away,' he says. 'I did the bass, the rhythm guitar, and the lead guitar up to my sort-of solo before James comes in at the end, all in the day, and pretty much most of the vocal. I rewrote a few of the lyrics afterwards, because the first draft has some pretty unpalatable stuff in there. But I did work really fucking hard! The funeral went on and on – I don't think I've ever been in the studio for such a long time.'

While its opening suggestion of 'Anarchy In The UK' – 'I don't know what I am for, but I know what I am against' – could serve as Wire's epitaph, 'OneManMilitia's intemperate chunderpunk challenges any number of preconceptions, not least about how a band into a fifth decade of continuous activity is supposed to close out its fifteenth album. Alternatively, it's a case of Wire doing a John Lydon and taking ownership of his own caricature. Either way, Bradfield and Moore were happy to play along.

'Obviously, I could hear where he was going with it,' says

James. 'I thought, "OK. That's one vocal I don't have to worry about." I just stayed away from him while he was doing it and then really enjoyed being John McGeoch again.'

The biggest fly in the ointment was getting clearance to use the Sex Pistols sample. Even after Moore had recorded his own version of the drumbeat, the Manics had to pay publishing royalties for approximating the drum pattern, even though Cook's version bore no resemblance to the original song's, played by Scott Asheton, who of course is sadly no longer around to reap the benefit. No fun, at all, indeed.

168.

Johatsu

Recorded: Door To The River Studios, Newport; Rockfield
    Studios, Monmouthshire
Producers: Dave Eringa and Loz Williams
Released: 14 February 2025 (*Critical Thinking* [Japan
    CD bonus track; Special Vinyl Edition 7-inch single],
    Columbia)

> 'Dreams stay with you.'
>   – Big Country, 'In A Big Country'

The latest in a line of great Manics ghost songs, at least 'Johatsu's
confinement as a Japanese bonus track was apt. Its subject is the
people who disappear, typically when faced with Japan's societal
shame for failure in professional or personal spheres, or to escape
hostile environments: as the lyric has it, 'the dead who don't die'.

The key line of the chorus is a *jōhatsu's* secret message to the
world they left behind: 'I want you to know that I'm not a ghost
yet'. The chorus also features one of James Dean Bradfield's sas-
siest feats of metrical escapology, fitting 'Domestic abuse victims,
violence and debt' into a catchy frame. 'I was really proud of
that!' he says. 'It's a bit out there, though not insensitive. I loved
"Johatsu" for a long time, but nobody else really was up for it,
so it got left out of the conversation.'

Demoed in January 2022, this was the first post-*The Ultra
Vivid Lament* recording, and may simply have been overlooked
in the accumulation of newer songs. It's a portal to its own self-
contained ecosystem, in this case the shopping arcades beneath
Japanese super-hotels, where jet-lagged tourists wander past
the one twenty-four-hour noodle bar or browse the 7-Eleven,

with just nocturnal workers and the furtive *jōhatsu* for company. 'They're spooky places,' says Bradfield. 'I love the idea of people not wanting to be part of each other. The song was trying to convey that spookiness.'

The flamboyant heel-clicking guitar flourishes and Wire's accentuated bass suggest The Smiths soundtracking a Tokyo noir thriller, maybe about a *jōhatsu* trying to evade discovery and the shady networks that exist to service their disappearance. The lyric even reads like a series of script directions: 'As sunlight falls over a broken life'; 'Scattered debris in the bible black air'.

There's clear resonance for the band's own history too, vis à vis Richey: their very own *jōhatsu*.

'I never thought about that until afterwards,' says Wire. 'But it has come to mind a few times, obviously. I must admit, though, it was more a journalistic lyric when I wrote it. I was in Japan having breakfast and reading *The Japan Times*. In the Arts section there was a report on the *jōhatsu*. So I wrote the lyric when I got home. Japan is a well of inspiration, it's the only place that just takes me to somewhere else, in a good way and a bad way. It sort of reorientates the creative mind.'

Fittingly the one that got away, 'Johatsu' tells its own singular story. And like every one of these 168 Manic Street Preachers songs, it's a story that demands to be heard.

Notes

Introduction

1 Chris Heath, 'Did Someone Order Gloom Service?', *The Face*, September 1998.

2 Danny Eccleston, 'A Rush Of Desperate Emotion', *MOJO*, February 2025.

Chapter 5: Motown Junk

1 Steven Wells, 'Single of the Week', *NME*, 19 August, 1989.

2 Ibid.

3 Bob Stanley, 'The Ugly Face of the New Art Riot', *Melody Maker*, 7 April 1990.

4 Ibid.

5 Rob Jovanovic, *A Version of Reason: The Search for Richey Edwards*, Orion, 2009, p. 78.

6 Sara Hawys Roberts and Leon Noakes, *Withdrawn Traces: Searching for the Truth about Richey Manic*, Virgin Books, 2019, p. 95.

7 Steven Wells, 'Scum On Feel The Noise!', *NME*, 4 August 1990.

8 Bob Stanley, 'Sidelines: Manic Street Preachers', *Melody Maker*, 4 August 1990.

9 Andy Peart, 'Profile: The Manic Street Preachers', *Sounds*, 25 August 1990.

10 Nick Robertshaw, 'Sade's Producer Is Trying To Stay Hungry', *Billboard*, 15 March 1986.

11 The Stud Brothers, 'Death or Glory', *Melody Maker*, 2 February 1991.

12 Nick Mitchell, 'Dave Eringa Interview', KMR Audio Blog, 17 July 2016: https://kmraudio.com/blogs/interview/dave-eringa-interview-part1

Chapter 9: Spectators Of Suicide

1 Greil Marcus, *Lipstick Traces: A Secret History of the Twentieth Century*, Faber, 2011, p. 54.

2 Ibid., p. 16.

3 Ibid., p. ix.

4 Guy Debord, *The Society of The Spectacle*, Rebel Press, 1994, p. 17.

5 Ibid., p. 10.

Notes

Chapter 14: Nat West-Barclays-Midlands-Lloyds

1 Antony Barnett, 'Holocaust Shame of Barclays', the *Observer*, 28 March 1999.
2 'Barclays banks on INS rebrand', *Design Week*, 23 April 1999.

Chapter 15: Born To End

1 In a further uncanny coincidence, the version of 'Fatman' on Southern Death Cult's self-titled posthumous 1983 compilation album was produced by future Manics associate Mike Hedges.

Chapter 16: Motorcycle Emptiness

1 Jon Savage, 'All Screwed Up: How Nirvana became anti-heroes for our time', the *Observer*, 15 August 1993.
2 Stuart Bailie, 'Non-Stop Neurotic Cabaret', *NME*, 30 May 1992.
3 Steve Bateman, Interview with Steve Brown, repeatfanzine.co.uk, 2010/ updated 2018.
4 Ibid.
5 S. E. Hinton and Francis Ford Coppola, *Rumble Fish* screenplay, 1983.
6 Ibid.

Chapter 17: Little Baby Nothing

1 Valerie Solanas, *SCUM Manifesto*, AK Press, 1996, p. 1.

Chapter 20: Condemned To Rock 'n' Roll

1 Nicky Wire performed an excerpt during a solo gig at Manics biographer Simon Price's Stay Beautiful club, 1 July 2006.

Chapter 21: From Despair To Where

1 Sue Sillitoe, 'Clive Langer & Alan Winstanley', *Sound On Sound*, July 1998.
2 Nick Mitchell, 'Dave Eringa Interview', KMR Audio Blog, 17 July 2016.

Chapter 22: Sleepflower

1 Simon Witter, 'Glam Rock: Manic Street Preachers', *Sky*, July 1993.

Chapter 23: La Tristesse Durera (Scream To A Sigh)

1 Dave Eringa and Tom Doyle, 'The Secret Diary of the Manic Street Preachers', *Melody Maker*, 17 July 1993.
2 Richey Edwards, 'Manics Go Goldmining', *Melody Maker*, 19 June 1993.

Chapter 25: Gold Against The Soul

1   Edwards, 'Manics Go Goldmining', 1993.

Chapter 26: Donkeys

1   Simon Price, *Everything (A Book about Manic Street Preachers)*, Virgin Books, 1999, p. 111.

2   'Time For A Change', *Metal Hammer*, August 1993.

Chapter 27: Life Becoming A Landslide

1   David Bennun, 'All That Glitters', *Melody Maker*, 29 January 1994.

Chapter 29: Faster

1   From 'Band Interview' on *The Holy Bible* 10th Tenth Anniversary Edition DVD (Epic, 2004).

Chapter 30: P.C.P.

1   Mick Wall, 'Rant For Cover', *RAW*, 8 June 1994.

2   http://www.foreverdelayed.org.uk/msppedia/index.php?title=The_Holy_Bible_Tour_Programme

3   Frank Füredi, 'PC – The Philosophy of Low Expectations', *Living Marxism*, No. 62, December 1993: https://www.marxists.org/history/etol/newspape/living-marxism/no62-dec-1993.pdf

4   The 2019 Conservative manifesto was in fact co-authored by a former Revolutionary Communist Party member, Munira Mirza, the long-time political aide to Boris Johnson who became head of the Downing Street policy unit when Johnson became Prime Minister in 2019: https://www.bbc.co.uk/news/uk-politics-60257702

5   'The Right To Be Offensive', *Living Marxism*, No. 64, February 1994: https://www.marxists.org/history/etol/newspape/living-marxism/no64-feb-1994.pdf

6   Mick Hume, 'The Moral of the Story', *Living Marxism*, ibid.

7   Richard King, *Brittle With Relics*, Faber, 2022, p. 430.

8   David Owens, 'Richey Edwards: The Lost Tape Revealed', 1992 interview published by Wales Online, 17 May 2009: https://www.walesonline.co.uk/news/wales-news/richey-edwards-lost-tape-revealed-2106089

9   'Don't Believe The Type!', *Melody Maker*, 14 August 1993.

Chapter 31: Revol

1   https://tonyoursler.com/evol-1

2   http://www.foreverdelayed.org.uk/msppedia/index.php?title=The_Holy_Bible_Tour_Programme

3   Kim Gordon, *Girl in A Band*, Faber, 2016, p. 148.

4   'Mel Brooks Says It's His Job To "Make Terrible Things Entertaining"', NPR, 26 April 2018: https://www.npr.org/transcripts/605297774

Chapter 32: Yes

1   Octave Mirbeau, *The Torture Garden* quoted on the sleeve of *The Holy Bible*.

2   http://www.foreverdelayed.org.uk/msppedia/index.php?title=The_Holy_Bible_Tour_Programme

Chapter 33: Ifwhiteamericatoldthetruthforonedayit'sworldwould-fallapart

1   Kevin Young, 'God Made Men, Samuel Colt Made Them Equal', *Living Marxism*, No. 61, November 1993: https://web.archive.org/web/20000310104908/www.informinc.co.uk/LM/LM61/LM61_Guns.html

Chapter 34: Of Walking Abortion

1   Solanas, *SCUM Manifesto*, p. 1.

2   http://www.foreverdelayed.org.uk/msppedia/index.php?title=The_Holy_Bible_Tour_Programme

Chapter 35: Archives Of Pain

1   Simon Price, 'Archives Of Pain', *Melody Maker*, 3 December 1994.

2   Quoted in David Macey, *The Lives of Michel Foucault'*, Verso, 2019, p. 36.

3   Bradfield used Alex Silva's TR7 Rickenbacker amplifier, a mainstay of the engineer's tenure as guitarist/saxophonist in influential late eighties Cardiff band Papas New Faith.

Chapter 37: Mausoleum

1   Mika Akao, 'Richey James Talks About The Holy Bible', *Music Life*, September 1994: https://solitudegrey.wordpress.com/2020/12/01/richey-edwards-talks-about-the-holy-bible-music-life-sept-1994/

Chapter 39: Die In The Summertime

1   http://www.foreverdelayed.org.uk/msppedia/index.php?title=The_Holy_Bible_Tour_Programme

2   Ibid.

3 Stuart Bailie, 'Manic's Depressive', *NME*, 1 October 1994.

4 T.S. Eliot, *Collected Poems 1909–1962*, Faber, 1963.

5 William Shakespeare, *Hamlet*, Act III, Scene 1.

Chapter 40: The Intense Humming Of Evil

1 Bailie, 'Manic's Depressive', 1994.

Chapter 41: A Design For Life

1 Sean Moore quoted in *Escape From Memory*, Dir: Kieran Evans, Sky TV, 2017.

2 Damon Albarn quoted in *Britpop Now*, Dir: Geraldine Dowd, BBC TV, 1995.

3 Mike Hedges quoted in *Escape From Memory*, 2017.

4 Simon Price, 'And If You Need An Explanation: Manic Street Preachers interviewed', the *Quietus*, 2 June 2016: https://thequietus.com/interviews/manic-street-preachers-everything-must-go-interview-simon-price/

5 Bradfield recalls subsequently seeing Morrison at a cinema screening of David Cronenberg's *Crash*. 'I suddenly found myself getting annoyed: "Mark Morrison's haunting me!" Weird. Never spotted any J.G. Ballard influences in his work . . .'

Chapter 43: Elvis Impersonator: Blackpool Pier

1 Mike Hedges quoted in *Escape From Memory*, 2017.

2 Ibid.

Chapter 44: Kevin Carter

1 Kevin Carter quoted in Greg Marinovich and Joao Silva, *The Bang-Bang Club*, Arrow, 2001, p. 238.

2 Ibid., p. 248.

Chapter 50: Interiors (Song For Willem De Kooning)

1 Peter Schjeldahl, 'Different Strokes: The Late Work of Willem de Kooning', *Artforum*, Vol. 35 No. 5, January 1997: https://www.artforum.com/features/different-strokes-the-late-work-of-willem-de-kooning-2-2020_6/

Chapter 52: No Surface All Feeling

1 Phil Wilding, 'Manics Best Songs: In their Own Words', *Louder Sound*, 23 March 2022.

2 Alan Bleasdale's 1991 TV drama about a left-wing Labour council leader in a

northern English city, widely thought to be based on Derek Hatton, deputy leader of Liverpool City Council in the mid-eighties.

3   Stuart Bailie, 'Courage Against the Machine', *Vox*, July 1996.

Chapter 55: Prologue To History

1   Richard Lowe, 'Blackwood Calling', *Select*, October 1991.
2   Paul Ansell, *Scathe*, 2 February 1994.
3   Simon Price, 'Street Life', *Melody Maker*, 4 January 1997.
4   Chapter 1 of Welsh nationalist historian Gwyn A. Williams's book *When Was Wales?* (Black Raven, 1985) is titled 'Prologue of a History'.

Chapter 58: Ready For Drowning

1   Meic Stephens' original graffiti, the grammatically incorrect 'Cofiwch Tryweryn', was anonymously amended to 'Cofiwch Dryweryn', which has since been copied in many different locations across Wales. Subsequently enjoying a distinguished literary career, Stephens didn't publicly discuss the act until many years later: broadcaster Huw Stephens only discovered the full story of his father's vandalism when making a documentary about it.

Chapter 59: Tsunami

1   Marjorie Wallace, *The Silent Twins*, Chatto & Windus, 1988.

Chapter 64: Socialist Serenade

1   On 19 October 1996, five years prior to their audience with Fidel Castro, the Manics met Arthur Scargill backstage at Liverpool Royal Court during the *Everything Must Go* tour. A professed admirer of Stalin, Scargill's leadership of the National Union of Mineworkers was certainly not without dictatorial tendencies. His association with the band continued in 1999, when Scargill gave a speech at Cardiff's Centre for Visual Arts for the opening of Jeremy Deller's *Unconvention*, an exhibition 'based on the imagined visual arts tastes of the Manic Street Preachers', according to the artist.

Chapter 65: The Masses Against The Classes

1   Daniel Booth, 'The Truth Hurts', *Melody Maker*, 19 December 1998.

Chapter 68: Locust Valley

1   Ray Johnson died on Friday 13 January 1995 after diving from a bridge at eastern Long Island's Sag Harbor Bay and swimming out to sea. His death

was subsequently interpreted as his final work of art.

Chapter 72: Intravenous Agnostic

1 The 1993-released *Where You Been* features a rare instance of a band apparently quoting the Manics – see the adjacency of 'What Else Is New' to 'Motorcycle Emptiness'.

Chapter 73: Let Robeson Sing

1 Paul Robeson quoted in Hywel Francis, *Miners Against Fascism: Wales and the Spanish Civil War*, Lawrence & Wishart, 2012, p. 249.

Chapter 78: Epicentre

1 Greil Marcus, 'Real Life Rock Top 10', *Salon*, 11 March 2002: https://www.salon.com/2002/03/11/64/

Chapter 79: Baby Elián

1 Paula J. Pettavino and Geralyn Pye, 'Sport in Cuba: The Diamond in the Rough', *University of Pittsburgh Press*, 1994: https://www.pbs.org/stealing-home/sport/diamond.html
2 Ted Kessler, 'Some Bands Meet Tony Blair. We Play Cuba And Castro Turns Up', *NME*, 3 March 2001.

Chapter 85: 4 Ever Delayed

1 https://www.recordproduction.com/features/trevor-horn-talks-about-hook-end-manor-studios

Chapter 86: Judge Yr'self

1 Marcus, *Lipstick Traces*, p. 20.

Chapter 87: The Love Of Richard Nixon

1 According to Young biographer Jimmy McDonough, following the show in Columbia, South Carolina, the Stills-Young Band tour was due to travel onwards to Atlanta. Young, however, diverted to Memphis airport and sent Stills a telegram ('Dear Stephen, Funny how some things that start spontaneously end that way') ending with a quotation from T.S. Eliot's 'The Love Song of J. Alfred Prufrock': 'Eat a peach'.
2 Stephen E. Ambrose, *Nixon: Ruin And Recovery 1973–1990*, Simon & Schuster, 1991, p. 10.

Chapter 88: 1985

1 Led by another Chris Dean, this mid-eighties Yorkshire soul-punk trio aspired to 'Sing like The Supremes and walk like The Clash'. Members of the Socialist Workers Party, the band's 9 November 1984 performance on Channel 4 TV's *The Tube* was notable for lending a platform to the perfectly named Durham miner Norman Strike, whose address to the nation went unheard because his microphone was mysteriously switched off.

Chapter 97: Your Love Alone Is Not Enough

1 The cassette now also contained the song 'Rendition', which Bradfield had written from a separate lyric Wire gave him at the same time as 'Your Love Alone Is Not Enough'.

2 The title track of Pink Floyd's 1975 album, popularly assumed to be about Syd Barrett, the band's co-founder and main songwriter who was sacked in 1968 due to his increasingly erratic behaviour.

Chapter 103: Imperial Bodybags

1 The older brother of Tom Lord-Alge, who engineered the US mix of *The Holy Bible*.

Chapter 109: Marlon J.D.

1 The standout song from Big Black's 1986 debut album *Atomizer*, an everyday tale of smalltown anomie and arson.

Chapter 123: Rewind The Film

1 Gareth Grundy, 'An Artist? I'm A Polaroid Freak', the *Observer*, 30 October 2011.

2 John Aizlewood, 'Everything Must Grow Up', *Q*, July 2011.

Chapter 125: This Sullen Welsh Heart

1 Garson O'Toole: https://listserv.linguistlist.org/pipermail/ads-l/2010-February/096333.html

Chapter 131: Europa Geht Durch Mich

1 David Cameron quoted in the *Guardian*, 28 April 2014: https://www.theguardian.com/world/2014/may/27/david-cameron-jean-claude-juncker-eu-top-job

Sources and Further Reading

Unless credited otherwise, all quotes in this book are taken from the author's own interviews.

The following books proved useful:

Ballard, J.G. *The Complete Short Stories*, Vol. 1 & 2 (4th Estate, 2014)

Beckett, Andy. *When the Lights Went Out: What Really Happened to Britain in the Seventies* (Faber & Faber, 2009)

Beckett, Andy. *Promised You a Miracle: Why 1980–82 Made Modern Britain* (Penguin, 2016)

Beckett, Francis & Hencke, David. *Marching to the Fault Line: The Miners' Strike and the Battle for Industrial Britain* (Constable, 2009)

Collins, Neil. *International Velvet: How Wales Conquered the '90s Charts* (Calon, 2024)

Debord, Guy. *The Society of the Spectacle* (Rebel Press, 2014)

Evans, David. *The Holy Bible* (Bloomsbury, 2019)

Foucault, Michel. *Discipline and Punish: The Birth of the Prison* (Penguin, 1991)

Francis, Hywel. *Miners Against Fascism: Wales and the Spanish Civil War* (Lawrence & Wishart, 2012)

Goddard, Simon. *Songs That Saved Your Life: The Art of The Smiths 1982–87* (Titan Books, 2013)

Gordon, Kim. *Girl in a Band* (Faber & Faber, 2015)

Sources and Further Reading

Gray, John. *The Immortalization Commission: The Strange Quest to Cheat Death* (Penguin, 2012)

Harris, John. *The Last Party: Britpop, Blair and the Demise of English Rock* (Harper Perennial, 2004)

Hinton, S.E. *Rumble Fish* (Delacorte Press, 2013)

Ikeda, Mitch. *Forever Delayed: Photographs of the Manic Street Preachers* (Vision On, 2002)

Jones, Patrick. *Fuse/Fracture (Poems 2001–2021)* (Parthian, 2021)

Jones, Rhian E., Lukes, Daniel & Wodtke, Larissa. *Triptych: Three Studies of Manic Street Preachers' The Holy Bible* (Repeater, 2017)

Jovanovic, Rob. *A Version of Reason: In Search of Richey Edwards* (Orion, 2010)

King, Richard. *Brittle with Relics: A History of Wales 1962–1997* (Faber & Faber, 2022)

MacDonald, Ian. *Revolution in the Head: The Beatles' Records and the Sixties* (4th Estate, 1994)

Marcus, Greil. *Lipstick Traces: A Secret History of the Twentieth Century* (Faber & Faber, 2011)

Moore, Thurston. *Sonic Life* (Faber & Faber, 2023)

O'Leary, Chris. *Rebel Rebel: All the Songs of David Bowie from '64 to '76* (Zero Books, 2015)

Paterson, Harry. *Look Back in Anger: The Miners' Strike in Nottinghamshire 30 Years On* (Five Leaves Publications, 2016)

Phillips, Valerie. *Little Baby Nothings: Manic Street Preachers* (Longer Moon Farther, 2024)

Power, Martin. *Nailed to History: The Story of Manic Street Preachers* (Omnibus Press, 2010)

Price, Simon. *Everything: A Book About Manic Street Preachers* (Virgin, 1999)

Reynolds, Simon. *Rip it Up and Start Again: Postpunk 1978–1984* (Faber & Faber, 2006)

Roberts, Sara Hawys & Noakes, Leon. *Withdrawn Traces: Searching for the Truth about Richey Manic* (Virgin, 2019)

Savage, Jon. *England's Dreaming: The Sex Pistols and Punk Rock* (Faber & Faber, 1992)

Solanas, Valerie. *SCUM Manifesto* (AK Press, 1996)

Stephens, Huw. *Wales: 100 Records* (Y Lolfa, 2024)

Thomas, R.S. *Selected Poems* (Penguin, 2003)

Thomas, R.S. *Uncollected Poems* (Bloodaxe, 2013)

Turner, Robin. *Believe In Magic: Heavenly Recordings: The First 30 Years* (White Rabbit, 2020)

Unsworth, Cathi. *Season of the Witch: The Book of Goth* (Nine Eight, 2023)

Williams, Gwyn A. *When Was Wales?: A History of the Welsh* (Penguin, 1991)

Wire, Nicky. *Death of a Polaroid: A Manics Family Album* (Faber & Faber, 2011)

There is a lot of Manic Street Preachers-related material on the world wide web. Choose your search engine carefully and don't be evil. Special thanks to estimable music journalism archive rocksbackpages.com. The Manics fan-site foreverdelayed.org.uk is a terrific resource, particularly its song index, gigography and press archive. Anyone seeking to go deeper into *The Holy Bible* is strongly recommended to visit Yusef Syed's astonishing 'Manic Body Politic' at 227lears.com – the ultimate archive of pain.

Acknowledgements

First and last and always, thanks to Jenny and Hamish for guiding and supporting me every day. Their love alone really is enough.

Thanks to Matthew Hamilton at The Hamilton Agency for believing in this book before there even was a book. Very special thanks to Lee Brackstone at White Rabbit for taking on this project, then being its most committed champion and seeing it through to the finish. Thanks also to the team at Orion Books, in particular Georgia Goodall, Jenny Lord, Steve Marking, Sophie Nevrkla and Tom Noble.

This book exists because of James Dean Bradfield, Richey Edwards, Sean Moore and Nicky Wire. From our first meeting in 1994, Manic Street Preachers have been a fount of intelligence, inspiration, thoughtful conversation, great company and consistently wonderful music. My eternal gratitude goes to this remarkable band, in particular James and Nicky for devoting so much time and energy to this book: most obviously the many hours of interviews, but also in pointing me towards Newport's finest eateries, making excellent sandwiches, offering generous gifts of Welsh tea and gin, and sharing their deep knowledge of crisps. Special thanks to Loz Williams for transport and black metal coffee.

Defenders of the faith: Martin Hall, Michael Hall, Philip Hall, Terri Hall, Gillian Porter, Caffy St Luce and Robin Turner.

Thanks to John Mulvey and the staff of *MOJO* for enabling me to make room for the book and still work for the world's greatest music magazine.

I'd also like to thank the following people, all of whom gave help, advice or encouragement along the way: Dave Bedford, Stuart Braithwaite, Geoff Brown, Steve Gullick, Sarah Hampson, Mick Houghton, Paul Hutton, Steve Lamacq, Eric Longley, Simon McEwen, Ann Scanlon, Cathi Unsworth, Mark Wagstaff, Jenny Wylam and Robert Jamieson-Beesley, and John Yates.

And finally, thanks so much to Mitch Ikeda for use of his incredible photographs in the second plate section. Thanks also to Nicky Wire for his Polaroids on the cover, and to James Dean Bradfield, Pete Brown and Dave Eringa for the photographs in the first plate section.

About the Author

A journalist since 1988, Keith Cameron is currently a contributing editor at *MOJO*. He previously worked for *Sounds* and *New Musical Express*, and his writing has appeared in the *Guardian*, *The Times*, the *Sunday Times*, *Scotland on Sunday*, *Kerrang!* and *Q*. He is author of *Mudhoney: The Sound and the Fury from Seattle*, acclaimed by Mark Lanegan as 'the definitive book on '90s Seattle music'.